ESSENTIAL QUANTITATIVE METHODS

ESSENTIAL QUANTITATIVE METHODS

FOR BUSINESS, MANAGEMENT AND FINANCE

SIXTH EDITION

LES OAKSHOTT

First published 2016 by
PALGRAVE

Palgrave in the UK is an imprint of Macmillan Publishers Limited, registered in England, company number 785998, of 4 Crinan Street, London, N1 9XW.

Palgrave Macmillan in the US is a division of St Martin's Press LLC, 175 Fifth Avenue, New York, NY 10010.

Palgrave is a global imprint of the above companies and is represented throughout the world.

Palgrave® and Macmillan® are registered trademarks in the United States, the United Kingdom, Europe and other countries.

ISBN 978–1–137–51855–2

This book is printed on paper suitable for recycling and made from fully managed and sustained forest sources. Logging, pulping and manufacturing processes are expected to conform to the environmental regulations of the country of origin.

A catalogue record for this book is available from the British Library.

A catalog record for this book is available from the Library of Congress.

Printed in China

For Vicky, Andrew, Kim, Christina and Frederick

SHORT CONTENTS

LONG CONTENTS

LIST OF TABLES AND FIGURES

TABLES

FIGURES

PREFACE TO THE SIXTH EDITION

Many degree programmes these days include at least one compulsory course in statistics or quantitative methods, and there are also many undergraduate and masters programmes that have an elective in these areas. Students are therefore getting more exposure to analytical techniques and, with the reduction in class contact time, need resources to help them with what many find a difficult subject.

As with the previous edition, this edition uses a variety of methods to guide the student through the maze of techniques that make up the quantitative methods syllabus. Each chapter starts with any prerequisites. This normally refers to previous chapter(s) the student is expected to have read before tackling the current one. The objectives for the chapter are then set out, followed by an introduction to the material being covered. Each chapter then provides detail of a real case that is relevant to the chapter being studied. The purpose of these *Quantitative methods in action* (QMA) cases is to demonstrate how useful and relevant the particular technique is to society and business. So, for example, the QMA in Chapter 4 uses charts to show just how fast the Chinese economy has grown in the past 20 years. And the QMA in Chapter 10 investigates the hypothesis that waiting times in A&E are getting worse. Although the cases have often been simplified, they all provide motivation for the student to understand and be able to apply quantitative techniques.

Each chapter is written in a student-friendly manner and avoids the use of unnecessary mathematics and long-winded explanations. Charts and diagrams are used throughout to help understanding of complex issues. In order for a student to gain confidence in applying a technique, extensive use of in-text activities are used, with the solution given immediately after the activity. These in-text activities have been praised by many educators. Another innovation in the last edition was the *Did you know?* snippets. These snippets give some interesting facts that relate to, but are separate from, the topic being discussed. An example is the mention of Florence Nightingale as a brilliant statistician as well as a famous nurse (Chapter 4). Hopefully, students will come to see these snippets both as a welcome diversion from the main topic and an incentive to discover more about the rich field of mathematics and statistics.

Each chapter ends with a *Reflection* section allowing students to think about what they have learnt in that chapter. Also provided is a *Key points* section which nicely summarises the ideas and techniques explored in that chapter. Finally there is a *Further reading* section and a set of *Practice questions*.

For the sixth edition, the chapter on inventory control has been reinstated in this edition, following lecturer feedback. Also as a result of feedback, changes have been made in Chapters 8 and 9 to ensure that the text uses accepted statistical abbreviations. And in Chapter 8 more explanation has been provided on the important idea of the sampling distribution of the mean. Finally Excel has been updated to Excel 2013 and SPSS has been updated to version 22.

Online learning and resources

One change from the previous editions is that solutions to all practice questions have been placed on the comprehensive, freely available, companion website (http://www.palgrave.com/oakshott-eqm6). Also provided on this website are:

- Review questions, True/false questions and Multiple choice questions. Students can work through these questions online and get immediate feedback (including references to appropriate pages in the text).
- Further practice questions and solutions.
- A list of statistical and mathematical formula used in the book.
- Excel and SPSS datasets used in the text.
- A bonus chapter retained from previous editions, 'Taking account of randomness'.

A password protected area for the exclusive use of lecturers who adopt this text contains:

- Answers to end-of-chapter assignments.
- Additional questions and assignments.
- An online library of additional cases.
- PowerPoint slides for teaching purposes.

GUIDED TOUR OF THE BOOK

Prerequisites *tell you exactly what you need to know in order to fully understand the chapter*

PREREQUISITES
Some understanding of sampling methods (Chapter 3: *Collecting data: surveys and samples*) would be useful but is not essential.

OBJECTIVES
- To be able to distinguish between different types of data
- To be able to tabulate data into an ungrouped or a grouped frequency table, as appropriate
- To be able to use diagrams to present data, and to know how to draw appropriate conclusions from these diagrams
- To be able to use Excel and/or SPSS to produce professional-looking charts

Objectives *identify the key skills you will acquire by reading it*

Introduction *presents the major themes of the chapter*

INTRODUCTION
The human brain finds it difficult to make sense of a large quantity of data. However, when data is organized and presented in a diagrammatic form we find it much easier to pick out patterns. This is the opposite to computers which can easily process vast quantities of data but find pattern recognition extremely difficult. This chapter first discusses the type of data that you may come across, and then looks at the best ways of displaying it.

QUANTITATIVE METHODS IN ACTION

The growth of China's economy

The growth of China's economy has been astonishing and is now the second largest economy after that of the USA. Although its gross domestic product (GDP) has slowed slightly from 9.2% in 2013 to 7.7% in 2014, the economy is expected to continue to grow. To illustrate China's position in the world, the use of charts and graphics can be much more useful than numbers alone. Figure 4.1 shows quite dramatically how fast the GDP has risen since 1990. Figure 4.2 demonstrates how China has overtaken most of the developed countries between 2005 and 2013. The exception is the USA, which still has the largest economy in terms of GDP. However, in Figure 4.3 we compare the percentage change in GDP (at 2005 prices) between 1990 and 2013, for the major economies. This chart clearly shows that in terms of percentage growth China has outstripped all other countries, including the USA, by a large margin. We will look at these and other types of charts later in this chapter.

Quantitative methods in action *case studies demonstrate the real-life application of quantitative techniques in business and society*

DID YOU KNOW?
Florence Nightingale was a respected statistician as well as a famous nurse in the Crimean War. Along with her colleague William Farr she did much pioneering work in showing how poor hygiene was killing soldiers unnecessarily. She used diagrams and charts extensively in her work and she developed a polar area graph which was a bit like a pie chart. Using her diagrams she was able to persuade the government to improve sanitation in both military and civilian hospitals. Florence was made a Fellow of the Royal Statistical Society in 1858.

Did you know *snippets provide interesting facts on related topics*

> **example 3.1**
> Table 3.3 is a part of a list of students enrolled on a business studies course at a university.
>
> Say from this 'population' of 25 students you wanted to randomly select a sample of 5 students. How would you do it? You could use the student number (in this case conveniently numbered from 1 to 25) and then try and obtain a match using a stream of two-digit random numbers. For example, suppose you had the following random numbers: 78, 41, 11, 62, 72, 18, 66, 69, 58, 71, 31, 90, 51, 36, 78, 09, 41, 00, 70, 50, 58, 19, 68, 26, 75, 69, and 04. The first two numbers don't exist in our population but 11

Examples *present everyday scenarios representing realistic business problems*

*Activities, which
spring from the
examples, help
you apply the
right quantitative
technique to solve a
business problem*

(**activity** 3.2) You have been asked to obtain the views of the student population at your institution regarding car parking facilities within the campus. What method of data collection would you use?

The best method would probably be face-to-face interviews, but it is unlikely that you would have the resources for this approach. Telephone interviewing is probably not realistic because of the cost and the fact that students' telephone numbers might be difficult to obtain. This leaves you with either a postal or online questionnaire, both of which should be quite reasonable for this relatively simple type of survey.

Reflection

As you will have seen in this chapter, there are a number of different diagrams that can be used to represent a set of data. Choosing the most appropriate diagram is important if you want to be able to interpret the data correctly and to provide others with reliable information. A good chart should be technically correct but also visually stimulating. The use of Excel has made it easy to produce charts that are attractive to the eye, particularly if a limited

*Reflection considers
the major themes
of each chapter
and explores the
importance of the
topics learnt*

*Key points
summarize the
fundamentals of each
chapter and help to
reinforce Objectives*

Key points

- Data can be *continuous, discrete, ordinal or nominal*. The type of data determines the method to be used in its presentation.
- Data is normally *aggregated into tables*. For continuous and discrete data, these tables can be either *ungrouped* or *grouped*.
- For *group frequency tables*, the *class interval* needs to be decided and a *tally chart* used to help in the aggregation process.

Further reading

This text is only an introduction to the huge subject of time series and forecasting. There are a large number of more advanced models that can be used. If you have an interest in the subject and are good at maths then the text by Makridakis et al. (2008) gives a thorough coverage but is quite technical. Forecasting techniques are used in sports and the text by Eastaway and Haigh (2014) is worth reading. The Operational Research (OR) Society has

Further reading
*points the way to
additional study aids*

*Practice questions
invite you to revise the
key techniques you have
learned; a full solutions
manual is available at
http://www.palgrave.
com/oakshott-eqm6.*

http://www.**palgrave.com**/oakshott-eqm6

Solutions to all questions are freely available

Practice questions

1 You have just completed an analysis into the sales of a computer game over the past 3 years and the result is shown in Table 13.17.
   (a) Plot this series on graph paper.
   (b) From the raw data, calculate the centred moving average series and plot this on the graph. Comment on both series of data.

*Assignments involve you
in solving more lengthy
problems in order to further
develop your knowledge
and skills; answers are
provided for lecturers
at http://www.palgrave.
com/oakshott-eqm6.*

Assignment

Car insurance companies are interested in the probabilities of different coloured cars getting involved in accidents. For example, red cars have historically been involved in a disproportionate number of accidents. Conduct a survey to find the proportion of the different coloured cars on a stretch of road near you. Convert these proportions into probabilities. These will be your prior probabilities.

NOTES ON THE SIXTH EDITION

This edition, like the fifth edition, is divided into four parts:

Part I   Mathematical applications
Part II   Collecting and interpreting data
Part III   Probability and statistics
Part IV   Decision-making techniques

The purpose of this arrangement is to try to anticipate the way that lecturers organize their courses. Not all courses will cover all topics. Some introductory statistical courses only require basic statistical knowledge and may therefore require only Part II, whereas more advanced statistical courses may also require Part III. The material provided in Parts II and III is designed to be taught sequentially, whereas the chapters in Parts I and IV can be taught in any order. It is recommended, however, that students who do not feel confident with GCSE-level mathematics work through Chapter 1 (Revision mathematics) first, no matter what parts they study subsequently.

Although it is assumed that most students have used Excel before, it may not be the case that all students have met Excel 2013 or 2010, which have a different look and feel to them than earlier versions. To help these students more detailed instructions are provided as and when required. Although both Excel and SPSS are used in Part II of the text, greater emphasis has been placed on SPSS in Part III because SPSS is superior to Excel when it comes to more advanced statistics. Excel is still used in many of the chapters in Part IV, however.

As before, *Progress questions*, *Review questions*, *True/false questions* and *Multiple choice questions* can be found on the companion website (http://www.palgrave.com/oakshott-eqm6). These questions can be answered online, where immediate feedback is provided. Solutions to all *Practice questions* can now be found on the website.

ACKNOWLEDGEMENTS

The author wishes to thank all those people who either reviewed the last edition or commented on the plans for this one. Particular thanks to Dr. Charlotte Price of Warwick Business School whose thorough review of the 5th edition was most helpful. Special thanks also to Lauren Zimmerman, the Development Editor at Palgrave Macmillan whose dedication and eye for detail ensured a much improved manuscript.

The authors and publishers are grateful to the following for kindly granting permission.

The Bank of England for Figure 8.8: CPI Inflation Project

Bureau van Dfik Electronic Publishing for data from FAME database used in Figure 4.25: Company Information

BP for the data used in the following:

- Table 2.1: Oil price and oil consumption since 1990
- Figure 2.1 Line chart of oil consumption for the USA, China and the UK
- Figure 2.2: Index of oil price and consumption for the USA, China and the UK

Greater Manchester Police for Figure 6.1: Venn diagram produced by Greater Manchester police to prove Victorino Chua's guilt in the Stepping Hill hospital poison investigation

The following figures are reprinted courtesy of International Business Machines Corporation, © SPSS, Inc., an IBM Company. SPSS was acquired by IBM in October, 2009.

- Figure 4.24: Opening SPSS screen
- Figure 4.25: Company Information
- Figure 4.26: Variable details
- Figure 4.27: Drop-down menu for Frequencies
- Figure 4.28: Frequencies dialogue box
- Figure 4.29: The Viewer window
- Figure 4.30: Define pie chart data
- Figure 4.31: The chart editor
- Figure 4.32: The final pie chart
- Figure 4.33: Changing chart type
- Figure 4.34: Using Chart Builder to plot a histogram
- Figure 4.35: SPSS histogram for 'Turnover'
- Figure 5.13: Dialogue box to create summary statistics using SPSS
- Figure 5.14: Summary statistics from SPSS
- Figure 5.15: The Explore Menu
- Figure 5.16: Creating a simple boxplot in SPSS

- Figure 5.18: Using the chart builder for boxplots
- Figure 9.8: Independent samples t-test using SPSS
- Figure 9.9: Setting up the test in SPSS
- Figure 9.10: SPSS Output
- Figure 9.11: Setting up the paired t-test in SPSS
- Figure 9.12: Output for the paired t-test
- Figure 9.17: The SARS data and the Crosstabs routine
- Figure 9.18: Crosstabs routine with cell display
- Figure 9.19: Crosstabs routine with statistics display
- Figure 9.20: Part of the Crosstabs output
- Figure 9.21: Statistical output from Crosstabs
- Figure 10.15: The Scatter routine in SPSS
- Figure 10.17: Linear regression in SPSS
- Figure 10.18: Setting SPSS for regression analysis

Microsoft for the following:

- Figure 4.19: The Insert tab in Excel 2013
- Figure 4.20: Creating a Pie chart
- Figure 4.21: Creating a simple bar chart
- Figure 4.22: Adding horizontal axis labels
- Figure 4.23: Creating a line chart
- Figure 5.9: Excel worksheet for distance to work
- Figure 5.11: The completed worksheet
- Figure 5.12: The Excel worksheet with the formulae shown
- Figure 7.8: Use of Excel for Activity 7.12
- Figure 9.15: Spreadsheet for Activity 9.13
- Figure 9.16: Excel formulae for Activity 9.13
- Figure 10.10: Using Excel 2013 to create a scatter chart
- Figure 10.11: Excel's bivariate functions applied to data from Example 10.1
- Figure 10.12: Adding the regression equation to a scatter diagram
- Figure 10.13: Using the Excel Trendline Options
- Figure 11.15: The decision tree for Example 11.4 added to an Excel spreadsheet
- Figure 11.16: The Goal Seek dialogue box
- Figure 11.17: Result of using Goal Seek in Excel
- Figure 13.10: Excel worksheet showing the time series formulae for the multiplicative model
- Figure 13.11: Step 2 of the Chart Wizard in Excel
- Figure 14.6: Adding the Solver constraints
- Figure 14.7: Solution found by Solver
- Figure 14.8 Sensitivity report from Solver
- Figure 14.9: Adding a new product
- Figure 14.10: The sensitivity report after adding a new product
- Figure 14.14: The Excel model for Example 14.4
- Figure 14.15: Setting up Solver for first iteration
- Figure 14.16: Solver results after first iteration

- Figure 14.17: Setting up second iteration of Solver
- Figure 14.18: Final iteration of Solver
- Figure 14.19: Final result of the Solver analysis

Opinium Research for the data used in chapter 8, question 14.

I

MATHEMATICAL APPLICATIONS

REVISION MATHEMATICS

INTRODUCTION

The aim of this chapter is to provide the basic numeracy skills that will be needed in subsequent chapters. If you have any doubts about your knowledge of particular areas you are recommended to tackle the diagnostic tests that you will find throughout this chapter. If you do not achieve 100% success in any of these tests, try to find out where you went wrong by reading through the remainder of that section. The books listed in the further reading section may also be of help if you need additional practice.

Number and number operations

activity 1.1

Write down the answers to the following questions (without a calculator).

1 $4 + (-2)$ **2** $4 - (-4)$ **3** $5 + (-2) - (-4)$

4 $2 \times (-3)$ **5** $-15 \div (-3)$ **6** $\dfrac{-10}{2}$

7 $\dfrac{5}{0}$ **8** $\dfrac{0}{5}$ **9** $3 \times 2 + 8 \div 4$

10 $3 \times (2 + 8) \div 4$

Answers

1 2   **2** 8   **3** 7

4 −6   **5** 5   **6** −5

7 no solution (∞)   **8** 0   **9** 8

10 7.5

Number operations often confuse people, particularly when they involve positive and negative numbers. The easy rule is that like signs give a plus while unlike signs give a negative. This is summarized in Table 1.1.

Another problem is deciding the order in which to carry out a series of calculations. Questions 9 and 10 had the same numbers in the same order but in question 10 a bracket separated some of the figures. There is an order in which mathematical operations are performed. You may have come across the term '*bedmas*', which stands for 'brackets, exponent, division, multiplication, addition and subtraction'. This is not strictly correct as addition and subtraction have equal priority, as do multiplication and division. Where the operations have equal priority the order is taken from left to right. The main point to remember is that if you want a calculation to be done in a particular order you should use brackets to make the order clear. Most scientific calculators should use the bedmas system but it is worth checking with some simple calculations. These calculators will also have the bracket function to allow the order of calculation to be controlled.

Table 1.1 Number operations

Addition and subtraction	Multiplication	Division
+ (+) = +	+ × + = +	+ ÷ + = +
− (−) = +	− × − = +	− ÷ − = +
+ (−) = −	+ × − = −	+ ÷ − = −
− (+) = −	− × + = −	− ÷ + = −

Decimals, fractions and percentages

activity 1.2

1 Convert the following decimals to fractions in their simplest form.

    (a) 0.2   (b) 0.5   (c) 0.3$\dot{3}$ (d) 0.125   (e) 0.375

2 Convert the following fractions to decimals.

(a) $\dfrac{1}{10}$ (b) $\dfrac{1}{5}$ (c) $\dfrac{11}{3}$ (d) $\dfrac{2}{7}$ (e) $\dfrac{3}{8}$

(f) $\dfrac{7}{3}$ (g) $\dfrac{1}{100}$ (h) $1\dfrac{3}{4}$

3 Convert the following fractions to percentages.

(a) $\dfrac{1}{4}$ (b) $\dfrac{1}{2}$ (c) $\dfrac{1}{5}$ (d) $\dfrac{2}{3}$ (e) $\dfrac{3}{4}$

4 Convert the following percentages into fractions in their simplest form.

(a) 40%   (b) 45%   (c) 60%   (d) 12%   (e) 19%

5 Carry out the following calculations.

(a) $0.25 + 0.37$ (b) $\dfrac{1}{2} \times 3$ (c) $\dfrac{1}{2}$ of 46%

(d) $\dfrac{4}{5} + \dfrac{2}{3}$ (e) $\dfrac{3}{4} \times \dfrac{3}{2}$ (f) $\dfrac{3}{4} \div \dfrac{3}{2}$

(g) $0.25 \times \dfrac{1}{5}$ (h) 0.00025×3000

6 Round the following decimals to 3 decimal places.

(a) 1.5432   (b) 1.5438   (c) 1.5435   (d) 0.000843   (e) 100.2003

7 Write the following numbers to 3 significant figures.

(a) 1.5432   (b) 1.5438   (c) 1.5435   (d) 0.000843   (e) 100.2003

(f) 13 256   (g) 1.000561

8 Write down the following numbers in scientific notation.

(a) 25 438 176   (b) 1 600 000   (c) 0.00001776

Answers

1 (a) $\dfrac{1}{5}$ (b) $\dfrac{1}{2}$ (c) $\dfrac{1}{3}$ (d) $\dfrac{1}{8}$ (e) $\dfrac{3}{8}$

2 (a) 0.1   (b) 0.2   (c) $3.66\dot{6}$ (d) 0.2857   (e) 0.375

     (f) $2.33\dot{3}$ (g) 0.01   (h) 1.75

3 (a) 25%   (b) 50%   (c) 20%   (d) $66.66\dot{6}$%   (e) 75%

4 (a) $\dfrac{2}{5}$ (b) $\dfrac{9}{20}$ (c) $\dfrac{3}{5}$ (d) $\dfrac{3}{25}$ (e) $\dfrac{19}{100}$

5 (a) 0.62   (b) 1.5   (c) 23%   (d) $1\dfrac{7}{15}$ (e) $1\dfrac{1}{8}$

     (f) $\dfrac{1}{2}$ (g) $\dfrac{1}{2}$ or 0.05   (h) 0.75

6 (a) 1.543   (b) 1.544   (c) 1.544   (d) 0.001   (e) 100.200

7 (a) 1.54   (b) 1.54   (c) 1.54   (d) 0.000843   (e) 100

     (f) 13 300   (g) 1.00

8 (a) 2.5438176×10^{7} (b) 1.6×10^{6} (c) 1.776×10^{-5}

Fractions, decimals and percentages are used throughout this book and you need to be able to convert a number from one form to another. To convert from a fraction to either a decimal or a percentage all you need to do is to divide the numerator (the number above the line) by the denominator (the number below the line). For a percentage you also need to multiply by 100. To convert a decimal to a fraction you simply have to remember that the first digit after the decimal point is a tenth and the second digit is a hundredth and so on. For example, 0.2 is $\frac{2}{10}$ and this can be simplified by dividing the top and bottom by 2 to give $\frac{1}{5}$. The conversion of a percentage to a fraction is easier as the denominator of the fraction is always 100. So 40% is $\frac{40}{100}$ and this simplifies to $\frac{2}{5}$.

A frequent question asked by students is, how many decimal places should an answer be given to? There is no easy answer to this, although a good rule of thumb to use when analyzing data is to give one more place than in the original data. So if your data had one decimal place you should give your answer to two decimal places. Giving more decimal places implies that your answer is accurate to this number of decimals, which is misleading. However, numbers should only be rounded at the end of a calculation. If you round intermediate values you will introduce rounding errors into your calculations, which can cause major errors in your final figure.

When rounding, remember the rule that numbers below 5 are rounded *down* and numbers of 5 and above are rounded *up*. So 1.5432 is 1.543 to 3 decimal places but 1.5435 is 1.544 to 3 decimal places.

Another form of cutting down the number of digits in an answer is to give a stated number of *significant* figures. In many cases the two systems will give identical results, but the real difference with using significant figures is that zeros are only included when they are significant. Thus 0.01654 becomes 0.0165 to three significant figures while 1.01654 would become 1.02. Significant figures can also be used when handling large numbers. For example, 13 256 is 13 000 to 2 significant figures. The zeros have to be added to maintain the place value of the remaining numbers.

If very large or very small numbers are involved it is all too easy to make a mistake and accidentally lose a digit. To avoid this you can use *scientific* notation. Scientific notation is in the form of $a \times 10^b$ where a is a decimal number below 10 and b is the number of places the decimal point needs to be moved to arrive back at the original number. For example, 25 438 176 can be changed to 2.5438176×10^7 as the decimal place has been moved 7 places to the left. Scientific calculators use this method when the number exceeds a set number of digits, except that the base 10 is not displayed – a source of confusion among students!

Powers and roots

$\left(\begin{array}{c}\textit{activity}\\ \textbf{1.3}\end{array}\right)$ Write down the value of the following.

1 2^3 **2** 3^4 **3** $\left(\frac{1}{2}\right)^3$ **4** 2^{-3} **5** $\sqrt{81}$ **6** $\sqrt[3]{27}$

Answers

1 8   **2** 81   **3** $\dfrac{1}{8}$ **4** $\dfrac{1}{8}$ **5** 9   **6** 3

When a number is raised to a power (or exponent) the number is multiplied by itself that number of times. So 2^3 means $2 \times 2 \times 2 = 8$. Powers take precedence in an expression after any brackets. In the calculation of $2 + 6 \times 3^2 - 4$, the order of calculation is as follows.

$$3^2 = 9, \quad 9 \times 6 = 54, \quad 54 + 2 - 4 = 52$$

Elementary algebra

activity **1.4**

1 Simplify the following expressions.

(a) $x + x^2 + y + 2x + 3x^2$ (b) $\dfrac{2x}{x}$ (c) $\dfrac{2x}{y}$ (d) $\dfrac{x^3}{x^2}$

(e) $\dfrac{x^2 - 4}{(x + 2)}$

2 Evaluate the expressions given in question 1 when $x = 2$ and $y = 4$.

3 Solve the following equations.

(a) $4x - 5 = 9$ (b) $\dfrac{7x - 4}{2} = 2x + 4$ (c) $x^2 + 4 = 20$

(d) $\dfrac{1}{x} = 10$ (e) $x^2 - 4x + 3 = 0$ (f) $2x^2 - 6x - 3 = 0$

Answers

1 (a) $4x^2 + 3x + y$ (b) 2   (c) $\dfrac{2x}{y}$ (d) x (e) $x - 2$

2 (a) 26   (b) 2   (c) 1   (d) 2   (e) 0

3 (a) 3.5   (b) 4   (c) ± 4 (d) 0.1   (e) 1 or 3
       (f) -0.436 or 3.436

Most students who have not studied mathematics beyond GCSE level find algebra difficult. The idea of replacing numbers by letters is quite abstract and many students do not understand the need for it. Unfortunately some understanding of algebra is essential if you are to successfully complete a quantitative methods course and many chapters in this book assume this understanding.

There are many algebraic techniques but the most important as far as this book is concerned is to be able to solve equations. To achieve this it is necessary to remember that whatever you do to one side of the equation you must do to the other. In solving

$$\frac{7x - 4}{2} = 2x + 4$$

the following steps are carried out:

1 Multiply both sides by 2. The equation then becomes $7x - 4 = 4x + 8$.
2 Subtract $4x$ from both sides to give $3x - 4 = 8$.

3 Add 4 to both sides to give $3x = 12$.

4 Divide both sides by 3.

This gives the answer $x = 4$.

When the unknown variable is raised to a power, the method of solving the equation becomes more complicated and in some cases it is necessary to resort to numerical methods. Quadratic equations are those involving x^2 and the method of solution depends on the equation. For $x^2 + 4 = 20$ the solution follows the method already described. That is, subtract 4 from both sides

$$x^2 = 16$$

and then take the square root of both sides

$$x = \sqrt{16}$$
$$= \pm 4$$

Notice that both $+4$ and -4 are solutions since $(-4)^2 = 16$.

Some quadratic equations can be *factorized*. To factorize an expression we need to find two factors that when multiplied together give the original expression. $x^2 + 2x = 0$ can be factorized by noting that x is a common factor to both terms. If we take out the x we get $x(x + 2) = 0$ and both x and $(x + 2)$ are factors of the original expression. The modified equation is easier to solve than the original as we can see that the equation is true when either $x = 0$ or $(x + 2) = 0$. That is, $x = 0$ or $x = -2$.

For $x^2 - 4x + 3 = 0$ we need to find two brackets that when multiplied together give these terms. Factorizing this type of expression can involve some trial and error but in this case it is fairly easy and will be

$$(x - 3)(x - 1) = 0$$

If you multiply the two brackets you get

$$x^2 - 3x - x + 3 = 0$$

which is the same as the original since $-3x - x = -4x$.

The solution to this equation is either

$$x - 3 = 0 \text{ or } x - 1 = 0$$

So x is either 1 or 3.

Factorizing only works easily for a small number of quadratic expressions, and a more general method is to use a formula. If the expression is in the form $ax^2 + bx + c = 0$, the formula is:

$$x = \frac{-b \pm \sqrt{b^2 - 4ac}}{2a}$$

For example, to solve $2x^2 - 6x - 3 = 0$, we first note that $a = 2$, $b = -6$ and $c = -3$

$$\text{so } x = \frac{-(-6) \pm \sqrt{(-6)^2 - 4 \times 2 \times (-3)}}{2 \times 2}$$

$$= \frac{6 \pm \sqrt{36 + 24}}{4}$$

$$= \frac{6 \pm 7.74597}{4}$$

$$= -0.436 \text{ or } 3.436$$

Indices and logs

activity 1.5

1 Simplify the following expressions.

(a) $2^3 \times 2^5$

(b) $3^2 \times 3^3$

(c) $2^3 \times 8^4$

(d) $\dfrac{10^5}{10^2}$

(e) $(2^3)^2$

(f) $a^x \times a^{2x}$

(g) $b^5 \times c^5$

(h) $\dfrac{a^x}{a^y}$

(i) $(a^x)^y$

(j) $\dfrac{a^{2x}}{a^{5x}}$

(k) $16^{3/2}$

2 Solve for x:

(a) $10^x = 15$

(b) $e^x = 1.6$

(c) $25 = 10 \times (1.1)^x$

(d) $1.8 = \dfrac{3^{5x}}{3^x}$

(e) $5^{2x+3} = 12 \times 6^{4x}$

Answers

1 (a) $2^8 = 256$ (b) $3^5 = 243$ (c) $2^{15} = 32768$ (d) $10^3 = 1000$
   (e) $2^6 = 64$ (f) a^{3x} (g) $(bc)^5$ (h) a^{x-y}
   (i) a^{xy} (j) a^{-3x} (k) 64

2 (a) 1.176 (b) 0.470 (c) 9.614 (d) 0.1338 (e) 0.5935

In Section 1.4 we saw that if a number is multiplied by itself a number of times then we can simplify the expression by the use of indices – so that $2 \times 2 \times 2 = 2^3$. In general the product of $a \times a \times a \ldots$ is written as a^n. We say that the *base* (a) is raised to the power of n.

There are 3 important formulae for indices and these are:

$$a^m \times a^n = a^{m+n}$$
$$a^m \div a^n = a^{m-n}$$
$$(a^m)^n = a^{mn}$$

Therefore, providing the bases are the same, you can add or subtract the powers.

So $2^3 \times 2^5 = 2^{3+5}$
$$= 2^8$$
$$= 256$$

and $\dfrac{10^5}{10^2} = 10^{5-2}$
$$= 10^3$$
$$= 1000$$

If m and n have the same value (say x) then $a^x \div a^x = a^0$.

As this expression must also equal 1, it follows that $a^0 = 1$. Also $a^1 = a$.

The power can be negative or fractional. $1/a^n$ can also be written as a^{-n}, and $a^{1/2}$ is the same as $\sqrt{a}$.

We could simplify $16^{3/2}$ to $((16)^{1/2})^3$. Since the square root of 16 is 4, then $4^3 = 64$.

We can rewrite $Y = a^x$ as $x = \log_a Y$. The word *log* is short for *logarithm* and this expression is read as x equals log of Y to the base a. There are only two bases you need worry about; these are base 10 and base e. These bases can be found on all scientific calculators; log to base 10 is usually written as *log*, and log to base e is written as *ln*.

There are three important formulae for logs that apply to all bases and these are:

$$\log(uv) = \log u + \log v$$
$$\log(u/v) = \log u - \log v$$
$$\log x^n = n \log x$$

The importance of logs as far as this book is concerned is the ability to use the laws of logs to solve certain types of equations. For example, to solve $5^{2x+3} = 12 \times 6^{4x}$ you would carry out the following steps.

$$\log(5^{2x+3}) = \log(12 \times 6^{4x})$$
$$(2x + 3)\log 5 = \log 12 + \log 6^{4x}$$
$$2x \log 5 + 3 \log 5 = \log 12 + 4x \log 6$$
$$2x \log 5 - 4x \log 6 = \log 12 - 3 \log 5$$
$$2x(\log 5 - 2 \log 6) = \log 12 - 3 \log 5$$
$$2x = \frac{\log 12 - 3 \log 5}{\log 5 - 2 \log 6}$$
$$2x = \frac{1.0792 - 3 \times 0.6990}{0.6990 - 2 \times 0.7782}$$
$$2x = \frac{-1.0178}{-0.8574}$$
$$2x = 1.1871$$
$$x = 0.5935$$

Mathematical symbols

activity **1.6**

What do the following symbols stand for?

1 $<$ 2 $\leq$ 3 $>$ 4 $\geq$ 5 $\neq$ 6 $\cong$ 7 $\sum$

Answers

1 less than	2 less than or equal to
3 greater than	4 greater than or equal to
5 not equal to	6 approximately equal to
7 the sum of	

We will be using all these symbols in later chapters of the book, particularly the summation sign. If you see the expression $\sum x$ it means you should add up all the values of x, while $\sum xy$ means multiply the pairs of x and y before summing them. For example, in Table 1.2 there are two columns of numbers which I have called x and y.

From Table 1.2 $\sum x = 2 + 1 + 4 + 6 + 4 \quad = 17$

$$\sum xy = 14 + 5 + 8 + 18 + 16 = 61$$

$$\sum x^2 = 4 + 1 + 16 + 36 + 16 = 73$$

If your calculator has the SD or Statistical Data function many of these calculations can be done automatically for you.

Table 1.2 Use of the summation sign

x	y	xy
2	7	14
1	5	5
4	2	8
6	3	18
4	4	16

Graphs and straight lines

activity
1.7

Which of the following equations represent straight lines?

1 $y = 2x + 5$ **2** $y + 4x = 20$ **3** $y = 8$ **4** $y = x$ **5** $y = x^2$

Answers
All except equation 5.

The equation of a straight line is $y = mx + c$, where m is the gradient and c is the value of y when $x = 0$ (often referred to as the *intercept* on the y-axis). Equation 1 is obviously a straight line with $m = 2$ and $c = 5$. Equation 2 is also a straight line and this may be easier to see if you subtract $4x$ from both sides of the equation.

That is: $y = 20 - 4x$

or $y = -4x + 20$

This equation is now in the standard form and you should see that $m = -4$ and $c = 20$. Equation 3 is another straight line but this is a special one. This could be written as $y = 0x + 8$ and you will see that $m = 0$; that is, the gradient is zero. This can be therefore be represented as a *horizontal* line. Equation 4 can be written as $y = x + 0$, so this represents a straight line with a gradient of 1 and c of 0. This line passes through the origin of the graph (that is, $x = 0$, $y = 0$). Equation 5 is *not* a straight line since y increases as the *square* of x. The graphs of these equations are shown in Figure 1.1.

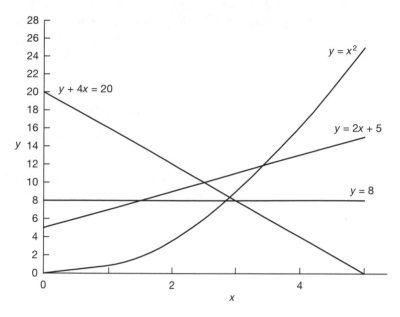

Figure 1.1 Graph for Activity 1.7

Solving linear equations graphically

activity
1.8

Plot the equations $2y + x = 8$ and $y + 2x = 7$ on the same graph and write down the coordinates of the point of intersection.

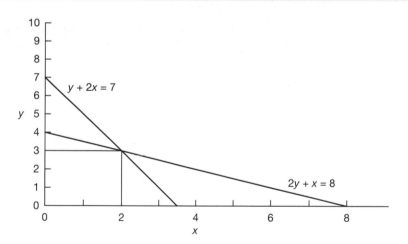

Figure 1.2 Solving equations graphically

You should have obtained the graph shown in Figure 1.2. The point of intersection of the two lines is at the point $x = 2$, $y = 3$. This can be written as (2,3). In this example the coordinates of the point of intersection were both whole numbers, which made it easy to read from your graph. Unfortunately this is not always the case and accurately reading fractional values from a graph is difficult. A better method is the algebraic method of *simultaneous equations*.

Solving linear equations simultaneously

Solve the equations given in Activity 1.8 simultaneously.

All being well, your answer agreed with the graphical method. The method of solving simultaneous equations I prefer is the method of *elimination*. To use this method the two equations are written down as follows:

$$y + 2x = 7 \tag{1}$$
$$2y + x = 8 \tag{2}$$

The coefficients of either x or y must be equal in the two equations and this is achieved by multiplying *both* sides of equation (1) by 2.

The equations can now be *subtracted*:

$$2y + 4x = 14$$
$$\underline{2y + x = 8}$$
$$3x = 6 \quad (y \text{ has now been 'eliminated'})$$

That is $x = 2$

This value of x can now be substituted back into either equation (1) or (2) to give the value of y. Using equation (2):

$$2y + 2 = 8$$
$$2y = 6$$

Therefore $y = 3$

Inequations

activity 1.10

1   What do the following inequations mean?
   (a) $y + 2x \leq 7$
   (b) $2y + x \geq 8$

2   How would you represent these two inequations graphically? And what does the term 'intersection' mean in this case?

Answers

1   Inequation (a) means that the sum of the left hand side of the equation must be less than or equal to 7; that is, the sum cannot be greater than 7. Inequation (b) means that the sum of the left hand side of the equation must be at least 8; it cannot be less.

2 Whereas an equation can be represented by a straight line, an inequation is represented by a *region*. The equation $y + 2x = 7$ forms the *boundary* of the region represented by the inequation $y + 2x \leq 7$. Similarly the equation $2y + x = 8$ forms the boundary of the region $2y + x \geq 8$. The region can only be on one side of the boundary and this can be found by inspection; that is, a point is investigated to see if it satisfies the inequation. The easiest point to try is the origin ($x = 0$, $y = 0$), except when the boundary passes through this point. When the region has been found it needs to be identified. This can be done by shading. The normal convention is to shade the *unwanted* region and this is the convention adopted in this book. You can see this in Figure 1.3.

The intersection of regions is the area on the graph that satisfies *all* inequations. In this example, the area is represented by ABC. Any point within this area (including the boundaries) satisfies both inequations.

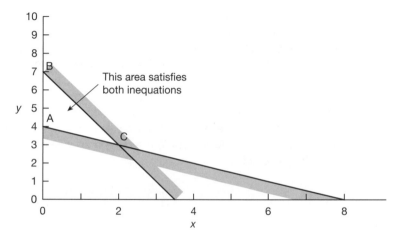

Figure 1.3 Graph for Activity 1.10

Further reading

There are a number of texts that are designed to help the student with basic mathematics such as Rowe (2002) and Morris (2007). There are also many online sources such as the BBC's Skillswise (www.bbc.co.uk/skillswise/numbers/wholenumbers/) which is part of their online learning support series (www.bbc.co.uk/learning/subjects/maths/shtml).

KEEPING UP WITH CHANGE: INDEX NUMBERS

OBJECTIVES

- To be able to calculate a simple one-item index
- To be able to calculate the Laspeyres' index
- To be able to calculate the Paasche's index
- To understand how the different consumer price indices are calculated, and to be able to use the RPI to deflate financial data

INTRODUCTION

An index is a means of comparing changes in some variable, often price over time. This is particularly useful when there are many items involved and when the prices and quantities are in different units. The best-known index in the UK is the *retail price index* (RPI) although the *consumer price index* (CPI) is becoming more prominent now that it is the official measure of inflation when it comes to up-rating public sector pensions and benefits. Both indices compare the price of a 'basket' of goods from one month to another. This chapter looks at the construction and use of different types of indices.

As a start we will use the idea of an index to see how the price and consumption of oil have changed from 1990 to 2014. This type of index is called a *simple index* as only one variable is involved.

QUANTITATIVE METHODS IN ACTION

Is the demand for oil increasing?

There are reckoned to be 1700.1 billion barrels of oil reserves worldwide (source: BP). It is estimated this will last 52.5 years at current consumption. Although new sources of oil are being found (e.g. from shale rock), oil is not a renewable resource – the world will eventually have to survive without oil.

Global oil consumption increased by 0.8 million barrels per day (b/d), or 0.8%, during 2014. China recorded the highest increase at +390,000 b/d. However, during 2014–15 the demand for oil plummeted, and as a consequence the average price of a barrel of Brent crude oil fell to less than $100 during 2014. This has benefitted the UK in that it helped inflation to fall to a record low.

Records of oil consumption and price for every country in the world are available since 1965 from the BP website (http://www.bp.com). Part of this data for the USA, China and the UK has been downloaded and is shown in Table 2.1. A chart of the consumption data is shown in Figure 2.1. Oil price is given at 2014 prices, and you will see the reason for this later in the chapter.

What do these figures and chart tell us? It is immediately obvious that the USA has a far greater consumption than either China or the UK. It is also clear that China's consumption has increased considerably since 1990. However, as the magnitude of the consumption for each country is so different, it is difficult to make direct comparisons. We will see in this chapter how the use of index numbers allows comparisons to be made even when the magnitude of the figures is so different.

Table 2.1 Oil price and oil consumption (in thousand barrels daily) since 1990

	1990	1991	1992	1993	1994	1995	1996	1997	1998	1999	2000	2001	2002
Price[1]	42.97	34.77	32.60	27.80	25.27	26.43	31.19	28.16	18.47	25.54	39.17	32.68	32.93
USA	16988	16713	17033	17236	17719	17725	18309	18621	18917	19519	19701	19649	19761
China	2320	2520	2736	3047	3115	3394	3722	4120	4216	4452	4766	4859	5262
UK	1754	1753	1771	1788	1778	1759	1798	1754	1743	1729	1704	1704	1700

	2003	2004	2005	2006	2007	2008	2009	2010	2011	2012	2013	2014
Price[1]	37.09	47.96	66.09	76.50	82.65	106.94	68.05	86.31	117.09	115.14	110.42	98.95
USA	20033	20732	20802	20687	20680	19490	18771	19180	18882	18490	18961	19035
China	5771	6740	6923	7437	7817	7937	8212	9266	9791	10231	10664	11056
UK	1723	1766	1806	1788	1716	1683	1610	1588	1532	1520	1494	1501

[1]Price is $ per barrel at 2014 prices.
Source: BP Statistical Review of World Energy, 2015.

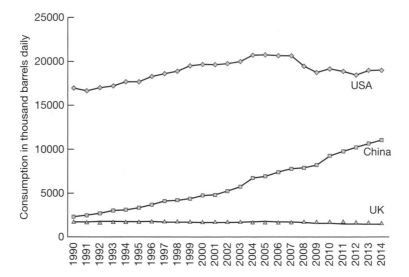

Figure 2.1 Line chart of oil consumption for the USA, China and the UK

Source: BP Statistical Review of World Energy, 2015.

Simple indices

From Table 2.1 we see that between 1990 and 2014 the price of a barrel of oil rose by $55.97. But how much had it gone up relative to the price in 1990? If 1990 is used as a base, it becomes possible to compare changes in price with this base. The base is given a value of 100: a price increase would result in a value greater than 100, whereas a price decrease would result in a value less than 100. Thus if $42.97 is equivalent to 100, then $98.95 is equivalent to

$$\frac{100}{42.97} \times 98.95 = 230.3$$

The value 230.3 is called the *price index*, and 1990 is the *base year*. To calculate the percentage change we do the following calculation:

$$\frac{230.3 - 100}{100} \times 100 = 130.3\%$$

This means that the price in 2014 is 130.3% of what it was in 1990. As you see, to find the percentage increase we simply take 100 away from the index (if the index was below 100, we would, of course, take the index away from 100, which would represent a decrease in the value relative to the base).

If p_n represents the price in the current year (year n) and p_0 represents the price in the base year, then the price index is:

$$\frac{100}{p_0} \times p_n$$

More normally this is expressed as:

$$\frac{p_n}{p_0} \times 100$$

The change in the oil consumption can also be represented by an *index number*. In this case we are calculating the change in quantity, so the formula is:

$$\frac{q_n}{q_0} \times 100$$

where q_0 represents the quantity at the base year and q_n the quantity at year n.

For the USA, the quantity index for 2014 using 1990 as the base year is therefore:

$$\frac{19035}{16988} \times 100 = 112.0$$

The USA has thus shown a 12% increase in oil consumption between 1990 and 2014.

activity
2.1

Use Excel to calculate both the price index and the quantity index for all three countries. Plot each index on the same chart, and explain what the chart tells you about the change in price and consumption over the 24-year span.

The chart in Figure 2.2 shows that from 1990 to 2003 the price of oil was fairly stable, but after 2003 the price of oil (in today's prices) started to rise rapidly. The

Figure 2.2 Index of oil price and consumption for the USA, China and the UK
Source: BP Statistical Review of World Energy, 2015.

price fell in 2009 due to the world recession (and hence a reduction in the demand for oil). The price then rose again until 2011 but has been on a steady decline since then. This decline is partly due to increased production by the USA and OPEC and partly due to weak consumption growth. What is very clear from the chart is that China has shown a dramatic increase in consumption over the entire 24-year period.

example
2.1

The resources used in the manufacture of glass-fibre boats include resin, glass-fibre mat and labour. The price of each of these resources varies and the average price during each of the years 2013 to 2015 is shown in Table 2.2.

Table 2.2 Price data for Example 2.1

Item	2013	2014	2015
Resin	£0.25/l	£0.20/l	£0.18/l
Mat	£0.16/m²	£0.16/m²	£0.20/m²
Labour	£5.50/hour	£5.85/hour	£8.30/hour

activity
2.2

Calculate the index for each item using 2013 as the base year.

You should have obtained the table shown in Table 2.3.

Table 2.3 Price index for Activity 2.2

Item	2013	2014	2015
Resin	100	80	72
Mat	100	100	125
Labour	100	106	151

You can see that the index for resin has shown a decrease while labour has shown the largest increase. But what does this tell you about the cost of production? Is it possible to combine the data in some way so that an aggregate index can be obtained?

(activity 2.3) Could you obtain an aggregate index simply by adding the prices together for each year?

There are two problems with this approach: first, the items are in different units; you have litres, square metres and hours; and second, the importance of each item might be different. If labour is the dominant cost then the aggregate index should reflect this fact. To overcome these problems each item is weighted according to its importance. When this is done you have a *weighted aggregate index*.

Weighted aggregate indices

In order to weight an index it is necessary to have information on the importance of each item. For the boat example, this could be done by recording the quantities used in its production.

(example 2.2) The quantities required in the production of a boat vary from year to year as production methods change. This can be seen in Table 2.4.

Table 2.4 Quantity data for Example 2.2

Item	2013	2014	2015
Resin	50 l	48 l	48 l
Mat	200 m²	210 m²	215 m²
Labour	30 hours	27 hours	23 hours

(activity 2.4) How might you use the information in Examples 2.1 and 2.2 to create an aggregate index?

Since price × quantity equals the cost of that item, the aggregate index could be obtained as:

Total cost of production at current prices
———————————————————————————
Total cost of production at base year prices

There is, however, one problem with this definition. What quantities should we use? Both price and quantities have varied from year to year and for comparison purposes we need to use the same quantities for the numerator and denominator of the index. The choice is to use either the base year quantities or the current year quantities. When you use the former you have a base weighted or *Laspeyres'* index, and when you use the latter you have a current weighted or *Paasche's* index.

Laspeyres' index

The definition of the Laspeyres' index is:

Total cost of base year quantities at current prices
———————————————————————————
Total cost of base year quantities at base year prices

Using p to represent price and q to represent quantity, this definition can be expressed as:

Sum of current prices times base quantities

$$\text{Laspeyres' index} = \frac{\Sigma p_n q_0}{\Sigma p_0 q_0} \times 100$$

Sum of base prices times base quantities

In order to calculate this index for the boat example, you may find it useful to write the data from Examples 2.1 and 2.2 into another table (Table 2.5).

Table 2.5 Price and quantity combined

Item	2013		2014		2015	
	Price	Quantity	Price	Quantity	Price	Quantity
Resin	£0.25	50	£0.20	48	£0.18	48
Mat	£0.16	200	£0.16	210	£0.20	215
Labour	£5.50	30	£5.85	27	£8.30	23

activity **2.5**

Calculate the Laspeyres' index for 2014 and 2015 using 2013 as the base year.

Each year needs to be calculated separately. These calculations are tabulated in Tables 2.6 and 2.7.

Table 2.6 Calculation of Laspeyres' index for 2014

p_0	q_0	p_n	$p_0 q_0$	$p_n q_0$
0.25	50	0.20	12.5	10.0
0.16	200	0.16	32.0	32.0
5.50	30	5.85	165.0	175.5
		Sum	209.5	217.5

Table 2.7 Calculation of Laspeyres' index for 2015

p_0	q_0	p_n	$p_0 q_0$	$p_n q_0$
0.25	50	0.18	12.5	9.0
0.16	200	0.20	32.0	40.0
5.50	30	8.30	165.0	249.0
		Sum	209.5	298.0

$$\text{So the Laspeyres' index for 2014} = \frac{217.5}{209.5} \times 100 = 103.8$$

$$\text{and for 2015 it is} = \frac{298.0}{209.5} \times 100 = 142.2$$

You can see from these calculations that there has been a dramatic increase in the index from 2014 to 2015. This was due to the large increase in labour costs that took place during 2014 to 2015.

Paasche's index

The definition of the Paasche's index is:

$$\frac{\text{Total cost of current year quantities at current prices}}{\text{Total cost of current year quantities at base year prices}}$$

This can again be expressed in algebraic form as:

Sum of current prices times base quantities

$$\text{Paasche's index} = \frac{\Sigma p_n q_n}{\Sigma p_0 q_n} \times 100$$

Sum of base prices times base quantities

activity 2.6

Calculate the Paasche's index for the boat building example.

A table can again be used in the calculation. The calculations for 2010 are shown in Table 2.8.

Table 2.8 Calculation of Paasche's index for 2014

p_0	q_0	p_n	$p_0 q_0$	$p_n q_0$
0.25	48	0.20	12.00	9.60
0.16	210	0.16	33.60	33.60
5.50	27	5.85	148.50	157.95
		Sum	194.10	201.15

So the Paasche's index for 2014 $= \dfrac{201.15}{194.1} \times 100 = 103.6$

If you repeat these calculations for 2015 you should find that the sum of $p_0 q_n$ is 172.9 and the sum of $p_n q_n$ is 242.54. So the Paasche's index for 2015 is:

$$\frac{242.54}{172.9} \times 100 = 140.3$$

Both indices give similar results for this data and in general there will not be a great difference between the two unless the weights (quantities) are very different. Table 2.9 summarizes the advantages and disadvantages of each index.

Table 2.9 Comparison of the two indices

	Laspeyres' index	Paasche's index
Ease of calculation	Denominator only calculated once	Denominator recalculated each year
Quantities required each year	No, only base quantities required	Yes
Comparability	Direct comparison from year to year	No direct comparison
Accuracy	Weights quickly become out of date	Reflects consumption patterns in current year

In practice the Laspeyres' index is the most commonly used index and the base year is redefined at regular intervals. When the base year is redefined it is a good idea to recalculate the index for previous years. For example, the figures below represent an index for the years 2007 to 2015. The base year was 2007 but it has been decided to change the base year to 2015.

2007	2008	2009	2010	2011	2012	2013	2014	2015
100	105.6	108.9	121.2	142.3	145.1	147.9	148.8	153.1

The index in 2007 becomes

$$\frac{100}{153.1} \times 100 = 65.3$$

activity 2.7

Calculate the index for each subsequent year.

You should have obtained the following figures:

2007	2008	2009	2010	2011	2012	2013	2014	2015
65.3	69.0	71.1	79.2	92.9	94.8	96.6	97.2	100

Consumer price indices

Two very important indices are the retail price index (RPI) and the consumer price index (CPI). They both show how prices have changed (usually upwards!) over the years and are a determining factor in deciding how interest rates, wages, pensions and tax allowances for instance are changed. Both indices measure the change in the price of a 'basket' of goods and are used as a measure of inflation although the government inflation target is based in the CPI. The RPI covers some 650 items divided into 14 groups, such as food, housing and motoring expenditure. Each component of the index is given a weight to represent the importance of that item and the weights are updated annually by the *family expenditure survey*. Prices of each item in the index are checked monthly. The weights used in the RPI are designed for the 'average' family and are not representative of high income groups or pensioners. The CPI is similar but excludes things like council tax and other housing costs; however, its weights cover all income groups. It also includes some financial services and follows international definitions.

The current RPI is based on prices of goods in January 1987, and at this date the index was given a value of 100. In January 2014 the RPI was 252.60, so a basket of goods costing £100 in 1987 would have cost £252.60 in January 2014. This means that prices according to the RPI have increased by 152.6% (252.6 − 100) during this period.

DID YOU KNOW?

In the 2010 June budget the Chancellor of the Exchequer George Osborne announced that in future, public sector benefits and pensions will be linked to the CPI and not the RPI. Over the past 20 years the CPI has only been greater than the RPI on 3 occasions so in general annual increases will be lower than if the RPI had been used.

activity
2.8

The RPI in November 2013 was 252.1 and the CPI was 127.0. A year later the value of the two indices was, respectively, 257.1 and 128.2. Compare the rates of inflation given by these two indices.

The change in the RPI during the year 2013/4 was $257.1 − 252.1 = 5.0$, so the percentage change relative to November 2013 is $5.0/252.1 \times 100 = 2.0\%$. An alternative way of calculating the percentage change is $257.1/252.1 = 1.020$, which is a 2.0% change.

Similarly, for the CPI the change during the same period is $128.2/127.0 = 1.009$, which is a 0.9% change. So inflation is rising faster according to the RPI (the way that the Office for National Statistics [ONS] calculates the annual inflation rate is slightly more complicated, but the principle is the same).

Inflation makes the value of a £1 now worth less in the future. Likewise a £1 in the past is worth less now. This means that a company's cash flow or a person's salary should be *deflated* to allow for inflation. When we do this, we usually talk about the *real* change in cash flow or earnings.

The next example illustrates a company's turnover during a 6-year period.

example
2.3

A company's turnover (in £m) since 2008 has been as follows:

2008	2009	2010	2011	2012	2013
2.3	3.3	4.1	4.2	4.4	4.7

It looks as if turnover has been steadily increasing, but at the same time the CPI has also been increasing. The average value of the CPI since 2008 has been as follows:

2008	2009	2010	2011	2012	2013
108.5	110.8	114.5	119.6	123.0	126.1

Source: Monthly Digest of Statistics. Adapted from data from the Office for National Statistics licensed under the Open Government Licence v.3.0.

Although the turnover has increased from £2.3m to £3.3m between 2008 and 2009, the CPI has increased from 108.5 to 110.8. This means that the CPI has changed by $110.8/108.5 = 1.021$, or 2.1%. £3.3m is therefore only really worth $£3.3/1.021 = £3.23m$ at 2008 prices. An easier way to deflate an amount is as follows

$$\text{Value now} = \frac{\text{Value then} \times \text{CPI then}}{\text{CPI now}}$$

So using our example, the £3.3m turnover in 2009 becomes

$$3.3 \times \frac{108.5}{110.8} = £3.23m$$

activity 2.9

Calculate the deflated turnover for the remainder of the years.

You should have obtained the figures below:

2008	2009	2010	2011	2012	2013
2.30	3.23	3.89	3.81	3.88	4.04

The picture is now of rising turnover until 2010, when it levels off before rising again a year later. This can be seen clearly in Figure 2.3.

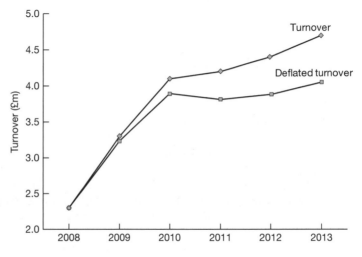

Figure 2.3 Chart for Activity 2.9

Reflection

Indices are as common today as averages, but as with averages, many people do not really understand what an index is. For example, when inflation is quoted as (say) 3%, how many people really understand that this means that the retail (or consumer) price index has increased by 3%? The RPI in November 2013 was 252.1.0, whereas for the same month a year later it was 257.1, a change of 5 points in the index. In percentage terms, however, this represents a change of 2.0%, and this is used as one measure of inflation.

Another complicating factor is that there are different measures of inflation. The RPI was the most common index. It was used to adjust pensions and showed the effect of inflation on household expenditure. However the UK government's preferred measure is now the CPI, and this is now used as a measure of inflation when uprating pensions and benefits. So between 2013 and 2014 the CPI was only 1%, which is half that of the RPI! There are several other indices used in the UK such as tax and price index (TPI) which includes income tax paid and allows the government to see what increase in pay is needed to compensate for tax rises.

Indices can be used to monitor all kinds of prices and commodities. The oil price data shown above in *Quantitative methods in action* might not be an obvious set of data to make into an index, but as you saw, the index helps enormously in comparing the volumes of oil consumption in the different countries. From Figure 2.2, we can see clearly the rapid rise in China's oil consumption between 1990 and 2014. What this chart doesn't tell us is what the future consumption of oil will be. Although BP has estimated that there are 52.5 years of oil reserves remaining, this figure is based on current consumption and reserves.

Key points

- An *index* allows changes in a variable to be compared over a period of time.
- The *base index* is given a value of 100, so an index value below 100 means a decrease and a value above 100 means an increase. As the base is 100, these changes can also be expressed in percentage terms.
- For a single item or variable, a *simple index* can be used.
- Where several items are involved, it is necessary to use a *weighted aggregate index*.
- There are two main *weighted indices*. These are *Laspeyres' index*, which is a base weighted index, and *Paasche's index*, which is a current weighted index.
- The Laspeyres' index is easier to use but soon gets out of date, while the Paasche's index reflects consumption patterns in the current year.
- The *retail price index* (*RPI*) and *consumer price index* (*CPI*) use consumption patterns as weights. These are derived from a family expenditure survey.
- The RPI and CPI are used as measures of *inflation*, and allow financial data to be *deflated*. The CPI is the index favoured by the UK government and is used to up-rate public sector pensions and benefits.

Further reading

Most general quantitative method texts have a chapter on index numbers. The text by Curwin and Slater (2013) gives a good coverage, particularly on the differences between RPI and CPI. There are many on-line sources particularly from the Office of National Statistics (ONS). The ONS website for all sources of economic data including the RPI and CP is www.ons.gov.uk.

http://www.**palgrave.com**/oakshott-eqm6

Solutions to all questions are freely available

Practice questions

1   Labour costs (in £000s) for an engineering company over the last 10 years has been as follows

2006	2007	2008	2009	2010	2011	2012	2013	2014	2015
50.1	65.3	68.6	72.0	76.6	78.3	88.7	90.5	99.3	112.9

Convert these costs into an index using 2002 as the base year.

2   The cost of an 'average' laptop computer has fallen over the last 3 years

Year 1   £650   Year 2   £580   Year 3   £410

Create an index of laptop prices using year 1 as the base year.

3   A manufacturer of greeting cards requires ink, card and production staff to produce its range of cards. The estimated cost of each resource over the past 3 years is as follows:

Resource	2013	2014	2015
Ink (£ per litre)	£0.55	£0.58	£0.76
Card (£ per m²)	£0.05	£0.05	£0.08
Labour (£ per hour)	£6.50	£6.90	£7.00

Create a simple index for each resource and comment on which resource has increased the most.

4   In addition to the cost data for the greeting card manufacturer in question 3 the quantities of each resource used over the past 3 years is as follows.

Resource	2013	2014	2015
Ink (litres)	4000	5000	3000
Card (m²)	115 000	124 000	110 000
Labour (number)	25	34	30

(a) Calculate the Laspeyres' index for 2014 and 2015 using 2013 as the base year.

(b) Calculate the Paasche's index for 2014 and 2015 using 2013 as the base year.

(c) Comment on the change in both indices over the 3 years.

5   The price and quantity consumed in a normal week of 3 items of food for a family are as follows:

	2005		2015	
	Price	Qty	Price	Qty
Bread	28p/loaf	6 loaves	78p/loaf	6 loaves
Milk	20p/pint	15 pints	150p/pint	12 pints
Tea	96p/packet	1 packet	75p/packet	2 packets

(a) Calculate the Laspeyres' index for 2015 using 2005 as the base year.

(b) Calculate the Paasche's index for 2015 using 2005 as the base year.

6   A person has a portfolio of 4 shares. The price and quantity of shares held between 1998 and 2011 are as follows:

	1998		2011	
Share	Price	No. held	Price	No. held
Company A	160	200	520	500
Company B	350	650	265	250
Company C	105	600	140	400
Company D	53	100	159	200

(a) Calculate the Laspeyres' index for 2011 using 1998 as the base year.

(b) Calculate the Paasche's index for 2011 using 1998 as the base year.

7. A company employs a range of employees in their factory, from unskilled workers to supervisory staff. The number in each group over the last few years has been as follows:

Staff	Year 1		Year 2		Year 3	
	Hourly wage (£)	No. employees	Hourly wage (£)	No. employees	Hourly wage (£)	No. employees
Supervisor	12	10	14	12	15	15
Skilled	9	120	10	160	11	160
Unskilled	6	200	7	200	8	180

(a) Create a simple index for wages for each staff group, using year 1 as the base year. Which group of employees has increased its wages the most?

(b) Calculate the Laspeyres' index using year 1 as the base year.

(c) Calculate the Paasche's index using year 1 as the base year.

(d) Comment on the change in both indices over the 3 years.

8 The price of a house in a residential district fell from £140 00 in 2004 to £105 000 in 2008. What was the real drop in price if the retail price index changed from 186.7 in 2004 to 214.8 in 2008?

9 A company's turnover (in £m) since 2005 has been as follows:

2005	2006	2007	2008	2009	2010
15.3	10.3	12.1	15.2	24.4	34.7

What has been the real turnover if the value of the RPI for each of these years has been as follows?

2005	2006	2007	2008	2009	2010
192.0	198.1	206.8	214.8	213.7	223.6

10 The following table gives the number employed by each department and the average salary for that department. Calculate Laspeyres' index and Paasche's index for 2011 using 2003 as the base year.

	2003		2011	
	Number employed	Av. salary (£000s)	Number employed	Av. salary (£000s)
Sales	120	7.5	158	9.0
Admin.	41	10.0	52	12.5
Clerical	25	8.0	30	10.0
Managerial	21	18.0	25	22.4

(*Source*: Payroll Department)

11 Using the information on the price and quantities used of given materials in 2006 and 2011, calculate for these years:
(a) the Laspeyres' index
(b) the Paasche's index

	2006		2011	
Material	Price (£)	Quantity	Price (£)	Quantity
A	3.63	3	4.49	2
B	2.11	4	3.26	6
C	10.03	1	12.05	1
D	4.01	7	5.21	5

12 (a) For the following data on the price of a security over 6 months, construct a fixed base index (use August = 100).

Month	Aug	Sept	Oct	Nov	Dec	Jan
Price	155	143	120	139	165	162

(b) By what percentage has the security price changed between:
   (i) August and January?
   (ii) September and December?

13 The following table gives the average weekly wage and the average retail price index (RPI) for the years 2008–2010:

Year	2008	2009	2010
Av. weekly wage (£s)	255.1	271.3	290.7
Av. RPI	214.8	213.7	223.6

Deflate the wage figures to 2008 values. Comment on the 'real value' of wages over this period of time.

14 The price of a house in a residential district fell from £62 000 in 2008 to £57 500 in 2010. What was the real drop in price? (Use the RPI figures from question 12.)

15 (a) The RPI figures in Question 12 used January 1987 as the base period (that is, January 1987 = 100). Construct a table of RPIs using the 'average' figures quoted for the years 2008–2010 with 2008 as the base period.
   (b) By what percentage has the average RPI changed between:
     (i) 2008 and 2009?
     (ii) 2008 and 2010?
     (iii) 2009 and 2010?

Assignment

You are to use the internet to investigate the composition of the CPI and how it is updated. You should use graphs and diagrams to illustrate its composition and provide examples of how the index is calculated. Discuss how useful this index would be to:

(a) the government as a means of controlling inflation
(b) a union for wage negotiation purposes
(c) a pensioner in deciding how well off he or she is likely to be next year.

Finally, comment on the accuracy of the index and how it compares to the RPI.

II

COLLECTING AND INTERPRETING DATA

3 COLLECTING DATA: SURVEYS AND SAMPLES

OBJECTIVES

- To understand the difference between a sampling frame, a sample and a population
- To understand the difference between probabilistic and non-probabilistic sampling
- To know how to select the correct sampling method in different situations
- To understand how to design a questionnaire

INTRODUCTION

Many decisions made by businesses and by the government are the result of information obtained from sample data, as it is often too costly or impractical to collect data for the whole population.

Data may already exist or may have to be collected. When we have to collect our own data, we call it *primary* data. When it already exists, as in government statistics, we call it *secondary* data. The collection of data can take many forms, but in this chapter we will concentrate on data that is collected by carrying out surveys. For example, during both the Scottish referendum in 2014 and the UK General Election in 2015, many surveys were undertaken by market research companies. The purpose of these surveys was not just to try and understand how people might vote but also to look at attitudes to issues and leaders, for example. Most of these surveys would have been conducted by telephone or face-to-face, although in some other less urgent surveys, people are sent questionnaires by post or email, or they complete a questionnaire online.

In the surveys undertaken during the Scottish referendum and the UK General Election, a lot of care would have gone into selecting a representative sample of the target population. The samples had to be representative of the gender, age profile and political persuasion of the population being surveyed, as well as other attributes that might be considered to affect people's voting intentions or views. The number of people being surveyed would also be calculated to ensure that a specified level of accuracy was obtained. However, in the case of the UK General Election in 2015, the pollsters were predicting a 'hung' parliament. In actual fact the conservatives had a small majority over all other parties. So even with large samples, surveys can and do lead to erroneous results. A fuller discussion of accuracy issues when taking samples of data is given in Chapter 8.

As well as discussing ways of collecting samples of data, this chapter also discusses questionnaire design because it is very important to ensure that the type and wording of questions is given proper attention if the analysis is to be of use. Finally we will look at sources of secondary data available on the internet, as well as how to use search engines more effectively.

QUANTITATIVE METHODS IN ACTION

The Scottish referendum 2014

A big event in the UK in 2014 was the Scottish referendum. People over age 16 living in Scotland were given the opportunity to answer yes or no to the question 'Should Scotland be an independent country?' Although at one time it looked as if the Yes campaign might have won an historic victory, in the end the result was NO 55.3% and YES 44.7%; 3,623,344 people voted, which was an 84.6% turnout.

After the vote a great deal of analysis was done by pollsters and others to understand why voters voted the way they did. Lord Ashcroft Polls asked referendum voters what influenced their decision and whether they would reveal it to others. Two thousand forty-seven adults who voted were interviewed either online (831) or by telephone (1216). The questions they were asked included:

- How did you vote?
- When did you finally make up your mind how to vote in the referendum?

- What were the two or three most important issues in deciding how you ultimately voted?

They were also asked to rank the reasons that people gave for voting the way they did. The responses to the question on how they voted were analysed by gender, age and what political party they supported. Table 3.1 below is based on the responses to the question 'How did you vote?' Some interesting results have been included in the table. As you can see, women were less likely to vote yes than men. It is also clear that older voters were less likely to vote yes, with only 27% of people over age 65 voting in this way. There were no surprises with how the supporters of either the conservatives (generally seen as an English political party) or the Scottish National Party (SNP) voted.

We will discuss issues of obtaining a representative sample and how to interpret the results later in this chapter.

Table 3.1 Percentage that voted YES in the Scottish referendum

Category	% that voted YES
All	45
Men	47
Women	44
Age 16–24	51
Age 25–34	59
Age 35–44	53
Age 45–54	52
Age 55–64	43
Age 65+	27
Conservative	5
SNP	86

Source: Lordashcroftpolls.com

The basics of sampling

I am sure that you have been a *respondent* in a survey at least once in your life. Have you filled in a *questionnaire* or been stopped in the street and asked some questions? You no doubt know that the purpose of a survey is for some organization or person to obtain *information* about some issue or product. This information could range from what television programme you watched last night to your views on the government of the day.

A survey only collects information about a small subset of the *population*. The word 'population' can and often does refer to all the people in Britain or a town, but for statisticians it is also a general term used to refer to all groups or items being surveyed. For instance, it could refer to the viewing habits of all children in a town or, as you will see in a later chapter, it could refer to the weights of jars of coffee produced by a company during a week. The alternative to a survey is to question every member of the population, and when this is done it is called a *census*. Unfortunately it is expensive and very difficult to carry out a census, and also unnecessary. A survey of a small subset of the population, called a *sample*, can give surprisingly accurate results if carried out properly. Unfortunately, if not carried out correctly, the results can at best be unreliable and at worst misleading. Before you carry out a survey you need answers to several questions, such as:

- What is the purpose of this survey?
- What is my *target* population?
- Do I have a list of the population?
- How can I avoid bias in my sample?
- How accurate do I want my survey to be?
- What resources do I have at my disposal?
- How am I going to collect the required data?

DID YOU KNOW?

The 2011 census was estimated to have cost the taxpayer £460m (Cabinet Office estimate) – the most expensive ever.

There has been a census in the UK every 10 years since 1801.

The census in 2011 is expected to be the last one. Other sources of information such as the electoral roll, GP records, tax returns and school enrolments will probably be used instead.

It is crucial to be clear about the purpose of the survey. Not only will this dictate your target population but it will also allow you to formulate your questionnaire correctly. For example, if you are interested in consumers' opinion of a new alcoholic drink it would be pointless targeting people under 18 (and unethical). The target population should contain every person who is likely to buy your product or whose views you are particularly interested in.

Once you have selected your target population, you need to determine whether there is any list that would allow you to identify every member of the population. This list is called a *sampling frame*, and examples include the electoral register, a company's personnel records or even a list of all serial numbers of cars built by one car manufac-turer last year. Sometimes a sampling frame is simply not available or is too difficult to obtain, in which case achieving a *representative* sample will be more difficult, but not necessarily impossible.

| *activity* **3.1** | What would be your target population for a survey on motorway tariffs, and would there be a sampling frame available? |

If you were only interested in the views of British car drivers then anyone holding a UK driving licence would form your target population. A suitable sampling frame would be records held by the DVLC at Swansea. It would not be 100% accurate as drivers might have changed address and not informed the DVLC, or they might have died.

Once your target population has been chosen and an appropriate sampling frame identified, it is necessary to choose your sample. If the sample is chosen badly your results will be inaccurate due to *bias* in your sample. Bias is caused by choosing a sample that is unrepresentative of the target population. For example, perhaps you wanted to discover people's views on whether a sports field should be sold to a prop-erty developer. If your sample contained a large number of people from the local football club, then the sample is likely to be biased in favour of one particular group! To avoid bias you need to ensure that your sample is *representative* of the target popu-lation. You will see how this can be achieved later.

DID YOU KNOW?

In the US Presidential Election in 1936 between Alfred Landon and Franklin Roosevelt the *Literary Digest* sent out 10 million post cards asking people how they would vote. The magazine received almost 2.3 million back, and the result suggested that Landon was leading Roosevelt by 57% to 43%. A young pollster named George Gallup also did a survey but on a much smaller sample. He correctly predicted that Roosevelt would win easily. In the event Roosevelt went on to win with 60% against just 37% for Landon. The reason why the *Literary Digest* did so badly was that they used a directory of car owners and the telephone directory, which gave them a biased sample because only the better-off had cars or telephones. Gallup had used a much more representative sample.

The purpose of a survey is to obtain information about a population. All other things being equal, the accuracy of the sample results will depend on the sample size; the larger the sample, the more accurate the results. A large sample will clearly cost more than a small one, although the method that is employed to collect the data will also determine the accuracy and cost of the survey. Methods of data collection range from the use of postal questionnaires to 'face-to-face' interviews. Some methods of data collection are expensive but guarantee a good response rate, while others are cheap to administer but are likely to produce quite a poor response. Table 3.2 compares the main methods of collecting data.

Table 3.2 Methods of data collection

	Postal questionnaire	Telephone interviewing	Face-to-face interviewing	Online
Cost	Low	Moderate	High	Low
Response rate	Low	Moderate	High	Moderate
Speed	Slow	Fast	Fast*	Fast
Quantity of information collected	Limited	Moderate	High	Limited
Quality of information collected	Depends on how well the questionnaire has been designed	Good	High	Depends on how well the questionnaire has been designed

*The speed of collecting the data will be high but travelling time by the interviewers may need to be considered.

(activity 3.2) You have been asked to obtain the views of the student population at your institution regarding car parking facilities within the campus. What method of data collection would you use?

The best method would probably be face-to-face interviews, but it is unlikely that you would have the resources for this approach. Telephone interviewing is probably not realistic because of the cost and the fact that students' telephone numbers might be difficult to obtain. This leaves you with either a postal or online questionnaire, both of which should be quite reasonable for this relatively simple type of survey.

There are two types of sampling procedures for obtaining your sample. The first is *probabilistic* sampling, which requires the existence of a sampling frame. The second method is *non-probabilistic* sampling, which does not rely on a sampling frame. Probabilistic sampling is the most important form of sampling as it allows you to use probability theory to calculate the probability that a particular sample could have occurred by chance.

DID YOU KNOW?

During the 2010 General Election in the UK a crisp manufacturer was seen giving away packets of crisps outside King's Cross station. The crisp packets were coloured red (for Labour), blue (for the Conservatives) and yellow (for the Liberal Democrats). Each of these different coloured packets were in 3 identical bins which had the picture of the party leader on the front. This was a publicity stunt by the crisp manufacturer but could the number of the different coloured packets taken at any one time reveal the popularity of each of the leaders? (*Source:* BBC News Magazine, 6 January 2011).

Think of as many reasons as you can why the data might lie.

Questionnaire design

Questionnaire design is more of an art than a science and there is no universal design that would be suitable for all situations. The actual design will depend on factors such as:

■ the type of respondent (for example, business, consumers, children)
■ the method of data collection (postal, telephone, face-to-face or online)
■ the resources available.

However, even though no two questionnaires will be identical, it is possible to make a list of some 'dos and don'ts' that should apply to most questionnaires. The most important ones are:

- Do make each question brief and the wording clear and concise with minimal use of jargon. It shouldn't be necessary to explain to the respondent the meaning of a particular question.
- Do keep the length of the questionnaire to a minimum. A maximum of around 20 questions is probably a good guide for most surveys.
- Do make the questions simple to answer.
- Do make the questions as specific as possible. A question such as '*Are you a heavy smoker?*' could be interpreted differently by different respondents. It would be much better to give ranges such as '*Do you smoke less than 10 cigarettes a day?*', '*Between 10 and 20?*' and '*Over 20?*'
- Do have a logical sequence to the questions.
- Do start with simple questions such as gender, leaving more complicated questions for later in the questionnaire.
- Don't leave the most important question to last. There is a risk that if a respondent becomes bored with answering a questionnaire he or she may not complete the final section.
- Don't use leading questions. For example, '*What are your views on the level of indirect taxation in the UK?*' is better than '*Do you agree that indirect taxation in the UK is too high?*'
- Do try and avoid asking personal questions. Even information on salary is considered by many people to be personal and most respondents prefer to have salary ranges to select. It is often better to ask this type of question later in the questionnaire. If it is necessary to collect really personal information, a face-to-face interview is essential using experienced interviewers.
- Do use a filtering method if not all questions are applicable to all respondents. For example, '*Did you watch Eastenders last night?*' may then be followed by questions relating to this episode. To avoid asking non-viewers these questions you will need to have an instruction that allows these non-viewers to jump to the next appropriate question.
- Don't ask two questions in one. A question such as '*Is your job interesting and well paid?*' is unlikely to be answered with a simple yes or no.
- Don't ask questions that rely on memory. Asking respondents if they watched *Eastenders* last night is acceptable, but asking if they watched it last week or last month will not necessarily produce very reliable results.
- Don't ask hypothetical questions. Asking someone what he or she would do under a hypothetical situation (such as winning the National Lottery) is unlikely to lead to reliable results. In some surveys this type of question cannot be avoided, but extra care should be taken in its wording.
- It is generally better to use close-ended questions (see later) rather than allow open answers. However, do allow for the fact that your selection of responses might not be complete by having an 'other' category.

For example, '*What type of property do you live in?*'
Terraced house   Semi-detached   Detached   Flat

This question needs an '*Other*' category since you might find someone who lives on a boat or in a windmill!

- Make the questionnaire attractive and easy to complete. Microsoft Word allows you to create forms for use as questionnaires and you can then distribute these forms as an email attachment if this is appropriate for your sample.
- Do conduct a pilot survey on a small but *representative* sample of the target population. This will test out your design and allow you to fine tune it.

Having looked at some of the more important dos and don'ts of questionnaire design we now need to consider the format of the questions and the most effective method of obtaining reliable responses. Questions are of two forms: *close-ended* questions and *open-ended* questions. Close-ended questions give the respondents a choice of answers and are generally considered much easier to answer and to analyze. However, the limited response range can give misleading results. Open-ended questions, such as '*Why did you buy this product?*', allow respondents more flexibility in the type of response (you may get answers that you hadn't though of), but of course this type of question is difficult to analyze. Close-ended questions are the most commonly used type and can take many forms, such as:

- *Dichotomous questions* These are questions that have only two answers, such as yes or no.
- *Numeric* Some questions ask for a single number, such as the distance travelled to work each day. Where the question is personal (for example, earnings or age) it is best to give a range, such as:

  Less than £20 000   £20 000 to £30 000   Over £30 000

- *Multiple choice* Respondents select from three or more choices (the question on salary above is an example of a multiple choice question).
- *Likert scale* The question is a statement, such as '*Taxes should be increased to pay for a better health service*', and respondents indicate their amount of agreement using a scale similar to the one below.

  Strongly agree   Agree   Neither agree   Disagree   Strongly
  *   nor disagree   disagree*

- *Semantic differential* With this type of question only two ends of the scale are provided and the respondent selects the point between the two ends that represents his views. For example, '*The leisure facilities in my town are*':

  Excellent _____ Poor

- *Rank order* Respondents are asked to rank each option. This type of question is useful if you want to obtain information on relative preferences, but is more difficult to analyze. The number of choices should be kept to a minimum.

Once the questionnaire has been designed you need to decide how to collect the data. Some methods require a sampling frame while others do not.

Simple random sampling

With this method every member of the target population has an *equal* chance of being selected. This implies that a sampling frame is required and a method of *randomly* selecting the required sample from this list. The simplest example of this technique is a raffle where the winning ticket is drawn from the 'hat'. For a more formal application a stream of *random numbers* would be used. Random numbers are numbers that show no pattern; each digit is equally likely. A table of random numbers is given in the Appendix. The method of simple random sampling using random numbers is quite easy to apply, although tedious, as you will see from Example 3.1.

example **3.1**

Table 3.3 is a part of a list of students enrolled on a business studies course at a university.

Say from this 'population' of 25 students you wanted to randomly select a sample of 5 students. How would you do it? You could use the student number (in this case conveniently numbered from 1 to 25) and then try and obtain a match using a stream of two-digit random numbers. For example, suppose you had the following random numbers: 78, 41, 11, 62, 72, 18, 66, 69, 58, 71, 31, 90, 51, 36, 78, 09, 41, 00, 70, 50, 58, 19, 68, 26, 75, 69, and 04. The first two numbers don't exist in our population but 11 does – it is student D. Jeffrey. The next two numbers do not exist but 18 does, and so on. The final sample is numbers 11, 18, 09, 19 and 04, which are students D. Jeffrey, S. Moore, G. Godfrey, F. Muper, and C. Meng.

The majority of random numbers were redundant in this case because the population was so small. In practice the population would be much larger, but the method remains essentially the same. Most sampling frames are held on computer these days so it is much easier to use the computer to select the sample.

activity **3.3**

Randomly select another sample of 5 students from the list in Table 3.3 using the random numbers: 09, 55, 42, 30, 27, 05, 24, 93, 78, 10, 69, 09, and 11.

Table 3.3 List of students enrolled on a business studies course

Number	Name	Gender
1	N. Adams	Male
2	C. Shah	Male
3	B. Booth	Female
4	C. Meng	Male
5	A. Ho	Male
6	D. Drew	Male
7	K. Fisher	Female
8	P. Frome	Male
9	G. Godfrey	Male
10	J. Bakoulas	Male
11	D. Jeffrey	Female

(continued)

Table 3.3 (continued)

Number	Name	Gender
12	H. Jones	Male
13	M. Li	Male
14	N. King	Female
15	K. Lenow	Male
16	A. Loft	Female
17	T. Georgiou	Female
18	S. Moore	Female
19	F. Muper	Female
20	R. Muster	Female
21	A. Night	Male
22	J. Nott	Male
23	L. Nupper	Male
24	K. Khan	Male
25	O. Patter	Female

You should have noticed that number 09 occurs twice. What did you do in this case? For practical reasons you should have ignored the second 09 and chosen the next number, 11, instead. Your final sample should have been: G. Godfrey, A. Ho, K. Khan, J. Bakoulas and D. Jeffrey.

How representative of the target population are these samples? Since the population is so small it is a simple matter to compare each sample with the population. For instance, there are 15 male and 10 female students, which is a proportion of 60% males to 40% females. In the first sample there were 2 males out of 5, a proportion of 40%, and in the second there were 4 males, a proportion of 80%. From this you can see that the first sample was an underestimate of the true number of males, while the second was an overestimate. Another sample could be different again, and you may even get a sample of all the same sex. This variation is called *sampling error* and occurs in all sampling procedures. In Chapter 8 you will be shown how to quantify this error.

It is possible to reduce the sampling error by a slight modification to the simple random sample method. This is applicable when the target population can be categorized into groups or *strata*.

Stratified sampling

Many populations can be divided into different categories. For example, a population of adults consists of the two sexes, the employed and unemployed, and many other categories. If you think that the responses you will get from your survey are likely to be determined partly by each category, then clearly you want your sample to contain each category in the correct proportions.

activity
3.4

Using the random numbers 09, 55, 42, 30, 27, 05, 25, 93, 78, 10, 69, 09, 11, 99, 21 and 01, obtain a sample of size 5 that contains the correct proportion of each sex.

Your probably realized that your sample should contain 3 males (60% of 5). In order to ensure that you will get exactly 3 males, you should first of all have separated out the two sexes and then obtained two simple random samples, one of size 3 and one of size 2, as shown in Table 3.4.

Table 3.4 Table ordered by gender

Number	Name	Sex
1	N. Adams	Male
2	J. Bakoulas	Male
3	D. Drew	Male
4	P. Frome	Male
5	G. Godfrey	Male
6	A. Ho	Male
7	H. Jones	Male
8	K. Khan	Male
9	K. Lenow	Male
10	M. Li	Male
11	C. Meng	Male
12	A. Night	Male
13	J. Nott	Male
14	L. Nupper	Male
15	C. Shah	Male

Number	Name	Sex
1	B. Booth	Female
2	K. Fisher	Female
3	T. Georgiou	Female
4	D. Jeffrey	Female
5	N. King	Female
6	A. Loft	Female
7	S. Moore	Female
8	F. Muper	Female
9	R. Muster	Female
10	O. Patter	Female

The two populations have been re-numbered, although this is not essential. The first sample consists of students 9, 5 and 10, that is K. Lenow, G. Godfrey and M. Li, while the second sample consists of students 9 and 1, that is R. Muster and B. Booth.

Stratified sampling is a very reliable method but it does assume that you have a knowledge of the categories of the population. Stratified sampling is often used in conjunction with the next method.

Multi-stage sampling

If the target population covers a wide geographical area then a simple random sample may have selected respondents in quite different parts of the country. If the method employed to collect the data is of the face-to-face interview type, then clearly a great deal of travelling could be involved. To overcome this problem the area to be surveyed is divided into smaller areas and a number of these smaller areas randomly selected. If desired, the smaller areas chosen could themselves be divided into smaller districts and a random number of these selected. This procedure is continued until the area is small enough for a simple random sample (or a stratified sample) to be selected. The final sample should consist of respondents concentrated into a small number of areas. It is important that the random sample chosen from each area is the same proportion of the population or bias towards certain areas could result. As it is, bias is likely to occur as a result of similarity of responses from people within the same area, but this is the price you pay for reduced travelling time.

activity
3.5

You have been asked to obtain a representative sample of television viewers from across Britain using the multi-stage sampling method. How would you select the sample?

The country could be split into counties, or perhaps television regions might be more appropriate in this case. A number of these would be chosen at random, and these areas subdivided into district councils. A random sample of districts within each chosen region could now be selected, and the selected districts divided into postal areas. A random sample of residents within each chosen postal area could then be chosen using the register of electors.

Figure 3.1 illustrates this process in diagrammatic form. At each level you are taking a random sample. Note that it is not until you get to the individual elector that you carry out the actual survey.

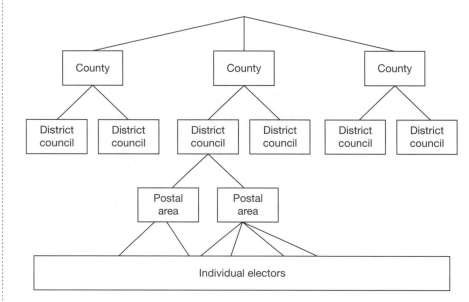

Figure 3.1 Multi-stage sampling

Cluster sampling

Cluster sampling is similar to multi-stage sampling and is used when a sampling frame is not available. Again a large geographical area is divided into a number of smaller areas called *clusters*. If necessary these clusters can be further subdivided to obtain clusters which are small enough for *all* members of the cluster to be surveyed. As with multi-stage sampling, a bias will result due to similarities in responses from members of the same cluster. The difference between cluster sampling and multi-stage sampling is that since individual members of a cluster cannot be identified in advance, it is necessary for all members to be surveyed. Random sampling is therefore *not* involved.

activity
3.6

How would you apply cluster sampling to the population referred to in Activity 3.5?

You would carry out the same procedure to obtain a selected number of postal districts, but these districts could be further subdivided so that individual streets were identified. All households of selected streets would then be surveyed.

Systematic sampling

This method is normally used with a sampling frame but it can also be used where a sampling frame is not available. However, in this case the size of the population must be known. The idea is that every nth member of a population is selected, where the value of n is determined by the size of the population and by the required sample size. For instance, if a 5% sample is to be selected from a population of size 1000, then every 50th person will be selected. The start of the sequence is usually chosen at random. For example, if a 20% sample was to be selected from the student population given in Table 3.3, every 5th person would be selected. If you started with, say, the third student, your sample would consist of B. Booth, P. Frome, M. Li, S. Moore and L. Nupper.

activity
3.7

You have been asked by a local newspaper to find out what people thought of a particular film that is showing at the local cinema. How would you obtain a sample of 10 people?

Clearly it would be pointless asking people who hadn't seen the film, so your target population would be those people who had recently seen it. The easiest method would be to wait outside the cinema and select people as they left. If there were 300 people watching the film then you would need to stop every 30th person.

Table 3.5 Details taken from a register office's records

Name	Date of marriage	Nationality
Mr A. Tan	21/3/93	British
Miss N. Taylor	21/3/93	British
Mr F. Barker	22/3/93	British
Miss F. Addai	22/3/93	Australian
Mr T. Barry	22/3/93	British
Ms K. Larch	22/3/93	Canadian

Systematic sampling is a very quick and efficient method of obtaining a sample. The sample should be random, provided there is no pattern in the way people are ordered in the population. For example, if a population consists of married couples then it is possible for the sample to consist of all husbands or all wives. To illustrate this point Table 3.5 refers to records taken from a register office. If you took a systematic sample that selected every second person and you started at F. Barker, all your sample would be males.

Quota sampling

I am sure that you have seen an interviewer in a town centre with a clipboard waiting to pounce on some unsuspecting individual! The interviewer is in fact looking for particular groups of individuals who meet the categories that he or she has been asked to interview. Within each group there will be a number or *quota* of people required and the survey is complete when the quotas have been reached. Quota sampling is a non-probabilistic version of stratified sampling. The quotas within each group should, like stratified sampling, reflect the proportions within the target population.

activity **3.8**

You want to obtain the views of the local population on the creation of an out-of-town shopping complex. You are told that 30% of the population is aged between 12 and 20, 60% is between 20 and 60, and 10% is over 60. You want a sample of 100 individuals. How would you go about choosing your sample?

Your first decision must be the location and time of the survey. An obvious choice would probably be the town centre on a Saturday when many people are out shopping. To reflect the fact that 30% of the population is aged between 12 and 20 you want a quota of 30 individuals in this age range. Similarly, for the other two age bands you would want 60 and 10 individuals respectively.

Quota sampling is a cheap and quick method of obtaining a sample. It is a particularly popular method for market research surveys and opinion polls. Its main disadvantage is that the sample could be heavily biased in favour of one particular group. For instance, in the case of the shopping centre the group of people who do not shop in the town centre will be omitted.

Other sampling methods

There are three other non-probabilistic sampling methods that are sometimes used. These are *judgemental, purposive* and *snowball* sampling. With judgemental sampling the researcher makes a judgement about what constitutes a representative sample. If a government agency was interested in the effects on people's health of car exhaust fumes they would choose areas near cities or motorways to obtain the sample. They would not choose rural areas, except perhaps for a control group.

Purposive sampling is where certain members of the population are purposefully chosen. For example, customers holding store loyalty cards might be asked about planned improvements to the store.

Snowballing is where a sample is chosen using one of the methods mentioned in this chapter and then additional members of the population are generated from this sample. An example could be in the investigation of the mis-selling of pensions that occurred in Britain during the late 1980s. A sample of pensioners could be obtained and any person who was persuaded to leave their occupational pension scheme would be asked to name other people they knew who were also affected. In this way the sample size could be increased.

activity **3.9**

A market research company is interested in consumers' reaction to a new brand of sun cream. What type of sampling method should they adopt?

Although most of the methods mentioned in this chapter would be suitable, judgemental sampling might be the best method to use in this situation. The researcher's judgement together with sales information could be used to select a few holiday resorts where it is likely that the product is being used. Once a resort has been chosen the researcher could use his or her judgement as to which age range should be sampled and at what time of the day the survey should be conducted.

Obtaining research data from on-line sources

In many cases it is unnecessary to carry out a survey as the relevant data has already been collected and published. When data has already been collected we say that it is *secondary data*. Much of the data collected by governments is available, free and usually reliable. In the UK the government has created a website, www.data.gov.uk, where links to 5600 datasets are made available. These include datasets for central and local government as well as for other public sector bodies. The project is ongoing and more datasets will be added in the future. In the USA the equivalent site is called www.data.gov. Most countries in the developed world publish some statistics. In China for instance the National Bureau of Statistics of China publishes economic statistics at www.stats.gov.cn/english. Census data is also available for many countries and in the UK this can be found through the www.data.gov.uk website.

The World Bank (http://data.worldbank.org/) has an open data policy and data on 200 countries can be found. Much of this data is related to developing countries and can be used in poverty assessment for example. The United Nations also has freely available datasets at http://data.un.org.

An interesting on-line source is 'Internet World Stats' (www.internetworldstats.com) which is an international website that features up-to-date world internet usage, population statistics and internet market research data for over 233 individual countries and world regions.

Another useful source is 'NationMaster' (www.nationmaster.com/index.php) an American-owned site which has a huge collection of data from such sources as the CIA World Factbook, UN and OECD. The site allows you to generate maps and graphs on all kinds of statistics.

Other sources of data include national newspapers, *Financial Times* and others for stock market and commodity prices, and the organizations themselves, for instance CAA for UK airline statistics. Whatever your interest there is almost certain to be data available somewhere, although not necessarily free and not necessarily in the format required.

You can of course use search engines to find relevant data or information. When searching for a particular on-line source of data you need to think carefully about the search terms to be used and the search engine you use. Google is currently the search engine of choice as it covers the largest number of website pages and is extremely fast. It also uses a 'crawler' engine that follows hyperlinks from page to page. When using Google or any other search engine it is useful to bear the following tips in mind.

- Keep it simple.
- Use terms that are more likely to be on a page rather than in a book or a person's memory, so if you are searching for 'statistical data on car manufacturers' you could type 'car manufacturer statistics'.
- Use as few terms as possible. Every word you use is included in the search and will limit the results you get. You can always add more words in subsequent searches. So for 'car manufacturer statistics' you might need to add the year of interest.

- You can use double quotes around groups of words and this will tell Google only to look for pages where these words are together. This will reduce the number of hits considerably but you may miss relevant pages (by searching on "car manufacturer statistics" the number of hits is reduced from about 75 million to 690 000!).
- Use a minus sign to omit pages that contain specific terms, so if you don't want to include Honda cars you would put '-honda' at the end of the search.
- If you want to search for car manufacturers or statistics you would put 'OR' between the search terms. This would look for pages with either car manufacturers or statistics. This can double the number of hits so should be used sparingly.
- You can limit the search to specific sites, so to search for Australian websites you would add 'site:au'.
- Google has an advanced search facility which makes it easy to include many of the above ideas.

(For further information on the technique of searching see www.google.com/support/websearch/?hl=en-GB)

The one disadvantage of on-line data (or even printed data) is that the quality is sometimes unknown. This is less of a problem with official sources, although it is still important to ensure that you know how the data was collected and any particular circumstances that have made the data inaccurate or distorted in some way. This information is usually given in notes at the end of the publication or in footnotes to the relevant table. Unfortunately the accuracy of unofficial sources of data is often of dubious quality and some checking may be needed to ensure it is acceptable to use. You should anyway give the full reference (URL) of the website, any authors mentioned and the data when you accessed it.

Reflection

Sampling is very important in today's complex society. Companies are always keen to find out what consumers think about their products, and governments need to obtain views on all kinds of issues. Surveys are very frequent around the time of elections and in the UK 2015 General Election market research companies carried out many surveys to find out people's views on election issues. The primary intention of these surveys was to try and predict the make-up of the future government. As it happened all surveys (apart for the exit poll) failed to predict the conservatory victory. Many explanations have been provided including a late swing to the conservatives and to people not being truthful when asked their voting intentions. The issue of how truthful people are in answering a pollsters questions is quite important. For example, when there is a question of income some respondents may have income they do not wish to disclose, particularly if they are on benefits. Face-to-face interviews will usually give more reliable results, provided that the questions are well thought-out and experienced interviewers are used.

Another issue with surveys is that they need a great deal of planning and research. It is easy to rush into a survey only to find later that a vital question has been missed. It is also easy to ask too many questions and either to find that the respondents do not complete the questionnaire or that the sample size is insufficient to provide meaningful analysis. This latter point is particularly important when you hope to analyze results by several categories and subcategories such as gender, age and income. Each additional category can double the number of respondents required.

To resolve many of these challenges it is essential that a pilot survey be conducted first. A pilot survey is a small-scale version of the full survey, although it must be large enough that some analysis can be attempted. The pilot survey should also allow the issue of non-response to be highlighted. Response rates vary from survey to survey, but 30% is usually considered to be quite good; for some methods, such as postal surveys, the response rate can be in single figures.

The type of survey method is, of course, another very important consideration. Probabilistic sampling methods are the most accurate but require a sampling frame and are generally more expensive than non-probabilistic methods. Election surveys normally use probabilistic sampling methods because accuracy is paramount. Non-probabilistic methods can be used when accuracy is not that important or when general patterns only are required. The crisp manufacturer which gave away packets of crisps during an election campaign was not doing it for scientific reasons, although some people might have interpreted the findings too literally. Just because one bin had less crisps in it than another doesn't necessarily mean that this leader was most popular – perhaps this bin was closest to the station, and people came across it first. Of course, we don't know how frequently the bins were refilled or whether the crisps were all the same flavour. This example, though, does highlight how important it is not to take statistics at their face value; you need to look behind the figures first. We will come back to this theme in later chapters.

Key points

- It is generally impractical to question or observe every member of the *target population*, so a sample of this population is selected instead.
- To obtain data from a population of people you normally carry out a survey. This survey can be done by post, by telephone, face-to-face and online. Each method has its advantages and disadvantages. A face-to-face survey normally gives you the best response rate but is more costly than other methods.
- Whatever method you use the sample should be representative of the target population.
- *Probabilistic* sampling methods will give you a representative sample but require a sampling frame.
- *Non-probabilistic* sampling is generally quicker to carry out but may not be completely representative of the target population.
- Table 3.6 summarizes the different sampling methods available.

Table 3.6 A summary of the sampling methods available

	Sampling frame available (probabilistic sampling)	Sampling frame not available (non-probabilistic sampling)
Population resides in one place	Simple random sampling Systematic sampling	Systematic sampling (if the size of the population is known) Judgemental sampling Purposive sampling
Population geographically scattered	Multi-stage sampling	Cluster sampling Judgemental sampling
Population is defined by categories	Stratified sampling	Quota sampling
Population is small and unknown		Snowballing

- When you carry out any sort of survey you need to use a questionnaire. The design of the questionnaire needs to be carefully formulated and tested using a pilot survey.

- Data that you collect yourself is called *primary* data. However data on all kinds of business issues are often available either in paper format or more likely on-line. Data obtained in this way is called *secondary* data. When searching for particular data using a search engine you need to think carefully about the search terms used.

Further reading

There are a huge number of quantitative methods and statistical texts that cover the collection of data. Some like Morris (2011) and Curwin and Slater (2013) cover similar material to this text. Collis and Hussey (2013) is a more general text on business research methods. Fowler (2013) is a very detailed text on survey research methods and would be ideal for anyone having to design their own survey.

http://www.**palgrave.com**/oakshott-eqm6

Solutions to all questions are freely available

Practice questions

1 In a Business Studies course at a university there are 320 students in year 1, 250 students in year 2 and 230 students in year 3. There are approximately 60% female students and 40% male students in each year. A survey of 50 students is to be taken to find their views on a course change. How many students of each gender should be selected from each year?

2 A town with historical connections has received a grant of £20m in order to improve its tourist facilities. The town councillors have decided to ask a representative sample of residents how the money should be spent. Given that expenditure for the survey must be kept to a minimum suggest ways in which a representative sample of residents can be chosen.

3 In preparation for the London 2012 Olympics, a survey of the British public is to be undertaken into the form of the opening ceremony. What type of survey should be undertaken and how would the respondents be chosen?

4 Criticize the following questionnaire into people's smoking habits.

Questionnaire on smoking habits	
1 How old are you?	☐
2 What is your marital status?	Single/married/cohabiting
3 Does your partner smoke?	Yes/No
4 How many cigarettes do you smoke a day?	☐
5 Do you understand the health risks of smoking?	Yes/No
6 Would you consider giving up if	
The price increased?	☐
A relative died of cancer?	☐
There were financial incentives for doing so?	☐
7 Did your parents smoke?	Yes/No
8 Which socio-economic class do you belong to?	
A	☐
B	☐
C1	☐
C2	☐
D	☐
E	☐

5 Which of the following are likely to have a sampling frame?

1 Students at a university

2 Employees of a company

3 Concert goers

4 Shoppers at a shopping mall

5 Members of a social networking group

6 Table 3.7 represents a target population.

Table 3.7 Population for Question 6

Name	Sex	Age	Newspaper read
Alan	M	23	*Guardian*
Steve	M	36	*The Times*
Jane	F	47	*Mirror*
Chris	M	36	*Mirror*
Julie	F	41	*Sun*
Stuart	M	37	*Mirror*
Jill	F	37	*Telegraph*
John	M	38	*Express*
Kim	M	48	*Sun*

(a) Using the random numbers 2, 9, 4, 3, 6, 7, select a simple random sample of sample size 3. What is the average age of your sample and what newspapers do they read?

(b) Stratify your sample by sex and repeat part (a).

(c) If a systematic sample of size 3 was required and the first person chosen was Steve, who would be the second person chosen?

7. Choose a large group of friends (at least 20), and write their names down in alphabetical order. From this list select a random sample of 4 using the following methods:

(a) Simple random sample

(b) A sample stratified by sex

(c) A systematic sample

From this sample obtain their average age and the course each is following.

8 You have been asked to conduct a survey into people's views of the council tax. What would be the target population and what would be a good sampling frame?

9 A football club wants to obtain the views of its supporters on a possible rise in admission charges. It has decided to obtain a simple random sample of members of the supporters' club. Comment on this proposal and suggest alternative target populations and sampling methods.

10 You have been asked to conduct a survey into the attitudes of school leavers to higher education. You intend to carry this out using the face-to-face interview method. How would you obtain your sample?

11 You have been asked to obtain the reaction to the proposal to pedestrianize your local town centre. What survey methods would you use?

12 A clothing company has just been approached by a students' union to supply a range of products suitable for the student market. However, the company wants some evidence that the market would be viable. You have been asked to help design a survey to discover if the students would be prepared to purchase their clothes from this company and what kind of price they would be prepared to pay.

(a) You are considering using either stratified or quota sampling to obtain your sample. Explain the differences between the two methods and discuss which method you think would be most suitable. State what categories or 'strata' you might want to consider for this problem, giving reasons why you think that these categories are important.

(b) Would multi-stage sampling be worth considering for this problem?

(c) Discuss the types of problems that might arise, both during the design phase and the survey itself. How might you overcome these problems?

13 A company wishes to carry out a survey of its employees to monitor their views on the future of the company. A departmental breakdown of the company's 200 employees is as follows:

Shop-floor/warehouse	80	Accounts	15
Service engineers	15	Personnel	10
Quality control	20	Administration	25
Marketing and sales	25	Catering	10

A survey of 40 employees is to be conducted. A sampling frame is available, listing the employees by surname in alphabetical order, independent of department.

(a) Explain how the following sampling methods could be carried out to obtain the sample of 40 employees:

- simple random sampling
- systematic sampling
- stratified sampling
- quota sampling.

(b) Discuss the benefits and drawbacks of using quota sampling to obtain the sample of 40 employees.

14 A university is considering introducing a third semester so that students can complete their degrees in 2 years by remaining at the university over the summer vacation. To help the university decide whether this would be acceptable to staff and students, it wants to conduct a survey to establish the views of a cross-section of the university community.

(a) In the context of this problem, describe the terms:

- target population
- sampling frame
- stratified sampling
- multi-stage sampling.

(b) Design 5 questions that you might ask the respondents to the survey. Explain how these questions would help you to satisfy the aims of the survey.

(c) What type of data collection method would you use (postal, telephone or face to face)?

15 Give as many reasons as you can why the scenario illustrated in *Did you know?* on page 34 would not give an accurate picture of the popularity of each party leader.

Assignment   Conduct a survey on some aspect of the quality of current television programmes. It is important that you do some research into the relevant issues and then conduct a survey using a questionnaire of your own design.

Information that you collect from your respondents might include:

- Viewing habits (that is, number of hours spent watching television, favourite programmes, and so on).
- Views on the quality of the programmes watched.
- What improvements they would like to see.
- Demographic information such as age, gender, occupation, and so on.

FINDING PATTERNS IN DATA: CHARTS AND TABLES

PREREQUISITES
Some understanding of sampling methods (Chapter 3: *Collecting data: surveys and samples*) would be useful but is not essential.

OBJECTIVES
- To be able to distinguish between different types of data
- To be able to tabulate data into an ungrouped or a grouped frequency table, as appropriate
- To be able to use diagrams to present data, and to know how to draw appropriate conclusions from these diagrams
- To be able to use Excel and/or SPSS to produce professional-looking charts

INTRODUCTION
The human brain finds it difficult to make sense of a large quantity of data. However, when data is organized and presented in a diagrammatic form we find it much easier to pick out patterns. This is the opposite to computers which can easily process vast quantities of data but find pattern recognition extremely difficult. This chapter first discusses the type of data that you may come across, and then looks at the best ways of displaying it.

QUANTITATIVE METHODS IN ACTION

The growth of China's economy

The growth of China's economy has been astonishing and is now the second largest economy after that of the USA. Although its gross domestic product (GDP) has slowed slightly from 9.2% in 2013 to 7.7% in 2014, the economy is expected to continue to grow. To illustrate China's position in the world, the use of charts and graphics can be much more useful than numbers alone. Figure 4.1 shows quite dramatically how fast the GDP has risen since 1990. Figure 4.2 demonstrates how China has overtaken most of the developed countries between 2005 and 2013. The exception is the USA, which still has the largest economy in terms of GDP. However, in Figure 4.3 we compare the percentage change in GDP (at 2005 prices) between 1990 and 2013, for the major economies. This chart clearly shows that in terms of percentage growth China has outstripped all other countries, including the USA, by a large margin. We will look at these and other types of charts later in this chapter.

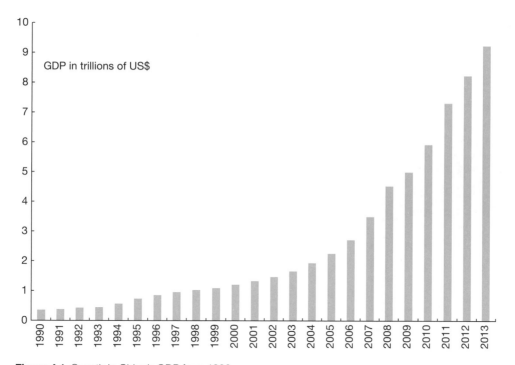

Figure 4.1 Growth in China's GDP from 1990

Source: The World Bank: World Development Indicators, http://databank.worldbank.org/data/views/variableselection/selectvariables.aspx?source=World-Development-Indicators.

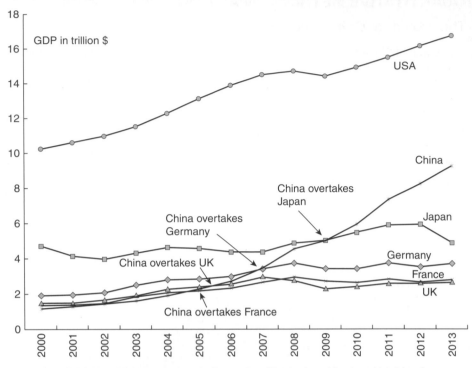

Figure 4.2 Growth of China's economy relative to other major economies

Source: The World Bank: World Development Indicators, http://databank.worldbank.org/data/views/variableselection/selectvariables.aspx?source=World-Development-Indicators.

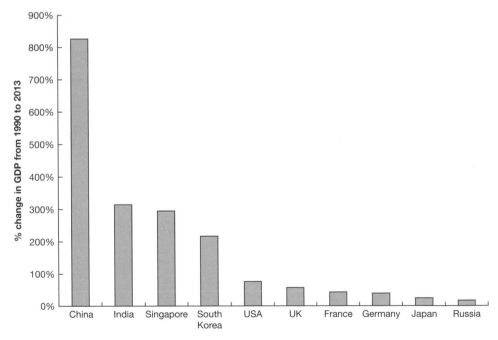

Figure 4.3 Percentage change in GDP (at 2005 prices) between 1990 and 2013

Source: The World Bank: World Development Indicators, http://databank.worldbank.org/data/views/variableselection/selectvariables.aspx?source=World-Development-Indicators.

Data classification

If your idea of data is simply lots of numbers then you may be surprised to learn that there are several different classifications or *levels of measurement*. Knowing which category your data falls into is very important as it determines what type of statistical analysis you perform. There are four levels of measurement. These are:

1 *Continuous data* Data that is measured on a scale, such as weight or temperature. The scale can be subdivided into as many intervals as required, depending on the accuracy of the measuring equipment. Using ordinary kitchen scales, for instance, you might record the weight of an item as 435 g; on more accurate scales the weight might be shown to be 434.8 g; and using laboratory-type scales you might be able to record the weight to three decimal places or more. Time is also continuous as it is measured using a clock, although it can be treated as discrete (see below). To complicate matters further, continuous data can be further subdivided into *interval-scale data* or *ratio-scale data*. An interval scale has no true starting (zero) point, so although it is possible to comment on the interval between measurements, it is not possible to compare the ratio of one to the other. For example, temperature (in Celsius and Fahrenheit) is measured on an interval-scale: you can say that 24C is twelve degrees hotter than 12C, but you cannot say that 24C is twice as hot as 12C. Ratio-scaled data, on the other hand, can be compared on a ratio basis as well as on an interval basis. For example, weight is measured on a ratio scale; 24 kg is twice as much as 12 kg, as well as being 12 kg different. For practical purposes this distinction makes little difference and most statistical packages (for example, SPSS) ignore this distinction.

2 *Discrete data* Data that takes on whole values. The obvious example of discrete data is data obtained by counting, such as the number of defective items in a batch. An important aspect of discrete data is that it cannot be subdivided (for example, you can't have half a defective item). Other examples of data that can be treated as discrete include the cost of an item or shoe size. Time is really a continuous measure, but for practical purposes it is often treated as discrete: people usually work a defined number of hours (or fractions of an hour), for example, and they give their age as a whole number of years. However, simply rounding a continuous quantity to a whole number doesn't make it discrete.

3 *Ordinal data* Data that can be arranged in some meaningful order. An example of this type of data is the assessment consumers might give to a product. They might be asked to rate the product using a score from 1 to 5, where 5 is 'excellent' and 1 is 'poor'. Although 5 is better than 1, it is not necessarily 5 times better or even 4 points better. One point that should not be forgotten is that just giving a numerical value to a category does not make it discrete data. You cannot do anything with this number apart from saying something like 'the higher the number, the better' (or 'the worse', for that matter).

4 *Nominal data* Data that does not have a numerical value and can only be placed in a suitable category. An example of this is hair colour or choice of newspaper. All we can do with nominal data is to separate it into its categories.

Ordinal and nominal data are usually referred to as *categorical data*.

To summarize:

- *Ratio data* Statistically the highest level of data. It has a defined zero so that data can be compared by interval and ratio.
- *Interval* There is no defined zero, so we can only compare intervals.
- *Discrete* It is meaningful to give data only in whole numbers. Discrete data is usually obtained by counting.
- *Ordinal* Ordinal data has order, but the interval between measurements is not meaningful.
- *Nominal* Nominal data has no order, and little statistical analysis can be done with this data.

The further you go down the hierarchy, the less the statistical analysis that can be carried out on the data. An important point to note, though, is that data can be manipulated downwards but not upwards. For example, data on ages could be placed into groups, such as: group 1, less than 20; group 2, from 20 to 30; etc. This could then be treated as ordinal data. It is of course not possible to give nominal data (such as mode of travel) a number, and then to treat the numbers as ordinal data.

(*activity*
4.1)

How would you define the following sets of data?

(a)   Measurement of the weights of jars of coffee.
(b)   Choice of summer holiday.
(c)   Weekly earnings by employees at a factory.
(d)   Numbers of students following a business studies course.
(e)   Market research survey into consumer reaction to a new product.

You should have defined (a) as ratio data since weight will be measured using either the metric or imperial system. (b) is nominal data since choice will be destination or home/abroad. (c) will be discrete since employees will earn an *exact* amount, such as £182.55. (d) is also discrete since the number can be found by counting. (e) could be either ordinal or nominal. It would be ordinal if you were asked to give a numerical score and nominal if you were simply asked to say whether you liked or disliked the product.

Tabulation of data

(*example*
4.1)

A small survey was carried out into the mode of travel to work. The information in Table 4.1 relates to a random sample of 20 employed adults.

Table 4.1 Data for Example 4.1

Person	Mode of travel	Person	Mode of travel
1	car	11	car
2	car	12	bus
3	bus	13	walk
4	car	14	car
5	walk	15	train
6	cycle	16	bus

7	car	17	car
8	cycle	18	cycle
9	bus	19	car
10	train	20	car

activity 4.2

How would you classify this data?

This data is categorical (nominal) since mode of travel does not have a numerical value. This information would be better displayed as a frequency table (Table 4.2).

Table 4.2 Frequency table

Mode of travel	Frequency	Relative frequency (%)
Car	9	45
Bus	4	20
Cycle	3	15
Walk	2	10
Train	2	10
Total	20	100%

Frequency is simply the number of times each category appeared. As well as the actual frequency, the *relative frequency* has been calculated. This is the frequency expressed as a percentage and is calculated by dividing a frequency by the total frequency and multiplying by 100. (*Note:* Some textbooks express relative frequency as a *proportion* and obtain it by dividing the frequency by total frequency. The sum of the proportions therefore adds to 1 instead of 100%).

The order in which you write these down is not important, although ordering by descending size of frequency makes comparison clearer.

example 4.2

The data in Table 4.3 gives the number of foreign holidays sold by a travel agent over the past four weeks.

activity 4.3

How would you classify the data in Table 4.3, and what can you deduce from the figures?

Table 4.3 Data for Example 4.2

Day	No. sold	Day	No. sold
Monday	10	Monday	13
Tuesday	12	Tuesday	10
Wednesday	9	Wednesday	12
Thursday	10	Thursday	8
Friday	22	Friday	12
Saturday	14	Saturday	12

(continued)

Table 4.3 (continued)

Day	No. sold
Monday	11
Tuesday	18
Wednesday	10
Thursday	10
Friday	11
Saturday	9

Day	No. sold
Monday	11
Tuesday	13
Wednesday	10
Thursday	14
Friday	13
Saturday	12

Can the travel agent sell a fraction of a holiday? Assuming that a holiday is a holiday regardless of the duration or the cost, then this is clearly discrete data and would have been obtained by counting. By examining the figures you should see that 10 sales occurs most frequently, although there is a range from 8 to 22 sales. To enable this information to be seen more clearly you could aggregate the data into a table (Table 4.4).

Table 4.4 Frequency table for Example 4.2

Number sold	Frequency
8	1
9	2
10	6
11	3
12	5
13	3
14	2
More than 14	2

This table is called an *ungrouped frequency table*, since the numbers sold have not been grouped. This table is a useful way of summarizing a small set of discrete data. There are two extreme values or *outliers* of value 18 and 22 sales and these have been included by the use of a 'more than' quantity. From this table you can see that between 10 and 12 holidays are usually sold each day.

example **4.3**   Table 4.5 gives the number of bolts produced by a machine each hour over the past 65 hours, while Table 4.6 gives the length in mm of 80 of these bolts.

Table 4.5 Hourly rate of bolt production

184	250	136	178	231	158	197	159	141	218
223	156	124	177	298	175	231	218	117	149
169	119	174	171	191	202	214	138	127	254
177	181	189	201	198	165	140	100	147	188
296	237	223	267	147	112	238	139	165	125
165	188	230	150	127	251	182	139	159	179
230	183	166	163	194					

Table 4.6 Length of bolts (mm)

49.9	53.8	61.3	45.8	51.2	44.5	55.3	51.4	84.1
55.7	52.7	68.7	52.5	58.8	37.8	44.1	49.9	43.8
64.1	35.9	46.4	45.1	30.6	45.9	54.8	54.0	49.3
46.8	46.5	52.2	33.3	42.9	47.7	46.2	40.5	36.8
47.5	46.3	70.2	35.5	56.7	56.0	56.5	49.5	57.5
52.0	36.8	46.3	42.4	30.2	49.5	36.3	44.6	45.1
30.0	47.0	52.1	53.0	46.1	50.5	56.0	50.9	42.7
42.1	51.2	49.0	49.9	54.4	53.2	43.0	41.3	49.7
42.9	61.1	41.7	35.7	45.0	59.2	60.6	44.7	

activity
4.4

> Look at the data in Table 4.5 and Table 4.6. Can you deduce anything about how many bolts are produced each hour or the length of each bolt? Would it help if ungrouped frequency tables were created, as in Activity 4.3?

I expect that you found it quite difficult to draw many conclusions from the data. For Table 4.5 you might have identified the range of production as between 100 and 298 bolts per hour, but what is the 'normal' production rate? Similarly, the smallest bolt is 30.0 mm and the largest is 84.1 mm, but what size are the majority of the bolts? An ungrouped frequency table for either set of data would not be very helpful for two reasons: for both data sets the range of the data is large, which would necessitate a large table, and for Table 4.6 the data is continuous. Continuous data can, by definition, take on any value, so what values would you use in your table? To overcome these problems a *grouped frequency table* is produced. A grouped frequency table is similar to an ungrouped table except that intervals are defined into which the data can be grouped. The number and size of each interval depends on the quantity and range of your data. In general you would have between 8 and 15 intervals and the width of each interval, or the *class interval*, should be a convenient number such as 10, 20, 25 etc. In the case of Table 4.5 the range is 298 − 100 = 198, and a class interval of 20 would give you 10 intervals, which is about right. The first interval would be 100 to 119; the second 120 to 139, and so on. Once you have decided on the size of each interval you need to allocate each value to one of the intervals. This can be done by using a *tally chart*. A tally chart is simply a foolproof means (or nearly) of ensuring that all items have been allocated. You start with the first value, in this case 184, and find the relevant interval, which is 180 to 199. A '|' is placed in this row. You then do the same with subsequent values, except that when you have four | s in a row you would draw a line through the group to make the total of 5. This has been done for you in Table 4.7.

Table 4.7 Tally chart

Class interval	Tally
100 to 119	IIII
120 to 139	HH III
140 to 159	HH HH

(continued)

Table 4.7 (*continued*)

Class interval	Tally
160 to 179	⊹⊹⊹ ⊹⊹⊹ |||
180 to 199	⊹⊹⊹ ⊹⊹⊹	
200 to 219	⊹⊹⊹
220 to 239	⊹⊹⊹ |||
240 to 259	|||
260 to 279		
280 to 299	||

The next stage is to add up the tally in each interval to give you the frequency. The final grouped frequency table is as shown in Table 4.8. From this table it appears that the rate of production is quite variable, although the rate is unlikely to be less than 120 or more than 240 bolts per hour.

Table 4.8 Grouped frequency table

Interval	Frequency	Relative frequency (%)
100 to 119	4	6.2
120 to 139	8	12.3
140 to 159	10	15.4
160 to 179	13	20.0
180 to 199	11	16.9
200 to 219	5	7.7
220 to 239	8	12.3
240 to 259	3	4.6
260 to 279	1	1.5
280 to 299	2	3.1
Total	65	100

How would you group the data in Table 4.6? You might decide on a class interval of 5 mm, which would give you 11 intervals. Since the smallest length is 30 mm the first group would start at 30 mm; the second at 35 mm, and so on. But what should the end of each group be? If you used 34 mm you would not be able to allocate a value between 34 and 35 mm. You cannot use the same figure for both the end of one group and the start of the next because this would allow a value to be added to more than one group. It is essential that a value can go into *one, and only one*, interval, so the ranges must be designed to guarantee this. Since the data is continuous the length can be quoted to any degree of accuracy, so the end of each group would be defined as *under* 35 mm and under 40 mm, and so on. In this way a length of 34.9 mm would be in the first group while 35.0 mm would be in the second group.

activity **4.5**   Obtain the grouped frequency table for the data in Table 4.6. What can you deduce about the length of bolts produced?

You should have obtained Table 4.9. If you look at this table the *distribution* of the lengths is clearer. 77.5% of the values are between 40 mm and 60 mm, with few over 60 mm or less than 40 mm.

Table 4.9 Grouped frequency table for the length of bolts

Interval	Frequency	Relative frequency (%)
30 to under 35 mm	4	5.00
35 to under 40 mm	7	8.75
40 to under 45 mm	14	17.50
45 to under 50 mm	23	28.75
50 to under 55 mm	16	20.00
55 to under 60 mm	9	11.25
60 to under 65 mm	4	5.00
65 to under 70 mm	1	1.25
70 to under 75 mm	1	1.25
75 to under 80 mm	0	0
80 to under 85 mm	1	1.25

In both these examples the class intervals were the same for the whole distribution; that is, 20 in the first case and 5 in the second. However, it is not necessary for the intervals to be equal and you may have two or more different intervals in the same table. In Table 4.9 you might decide to condense the last four intervals into one since the frequencies in these intervals are small. If you do this your last interval will be 65 to under 85 mm, which has a frequency of 3. It is also possible to have an *open* interval at the beginning or end, such as greater than 70 mm or less than 30 mm. However, only use open intervals if you really have to and only if there is a relatively small number of items in this interval.

Diagrammatic representation of data

Although frequency tables can give you more information than the *raw* data, it can still be difficult to take in all the information that is inherent in the data. Diagrams can help provide this additional information and also display the data in a more visually attractive manner. You do lose some detail but this is a small price to pay for the additional information that diagrams provide. There are several types of diagram and the choice depends mainly on the type of data, but also on your intended audience.

These days most people will use a spreadsheet when producing diagrams. Spreadsheets can produce high-quality charts which can be easily updated if the data changes. However, some experience of drawing diagrams by hand is still useful.

example
4.4

The sales by department of a high street store over the past three years are shown in Table 4.10.

Table 4.10 Sales by department and year

	2012	2013	2014
Clothing	£1.7m	£1.4m	£1.4m
Furniture	£3.4m	£4.9m	£5.6m
Electrical goods	£0.2m	£0.4m	£0.5m
Total	£5.3m	£6.7m	£7.5m

An inspection of the data in Table 4.10 reveals that the total sales have increased over the three years, although clothing has shown a decline. Diagrams should help bring out these and other differences more clearly.

Pie charts

When you want to compare the relative sizes of the frequencies a pie chart is a good choice of diagram. It is normally used for categorical data and each category is represented by a segment of a circle. The size of each segment reflects the frequency of that category and can be represented as an angle. It is rare for people to draw a pie chart by hand as a protractor is required to measure the angles, but if you need to, the angle is calculated by working out the percentage of the category and then multiplying by 360. For example, for the sales for 2014 in Example 4.4 the angle would be calculated as follows:

$$\text{Clothing as a percentage is } \frac{1.4}{7.5} \times 100 = 18.7\%$$

$$\text{The angle is therefore } \frac{18.7}{100} \times 360 = 67°$$

The complete pie chart for the sales for 2014 is shown in Figure 4.4. This diagram demonstrates that the furniture department has contributed the bulk of the total sales for this year. (Note: adjustments have been made to allow for rounding errors.)

Bar charts

Although pie charts tend to be a popular means of comparing the size of categories they have the disadvantage that they are not suitable for displaying several sets of data

Figure 4.4 Pie chart for sales in 2014

simultaneously. You would, for instance, need three separate pie charts to represent the data in Table 4.10. A *simple bar chart* is another useful method of displaying categorical data, or an ungrouped frequency table. For each category a vertical bar is drawn, the height of the bar being proportional to the frequency. The diagram in Figure 4.5 shows the total sales in the form of a simple bar chart.

When a category is subdivided into several subcategories the simple bar chart is not really adequate as you would need a different bar chart for each subcategory. A *multiple bar chart* is used when you are interested in changes in the components but the totals are of no interest. Figure 4.6 is a multiple bar chart for the data in Table 4.10.

If you are interested in comparing totals and seeing how the totals are made up a *component* bar chart is used. Figure 4.7 is a component bar chart for the data in Table 4.10. In this figure you can see the variation in total sales from year to year as well as seeing how each department contributes to total sales. If you are more interested in the proportion of sales in each department a *percentage* bar chart may be of more interest. This is shown in Figure 4.8. This chart is rather like the pie chart but has the advantage that several sets of data can be displayed simultaneously.

Line graphs

When data is in the form of a *time series* a line graph can be a useful means of showing any trends in the data. Figure 4.9 is a line graph for the total sales given in Table 4.10

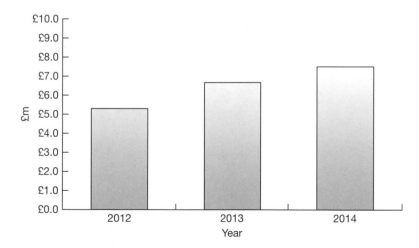

Figure 4.5 A simple bar chart of total sales

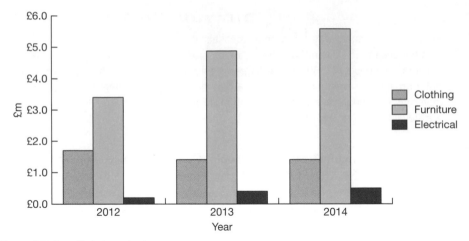

Figure 4.6 A multiple bar chart

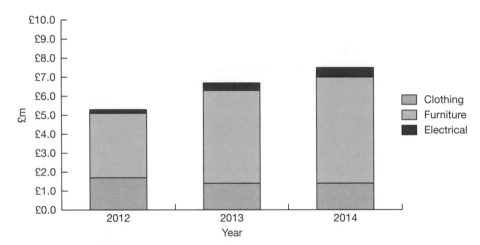

Figure 4.7 A component bar chart

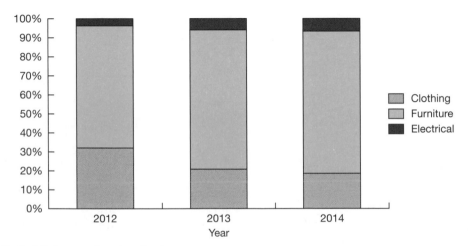

Figure 4.8 A percentage bar chart

and clearly shows the rise in sales over the three years. When this type of diagram is shown in company publications you will often find that the scale on the *y*-axis is broken. This will exaggerate the growth in sales or other measure and can be misleading unless you are aware of what is going on. This can be justified if none of the values are near zero, but in this case the break in the scale should be clearly shown. Figure 4.10 shows how this should be done.

We will be looking at line graphs in more detail in Chapter 13.

Figure 4.9 Line graph

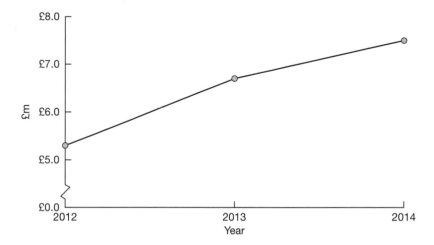

Figure 4.10 Line graph with adjusted scale

activity
4.6

Use Figures 4.4 to 4.10 to summarize how the sales have varied by department and year.

You should be able to deduce that:

- Total sales have increased over the three years, although the largest increase was between 2012 and 2013.
- Most of this increase has been the result of sales of furniture.
- Clothing has shown a decrease in sales from 2012 to 2013 but has then remained steady.
- The sales of clothing as a proportion of total sales has declined, while the proportion of electrical sales has increased.

Histograms

For grouped frequency tables a different type of diagram is normally used. This diagram is called a *histogram* and although it may look like a bar chart there are some important differences. These are:

- The horizontal axis is a continuous scale, just like a normal graph. This implies that there should not be gaps between bars unless the frequency for that class interval really is zero.
- It is the *area* of the bars that is being compared, not the heights. This means that if one class interval is twice the others then the height must be halved, since area = width × height.

The histogram shown in Figure 4.11 is for the lengths of bolts given in Example 4.3 and uses an equal class interval of 5 mm.

If the last four intervals were combined, the last class interval would be 20 mm. In this case the frequency of 3 should be *divided* by 4 (since 20 is 4 × 5) to give 0.75 and the histogram would have to be redrawn as shown in Figure 4.12. Where there are several different class intervals it is normal practice to divide each frequency by the corresponding class width. The resulting values are called the *frequency density*.

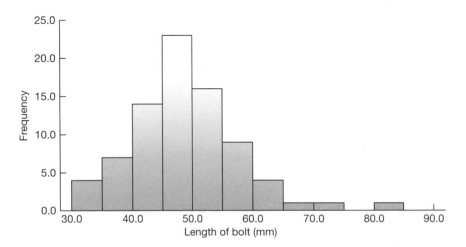

Figure 4.11 Histogram of length of bolt

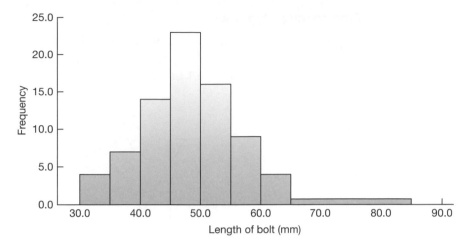

Figure 4.12 Histogram with unequal class intervals

When you draw histograms for discrete data there is a problem in that there is a gap between the end of one interval and the start of the next. You can get round this problem by extending each interval half way to the next or last interval. Thus for the example of the rate of production of bolts, the intervals would become 100.5 to 119.5 and 119.5 to 139.5, and so on.

activity
4.7

Draw a suitable chart for the production rate data (Table 4.5).

You should have drawn a histogram like the one in Figure 4.13.

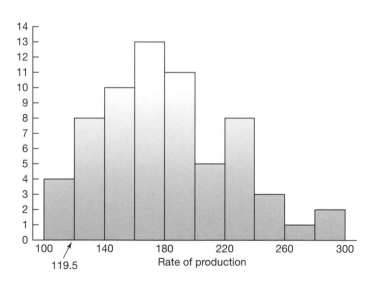

Figure 4.13 Histogram for discrete data

Frequency polygons

To get a better idea about how the data is distributed across the range of possible values of the data, you can join up the mid points of the top of each bar of the histogram. This is shown in Figure 4.14 for the bolt length data.

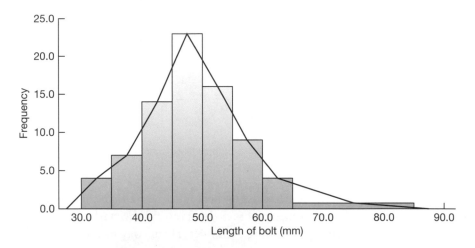

Figure 4.14 Histogram with mid points joined up

If the bars are now removed, you are left with a picture of the shape of the underlying distribution of the data. The area under the frequency polygon is the same as the area under the original histogram (Figure 4.15).

This diagram can be quite useful if you want to compare different distributions, as it is possible to plot more than one frequency polygon on the same graph. This is not possible with the other diagrams you have met, as they would look too confusing.

Another important use of the frequency polygon is to categorize the shape of the distribution in terms of its degree of symmetry. A distribution that is perfectly balanced is called *symmetrical*, whereas a distribution which has its peak offset to one

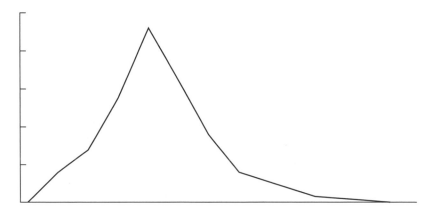

Figure 4.15 Frequency polygon

side is called *skewed*. If the peak is to the left, the distribution is called *right* or *positive* skewed, whereas if the peak is to the right, the distribution is called *left* or *negative* skewed. This may sound illogical but you will discover the reason for this convention in the next chapter. I find it easier to look at the *tail* of the distribution. If the tail is to the right it is right skewed and if the tail is to the left it is left skewed. The diagrams in Figure 4.16 may help you appreciate the differences.

Right skewed   Symmetrical   Left skewed

Figure 4.16 Distribution shapes

activity
4.8

How would you define the shape of the distribution of bolt lengths?

The distribution is approximately symmetrical, although it has a slight right skewness to it.

Ogive

Another diagram can be created by plotting the *cumulative* frequencies. Cumulative frequency is simply a running total of the frequencies. The cumulative frequencies for the bolt length data are shown in Table 4.11.

The percentage cumulative frequencies have also been calculated as you will find that the use of percentages has certain advantages. The cumulative frequency graph or *ogive* can now be drawn. The *upper* boundaries of each class interval are plotted against the (%) cumulative frequencies, as shown in Figure 4.17.

Table 4.11 Calculation of cumulative frequencies

Interval	Frequency	Cumulative frequency	% cumulative frequency
30 to under 35 mm	4	4	5.00
35 to under 40 mm	7	11	13.75
40 to under 45 mm	14	25	31.25
45 to under 50 mm	23	48	60.00
50 to under 55 mm	16	64	80.00
55 to under 60 mm	9	73	91.25
60 to under 65 mm	4	77	96.25
65 to under 70 mm	1	78	97.50
70 to under 75 mm	1	79	98.75
75 to under 80 mm	0	79	98.75
80 to under 85 mm	1	80	100.00

Figure 4.17 Ogive

This is a very useful diagram and you will meet this again in the next chapter. For the purposes of this chapter you can treat this graph as a *less than* graph, since the upper-class boundaries were plotted against the cumulative frequencies. So, for example, 13.75% of the lengths are below 40 mm.

activity
4.9

Determine the proportion of lengths that are:
(a) below 50 mm   (b) below 41 mm   (c) above 63 mm

The answer to (a) can be read directly from the grouped frequency distribution and is 60%. However, for both (b) and (c) you should use the ogive to *interpolate* between two boundaries. To do this you should draw a vertical line up from the x-axis at the appropriate value to meet the ogive. You can then draw a horizontal line from this point until it meets the y-axis and then it is a matter of reading the cumulative frequency from this axis. This has been done for you in Figure 4.18.

You will see from the diagram that I have drawn lines for all three lengths. The cumulative frequency for (a) is 60% as it should be. The cumulative frequency for (b) is approximately 17%, so 17% of lengths are below 41 mm. The cumulative frequency for (c) is approximately 94% but, as you were asked to find the proportion above 63 mm, you then need to subtract 94 from 100, that is 6%.

Other diagrams

There are many other diagrams that can be used to represent data. The simplest is a pictogram which just uses a picture to represent a quantity. So for the sales at a high street store (Example 4.4) a picture of a money bag could be used to represent £200 000. So for clothing in 2012 you would need 8 and half bags to represent £1.7m. This is a popular diagram to use in magazines as it is visually appealing and requires little knowledge of statistics.

There are also *surface* charts, *area* charts, *doughnut* charts, *bubble* charts and *radar* charts as well as three dimensional bar charts. However apart for some specialized

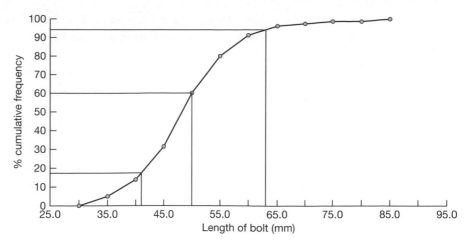

Figure 4.18 Using the ogive

uses these charts don't generally provide any more information than the ones we have already met, and in some cases can even confuse.

One other diagram that can be useful, particularly when there is little data, is a *stem and leaf* plot. In this plot the most significant digit is the stem and the least significant digit is the leaf. So in the length of bolt data where the data varies between 30 mm and 80 mm the stem would be represented by the tens unit (3 to 8) and the leaf by the remaining digit (the decimal value would be ignored). We normally add the leaf values in the order they come in the data and then redraw the diagram with the leaves arranged in order on each stem.

activity
4.10

Draw a stem and leaf plot for the length of bolt data.

If we used the values 3 to 8 as the stem we would only have 6 values making up the stem which is a little low. In these situations it is useful to split the stem unit into 2 so for the value 3 the first stem value would be used for values 30 to 34 and the second value used for the values 35 to 39.

After ordering the leaf values you should have got the 'diagram' represented by Table 4.12.

Table 4.12 A stem and leaf plot of the length of bolt data

```
Frequency        Stem & Leaf
    4.00            3 . 0003
    7.00            3 . 5556667
   14.00            4 . 01122222334444
   23.00            4 . 55555666666677799999999
   16.00            5 . 0011122222333444
    9.00            5 . 556666789
    4.00            6 . 0114
    3.00      Extremes  (>=68)

                 3|3 represents 33 mm
```

The 3 values above 65 mm can be represented as *outliers* as shown. This diagram clearly shows the shape of the distribution and can be quick and easy to produce. It can also be used when you are comparing two sets of data as you can use a *back* to *back* stem and leaf plot where one set of leaves is to the left of the stem and other to the right. As we will see later we can also use this diagram to obtain statistical information about the data.

Creating charts with Excel 2013

Very few people draw charts by hand these days, as it is much easier to use a spreadsheet, such as Excel. Charts produced by a spreadsheet also look more professional, and they can be immediately updated if the data changes. When drawing charts in Excel, you can choose whether to create the chart as an object in the same worksheet as the data or to create the chart in a new sheet. Being able to see the chart next to the data can be useful, but if you want to print out the chart or to copy and paste it in another document, it is often easier to create it in a new sheet.

The version of Excel used in this text is Excel 2013. This version is similar to Excel 2010 in that it uses the idea of a 'Ribbon', which replaced the menus and toolbars used in earlier versions. The ribbon has seven tabs which include Home, Insert, Page Layout, Formulas, Data, Review and View, as before. Within each tab, commands are grouped logically, so in the Insert tab there is a Charts group which contains all the charts found in earlier versions of Excel. The difference between Excel 2010 and Excel 2013 is that has been made much easier to create a perfect chart. There is even a tab that recommends the best chart or charts for your data. Another new innovation is the Quick Analysis gallery. When you highlight a range of cells, you will find a quick analysis button appearing, and by clicking on it, you can do a range of analyses, including creating a chart. We will see this in the following pages.

The basic Excel workbook with data from Table 4.10 (page 60) is shown in Figure 4.19.

Figure 4.19 The Insert tab in Excel 2013
Used with permission from Microsoft.

<table>
<tr><td>*activity*
4.11</td><td>Use Excel and data provided in Table 4.10 (page 60) to create:
1 A pie chart for sales in 2014
2 A simple bar chart of total sales for each of the three years
3 A multiple bar chart for sales by year and department
4 A component bar chart
5 A percentage bar chart
6 A line graph for the total sales over the three years</td></tr>
</table>

For each chart you can either use the `Insert` tab or the `Quick Analysis` gallery. The charts produced are the same ones that were shown earlier in the chapter, and you will be referred back to these charts.

1 Pie chart

Highlight cells A6 to A8, and while holding down the <Ctrl> key on your keyboard, highlight cells D6 to D8. Click on the `Insert` tab, then `Pie` and choose the one you want. This screen is shown in Figure 4.20. You can move the chart to a new sheet (recommended) or leave as an embedded chart. In both cases you will be able to choose a chart layout and format. The pie chart can be seen in Figure 4.4 (page 60).

2 Simple bar chart

Vertical bar charts are called *Clustered Column* charts in Excel. Highlight cells B10 to D10 and then click on the `Quick Analysis` gallery at the bottom right hand corner of cell D10. Then click on `CHARTS` then `Clustered Column`. This screen is shown in Figure 4.21. If you right-click inside the chart area, you can move the chart to a new sheet. In the `Charts tab` you can add the horizontal axis labels by clicking on the `Design group` and selecting `Data` and `Edit` under the Horizontal (Category) Axis labels (see Figure 4.22). You can also select an appropriate chart layout and add titles to both axes. The final chart can be seen in Figure 4.5 (page 61).

Figure 4.20 Creating a pie chart
Used with permission from Microsoft.

Figure 4.21 Creating a simple bar chart
Used with permission from Microsoft.

Figure 4.22 Adding horizontal axis labels
Used with permission from Microsoft.

3 Multiple bar chart

Proceed as before, but this time highlight cells A6 to D8. Add the years to the horizontal axis and choose a chart layout as before. The final chart can be seen in Figure 4.6 (page 62).

4 Component bar chart

A component bar chart is called a *Stacked Column* chart in Excel. It can be found under More Charts in the Quick Analysis gallery. Proceed exactly as before. The final chart can be seen in Figure 4.7 (page 62).

5 Percentage bar chart

This is exactly the same as before except that 100% *Stacked Column* is chosen. This chart can be seen in Figure 4.8 (page 62).

6 Line graph

To display a line graph, highlight the totals as in the simple bar chart. In the *Design* ribbon select the chart with markers, as shown in Figure 4.23. The chart can be seen in Figure 4.9 (page 63). Note that, as mentioned earlier, the *y*-axis for this chart need not be started at zero. However, when this is done, it is good practice to show a break in the scale (Figure 4.10, page 63). Unfortunately this cannot be achieved automatically in Excel.

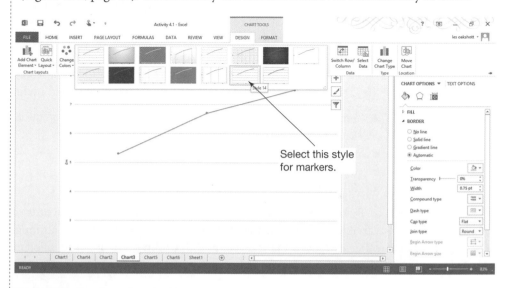

Figure 4.23 Creating a line chart
Used with permission from Microsoft.

Creating charts with IBM SPSS statistics

The advantage with Excel is that almost every workplace has a copy of it and people are familiar with the package. The charts it produces are on the whole professional-looking and easy to create. Excel is a general-purpose package and does lots of things reasonably well. It can, for instance, do data analysis; be used as a simple database; be used as an optimizing tool; and even be used as a word processor! In addition it can, in conjunction with the powerful Visual Basic editor, be used for all kinds of advanced modelling purposes. Although Excel can (and often is) use as a word processor, however, most people would prefer to use a dedicated word processor package such as Microsoft Word™. So it is with statistical packages. Several packages are dedicated to statistical work, and one of the most popular is IBM® SPSS Statistics software V22 (referred to as SPSS® from now on).

Before getting started with SPSS, it is recommended that you become familiar with the basic principles of the package. There is a very good help facility within SPSS which contains an online tutorial. There is also a contextual help system within the package: this can be activated by pointing the mouse at the feature you are unsure about and right-clicking the mouse button.

Basic ideas behind SPSS

SPSS is similar to other Windows-based packages, and features a title bar, a menu bar and a toolbar. The first screen you normally see is shown in Figure 4.24.

The basic outline looks similar to Excel in that there are rows and columns. This is where the similarity ends, however. The first difference you will notice is that there are two screens or views: a Data View and a Variable View (see Figure 4.24); you click on a tab to switch between views. Another major difference is the way you refer to data in SPSS. With Excel you can have a column or row of data, and it is possible to apply some limited formatting to the row, to the column, or to individual cells. In SPSS, in contrast, each row of data is called a *case* and each column is called a *variable*. This terminology has arisen because SPSS was originally designed to analyze survey data (SPSS stands for Statistical Package for the Social Scientist). In analyses of survey data, each case represented a respondent and each variable represented the response to a particular question. However, it is possible to analyze variables quite independently of each other.

The data shown in Figure 4.25 contains information on a selection of companies in the UK (*Source*: FAME database). The information obtained included the following:

- *Company* Type of company ('Public quoted', 'Public not quoted', 'Private limited', 'Private unlimited' and 'Public aim').
- *Emp* Number of employees.
- *Turnover* (in £000s).
- *SIC* Standard industrial classification.

Before we look at the Variable View screen, a few words on how SPSS defines variables will be useful. The default type is Numeric, although there are several other categories that can be used, including String (text). For numeric data there is also a sub-type or measurement type (Measure), which can be Scale, Ordinal or

Figure 4.24 Opening SPSS screen
Reprint courtesy of International Business Machines Corporation, © International Business Machines Corporation.

Figure 4.25 Company information
Reprint courtesy of International Business Machines Corporation, © International Business Machines Corporation.
Data from FAME database published by Bureau van Dfix Electronic Publishing.

Nominal. (Note that SPSS does not distinguish between ratio, interval and discrete data.) If we want a *discrete* variable, we need to set the number of decimal places to zero. In our data, *Emp* and *Turnover* are scale variables, while *Company* and *SIC* are nominal.

Figure 4.26 is the Variable View and gives details of our four variables. Notice that the Label field allows us to give a longer description of the variable. The Values field

Figure 4.26 Variable details
Reprint courtesy of International Business Machines Corporation, © International Business Machines Corporation.

allows us to add further information to ordinal or nominal data. In our case, codes were used for company type: 1 = *Public quoted*, 2 = *Public not quoted*, etc. These do not affect any calculations we do, but they make output clearer (see Figure 4.29). It is also possible to define missing values. In our case the number 9 was used to represent values that were missing in *Emp* and *Turnover*.

Charts in SPSS

There are two ways of getting charts in SPSS. The first and simplest way is through the `Analyze` menu. Click on `Analyze`, then `Descriptive Statistics`, then `Frequencies` (see Figure 4.27).

Figure 4.27 Drop-down menu for `Frequencies`
Reprint courtesy of International Business Machines Corporation, © International Business Machines Corporation.

When you click on `Frequencies` you get the options shown in Figure 4.28. Highlight `Type of company` and click the right-facing arrow. Then click on `Charts`: you will be offered a choice of bar charts, pie charts and histograms. Bar charts and pie charts are applicable for ordinal and nominal data. We will choose `Bar charts`. You also have a choice of displaying the chart values as `Frequencies` or `Percentages`; we will choose `Frequencies`. Press `Continue`.

We don't need a list of frequencies, so we remove the tick form `Display frequency tables`. Press `OK` to initiate the SPSS processor.

All SPSS output is added to the `Viewer` window (Figure 4.29). This window has two sections or panes. The left-hand pane is called the outline pane, and the right-hand pane is the display pane. To see the bar chart properly, we need to scroll down the display pane. You can see that the largest number of companies is *Private limited*.

Figure 4.28 `Frequencies` dialog box
Reprint courtesy of International Business Machines Corporation, © International Business Machines Corporation.

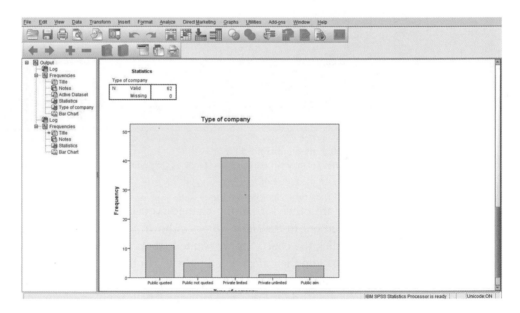

Figure 4.29 The `Viewer` window
Reprint courtesy of International Business Machines Corporation, © International Business Machines Corporation.

(*activity*
4.12)
Create a pie chart of the variable *Type of company*.

Although you can create a pie chart in a similar way as we did for the bar chart, SPSS version 22 has a powerful chart builder that allows you to preview a chart as you are building it. Click on `Graphs` and then `Chart Builder`. Make sure that `Gallery` is selected and drag the picture of a pie chart into the preview screen (in other charts you will have a choice of chart subtype). Drag *Type of company* into Slice by? and in the Element properties change statistic to *percentage* and click Apply. You should get the screen as seen in Figure 4.30. You can add a title by clicking on Titles/Footnotes and adding a title into the Content box. Click OK.

Figure 4.30 Define pie chart data
Reprint courtesy of International Business Machines Corporation, © International Business Machines Corporation.

There are other formatting changes you can do but most other embellishments are carried out in the *chart editor* as shown in Figure 4.31. To enter the chart editor double-click the chart. Say we wanted labels and the percentages in each slice. Click Elements and then Show Data Labels. In the Labels boxes have *Type of company* and *percentages* in Displayed and *Count* Not displayed. If you want you can have the labels outside the pie and prevent labels from overlapping others and you can also manually move the labels around. You can also hide the legend from the options menu. When you have completed the editing go to File and then Close to return to the SPSS Viewer. The final pie chart is shown in Figure 4.32.

You can easily change the chart type in the chart editor by clicking on the Variables tab in the Properties window. Change the element type to Bar and click Apply and you immediately get the bar chart shown in Figure 4.33. Note however that not all chart types are suitable for all types of data and unsuitable ones will be greyed out. For instance you couldn't plot a histogram with *Type of company*!

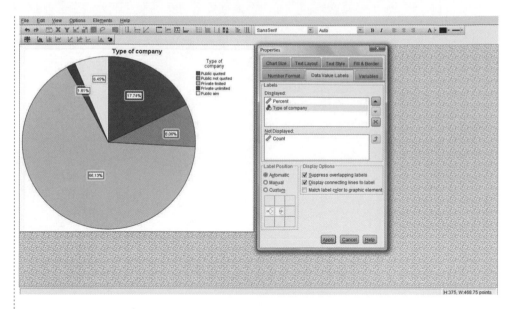

Figure 4.31 The chart editor
Reprint courtesy of International Business Machines Corporation, © International Business Machines Corporation.

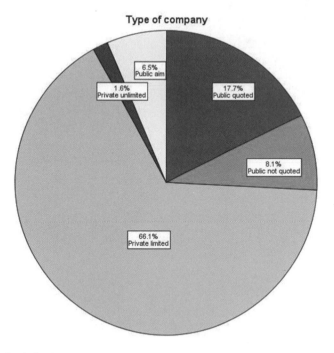

Figure 4.32 The final pie chart
Reprint courtesy of International Business Machines Corporation, © International Business Machines Corporation.

The final chart we shall look at is a *Histogram*, which again can be built using the Chart Builder. As a histogram requires continuous data (called *scaled* data in SPSS) we will use *Turnover* for our histogram. The procedure is the same as for the pie

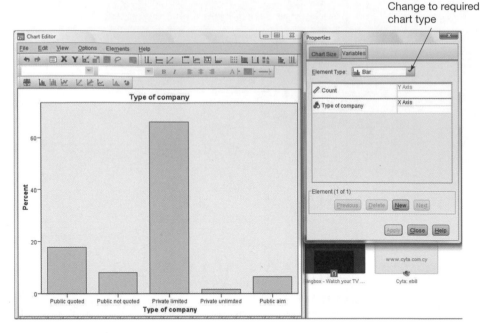

Figure 4.33 Changing chart type

Reprint courtesy of International Business Machines Corporation, © International Business Machines Corporation.

Figure 4.34 Using Chart Builder to plot a histogram

Reprint courtesy of International Business Machines Corporation, © International Business Machines Corporation.

chart except that we have a choice of 4 subtypes. We will use the first one – a simple histogram (see Figure 4.34). The histogram is shown in Figure 4.35. This chart clearly shows the (right) skewness of the distribution.

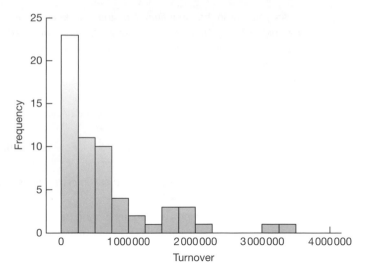

Figure 4.35 SPSS histogram for 'Turnover'
Reprint courtesy of International Business Machines Corporation, © International Business Machines Corporation.

DID YOU KNOW?

Charts can be used to mislead as well as clarify. Figure 4.36 is taken from the US Environmental Law Institute. The idea of the diagram is to show that fossil fuels get a bigger tax break than renewables. The diagram looks a bit like a pie chart but is totally misleading, with nothing to scale. Either the data (there are only 16 values) could be represented simply as a table or as a component bar chart.

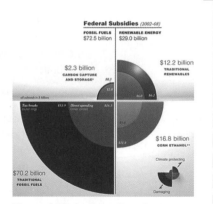

Figure 4.36 A misleading chart

Source: Straight Statistics, May 2011 (www.straightstatistics.org/article/who-ate-all-pies)
Figure source: US Environmental Law Institute

Reflection

As you will have seen in this chapter, there are a number of different diagrams that can be used to represent a set of data. Choosing the most appropriate diagram is important if you want to be able to interpret the data correctly and to provide others with reliable information. A good chart should be technically correct but also visually stimulating. The use of Excel has made it easy to produce charts that are attractive to the eye, particularly if a limited amount of colour is used. However, SPSS is becoming more popular and can produce more professional-looking charts.

Many published diagrams are misleading (sometimes intentionally!). One of the most common mistakes – but fortunately not usually misleading – is the use of bar charts for continuous data. One reason for this is that Excel does not have a histogram as one of its standard charts. Another reason might be that histograms are seen as too technical for the lay reader.

As you saw in the *Quantitative methods in action* at the start of this chapter, diagrams can help portray the rapid growth of the Chinese economy. Although all three charts give the same story, each one adds to the general picture of the rapidity of China's growth compared to most other countries.

Key points

- *Data* can be *continuous, discrete, ordinal or nominal*. The type of data determines the method to be used in its presentation.
- Data is normally *aggregated into tables*. For continuous and discrete data, these tables can be either *ungrouped* or *grouped*.
- For *group frequency tables*, the *class interval* needs to be decided and a *tally chart* used to help in the aggregation process.
- Several different types of diagram can be used to display the data more effectively.
- *Pie charts* can only be used for categorical data.
- *Bar charts* are normally used for categorical data and for discrete data.
- *Line graphs* can be used for time series data.
- *Histograms* are used either for continuous or for discrete data that has been aggregated into a frequency table. A histogram gives you an idea of the shape of the underlying distribution, but a *frequency polygon* will show this more clearly.
- If cumulative frequencies are plotted, a *cumulative frequency ogive* is obtained. This important graph allows you to obtain further information about the underlying distribution.
- Another useful diagram is a stem and leaf plot. This diagram allows the shape of the distribution to be seen and outliers can be highlighted.

Further reading

As with the previous chapter, all elementary statistical texts contain a chapter on presentation of data. Many texts such as Curwin and Slater (2013) use Excel, but some cover SPSS or Minitab (another statistical package) as well. There are also a large number of texts that specialize in SPSS, such as the one by Field (2013) and another by Pallant (2013).

http://www.**palgrave.com**/oakshott-eqm6

Solutions to all questions are freely available

Practice questions

1   How would you define the following sets of data?
    (a) The number of hours of sunshine each day at a seaside resort
    (b) The mean daily temperature at a seaside resort
    (c) Daily rainfall (in mm)
    (d) Scoring system for ice dancing

2   In the context of a survey into internet usage give an example of
    (a) Ratio data
    (b) Interval data
    (c) Discrete data
    (d) Ordinal data
    (e) Nominal data

3   A person keeps account of the number of text messages she has sent over the past 18 days and the results are shown in Table 4.13.

Table 4.13 Data for Question 3

Day	Texts sent	Day	Texts sent	Day	Texts sent
1	2	7	10	13	8
2	5	8	20	14	6
3	5	9	0	15	30
4	12	10	10	16	12
5	1	11	4	17	1
6	5	12	2	18	9

Summarize this data in the form of a frequency table using suitable class intervals and plot the data.

4   A survey was carried out into consumers' preference for different types of coffee. A sample of 20 people gave the following replies:

Person	Preference	Person	Preference
1	instant	11	ground
2	filter	12	instant
3	instant	13	ground
4	filter	14	filter
5	instant	15	instant
6	filter	16	instant
7	ground	17	ground
8	instant	18	filter
9	filter	19	instant
10	filter	20	filter

(a) Aggregate this data into a suitable table.
(b) Draw a pie chart of the data.
(c) Draw a simple bar chart of the data.

5   Table 4.14 represents the sales by department of a high street store. Using Excel or otherwise, draw a component bar chart and a multiple bar chart of the sales.

Table 4.14 Sales information for Question 5

Department	2009	2010	2011
Menswear	£2.7m	£4.9m	£6.3m
Furniture	£3.4m	£2.3m	£1.5m
Household	£2.5m	£2.4m	£2.5m
Total Sales	£8.6m	£9.6m	£10.3m

What conclusions can you make about the sales for this store?

6   Table 4.15 shows how the sales of Marla plc were broken down between the company's four sales regions during the years 2007 to 2011. Using Excel or otherwise,
(a) Draw a simple bar chart to show the total sales for the four-year period.
(b) Draw a component bar chart to show the sales for the years and how they were broken down between the four sales regions.
(c) Draw a multiple bar chart to compare the sales for each region.

(d) Draw a pie chart to show the breakdown of total sales in 2011.

(e) What can you conclude about the sales of Marla plc?

Table 4.15 Sales information for Question 6

Sales region	Year (Sales £m)				
	2007	2008	2009	2010	2011
S. West	4.0	2.0	2.2	3.6	3.7
South	6.0	4.9	2.5	3.2	3.7
S. East	7.6	9.1	5.2	4.3	4.2
Wales	1.5	1.4	1.4	1.5	1.6
Totals	19.1	17.4	11.3	12.6	13.2

7 The data below relates to the weight (in grams) of an item produced by a machine.

28.8	29.2	30.8	29.2	30.2	30.0	26.8	30.6	29.0	27.8	28.6
30.4	30.8	29.2	30.4	29.6	31.4	30.6	31.0	31.4	31.4	30.0
29.0	29.4	29.0	28.0	26.5	29.6	27.0	23.2	25.2	24.5	28.0
27.0	29.4	27.6	26.2	25.3	26.8	25.8	28.2	28.1	30.0	30.0
27.1	26.1	25.4	23.8	22.8	23.5	25.5	24.0	27.0	28.5	27.2
25.5	25.6	24.5	23.5	22.4	25.2	27.4	27.0	28.2	28.0	28.0
25.8	30.4	26.5	25.2	29.3	27.4	22.1	26.2	23.8	24.8	20.5
20.4	24.6	24.8								

(a) Aggregate this data into a suitable frequency table.

(b) Draw a histogram of the data.

(c) Draw a stem and leaf plot of the data.

(d) Draw a cumulative frequency ogive of the data and demonstrate how it could be used to provide further information about the distribution of weights.

(e) What conclusions can be made about the data from your diagrams?

8 Using the data given in Table 4.13 for Question 3 plot the data using a histogram.

9 The histogram in Figure 4.37 represents hours worked, taken from the British 2001 census. Describe what this histogram shows. How would you describe the shape of the histogram?

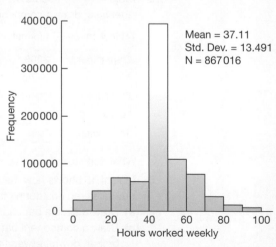

Mean = 37.11
Std. Dev. = 13.491
N = 867 016

Figure 4.37 Histogram of hours worked from the 2001 census

10   Table 4.16 shows the number of cars/vans per household taken from the 2001 British census. Using the Valid percentage column draw a pie chart and explain what this chart shows.

Table 4.16 Vehicles owned, taken from the 2001 national census

Cars/Vans Owned or Available for Use					
		Frequency	Percentage	Valid percentage	Cumulative percentage
Valid	No car	358 420	19.4	19.8	19.8
	1 car	761 398	41.3	42.1	61.8
	2 cars	537 155	29.1	29.7	91.5
	3 cars or more	153 602	8.3	8.5	100.0
	Total	1 810 575	98.2	100.0	
Missing	Not applicable (not in a household)	32 950	1.8		
Total		1 843 525	100.0		

11   Table 4.17 shows family type taken from the 2001 national census. Draw a bar chart using the Valid percentage column of this data and describe what it shows.

Table 4.17 Frequency table of family type taken from the 2001 national census

Family Type				
	Frequency	Percentage	Valid percentage	Cumulative percentage
Valid				
Lone parent – male	27 264	1.5	1.5	1.5
Lone parent – female	190 229	10.3	10.6	12.1
Married couple – no children	342 020	18.6	19.1	31.2
Married couple – children all belong to both members of couple	671 362	36.4	37.4	68.7
Married couple – children do not all belong to both members	63 983	3.5	3.6	72.2
Cohabiting couple – no children	80 237	4.4	4.5	76.7
Cohabiting couple – children all belong to both members	58 178	3.2	3.2	79.9
Cohabiting couple – children do not all belong to both members	46 005	2.5	2.6	82.5
Ungrouped individual (not in a family)	313 438	17.0	17.5	100.0
Total	1 792 716	97.2	100.0	
Missing Not applicable (not in a household/ student living away)	50 809	2.8		
Total	1 843 525	100.0		

12 Table 4.18 is taken from the 2001 national census. It shows the highest qualification held by men and women. Using level of education qualification as x-axis labels:

Table 4.18 Level of highest qualifications (aged 16–74), England, Wales and Northern Ireland by sex

	Sex		
	Male	Female	Total
No qualifications	165	187	352
Level 1	99	99	198
Level 2	107	124	231
Level 3	48	50	98
Level 4/5	117	117	234
Other qualifications/level unknown (England and Wales only)	51	28	79
Total	587	605	1192

(a) Plot a multiple bar chart of the data.
(b) Plot a component bar chart of the data.
(c) Plot a percentage bar chart of the data.
(d) Explain what these charts tells you about qualifications held by men and women in England, Wales and Northern Island.

13 The sickness records of a company have been examined and Table 4.19 shows the number of days taken off work through sickness during the past year.

Table 4.19 Information for Question 13

Days off work	Number of employees
Less than 2 days	45
2 to 5 days	89
6 to 9 days	40
10 to 13 days	25
14 to 21 days	5
22 to 29 days	2

Draw a histogram to represent this distribution and comment on its shape.

14 A survey carried out into 605 small and medium-size companies (SMEs) in the South of England revealed the information in Table 4.20 (overleaf) on average sales growth during a period of recession.

(a) Using Excel, plot the following charts:
  (i) A simple bar chart of the number of companies in each region
  (ii) A multiple bar chart with year as the x-axis labels
  (iii) A multiple bar chart with region as the x-axis labels
  (iv) A line graph of the average change in sales growth from 2008 to 2010
  (v) A pie chart of the sales growth for each region during 2008
(b) Write a paragraph summarizing your charts.

Table 4.20 Annual average % sales growth (from previous year) by region

Region	No. of companies	2008	2009	2010
South Western	63	17.3	−1.0	2.5
Southern	143	21.1	3.2	2.4
Eastern	77	11.9	7.6	0.6
South Eastern	48	50.5	25.5	−0.7
Outer London	78	17.3	1.7	2.3
Inner London	191	19.1	17.3	12.6

15 A high street store has gathered the following data about the value in £s of purchases made by a sample of 50 customers.

67.00 55.56 85.21 72.33 63.25 58.00 53.00 53.41 73.33 79.21
65.22 53.25 82.10 46.10 56.00 64.16 55.67 57.00 57.00 58.20
43.20 52.30 98.00 57.21 59.62 52.33 57.77 58.20 58.60 61.22
53.40 67.00 66.32 50.10 60.11 45.00 51.20 53.00 78.54 64.00
41.21 78.61 55.55 48.62 59.99 63.54 76.35 77.00 45.50 55.01

(a) Plot a histogram of the data using suitable class intervals and join up the mid points to form a frequency polygon. Describe the shape of the distribution.
(b) Plot a cumulative frequency ogive and find the following:
    (i)   The percentage of sales in excess of £70
    (ii) The percentage of sales between £52 and £72
    (iii) The value of purchases that are exceeded by 10% of sales.

Assignment

Find examples (at least three) of diagrams in newspapers, company reports and statistical publications. You should write a paragraph on each diagram discussing the following points:

- the conclusions that you can draw from the diagram
- whether a different diagram would be more informative
- how the diagram could be misleading (if applicable).

MAKING SENSE OF DATA: AVERAGES AND MEASURES OF SPREAD

PREREQUISITES
In order to fully understand this chapter you should have read Chapter 4 (*Finding patterns in data: charts and tables*).

OBJECTIVES
- To be able to calculate measures of central tendency (measures of location) and variation in the data (spread around the central location)
- To understand the advantages and disadvantages of different measures
- To be able to draw suitable charts to help calculate some of these measures
- To be able to use Excel and SPSS to visualize some of these measures

INTRODUCTION
Although tables and diagrams allow important features of data to be displayed, these methods of summarizing information are generally *qualitative* rather than *quantitative*. In order to provide more quantitative information, it is necessary to calculate statistical measures that can be used to represent the entire set of data. Two important measures of the data are its *location*, in terms of a typical or central value, and the *spread* or *dispersion* of the data around this central value. As we will see later in this chapter, the average and spread of data can be represented by a number of different statistics. One measure of average is the *median*, which is the middle value once the data has been sorted. A useful statistic to show spread is the *quantile*, which allows the data to be split into equal parts. The two most common quantiles are the *quartile*, which is a quarter, and the *decile*, which is a tenth. We shall meet the decile in the case represented in the *Quantitative methods in action*.

QUANTITATIVE METHODS IN ACTION

How wealthy are you?

Table 5.1 was produced as part of the distributional analysis to accompany the 2014 UK Budget. It is designed to give an idea of the impact of the budget on households. Gross (pre-tax) income for each household group is split into 10 equal deciles. Within each decile the median gross income is the middle of that income range. From this table you can discover which decile group you are likely to be in. So if you are a single adult earning £21,000, then you are likely to be in the sixth income decile. However, if you are in a two-adult household with the same income, then you are likely to be in the third decile.

Interestingly, if you are a two-adult, two-children family, then you only need to be in the fifth decile before you start paying tax at the 40% level (as of April 2015, 40% tax is normally charged on income over £42,385)!

Of course your actual income depends on many factors, including your qualifications and the type of job you have. It also depends on whether you work in the public or private sector. Figure 5.1 is taken from the Annual Survey of Hours and Earnings (ASHE) and compares statistics for these two sectors in the form of a *box and whisker* chart. The interpretation of this chart is slightly different to Table 5.1. The percentiles and quartiles represent the number of employees *below* a particular level. So in the private sector 90% of employees earn less than £57,089, whereas in the public sector 90% earn less than £49,111, which means that 10% earn more than these amounts. You will also see that the median is higher in the private sector. The difference between the two quartiles is one possible measure of the spread of the data (known as the *interquartile range*). You will meet this type of chart later in the chapter.

Table 5.1 Median 2014 gross income for each decile (£ p.a.) for different household compositions

Median gross income of households in decile	One adult (£)	One adult and one child (£)	Two adults (£)	Two adults and one child (£)	Two adults and two children (£)
Top decile	60,500	77,700	88,500	113,400	151,400
Ninth decile	39,800	49,300	58,300	74,700	91,100
Eighth decile	31,100	36,700	46,400	59,800	70,200
Seventh decile	24,800	30,900	37,900	49,200	59,900
Sixth decile	21,100	26,300	32,200	42,100	50,900
Fifth decile	17,600	24,700	27,200	35,600	44,200
Fourth decile	15,300	20,900	23,000	30,400	37,100
Third decile	13,200	17,000	19,900	26,400	32,000
Second decile	11,300	14,500	17,100	21,800	26,800
Bottom decile	8,600	10,700	13,300	15,300	19,700

Source: HM Treasury tax and benefit microsimulation model, 'Impact on households: distributional analysis to accompany Budget 2014'. Contains public sector information licensed under the Open Government Licence v3.0.

Figure 5.1 Distribution of full time gross employee pay in the public and private sectors 2014

Source: Adapted from data from the Office for National Statistics licensed under the Open Government Licence v.3.0. 'Annual Survey of Hours and Earnings, 2014 Provisional Results'. Table 13.7a Annual pay – Gross 2014.

Measures of location

I am sure that you have heard of the word *average*. An average is some kind of representative item within a set of possible items. The word *location* is used because, for numerical data, an average *locates* a typical value of some distribution. This is not as easy as it may seem as there could be several different values that would serve as this average figure.

example 5.1

The number of sales made by two salespersons over the past few days has been as follows:

Mike   3, 2, 1, 32, 2, 1, 1
Janet   0, 1, 4, 12, 10, 7, 8, 6

activity 5.1

What would be a good measure of the daily number of sales by each salesperson?

Six out of the seven values for Mike are between 1 and 3 sales per day, while for Janet the values are fairly evenly spread between 0 and 12 sales per day. Do you choose one of the existing values to represent the number of sales per day or do you choose a value that is in between?

There are in fact three different averages and each can give you different values. The next section defines each one and discusses the advantages and disadvantages of each.

The mean, median and mode

The *mean* is defined as the sum of all the values divided by the total number of values. So for Mike the mean number of sales per day is:

$$\frac{3 + 2 + 1 + 32 + 2 + 1 + 1}{7} = 6$$

Notice that the mean is not one of the values in the set of data. (A mean value can also be a fractional value even if the data values are themselves whole numbers.)

The mean of a set of numbers is normally referred to as $\bar{x}$ (x bar) and in symbols the formula for the mean is:

Sum of the n values

$$\bar{x} = \frac{\sum x}{n}$$

Number of items

activity 5.2

Find the mean number of sales per day for Janet.

You should have found that the mean for Janet is also 6. Is 6 sales a good measure of average for both data sets? Certainly for Janet a mean of 6 is quite a good representative value, but for Mike a value between 1 and 3 would be more typical. The problem with the mean is that it gives equal importance to *all* values, including any extreme values. In Mike's case the value of 32 is clearly influencing the mean. The *median* overcomes this problem by choosing the *middle* value of a set of numbers. In order to find this value the data is first ordered in ascending order as follows:

1, 1, 1, 2, 2, 3, 32

The middle value of this set of 7 numbers is 2, which is a more typical value.

activity 5.3

Find the median sales for Janet.

You should have found a slight problem here in that there is no single middle number. There are two middle numbers though, which are 6 and 7 and in this case you would take the mean of these two numbers which is 6.5. This is close to the mean value of 6, so in this case either of the two averages are equally suitable.

Which is the better average? This is a difficult question to answer as both have their advantages and disadvantages, as you can see in Table 5.2.

Table 5.2 Comparison of mean and median

	Mean	Median
One of the actual data items?	Not usually	Often
Equal contribution by all data items?	Yes	No
Influenced by extreme values (outliers)?	Yes	No
Easy to calculate?	Yes	No

The mean and median can both be used for numerical data but not for *categorical* data. The next activity illustrates this point.

activity 5.4

In Chapter 4 data from a travel to work survey was provided. This data is summarized in Table 5.3.

Which is the most typical mode of travel?

Table 5.3 Results of a travel to work survey

Mode of travel	Frequency
Car	9
Bus	4
Cycle	3
Walk	2
Train	2

Clearly the car is the most common mode of travel. The category that occurs the most frequently is called the *mode*. The mode can also be quoted for numerical data.

activity
5.5

What is the mode for the sales data of Example 5.1?

For Mike, 1 sale occurred most frequently so this is the mode for this group of numbers. However, there is no mode for Janet's sales data since each value occurs once only.

The mode has limited uses but it can be useful when the most common value or category is required. Can you imagine a shoe shop being interested in the mean or median size of shoe?

The mean, median and mode for a frequency distribution

It is relatively straightforward finding an average of a small set of data, but when large quantities of data are involved, or when the data is supplied in the form of a frequency table, the methods of calculation become more involved.

example
5.2

The ungrouped frequency table in Table 5.4 gives the daily number of sales made by the sales force of a double glazing company.

Table 5.4 Ungrouped frequency table

No. of sales	Frequency
2	3
3	7
4	9
5	6
6	5
7	2
8	1

activity
5.6

What is the mean number of sales made per day by the company's sales force?

The mean could be found by writing the value 2 three times, 3 seven times and so on. You would then add up all the values and divide by the total number of values, which is 33. However, a much easier method is to multiply 2 by 3, 3 by 7 and so on. This will give you the same sum as the longer method. If you let x be the number of sales and f the frequency, the procedure for calculating the mean can be seen in Table 5.5.

Table 5.5 Calculation of the mean

No. of sales x	Frequency f	fx
2	3	6
3	7	21
4	9	36
5	6	30
6	5	30
7	2	14
8	1	8
Total	33	145

The mean is therefore: $\dfrac{145}{33} = 4.4$ sales.

This calculation can be expressed in algebraic notation as follows:

$$\bar{x} = \frac{\sum fx}{\sum f}$$

←— Multiply f by x and sum

←— Sum of frequencies

---

activity 5.7

What is the median number of sales made per day?

The median for this set of values can be found by remembering that the median is the middle value. Since the data is already in ascending order it is a simple matter of locating the middle value, which will occur at the 17th frequency. If you write down the cumulative frequencies as shown in Table 5.6, you will see that the median must occur when $x = 4$.

Table 5.6 Calculation of the median

x	f	Cumulative f
2	3	3
3	7	10
4	9	19
5	6	25
6	5	30
7	2	32
8	1	33

---

activity 5.8

What is the modal value of sales?

The modal number of sales is easy to see since 4 sales occurs 9 times, which is the most frequent.

---

example 5.3

The group frequency table shown in Table 5.7 refers to the length of 80 bolts produced by a machine.

Table 5.7 Grouped frequency table

Interval	Frequency
30 to under 35 mm	4
35 to under 40 mm	7
40 to under 45 mm	14
45 to under 50 mm	23
50 to under 55 mm	16
55 to under 60 mm	9
60 to under 65 mm	4
65 to under 70 mm	1
70 to under 75 mm	1
75 to under 80 mm	0
80 to under 85 mm	1

This is a similar table to that in Example 5.2, except that x does not have a single value. In order to calculate the mean, the *mid value* is used for x. So the mid value for the interval 30 to under 35 would be 32.5. (You can assume that you can get as close as you like to 35mm.) Although this is an approximation, it is generally a very close one and is normally quite adequate.

activity 5.9

Calculate the mean for the data in Table 5.7.

Table 5.8 shows how the mean is calculated by making x represent the mid point of the range.

Table 5.8 Calculation of the mean and median for a frequency distribution

Interval	Mid point (x)	Frequency f	fx	Cumulative frequency	% cumulative frequency
30 to under 35 mm	32.5	4	130.0	4	5.00
35 to under 40 mm	37.5	7	262.5	11	13.75
40 to under 45 mm	42.5	14	595.0	25	31.25
45 to under 50 mm	47.5	23	1092.5	48	60.00
50 to under 55 mm	52.5	16	840.0	64	80.00
55 to under 60 mm	57.5	9	517.5	73	91.25
60 to under 65 mm	62.5	4	250.0	77	96.25
65 to under 70 mm	67.5	1	67.5	78	97.50
70 to under 75 mm	72.5	1	72.5	79	98.75
75 to under 80 mm	77.5	0	0.0	79	98.75
80 to under 85 mm	82.5	1	82.5	80	100.00
	Total	80	3910.0		

The mean is:

$$\frac{3910}{80} = 48.875 \text{ mm}$$

The mean using the raw data is 48.652 mm, so the value obtained using the frequency table is quite a good one. (If you want to check this calculation, the raw data can be found in Example 4.3 (Table 4.6 on page 57).)

activity 5.10

What is the median length of a bolt?

The problem with obtaining the median from a grouped frequency table is that the median is likely to lie within an interval. You could locate the required interval and then simply use the mid point as an estimate, but a better approximation is to interpolate within the interval. There are two methods of doing this extrapolation. The easiest method is graphical and if a cumulative frequency ogive is drawn the median frequency will be halfway up the y axis. It is often easier to use percentage cumulative frequency, as then the median frequency is 50%. Figure 5.2 is the cumulative

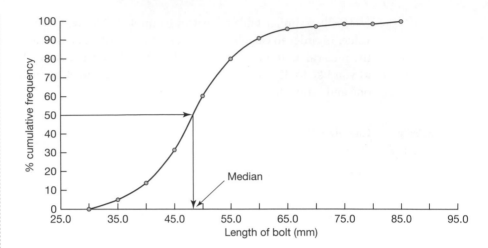

Figure 5.2 Ogive

frequency ogive for the length of bolts, and you will see that the median is around 48 mm, so 50% of bolts are below 48 mm in length and 50% above.

An alternative method is by calculation. If we look at Table 5.8 we see that 25 bolts are below 45 mm and 48 below 50 mm so the median (the 40th bolt) must be in the interval 45 to 50 mm. That is, the median is 45 plus a proportion of the 5 mm interval. As the median is represented by the 40th bolt it must be $40 - 25 = 15$ into this interval and since there are 23 bolts in the interval then 15/23 is the fraction of the interval. If we multiply this fraction by 5 we get the amount we must add on to 45. So the median will be:

$$45 + \frac{15}{23} \times 5 = 48.26\,\text{mm}$$

which agrees with the values obtained graphically.

We can write this calculation as a formula:

$$\text{Median} = l + w \left(\frac{\frac{n}{2} - F}{f} \right)$$

where l is the lower boundary of the median group, w is the width of the median group, n is the number of values, f is the frequency in the median group and F is the cumulative frequency up to the median group.

So in our example: $l = 45$; $w = 5$; $n = 80$; $f = 23$ and $F = 25$ and

$$45 + 5 \left(\frac{40 - 25}{23} \right) = 48.26, \text{ as before.}$$

A further method is to use a stem and leaf plot. In Activity 4.10 (page 69) we obtained a stem and leaf plot for the length of bolt data (see Table 5.9). As there is an even number of values we must take the average of the two middle two values which will be the 40th and 41st value. Counting from either end we get 47 and 49 mm and the mean of these two numbers is 48 mm which again agrees with the other two methods.

Table 5.9 A stem and leaf plot of the length of bolt data

```
Frequency      Stem &  Leaf
    4.00          3 . 0003
    7.00          3 . 5556667            The middle two values
   14.00          4 . 01122222334444
   23.00          4 . 55555666666677(79)99999999
   16.00          5 . 0011122222333444
    9.00          5 . 556666789
    4.00          6 . 0114
    3.00  Extremes    (>=68)

                      3|3 represents 33 mm
```

activity **5.11** What is the modal value of the length of bolts?

It is normal to talk about a *modal class* in a grouped frequency distribution, although it is possible to estimate a single value. The grouped frequency table in Example 5.3 (Table 5.7) suggests that the interval 45 to under 50 mm has the highest frequency of 23. A single estimate of the modal value could be obtained using the geometric method illustrated in Figure 5.3. You should see that this modal value is approximately 48 mm. You might have noticed that all three averages are very similar. This is because the underlying distribution is approximately *symmetrical*. If the distribution were *right* skewed the mean would be displaced to the *right* of the mode, and if the distribution were *left* skewed the mean would be displaced to the *left* of the mode.

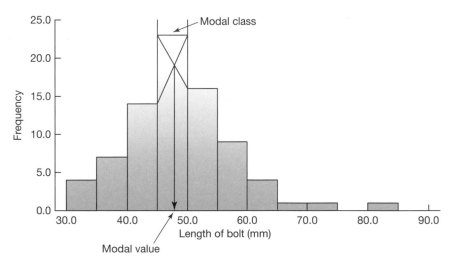

Figure 5.3 Graphical method for finding the mode

The median is between the two but closer to the mean. (Skewness was first discussed in Chapter 4.) Earnings data is a good example of a distribution that is right skewed.

(activity 5.12) The grouped frequency table in Table 5.10 refers to the weight of jars of coffee. What is the average weight of a jar according to this data?

Table 5.10 Grouped frequency table with open classes

Class interval	Frequency
less than 96 g	5
96 to under 98 g	10
98 to under 99 g	15
99 to under 100 g	27
100 to under 102 g	11
more than 102 g	2

The problem with Table 5.10 is the open classes. A mean needs a mid point for each interval, which this data clearly does not have. There is no satisfactory way of calculating the mean for grouped frequency tables with open classes, although some people say you should use the width of the previous or next interval. So the mid point of the first interval would be 95 g and 103 g for the last interval. This approximation *may* be justified if the number of items in the open intervals is small relative to the closed intervals. I think that for open intervals the median is a far better average to use. The median only requires the upper value of each interval and it is not necessary for the ogive to be complete. This is illustrated in Figure 5.4 where you will see that the median is about 99.2 g.

In the calculation of the mean, each value was given an equal weighting. However, there are some circumstances where this is not correct. The next activity illustrates a typical example.

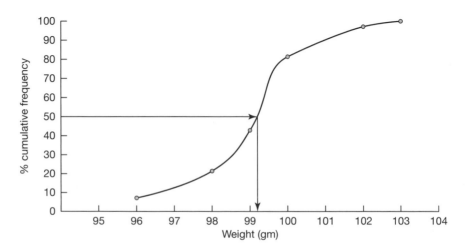

Figure 5.4 Median weight for jars of coffee

3 Add up all these squared differences.
4 Divide the total squared difference by one less than the number of data items (n). The reason for dividing by $n - 1$ and not n has to do with the fact that when you take a sample of data items the spread will be less than the spread of the population. To understand this, think of how many seven-foot people you know. There will be several seven-foot people in a country, and the spread of heights of the population will be influenced by these people. Yet if you take only a small sample, it is extremely unlikely that you will get any very tall or very short people, so the *sample* spread will be less than the *population* spread. Dividing by $n - 1$ helps to compensate for this. We will come back to this issue when we look at sample data in Chapter 8.

The statistic you have calculated – the variance – is one of the most important measures in statistics. However, as it is in squared units, it is usual to use the square root of the answer: this statistic is called the *standard deviation* and has the same units as the data. Standard deviation is a far more practical measure of spread and will be used extensively throughout this text.

The variance not only takes account of all data values but also magnifies the effect of values that are a long way from the mean. Data that is more spread out will have a larger variance than data that is clustered closer to the mean.

The procedure for calculating the variance for Mike's sales is shown in Table 5.11. Remember that the mean was 6.

Table 5.11 Calculation of the variance for Mike's sales

Sales	Difference	Difference squared
x	$x - 6$	$(x - 6)^2$
3	−3	9
2	−4	16
1	−5	25
32	26	676
2	−4	16
1	−5	25
1	−5	25
	Total	792

$$\text{Variance} = \frac{792}{7 - 1} = 132.0$$

The variance is usually represented by the symbol s^2:

$$s^2 = 132$$

The standard deviation, s, is $\sqrt{132}$

$$s = 11.5 \text{ sales per day}$$

Notice how the variance is affected by the outlier of 32 sales.

In algebraic terms the formula for the variance is:

Sum of the differences squared

$$s^2 = \frac{\sum (x - \bar{x})^2}{n - 1}$$

number of values −1

The problems with this formula are that it is tedious and can be inaccurate if the mean has been rounded. A better formula is:

Sum of squared x Sum of x all squared

$$s^2 = \frac{\sum x^2 - \frac{(\sum x)^2}{n}}{n - 1}$$

Table 5.12 illustrates how this formula is used in practice.

$$s^2 = \frac{1044 - \frac{(42)^2}{7}}{6}$$

$$= \frac{792}{6}$$

$$= 132 \text{ as before}$$

Table 5.12 Calculation of the variance using the modified formula

x	x²
3	9
2	4
1	1
32	1024
2	4
1	1
1	1
42	1044

activity 5.16

Calculate the variance and standard deviation for Janet's sales data.

Using the modified formula, you should have obtained Table 5.13.

Table 5.13 Calculation of the variance of Janet's data

x	x²
0	0
1	1
4	16
12	144
10	100
7	49

	8	64
	6	36
Totals	48	410

$$s^2 = \frac{410 - \dfrac{(48)^2}{8}}{7}$$

$$= \frac{122}{7}$$

$$= 17.4$$

The standard deviation, $s = 4.2$ sales per day.

This calculation demonstrates that, compared with Mike, Janet has a much smaller variation in her daily number of sales.

activity 5.17

It has been discovered that a mistake has been made in Janet's sales data given in Example 5.1. Her daily sales are all 3 less than they should be. What should the mean and standard deviation really be?

You should have found the mean to be 9, which is simply 3 more than originally quoted. However, the standard deviation hasn't changed at 4.2. Why is this? This can be explained if you look at Figure 5.6.

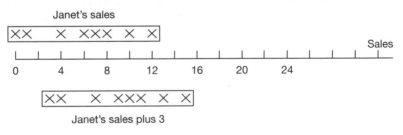

Figure 5.6 Standard deviation remains unchanged

The original values have been shifted 3 units to the right. The spread of the new values has not changed so the standard deviation will be the same.

activity 5.18

If Janet's sales should really be double the figures given in Example 5.1, what would the mean and standard deviation be in this case?

You should have found that both the mean and standard deviation have doubled. By doubling each value the spread has also doubled, as you can see in Figure 5.7.

Figure 5.7 Standard deviation doubles

The variance and standard deviation for a frequency distribution

A slightly different formula is used for a frequency distribution, to reflect the fact that frequencies are involved. The formula normally used for the variance is:

$$s^2 = \frac{\sum fx^2 - \dfrac{(\sum fx)^2}{\sum f}}{\sum f - 1}$$

As the sum of frequencies $\left(\sum f\right)$ is likely to be large (greater than 30), it is not really necessary to subtract 1 from the denominator. The formula then becomes:

Sum of $(f \times x^2)$ Sum of $(f \times x)$

$$s^2 = \frac{\sum fx^2}{\sum f} - \left(\frac{\sum fx}{\sum f}\right)^2$$

Sum of f

This is a little easier to use.

activity **5.19**

Calculate the variance and standard deviation of the data in Table 5.7 (page 94).

The value of x takes the same mid point value as in the calculation of the mean (Activity 5.9). The calculation is shown in Table 5.14.

Table 5.14 Calculation of standard deviation for a frequency distribution

Interval	x	f	fx	x²	fx²
30 to under 35 mm	32.5	4	130.0	1 056.25	4 255.00
35 to under 40 mm	37.5	7	262.5	1 406.25	9 843.75
40 to under 45 mm	42.5	14	595.0	1 806.25	25 827.50
45 to under 50 mm	47.5	23	1092.5	2 256.25	51 893.25
50 to under 55 mm	52.5	16	840.0	2 756.25	44 100.00
55 to under 60 mm	57.5	9	517.5	3 306.25	29 756.25
60 to under 65 mm	62.5	4	250.0	3 906.25	15 625.00

65 to under 70 mm	67.5	1	67.5	4 556.25	4 556.25
70 to under 75 mm	72.5	1	72.5	5 256.25	5 256.25
75 to under 80 mm	77.5	0	0.0	6 006.25	0.00
80 to under 85 mm	82.5	1	82.5	6 806.25	6 806.25
	Total	80	3910.0	39 118.75	197 350.00

The variance is therefore:

$$\frac{197\,350}{80} - \left(\frac{3910}{80}\right)^2 = 2466.875 - 2388.7656$$

$$= 78.1094 \quad \text{or} \quad 78.1$$

and the standard deviation:

$$s = \sqrt{78.1094}$$

$$= 8.8 \text{ mm}$$

Coefficient of variation

If two sets of data have similar means then it is easy to compare the variation by calculating their standard deviations. However, if the means are different then the comparisons of spread will not be so obvious.

activity
5.20

An electrical shop is comparing the delivery times of two products it sells. A smart-phone has a mean delivery time of 17 days with a standard deviation of 6 days, whereas a laptop computer has a mean delivery time of 11 weeks with a standard deviation of 1 week. Which product has the highest variability?

The problem here is not only that the means are quite different but also that the units are different (days in one case and weeks in the other). In order to compare the variability the coefficient of variation is calculated. This is defined as:

$$\frac{\text{standard deviation}}{\text{mean}}$$

This is usually expressed as a percentage by multiplying by 100.

For the smartphone the coefficient of variation is:

$$\frac{6}{17} \times 100 = 35.3\%$$

while for the laptop it is:

$$\frac{1}{11} \times 100 = 9.1\%$$

Therefore, relative to the mean, the smartphone has a larger spread or variation.

Box and whisker plots

A very useful diagram that summarizes information about the location and spread of a set of data is the *box and whisker plot*. The 'box' represents the middle 50% of the data and the extremities of the box are the quartiles Q_1 and Q_3. The median (Q_2) is marked and will obviously be inside the box. Each 'whisker' represents 25% of the data, and the extremities of the whiskers are the minimum and upper values of the data (or the class intervals).

> *activity*
> **5.21**
>
> Draw a box and whisker plot for the data given in Table 5.7 (page 94).
>
> The median (Q_2) of this data is 48 mm (see Activity 5.10) and the values of Q_1 and Q_3 are 44 and 54 mm respectively (Activity 5.15). The box and whisker plot is shown in Figure 5.8.

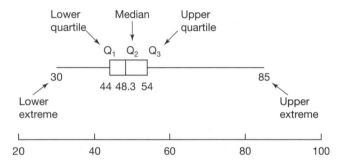

Figure 5.8 Box and whisker plot

Not only does this diagram give you an idea of the average and spread, it also tells you about the shape of the distribution of the data. If the box is small compared to the whiskers this indicates a distribution that is bunched in the middle with long tails. A box shifted to one side or the other indicates skewness, as does the position of the median within the box. In the case of the bolt lengths the right hand whisker is slightly longer than the left, suggesting a slight right skewness to the distribution. However, the median is close to the middle of the box so this skewness is small. The box and whisker plot is particularly useful when you have two or more distributions to compare.

This next activity shows you how you can analyse data that has an open class in a frequency table.

> *activity*
> **5.22**
>
> Table 5.15 shows data from the 2011 census on travel to work. What can you deduce from this data?

Table 5.15 Data from the 2011 census on travel to work

Description	Count	Percentage
Less than 2 km	4 426 231	20.44%
2 km to less than 5 km	4 871 520	22.49%
5 km to less than 10 km	4 613 143	21.30%
10 km to less than 20 km	4 082 459	18.85%
20 km to less than 30 km	1 536 518	7.10%
30 km to less than 40 km	682 642	3.15%
40 km to less than 60 km	618 261	2.85%
60 km and over	825 271	3.81%
Total	21 656 045	

Source: 2011 Census table DC7102EWla. Adapted from data from the Office for National Statistics licensed under the Open Government Licence v.3.0.

The analysis was carried out in Excel and the worksheet is shown in Figure 5.9.

Figure 5.9 Excel worksheet for distance to work
Used with permission from Microsoft.

What can you deduce from the bar chart in Figure 5.9? It is clearly right-skewed, with over 60% of people travelling less than 10 km to work. The modal group is the '2 km to less than 5 km' category, although there is not much difference in the height of the first three bars.

We now need to try to calculate some statistics from the data. Unfortunately, the mean and variance cannot be calculated because of the '60 km and over' category. However, the median can be estimated from the ogive: it is about 6 km. This means that for those people who travel to work, half the population travel fewer than 6 km and half travel more. The interquartile range can also be estimated from the ogive; this is about 13 km (15 – 2). This tells us that the middle 50% of the distribution covers a range of about 13 km. This can perhaps be better seen in the box and whisker plot in Figure 5.10, where the skewness is clear.

Figure 5.10 Box and whisker plot for distance to work

DID YOU KNOW?

How should you measure youth unemployment? The Office for National Statistics (ONS) revealed in January 2011 that the rate of youth unemployment was 18%, which was above the 17.8% rate seen in 1993. However when you look behind the figures you see that the ONS definition of youth unemployment is not the percentage of youths who are unemployed but instead is a percentage of the economically active (the employed and unemployed) excluding what the ONS call the 'inactive'. Inactive youths are primarily those who are in full-time education so, as more people go on to higher education, the denominator used in the calculation gets smaller. If the total number of youths and number of unemployed youths stays the same the rate of unemployment will rise as more youths enter higher education. If you recalculate the unemployment rate as a percentage of all youths the rate goes down to below 13%, which is less than it was at the previous peak. So, although youth unemployment is high, it is not as high as we were made to believe.

Source: http://straightstatistics.fullfact.org/article/youth-unemployment-bad-or-very-bad

---

Using Excel to calculate summary statistics

Before attempting Activity 5.23, you might want to go to the website to check that you understand how Excel deals with formulae and functions.

activity **5.23**

The following data sets show the sales made by the 20 staff in the sales department at the head office of Omega Computer Services plc, for the months of August and September 2014. Figures are in £s.

August 2014   21 900   12 400   9800   6800   13 050   14 900   15 250   8 900
16 451   13 230   16 450   12 890   13 670   14 700   10 430   11 670   13 200
11 100   19 800   15 700

September 2014   12 600   13 500   22 000   34 000   12 500   25 540   21 700
67 800   18 970   16 450   23 220   21 670   17 600   32 420   23 570   14 700
22 400   21 600   26 400   19 700

Use a spreadsheet to summarize both sets of data. In particular, find the mean sales for each salesman and the commission each would get in August based on a 1% commission rate.

The worksheet for Activity 5.23 is shown in Figure 5.11. Figure 5.12 shows the formulae used.

	A	B	C	D	E	F	G
1		Sales of Omega			Commission rate	1%	
2	Sales person	Aug-14	Sep-14	Mean sales	Commission in August		
3	1	£21,900	£12,600	£17,250	£219		
4	2	£12,400	£13,500	£12,950	£124		
5	3	£9,800	£22,000	£15,900	£98		
6	4	£6,800	£34,000	£20,400	£68		
7	5	£13,050	£12,500	£12,775	£131		
8	6	£14,900	£25,540	£20,220	£149		
9	7	£15,250	£21,700	£18,475	£153		
10	8	£8,900	£67,800	£38,350	£89		
11	9	£16,451	£18,970	£17,711	£165		
12	10	£13,230	£16,450	£14,840	£132		
13	11	£16,450	£23,220	£19,835	£165		
14	12	£12,890	£21,670	£17,280	£129		
15	13	£13,670	£17,600	£15,635	£137		
16	14	£14,700	£32,420	£23,560	£147		
17	15	£10,430	£23,570	£17,000	£104		
18	16	£11,670	£14,700	£13,185	£117		
19	17	£13,200	£22,400	£17,800	£132		
20	18	£11,100	£21,600	£16,350	£111		
21	19	£19,800	£26,400	£23,100	£198		
22	20	£15,700	£19,700	£17,700	£157		
23	Total sales	£272,291	£468,340				
24	Mean sales	£13,615	£23,417				
25	Median sales	£13,215	£21,685				
26	Modal sales	#N/A	#N/A				
27	Standard deviation	£3,546	£11,954				
28	Coefficient of variation	25.4%	49.8%				
29	Lower quartile	£11,528	£17,313				
30	Upper quartile	£15,363	£24,063				
31	IQR	£3,835	£6,750				
32							

Figure 5.11 The completed worksheet
Used with permission from Microsoft.

Figure 5.12 The Excel worksheet with the formulae shown
Used with permission from Microsoft.

activity 5.24

What does the N/A mean for the mode in Activity 5.23?

The mode is the value that occurs most frequently. As all the values are different then the data does not have a mode. Excel will give N/A (not applicable) when this occurs.

activity 5.25

What do the values of the mean and median tell you about the shape of the distribution of data?

If you look at the results you will see that the mean for both months is greater than the median. This means that the distribution is right skewed.

activity 5.26

Which month has the greatest spread of data?

The standard deviation in September is greater than in August, but then so is the mean. If you look at the coefficient of variation you will see that this statistic is twice as large in September, so this is evidence that there is more variation in this month. The interquartile range is also nearly twice the value in September.

Using SPSS to calculate summary statistics

Summary statistics can be produced using the Analyze Descriptive Statistics/ Frequencies dialog box as for charts (see Chapter 4). Figure 5.13 shows the dialog boxes required to calculate the summary statistics for the data from Activity 5.23; the output can be seen in Figure 5.14.

Figure 5.13 Dialog box to create summary statistics using SPSS

Reprint courtesy of International Business Machines Corporation, © International Business Machines Corporation.

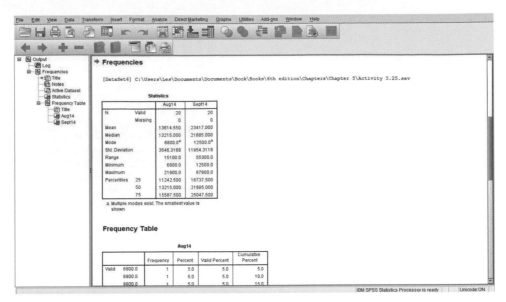

Figure 5.14
Summary statistics
from SPSS

Reprint courtesy of International Business Machines Corporation, © International Business Machines Corporation.

You can also use `Explore` under `Descriptive Statistics` in the `Analyze` menu (see Figure 5.15). This gives a wide range of statistics, most of which are not applicable to this chapter.

Figure 5.15 The
`Explore` menu

Reprint courtesy of International Business Machines Corporation, © International
Business Machines Corporation.

SPSS will also produce boxplots for you, which Excel doesn't do. The simplest method is to use the Explore routine again (see Figure 5.16). Click OK and you will get the boxplots shown in Figure 5.17.

Figure 5.16 Creating a simple boxplot in SPSS

Reprint courtesy of International Business Machines Corporation, © International Business Machines Corporation.

activity **5.27** : What can you conclude from the two boxplots about sales in August and September?

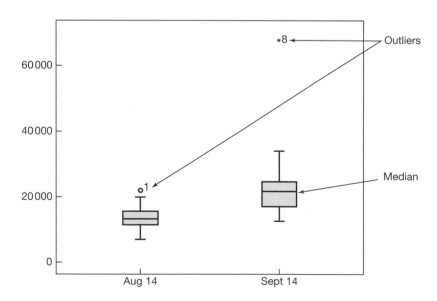

Figure 5.17 Boxplots for the sales data

Your answers here should be the same as your answers to Activity 5.25 and Activity 5.26. However, the boxplot compares the two sets of data quite nicely: you can clearly see that the sales are generally higher in September, and that the spread of sales in September is also higher. One extra feature that SPSS provides is the identification of outliers. As you can see in Figure 5.17, it has identified one value in August (£21 900) and one value in September (£67 800) as possible outliers. These are identified by case numbers (1 and 8).

Before we leave SPSS and boxplots, it is worth coming back to the way in which data is stored in SPSS. Remember that each row represents a case, and each column a variable (see Chapter 4). In the data from Activity 5.23, each case represented a sales-person. However, it could happen that the data is not matched in this way. If this is so, having two separate variables might not be the most appropriate way to represent the data. In such instances there could be a single variable (called 'Sales', say), and to differentiate between August and September a nominal variable (called 'Month', say) would be included. A code of 1 for August and 2 for September could be used.

When data is in this form you use the `Chart Builder` option under `Graphs`. The Y-axis is now 'Sales' and the `Category Axis` is 'Month', as you can see in Figure 5.18. The boxplot you get is exactly the same as in the previous method. This method of defining variables in SPSS will be used in subsequent chapters.

Figure 5.18 Using the chart builder for boxplots

Reflection

We cannot escape averages! We hear the word on the radio and television, and see it in newspapers. We hear about cricket averages, average alcohol consumption, average wage, and average life expectancy. But do people really understand what the word means? An understanding of the word 'average' is taken for granted; usually it refers to the mean, even when the median would be more informative.

Even when the median is used, it is not always called an average. For example, in one article the *Guardian* newspaper states, '50% of women have an independent income of less than £100 per week' ('Has Labour Delivered?', *Guardian*, 31 January 2005). Of course this means that 50% of women have an income greater than £100 per week, with some women earning substantially more than this – that is, the distribution will be right-skewed. The median is a very important measure of average, particularly when the data is skewed. If you were told that that you had scored 56% in an assignment and that the group mean was 60%, you might think that you had not done very well. However, if the median was 55%, your score would be in the top half of the group.

Measures of spread are also conspicuous by their absence in newspapers and the media generally. Yet when comparing sets of data for which the averages are close, being given measures of spread does help to differentiate between the datasets. As we shall see in subsequent chapters, we need the variance when making inferences about one or more samples of data. We shall also discover that for distributions that are symmetrical, over 99% of the data is within plus and minus 3 standard deviations of the mean.

As well as calculating measures of average and spread, we must not forget the importance of charts in summarizing a set of data. A chart gives us a full picture of a set of data and should always be a first step, even when more complicated statistical techniques are used on the data. Charts can also provide information on measures of average and spread when these cannot easily be calculated from the data. For example, a cumulative ogive gives the median and interquartile range.

Key points

- The *mean, median* and *mode* are measures of average; they *locate* the data.
- In a *symmetrical distribution*, the mean, median and mode are equal. In a *right-skewed distribution* the mean and median are greater than the mode; and in a *left-skewed distribution* they are less than the mode.
- The median is the *50% quartile*, and can easily be found from a cumulative frequency ogive. The median exists even when not all values are available at either the lower or upper end of the distribution.
- To describe a set of data fully, a measure of *spread* is required. The *range* is the simplest measure, but a better measure is the *interquartile range (IQR)*. The IQR uses the middle 50 per cent of the data and is therefore less influenced by extreme values.
- The best measure of spread is the *variance*. The square root of the variance is the *standard deviation*, which is in the same units as the data.
- When a constant figure is added to all the data items the standard deviation does not change, but it you multiply each data item by a constant figure the standard deviation will increase by the same proportion.
- When comparing the spread of two or more distributions, it is useful to compare the *coefficients of variation* for each as these take into account differences in the mean.
- A good visual summary of a frequency distribution is a *box and whisker plot*. This diagram can be used to compare several different distributions side by side.

Further reading

Most texts on quantitative methods and all elementary statistical texts will have a chapter on descriptive statistics. Straight Statistics and Sense about Science have produced a very useful free publication called *Making Sense of Statistics*. The pdf of this publication can be downloaded at www.straightstatistics.org/resources/making-sense-statistics. Another very interesting text and in the same vein is *The Tiger that Isn't: Seeing Through a World of Numbers* by Blastland and Dilnot (2007). Both these publications look at statistics from a commonsense perspective and show how statistics can often deceive unless we know what to look for.

http://www.**palgrave**.com/oakshott-eqm6

Solutions to all questions are freely available

Practice questions

1 The weekly gross pay of 5 employees was as follows:

   £160.24, £183.56, £155.00, £274.50, £174.34

   (a) Calculate the mean and median of the data. Which average may be more appropriate, and why?
   (b) Calculate the standard deviation of the data.
   (c) Recalculate the mean and standard deviation if:
       (i) each value is increased by £20
       (ii) each value is increased by 5%

2 The temperature at a particular Mediterranean resort was taken the same day each month for a year. The temperature in C for each month was

   16, 14, 19, 22, 25, 29, 33, 36, 30, 27, 24, 19.

   (a) what is the mean, median and modal value of the temperature? From the point of view of a holiday maker are any of these averages any use?
   (b) Calculate the standard deviation of the temperatures.
   (c) It was later found that the temperature gauge used was under-reading by 2C. How would this affect the mean and standard deviation?
   (d) Conversion of C to F is by the formula

   $$°F = °C \times 9/5 + 32$$

   Without converting each temperature find the mean and standard deviation of the temperature in F.

3 Which average(s) is most appropriate in each case?
   (a) The test scores of a class of students
   (b) The earnings of people in a particular industry
   (c) The weights of pre-packed food
   (d) Shoes stocked by a shoe shop
   (e) Sizes of parts produced by a machine

4 Table 5.16 shows the number of rejects from a production process. Find the mean and standard deviation.

   Table 5.16 Number of rejects from a production process

Number of rejects	Frequency
0	12
1	45
2	36

   (continued)

Table 5.16 (*continued*)

Number of rejects	Frequency
3	30
4	20
5	5
6	0

5   The following set of data refers to the daily Euro exchange rate to the British pound during the first 10 days of 2009

   1.0471, 1.0473, 1.0457, 1.0458, 1.0573, 1.0886, 1.1104, 1.1092, 1.1168, 1.1260

   (a) What is the mean and median of the exchange rate?

   (b) What is the standard deviation of the exchange rate?

   (c) Comment on the use of these statistics for this data.

6   The histogram given in Figure 5.19 refers to the weekly hours worked of British people as taken from the 2001 national census.

   (a) Estimate the mean, median and mode of hours worked

   (b) Estimate the standard deviation of hours worked. What assumption are you making to arrive at your estimate?

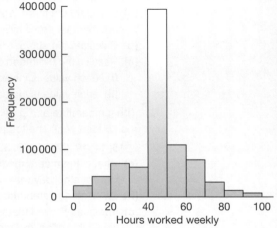

Figure 5.19 Histogram of hours worked from the 2001 census

7   The weighting given to coursework and exam for a quantitative methods course at a university is 40% coursework and 60% exam. If a student gets 74% for the coursework and 56% in the exam, what would be his or her average mark for the unit?

8   The average lifetime for 12 light bulbs is 180.6 hours. Another light bulb gave a lifetime of 200 hours. What would the mean lifetime be if this result was included?

9   The sickness records of a company have been examined and Table 5.17 shows the number of days taken off work through sickness during the past year.

Table 5.17 Data for Question 9

Days off work	Number of employees
Less than 2 days	45
2 to 5 days	89
6 to 9 days	40
10 to 13 days	25
14 to 21 days	5
22 to 29 days	2

(a) What is the mean number of days off work?

(b) What is the median number of days off work?

(c) What is the modal number of days off work?

(d) What is the interquartile range?

(e) What is the standard deviation?

(f) What is the coefficient of variation?

(g) Draw a box and whisker plot and comment on the shape of the distribution.

10 Items are manufactured to the same nominal length on two different machines, A and B. A number of items from each machine are measured and the results are shown in Table 5.18.

Table 5.18 Data for Question 10

Class interval (mm)	Frequency	
	Machine A	Machine B
20 to under 22	5	2
22 to under 24	12	5
24 to under 26	26	20
26 to under 28	11	25
28 to under 30	3	8
30 to under 32	0	2

(a) Find the mean, median and modal values for the two machines.

(b) Find the interquartile range and standard deviation for both machines.

(c) Calculate the coefficient of variation for both machines.

(d) Draw a box and whisker plot for both machines.

(e) Use your results from (a) to (d) to comment on the lengths of items produced by both machines.

11 Table 5.19 shows the wages paid last week to 45 part-time employees of a supermarket chain. Find the mean and the median wage.

Table 5.19 Data for Question 11

Wages (£s)	No. of employees
20 to under 30	2
30 to under 40	4
40 to under 50	6
50 to under 60	12
60 to under 70	11
70 to under 80	9
80 to under 90	1
	45

12 A company is involved in wage negotiations with the trade unions. The current gross weekly wages of the company's employees are summarized in the frequency table in Table 5.20. Two proposals are on offer:

Proposal 1: Give the employees an increase in pay equivalent to 10% of the current mean weekly wage.

Proposal 2: Give the employees an increase in pay equivalent to 12.5% of the current median weekly wage.

Compare the costs of the two proposals.

Table 5.20 Data for Question 12

Gross weekly wages (£s)	No. of employees
90 to under 110	14
110 to under 140	54
140 to under 160	16
160 to under 200	12
200 to under 240	2
	98

13   A firm purchases four main raw materials. Recently, the prices of these raw materials have increased by the percentages indicated in Table 5.21. This table also shows the estimated amount the company will spend per month on each raw material. The purchasing manager of the company has calculated that the average increase in raw material prices is 15%. Can you find an average that reflects more accurately the increase in costs that the company is likely to incur?

Table 5.21 Data for Question 13

Raw material	% increase in price	Mean expenditure per month (£)
Lead	10	3000
Copper	4	1000
Zinc	0	650
Adhesives	46	350

14   The production target of a manufacturer is 300 widgets per week. In the first ten weeks production has averaged 284.7 per week. What average must be reached in the final three weeks of the quarter for the original target to be achieved?

15   A salesperson travels 100 miles to Exeter at an average speed of 60mph. She then returns home at a more leisurely 50 mph. What was the average speed over the 200 miles covered? (No, it's not 55 mph!)

16   Miracle Fashions has recorded the sales made during a particular day and these are shown in Table 5.22.

Table 5.22 Data for Question 16

Value of sales (£)	Number of sales in this range
5 to less than 10	50
10 to less than 20	75
20 to less than 30	45
30 to less than 40	38
40 to less than 60	27
60 to less than 100	18

(a) Using your calculator's statistical mode or a spreadsheet, estimate:
   (i)   the total sales (in £) during this day
   (ii) the mean value of sales
   (iii) the standard deviation of the value of sales
   (iv) the coefficient of variation of the value of sales
(b) Why are your answers in part (a) only estimates?

(c) A fashion shop across the road has also carried out similar calculations and its coefficient of variation of the value of sales is 40%.
   (i) What can you deduce about the distribution of the value of sales between the two shops?
   (ii) Is this other shop likely to be more or less expensive than Miracle Fashions?
(d) Using the data in the table, draw a percentage cumulative frequency ogive, and from your ogive deduce:
   (i) the median value of sales
   (ii) the interquartile range of the value of sales
   (iii) the percentage of sales that were over £50

Assignment

A large bakery regularly takes samples of bread in order to ensure that its product meets quality specifications. Each loaf that is sampled is first weighed, and weight records of 765 'standard' sliced loaves have accumulated over the last few months. The Quality Control Manager would like these records analyzed and has aggregated the data into the frequency table in Table 5.23.

Table 5.23 Data for the assignment

Weight range	Number of loaves in this range
780 g to below 790 g	34
790 g to below 795 g	80
795 g to below 800 g	111
800 g to below 805 g	162
805 g to below 810 g	161
810 g to below 815 g	120
815 g to below 820 g	70
820 g to below 830 g	27

Analyze these figures and write a report to the Quality Control Manager. Your analysis should include graphs, diagrams and measures of location and spread of the data.

III

PROBABILITY AND STATISTICS

6 TAKING A CHANCE: PROBABILITY

OBJECTIVES

■ To be able to calculate simple probabilities

■ To be able to calculate probabilities of compound events using the rules of addition and multiplication

■ To know how to use probability trees to solve problems

■ To understand how to apply Bayes' theorem to modify probabilities when new information is received

INTRODUCTION

It is difficult to go very far in solving business problems without a basic understanding of probability. The 'laws of chance' underpin many decisions that are made in real life. For example, when we carry out a survey we need to know how the sample data relate to the target population. Our insurance premiums are determined by the chance of some mishap occurring, and quality control systems are built around probability laws. There are also many games of chance including card and dice games, horse racing and the National Lottery. This chapter contains all the basic rules and methods of probability that will be required in subsequent chapters.

QUANTITATIVE METHODS IN ACTION

Use of statistics in criminal cases

Statistics are increasingly being used by prosecutors to prove the guilt of a defendant in criminal proceedings. In some cases the statistics used can be quite complex, and many judges will not allow such evidence in court. However, in the case of the Stepping Hill nurse, Victorino Chua, the statistics used were quite basic, but nonetheless very effective.

During the summer of 2011, a number of patients suffered hypoglycaemic shock, causing their blood sugar levels to plunge to dangerously low levels. By the time the police were called in, two patients had died. Initially, foul play was not expected, but this changed over the weekend of 11–12 July 2011. Five patients on the male ward A1 suffered classic symptoms of insulin overdose. The following day a nurse discovered that several saline bags had been tampered with. Once it was clear that someone was trying to harm patients, Greater Manchester Police (GMP) started its biggest and most complex murder investigation. Named Operation Roxburg, it was to take GMP 18 months and required the examination of other hypoglycaemic incidents at Stepping Hill, as well as taking 3291 statements and analysing the shift patterns of over 4000 staff. The prosecution file exceeded 30000 pages, and more than 500000 pages of information were collated. Unfortunately, another nurse was initially accused of the murders, but after she spent 6 weeks in custody, it was shown that she was innocent.

Several measures were put into place at the hospital to prevent tampering with the saline bags, including CCTV and restricted access to drug storerooms. For 5 months there were no other suspicious incidents. However, this changed on 2–3 January 2012 when it was discovered that changes had been made to patients' prescription records, and incorrect doses had been administered. On 5 January 2012, Victorino Chua was arrested. As part of the evidence to prove that Chua was responsible for tampering with the saline bags police produced a Venn diagram (see Figure 6.1) plotting the suspicious hypoglycaemic episodes against the staff working the shifts when and where the episodes occurred. You will meet this diagram later in this chapter, but essentially it allows separate events to be depicted using circles, with any common elements being shown as an intersection of two or more circles. So in this case three events are shown: nursing staff on duty on 10 July 2015 on ward A1; on 11 July 2015 on ward A3; and on the 2 January night shift / 3 January early shift on ward A3. From this diagram it was clear that nurse Chua was common to all three episodes.

On 18 May 2015, Victorino Chua was convicted of murdering two patients, intentionally causing grievous bodily harm to another patient and attempting to intentionally cause grievous bodily harm to 21 other patients. On 19 May 2015, he was jailed for life, with a minimum of 35 years.

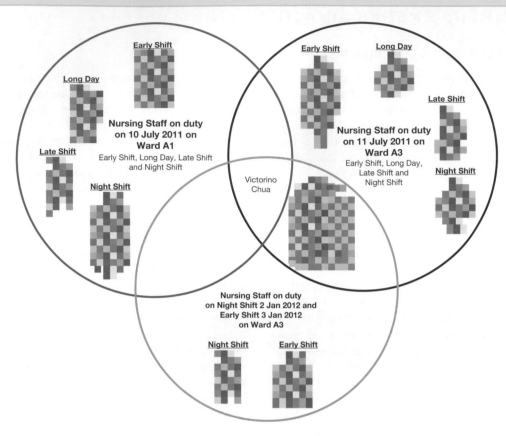

Figure 6.1 Venn diagram produced by Greater Manchester Police to prove Victorino Chua's guilt in the Stepping Hill Hospital poison investigation

Source: Reprinted courtesy of Greater Manchester Police.

Basic ideas

The value of a probability can be given either as a fraction, as a decimal or as a percentage. An event with a probability of zero is termed impossible, while an event with a probability of 1 or 100% is termed certain. Figure 6.2 may help you to picture the idea of the probability measure.

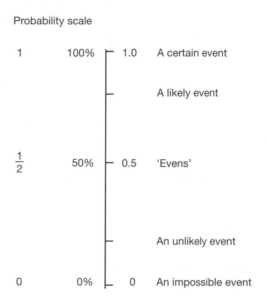

Figure 6.2 Probability scale

Probabilities can be obtained in a number of ways. The simplest is the *subjective* method where you estimate what you think the probability of a particular event will be. For example, a sales manager may estimate that the probability of high sales for a particular product is 60%. This figure may be based on market research or experience of a similar product, but it is unlikely to involve any calculations.

Another method is the *empirical* approach. This method uses measurement to estimate probabilities. For example, you may wish to determine the probability of a defective electrical component being produced by a particular' process. If you test 100 components and find 5 defective, then you would say that the probability of a defective component being produced is $\frac{5}{100}$ or 0.05. That is,

$$\text{probability} = \frac{\text{number of times a particular event occurred}}{\text{total number of trials or 'experiments'}}$$

The particular event here is finding a defective component and the 'experiment' is picking, testing and classifying a component as either good or defective.

activity **6.1** Toss a coin 10 times and use the above formula to calculate the probability of a head.

Did you get a probability of 0.5? This, as you will see shortly, is the 'correct' answer, but 10 tosses is a very small number of experiments. If you tossed the coin a further 10 times you would quite likely get a different answer. This is the basis of *sampling error*, which we shall come back to in Chapter 10. You will also see that the sampling error in this case could be reduced by tossing the coin a larger number of times; that is, the larger the number of tosses, the nearer you will get to a probability of 0.5.

However, to obtain the theoretical probability of a head you would use a different method, called the *a priori* approach. This is similar to the empirical approach, except that you can work out *in advance* how many times a particular event should occur. In the coin tossing activity you know that there is only one head, so that the probability of a head is $\frac{1}{2}$ or 0.5. If you picked a card from a pack, the probability of an Ace is $\frac{4}{52}$ or 0.0769, since there are 4 Aces in a pack. The definition can be written as:

$$\frac{\text{number of ways in which a particular event can occur}}{\text{total number of outcomes}}$$

This definition assumes that all outcomes are equally likely; that is, there is no bias associated with a particular outcome. This definition would not apply to, say, a race involving 10 horses, since the probability that any horse will win is unlikely to be 0.1. The *odds* would reflect such factors as form, jockey, trainer, etc.

$\left(\begin{array}{c}\textit{activity} \\ \textbf{6.2}\end{array}\right)$ You pick a card from a pack. What is the probability that it is a picture card?

To answer this question you would have listed the picture cards in a suit. These are Jack, Queen and King. Since there are 4 suits you should have decided that there will be $4 \times 3 = 12$ ways in which a particular outcome can occur. The probability of a picture card is therefore $\frac{12}{52} = 0.2308$.

The probability of compound events

It is frequently required to find the probability of two or more events happening at the same time. For example, an aircraft has many of its controls duplicated so that if one fails the other would still function. But what is the probability that both systems will fail? The way that probabilities are combined depends on whether the events are *independent* or whether they are *mutually exclusive*. Two (or more) events are said to be independent if the occurrence of one does not affect the occurrence of the other. The two aircraft systems will be independent if the failure of one system does not change the probability of failure of the other system. Two (or more) events are mutually exclusive if either event can occur, but not both. One card drawn from a pack cannot be a Jack and an Ace. However, a Jack and a Diamond are not mutually exclusive since the selected card could be both. When the set of all possible outcomes are known, they are said to be *mutually exhaustive*, and the sum of the probabilities of a set of outcomes that are mutually exclusive *and* mutually exhaustive must equal 1. For example, there are four suits in a pack of cards and the probability of selecting a card from a given suit is $\frac{13}{52}$ or 0.25. The sum of these probabilities is 1, since a card must come from one (and only one) of the suits. This idea will allow you to calculate a probability if the other or others are known. If, say, the probability of a defective component is 5%, then the probability that it is not defective is 95%.

Compound events can be more easily solved if a diagram is drawn. One useful diagram is the *Venn* diagram. A Venn diagram is made up of a square, the inside of which encloses all possible outcomes. The events of interest are represented by circles. The Venn diagram in Figure 6.3 represents two events, A and B. Event A is being dealt a Jack, which has a probability of $\frac{4}{52}$ or 0.0769, and Event B is being dealt an Ace, which also has a probability of $\frac{4}{52}$. The probability of being dealt either a Jack *or* an Ace is:

$$P(\text{Jack or Ace}) = P(\text{Jack}) + P(\text{Ace})$$
$$= 0.0769 + 0.0769$$
$$= 0.1538$$

However, if Event B is being dealt a Diamond then the two events overlap, as shown in Figure 6.4. If the two probabilities are now added, the intersection of the two events (shown shaded) will have been added twice. This intersection, which represents the case of being dealt a Jack of Diamonds (with a probability of $\frac{1}{52}$ or 0.0192), must be subtracted from the sum of the two probabilities. That is:

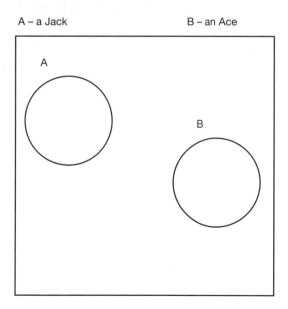

A – a Jack   B – an Ace

A

B

Figure 6.3 Venn diagram for mutually exclusive events

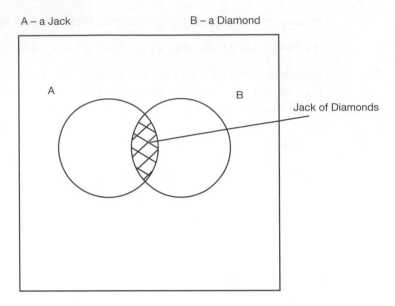

Figure 6.4 Venn diagram for events that are not mutually exclusive

$$P(\text{Jack or Diamond}) = P(\text{Jack}) + P(\text{Diamond}) - P(\text{Jack of Diamonds})$$
$$= 0.0769 + 0.25 - 0.0192$$
$$= 0.3077$$

In general if $P(A)$ means the probability of Event A and $P(B)$ the probability of Event B then:

$$P(A \text{ or } B) = P(A) + P(B) - P(A \text{ and } B)$$

This is known as the *addition rule*.

NOTE: If the two events are mutually exclusive, as in the first example, then there is no intersection and $P(A \text{ and } B)$ is zero.

activity **6.3**

The police regularly carry out spot checks on heavy goods vehicles. During one particular month the results are as shown in Table 6.1.

Assuming that these results are typical of all heavy goods vehicles on the road, what is the probability that if a vehicle was stopped at random it would either be overweight or the driver would have exceeded the allowed driving time?

Table 6.1 Results from checks on heavy goods vehicles

	Overweight	Not overweight	Total
Driving time exceeded	15	25	40
Driving time not exceeded	20	40	60
Total	35	65	100

The key to this question is the word *or*. And since it is possible both for the vehicle to be overweight and for the driver to have exceeded the permitted driving time, the events are not mutually exclusive. Using the addition law you should have obtained the following result:

$$P(\text{time exceeded}) = \frac{40}{100} \text{ or } 0.4$$

$$P(\text{overweight}) = \frac{35}{100} \text{ or } 0.35$$

$$P(\text{time exceeded and overweight}) = \frac{15}{100} \text{ or } 0.15$$

$$\text{So the } P(\text{time exceeded or overweight}) = 0.4 + 0.35 - 0.15$$

$$= 0.6$$

That is, there is a 60% chance that either the lorry would be overweight or the driver would have exceeded the driving time.

Conditional probability

If the probability of Event B occurring is dependent on whether Event A has occurred, you would say that Event B is conditional on Event A. This is written $P(B|A)$, which means the probability of B given that A has occurred.

When Event A and Event B are independent, $P(B|A) = P(B)$. Sampling without replacement is a good example of conditional probability. If two students are to be chosen randomly from a group of 5 girls and 4 boys, then the probability that the first person chosen is a girl is $\frac{5}{9}$ or 0.5556, and the probability that it is a boy is $1 - 0.556 = 0.4444$. The probability that the second person is a girl depends on the outcome of the first choice.

First choice	Probability of second choice being a girl
boy	$\frac{5}{8}$ or 0.625
girl	$\frac{4}{8}$ or 0.5

In the first case the number of girls remains at 5, but in the second case there are only 4 girls to choose from. Note that in both cases the total number of students left is 8, since one has already been chosen.

If you want to know the probability of the first student being a girl *and* the second student being a girl, you will need to use the *multiplication rule*. If the events are dependent, as in this example, the rule is:

$$P(A \text{ and } B) = P(A) \times P(B|A)$$

So $P(\text{girl and a girl}) = 0.5556 \times 0.5 = 0.2778$.

If two (or more) events are independent the rule simplifies to:

$$P(A \text{ and } B) = P(A) \times P(B)$$

For example, if an aircraft has a main and a back-up computer and the probability of failure of either computer is 1%, then the probability of both failing is $0.01 \times 0.01 = 0.0001$ or 0.01%.

activity
6.4

A light bulb manufacturer produces bulbs in batches of 50, and it is known from past experience that 5 of each batch will be defective. If two bulbs are selected without replacement from a batch, what is the probability that both will be defective?

The probability that the first bulb is defective is $\dfrac{5}{50} = 0.1$, but the probability that the second is defective is $\dfrac{4}{49} = 0.0816$, since the total number of bulbs has been reduced by one and there must be one less defective bulb. The probability that both bulbs are defective is therefore:

$$0.1 \times 0.0816 = 0.00816$$

This probability is very small, so if you did in fact get two defective bulbs you should be suspicious concerning the claimed defective rate. (This idea forms the basis of some quality control schemes.)

Tree diagrams

A very useful diagram to use when solving compound events, particularly when conditional probability is involved, is the tree diagram. This diagram represents different outcomes of an experiment by means of branches. For example, in the student example the two 'experiments' of choosing an individual can be represented by the tree diagram in Figure 6.5. The first experiment is represented by a small circle or node, and the two possible outcomes are represented by branches radiating out from the node. The event and probability are written alongside the branch. The second experiment is again represented by a node and you will notice that this node appears twice, once for each outcome of the first experiment. Branches again radiate out from each node, but notice that the probability is different depending on what happened in the first experiment.

You will see that the compound events have been written at the end of each route in Figure 6.5. If you add up these probabilities you will see that they sum to 1 (to 3 decimal places). This is because the routes are mutually exclusive and *mutually exhaustive*. They are mutually exclusive because one and only one of the routes can be followed, and they are mutually exhaustive because all possible routes have been shown. From this diagram various probabilities could be evaluated using the law of addition. For example, the probability of getting two students of the same sex is $0.2778 + 0.1667 = 0.4445$.

It is unlikely that you would use a tree diagram to solve a simple problem like this, but consider the problem in Example 6.1.

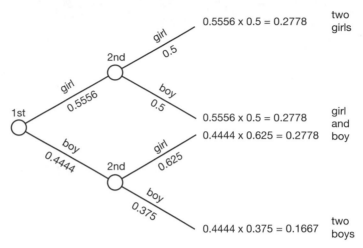

Figure 6.5 A tree diagram

example
6.1 The demand for gas is dependent on the weather and much research has been under-taken to forecast the demand accurately. This is important since it is quite difficult (and expensive) to increase the supply at short notice. If, on any particular day, the air temperature is below normal, the probability that the demand will be high is 0.6. However, at normal temperatures the probability of a high demand occurring is only 0.2, and if the temperature is above normal the probability of a high demand drops to 0.05. What is the probability of a high demand occurring if, over a period of time, the temperature is below normal on 20% of occasions and above normal on 30% of occasions?

The tree diagram is shown in Figure 6.6. Since the demand *depends* on temperature, the first node refers to temperature and there are three branches: below normal, normal and above normal. The probability of the temperature being normal is $1 - (0.2 + 0.3) = 0.5$. The compound probability for each route has been written at the end of the route, so that the probability of there being a high demand given that the temperature is below normal is $0.2 \times 0.6 = 0.12$. Since there are three routes where the demand could be high, the law of addition is used and the probability is:

$$0.12 + 0.10 + 0.015 = 0.235$$

activity
6.5 A company purchases electronic components in batches of 100 and the supplier guarantees that there will be no more than 5 defective components in each batch. Before acceptance of a particular batch the company has a policy of selecting without replacement two components for testing. If both components are satisfactory the batch is accepted and if both are defective the batch is rejected. However, if only one is defective another component is selected and if this is satisfactory the batch is accepted, while if it is defective, the batch is rejected. If the probability that a component is defective is 5%, what is the probability that the batch will be accepted?

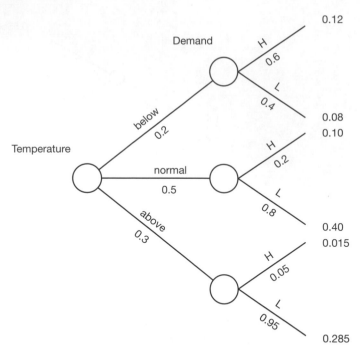

Figure 6.6 Tree diagram for Example 6.1

You could answer this question without a tree diagram, but it is strongly recommended that diagrams are used whenever possible. The diagram is shown in Figure 6.7 where it will be seen that each node has two outcomes: either OK or defective. At the start of the process the probability that the first selection will give a defective component is $\frac{5}{100}$ or 0.05, and the probability that it will be OK is 0.95. If the first component was defective, then the probability that the second is also defective is reduced to $\frac{4}{99}$ or 0.04040, since there is one less defective component *and* one less component in total. The remaining probabilities have been found using a similar reasoning.

The compound probabilities have been written at the end of each route together with the decision; that is, accept or reject. There are three routes where the decision is to accept, and the addition law can be used to give the probability that the batch will be accepted. That is:

$$0.90202 + 0.04602 + 0.04602 = 0.99406$$

The probability that the batch will be rejected is $1 - 0.99406 = 0.00594$. This can be confirmed by adding the probabilities separately.

As in Activity 6.4, it is unlikely that a batch would be rejected. However, if it was, you would have grounds to question the supplier about the true number of defective items in a batch. This type of problem comes under the category of quality control.

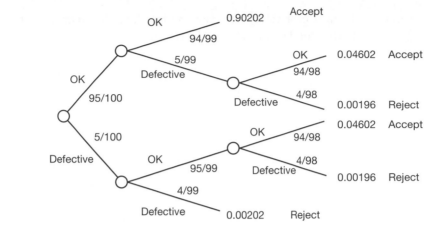

Figure 6.7 Tree diagram for Activity 6.5

Bayes' theorem

This theorem is based on the idea that in many situations we begin an analysis with some *prior* or initial probability estimate for the event we are interested in. This probability can come from historical data, previous experience, a pilot survey, and so on.

Then, we receive additional information from a survey, test, report, and so on, so that we are able to update our prior probability and calculate, using Bayes' theorem, what is known as our *posterior probability*. Consider Example 6.2.

example **6.2**

You are a manager of a company that manufactures 'set top' boxes for digital TV. There is a large demand for these boxes and retailers are urgently asking for delivery. To speed up delivery you could cut out the time-consuming testing of each box, but you are worried that defective boxes would then be returned, which would tarnish the company's reputation. From past experience you know that about 5% of boxes would be expected to be faulty.

As the manager, you select a box. What is the chance that it is faulty? Clearly it is 5% or 0.05. This is our *prior* probability. Perhaps it is possible to do a 'quick and dirty' test on the box, but you know that this test is not very reliable. It is believed that the test will indicate that the box is defective 20% of the time when it is in fact perfectly OK. If the box is defective the test should get it right 90% of the time; that is, the test is better at getting it right when the box is defective. This means that the test is *biased*.

If you do this quick test on a box and it fails, how do you revise your prior probability in the light of this result?

(*activity* **6.6**) Draw a probability tree showing the different outcomes when the test is applied to both a good and a defective box.

For each branch of the tree there are two outcomes of the test; either pass or fail. The probability tree with the probabilities added is shown in Figure 6.8.

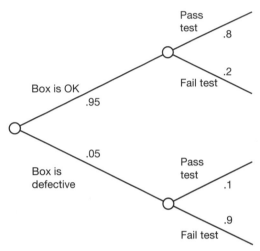

Figure 6.8 Probability tree diagram for Example 6.2

(*activity* **6.7**) Imagine that you have 1000 boxes to test. How many boxes would you have along the different branches?

As there are 1000 boxes, then 950 of these will be good boxes and 50 will be defective. Of the 950 good ones, there will 950 × 0.8 = 760 that pass the test while the remaining 190 will fail. Of the 50 that are defective, there will be 50 × 0.1 = 5 that pass the test while the remaining 45 will correctly fail it. This information has been added to the probability tree and you can see this in Figure 6.9.

(*activity* **6.8**) What is the probability that if you picked one of the 1000 boxes at random it would fail the test?

190 good boxes failed the test and 45 defective boxes failed the test. The total number that failed is therefore 190 + 45 = 235, and the probability that a box would fail the test is

$$\frac{235}{1000} = 0.235$$

(*activity* **6.9**) What is the probability that a box is defective given that it failed the test?

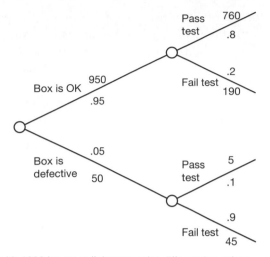

Figure 6.9 The tree with 1000 boxes split between the different branches

Out of the 235 boxes that failed the test, 45 came from boxes that were defective, so the probability that the chosen box is defective is $\frac{45}{235} = 0.1915$. So this new information has allowed us to revise our probability of a defective box from 5% to 19%.

activity **6.10**

Repeat the last three activities using 100 boxes.

You should have found that you still get the same probabilities even though you are dealing with fractions of a box when the boxes are defective. In fact it is not necessary to even consider the number of boxes at all as all you are really doing is multiplying probabilities together. Figure 6.10 is the formal probability tree diagram

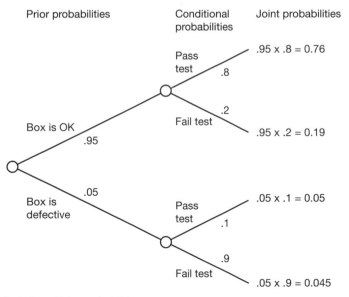

Figure 6.10 Calculation of joint probabilities

for the problem using Bayes' theorem. The probability of the test being correct or not is the *conditional* probability as it is conditional on the first branch of the tree. The probabilities at the end of the tree are the *joint* probabilities as they are obtained by multiplying the prior and conditional probabilities together. The probability that a box would fail the test is the sum of the relevant joint probabilities; that is, $0.19 + 0.045 = 0.235$, and this is the same value as we obtained before. The probability that the a box is defective given that it failed the test is called the *posterior* probability, and for our problem it is

$$\frac{0.045}{0.235} = 0.1915$$

To summarize this procedure:

- Construct a tree with branches representing all the prior probabilities.
- Extend the tree adding the new information obtained. Write the conditional probabilities on these branches.
- Calculate the joint probabilities.
- To obtain the posterior probabilities, divide the appropriate joint probability by the sum of the corresponding joint probabilities.

As a formula this is:

$$P(B|A) = \frac{P(B \, and \, A)}{P(A)}$$

where B is the event 'box is defective' and A is the event 'it failed the test'.

Bayes' theorem is a very powerful technique in solving probability problems and we will come back to an important application of this theorem when we look at decision trees in Chapter 11.

Permutations and combinations

Problems frequently exist where selections are made from groups of items. In these cases it is useful to be able to calculate the number of selections that are possible. The method used depends on whether the order of the selection is important or not. If it is, you should use *permutations*. The number of permutations, where r items are to be selected from a group of size n, is given by the formula:

$$^nP_r = \frac{n!}{(n-r)!}$$

where $n!$ is read as *factorial n* and means $(n-1) \times (n-2) \times (n-3) \times \dots$ For example, $5! = 5 \times 4 \times 3 \times 2 \times 1 = 120$. (Note: $1! = 1$ and by definition $0! = 1$.) If you have a scientific calculator you should find that it has a ^nP_r button, which is much easier than using the formula.

activity
6.11

Bank cheque cards usually have a 4-digit 'pin' number so that they can be used in a cash dispenser. What is the probability that a thief, finding your card, could hit on the correct combination at the first attempt?

The order is important here because, for example, 1234 is a different number from 4321. There are 10 possible digits (0 to 9) so the number of ways of selecting 4 from 10 is:

$$^nP_r = {}^{10}P_4$$

$$= \frac{10!}{(10-4)!} = \frac{10!}{6!}$$

$$= \frac{10 \times 9 \times 8 \times 7 \times 6 \times 5 \times 4 \times 3 \times 2 \times 1}{6 \times 5 \times 4 \times 3 \times 2 \times 1}$$

$$= 5040$$

So there is only a 1 in 5040 chance of the thief finding the correct permutation. As a probability this is:

$$\frac{1}{5040} = 0.000198$$

Where the order is *not* important, you would use *combinations*. The formula for this is as follows:

$$^nC_r = \frac{n!}{r!(n-r)!}$$

Again, most scientific calculators should contain this function.

$\left(\begin{array}{c}\textbf{\textit{activity}} \\ \textbf{6.12}\end{array}\right)$ | What is the probability of winning the National Lottery (Lotto) jackpot?

To win the jackpot you must correctly guess the 6 numbers drawn from the numbers 1 to 49. These numbers can occur in any order, so you would use the combination formula for this calculation. In this case $n = 49$ and $r = 6$, so:

$$^nC_r = {}^{49}C_6$$

$$= \frac{49!}{6! \times (49-6)!}$$

$$= \frac{49 \times 48 \times 47 \times 46 \times 44 \times 43!}{6! \times 43!}$$

$$= 13\,983\,816$$

This is nearly 14 million to 1!

Expected value

If you toss a coin 100 times, you would *expect* 50 heads and 50 tails. That is, the expected number of heads is $0.5 \times 100 = 50$. In general it is a long-run average, which means it is the value you would get if you repeated the experiment long enough. It is calculated by multiplying a value of a particular variable by the probability of its occurrence and repeating this for all possible values. In symbols this can be represented as:

$$\text{Expected value} = \sum px$$

where $\sum$ means the 'sum of'.

activity
6.13

Over a long period of time a salesperson recorded the number of sales she achieved per day. From an analysis of her records it was found that she made no sales 20% of the time, one sale 50% of the time and 2 sales 30% of the time. What is her expected number of sales?

The x in this case takes on values of 0, 1, and 2 and

$$\text{expected value is} = 0.2 \times 0 + 0.5 \times 1 + 0.3 \times 2$$
$$= 0 + 0.5 + 0.6$$
$$= 1.1 \text{ sales}$$

This is just like working out the mean value of a group of numbers, where the probabilities are the frequencies or 'weights'. And, just like the mean, the expected value will not necessarily be a whole number.

Expected values are frequently used to calculate expected monetary values, or EMV. This is illustrated in the next activity.

activity
6.14

An investor buys £1000 of shares with the object of making a capital gain after 1 year. She believes that there is a 5% chance that the shares will double in value, a 25% chance that they will be worth £1500, a 30% chance that they will only be worth £500 and a 40% chance that they will not change in value. What is the expected monetary value of this investment, ignoring dealing costs?

The EMV is found in a similar manner to the expected number of sales in Activity 6.1, that is:

$$0.05 \times 2000 + 0.25 \times 1500 + 0.3 \times 500 + 0.40 \times 1000$$
$$= 100 + 375 + 150 + 400$$
$$= £1025$$

So the EMV is £1025, an expected profit of £25.

Reflection

Probability affects all our lives. Most of us have bought a lottery ticket from time to time and know that the chance of winning the jackpot is very small. However, very few people know that the odds for the UK National Lottery are about 14 million to 1 against, and even fewer people would know how to calculate this figure. Even well-educated people find probability a difficult concept.

This is particularly so in court cases. An example in England from 1999 is the case of Sally Clark, who was convicted of killing two of her babies. The argument made by the paediatrician Sir Roy Meadow was that the chance of a baby from an affluent family dying from cot death was 1 in 8500, and that the chance of two babies in the same family dying from cot death is found by squaring this figure. This gives a probability of 1 in 73 million (or 0.000 000 013 7). The implication of this analysis is that two cot deaths in the same family should happen less than once a century in England – yet, in fact, double cot deaths occur almost every year. The problem with the initial analysis is its assumption that cot deaths in the same family are *independent*. Ray Hill, a professor in the Mathematics Department at Salford University, has shown that such deaths are not independent and has estimated that the chance is between 10 and 22 times greater that siblings of children who die of cot death will also die in the same way, as compared with children in the population as a whole ('Beyond reasonable doubt' by Helen Joyce: https://plus.maths.org/content/beyond-reasonable-doubt). When his figure is taken into account, the probability of two children dying of cot deaths in the same family is around 1 in 130000. As about 650000 children are born every year in England and Wales, we would then expect around five double cot deaths a year.

In convicting Sally Clark, the jury committed what is known as the 'Prosecutor's Fallacy'. This fallacy invites people to believe that the chance of a rare event happening is the same as the chance that the defendant is innocent. In actual fact it is simply the chance that a family chosen at random will experience a double cot death. With such a large population, the expected number of double cot deaths will be finite, even if the probability of this event happening is infinitesimally small.

Of course, as the two events are *not* independent, we should be using ideas based on conditional probability. This means that we should be using Bayes' theorem. And using Bayes' theorem it can be shown that the probability that Sally Clark's two babies died of natural causes was greater than 0.67 (https://plus.maths.org/content/beyond-reasonable-doubt). Unfortunately, judges will not allow the use of Bayes' theorem to be used in evidence, as it is felt to be too difficult to understand! However, as we saw in the *Quantitative methods in action* case at the start of this chapter, it is also possible to use relatively simple statistical tools to arrive at a conclusion.

(On 29 January 2003, Sally Clark's conviction was quashed by the Court of Appeal.)

Further reading

Probability is a wide subject and can be treated in many different ways. Students taking a maths or statistics degree would probably want a more mathematical text such as Swift and Piff (2014). A classic text is the one by Ross (2014). However, this is only for students with a good background in mathematics. For those students interested in sport and gambling, there are a number of texts that show how probability can improve their understanding of the issues involved. Examples are Haigh (2003) and Barboianu (2006). Haigh is a particularly easy-to-read text. There are also many resources that can help in understanding probability. *Plus* magazine (https://plus.maths.org/content) is aimed at schools but will be of interest to university undergraduates too.

http://www.**palgrave.com**/oakshott-eqm6

Practice questions

Solutions to all questions are freely available

1 What is the probability that if you toss 2 fair coins you get 2 tails?

2 What is the probability that if you toss 3 fair coins you get 3 tails?

3 What is the probability of 2 sixes when you throw 2 dice?

4 What is the probability of a score of 8 from throwing two dice?

5 Three cards are taken from a pack of cards (and not replaced). What is the probability that you get 3 aces?

6 Three cards are taken from a pack of cards (and not replaced). What is the probability that they are all red cards?

7   A bag contains 5 red discs, 3 yellow discs, and 2 green discs.
(a) A disc is picked from the bag. What is the probability that the disc will be:
(i)   red?
(ii)   yellow?
(iii) not yellow?
(b) Two discs are picked from the bag *with* replacement. What is the probability that the discs will be:
(i)   both red?
(ii)   1 red and 1 yellow?
(c) Repeat part (b) if the discs are picked *without* replacement.

8   What is the probability that if you pick a card from a pack it will be:
(a) an Ace?
(b) a red card?
(c) an Ace or a red card?

9   A box contains 50 light bulbs, of which 4 are defective. You purchase two bulbs from this box. What is the probability that both will be defective?

10   The probability that a double glazing salesperson will make a sale on a particular day is 0.05. What is the probability that over a three-day period the salesperson will make:
(a) 3 sales?
(b) exactly 1 sale?
(c) at least 1 sale?

11   A mail order firm knows that it will receive a 20% response rate to any literature it circulates. In a new geographic location 8 circulars are mailed as a market test. Assuming that the response rate is still applicable to this new location, calculate the probability of the following events:
(a) All 8 people respond
(b) No one responds
(c) Exactly 2 people respond

12   How might you try to assess the following probabilities?
(a) the probability that the FT index will rise in value tomorrow
(b) the probability that a jar of coffee, filled by an automatic process, will weigh less than the stated weight
(c) the probability that you might win the top prize in the National Lottery
(d) the probability that the ageing process will eventually be reversed

13   Three machines – A, B and C – operate independently in a factory. Machine A is out of action for 10% of the time, while B is out of action 5% of the time and C is out of action for 20% of the time. A rush order has to be commenced at midday tomorrow. What is the probability that at this time:
(a) All three of the machines will be out of action?
(b) None of the machines will be out of action?

14   A company is engaged in a civil engineering project.
The probability that the project will be delayed by bad weather is 0.3, while the probability that it will be delayed by geological problems is 0.2. What is the probability that the project will be delayed by both bad weather and geological problems?

15   A box contains 20 spark plugs, of which 6 are substandard. If two plugs are selected from the box without replacement, what is the probability that both will be substandard?

16 The probability of the FT 30 index rising on a particular day is 0.6. If it does rise then the probability that the value of shares in a publishing company will rise is 0.8. If the index does not rise then the publishing company shares only have a 0.3 probability of rising. What is the probability that tomorrow the publishing company's shares will rise in value?

17 A confectionery company launches three new products. From its own market research the company believes that the probabilities that each of their current retailers will adopt the new products for sale are as follows:

Aunty Dolleys mixture   0.9

Battys allsorts   0.6

Minty mints   0.7

The adoption of any one product is independent of the adoption of any other.
(a) What is the probability that the retailer will adopt all three products?
(b) What is the probability that the retailer will adopt at least one product?
(c) What is the probability that the retailer will adopt none of the products?

18 (a) A light bulb is to be selected at random from a box of 100 bulbs, details of which are given below.

Type of bulb	Defective	Satisfactory
60 watts	20	40
100 watts	10	30

Find:
(i) P(bulb is defective)
(ii) P(bulb is defective/selected bulb is 60 watts)
(b) Suppose that the company receiving the bulbs has a policy of selecting, without replacement, two bulbs from each box when it is delivered. It then applies the following decision rules:

If both bulbs are satisfactory then the box will be accepted.
If both bulbs are defective, the box is returned to the supplier.
If one bulb is defective, a third bulb is selected and the box is only accepted if this bulb is satisfactory.

What is the probability that a box, referred to above, will be accepted?

19 Marla plc is trying to decide whether it markets its new car immobilizer nationwide. The sales of the product will depend to some extent on the demand for car immobilizers, and the marketing department has suggested that the probability of high demand is 0.2 and medium to low demand is 0.8. However, it is possible to modify these probabilities by a market research exercise, but the probability that the research will be correct is only 0.6. What is the probability that the demand is really high given that the market research indicates that it will be high?

20 A simple screening test can be conducted to indicate if someone has a particular medical condition or not. However the test sometimes gives incorrect results. A false positive result (when the person does not have the condition) occurs 5% of the time and a false negative result (when the person has the condition) occurs 10% of the time. It is estimated that 2% of the population have the condition.

Draw a probability tree of the situation and mark on it all given probabilities. What is the probability that a person tested at random will not have the condition given that they test positive and what is the probability that they will have the condition given they test negative?

Assignment   Car insurance companies are interested in the probabilities of different coloured cars getting involved in accidents. For example, red cars have historically been involved in a disproportionate number of accidents. Conduct a survey to find the proportion of the different coloured cars on a stretch of road near you. Convert these proportions into probabilities. These will be your prior probabilities.

You are now given access to recent accident records for that stretch of road and discover that the probability that a red car will be involved in an accident is 0.03; a blue car 0.015; and all others 0.023. Given that there is an accident, what is the probability that the car involved is red?

7

THE SHAPE OF DATA: PROBABILITY DISTRIBUTIONS

PREREQUISITES

In order to fully understand this chapter you should have read through Chapter 4 (*Finding patterns in data: charts and tables*), Chapter 5 (*Making sense of data: averages and measures of spread*) and Chapter 6 (*Taking a chance: probability*).

OBJECTIVES

- To understand the difference between continuous and discrete probability distributions
- To be able to calculate binomial probabilities
- To be able to calculate Poisson probabilities
- To be able to use the Poisson distribution as an approximation to the binomial distribution
- To understand how the shape of the normal distribution is affected by the mean and standard deviation of the data
- To be able to use the normal distribution table
- To know how to use the normal distribution as an approximation to both the binomial and Poisson distributions

INTRODUCTION

This chapter examines some very important probability distributions. The *binomial distribution* is a discrete distribution, and is used when there are only two possible outcomes. The *Poisson distribution* is another discrete distribution, and is used for modelling rare events or events that occur at random. The final distribution you will meet is the *normal distribution*, and this (continuous) distribution has applications in almost all aspects of daily life, such as deciding whether the weight of a loaf of bread is outside acceptable limits or whether a child's height or weight is abnormal in some way.

QUANTITATIVE METHODS IN ACTION

Is goal scoring a random event?

In the 2014 football World Cup in Brazil there were 170 goals scored from 64 matches. The number of goals scored per game varied from 0 to 8 (the highest number was from the Brazil versus Germany semi-final match). If we look at the frequency of the number of goals scored per match we get Table 7.1.

If these are plotted on a bar chart you get Figure 7.1. What do this table and bar chart tell us? The mean is 2.65 goals per match, and the median is 3 goals per match. The distribution of goals scored is fairly symmetrical although there is a slight right skewness to it. What we shall look at later in this chapter is whether the number of goals scored is a random event; that is, can you predict the number of goals scored from a history of recent matches? If the answer to this question is no, then the event is random.

Table 7.1 Goals scored per 2014 World Cup match

No. of goals	0	1	2	3	4	5	6	7	8
Frequency	7	12	9	19	9	4	2	1	1

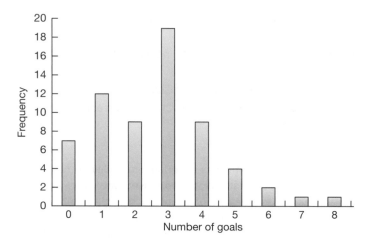

Figure 7.1 Bar chart of goals scored per World Cup match

Discrete and continuous probability distributions

The differences between discrete and continuous data were discussed in Chapter 4, but essentially discrete data is obtained by *counting*, whereas continuous data is obtained by *measurement*. So counting the number of loaves of bread baked over a period of time would give you data that only contained whole numbers (assuming that the bread is only sold as complete loaves), while recording the weight of each loaf of bread baked would give you data that could take on any value.

example
7.1

Data on the number and weight of a 'standard' loaf of bread were collected over a period of time and aggregated into Table 7.2.

Table 7.2 Frequency table for the data on the number and weight of loaves of bread

Number of loaves baked		Weight of each loaf	
Number	Frequency	Weight range	Frequency
20	8	770g to below 775g	3
21	12	775g to below 780g	17
22	24	780g to below 785g	44
23	26	785g to below 790g	100
24	35	790g to below 795g	141
25	35	795g to below 800g	192
26	30	800g to below 805g	191
27	28	805g to below 810g	150
28	21	810g to below 815g	90
		815g to below 820g	42
		820g to below 825g	14
		825g to below 830g	9

In order to compare the two data sets in more detail, diagrams could be used. A *bar chart* would be appropriate for the number of loaves baked, while a *histogram* is necessary for the weight data (see Chapter 4). These diagrams are shown in Figures 7.2 and 7.3.

The histogram gives you an idea of the underlying distribution of the data; that is, it shows you how the data is *distributed* across the range of possible values. This kind of distribution is called an *empirical* distribution because it is obtained by measurement or observation. There are also distributions that can be derived mathematically. The three most common distributions are the binomial distribution, the Poisson distribution and the normal distribution.

The binomial distribution

This is a discrete probability distribution and arises when

- a variable can only be in one of two states (an either/or situation)
- the probabilities of the two outcomes are known and constant from trial to trial
- the number of trials is known and constant
- successive events are independent.

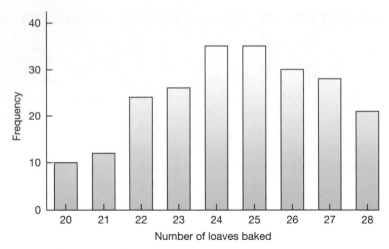

Figure 7.2 Bar chart for the number of loaves baked

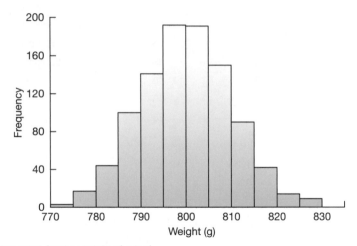

Figure 7.3 Histogram for the weight of a loaf

The obvious example to use here is a coin since it can be in one of two states, either a head (H) or a tail (T). However, the binomial distribution can be used in many applications, such as quality control where an item can be either defective or not defective.

If a coin is tossed once, there are only two outcomes with equal probability, but if you toss a coin twice (or toss two coins once), the outcome could be one of the following:

2 heads, or
2 tails, or
a head and a tail

There are two ways of getting a head and a tail, since either toss could result in a head or a tail. The best way of illustrating the outcomes is by means of a tree diagram.

Figure 7.4 shows that there are 4 'routes' to the tree. At the end of each route the number of heads has been indicated, together with the probability of that route. The number of ways of getting 2, 1, and 0 heads is 1, 2, and 1 respectively, and the probability of any route is $0.5 \times 0.5 = 0.25$ (or $(0.5)^2$). Therefore the probability of getting 1 head is $2 \times 0.25 = 0.5$.

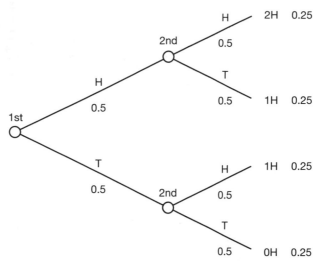

Figure 7.4 A coin tossed twice

activity 7.1

Draw the tree for the case where a coin is tossed three times. What is the probability of

(a) one head, and
(b) two heads?

The tree has become a little more complicated and is shown in Figure 7.5. The number of ways of getting 3, 2, 1, or 0 heads is 1, 3, 3, and 1 respectively and the probability of following any route is now $(0.5)^3 = 0.125$. The probability of getting 1 head is therefore $3 \times 0.125 = 0.375$ and the probability of getting 2 heads is also 0.375.

If you repeat this for 4 heads you should find that the number of ways of getting 4, 3, 2, 1, 0 heads is 1, 4, 6, 4, and 1 respectively, and the probability of following any route is $(0.5)^4 = 0.0625$. If you now write the number of ways of getting various combinations of heads in a table similar to the one below, you should see how easy it is to carry on the sequence.

1 toss				1		1		
2 tosses			1		2		1	
3 tosses		1		3		3		1
4 tosses	1		4		6		4		1

activity 7.2

Continue the sequence for 5 tosses of the coin.

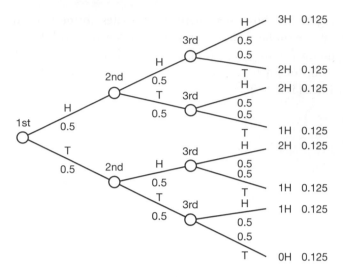

Figure 7.5 A coin tossed three times

For 5 tosses the sequence will be 1, 5, 10, 5, 10, 5, 1 since $1 + 4 = 5$ and $4 + 6 = 10$. This is known as *Pascal's triangle* and it gives you the number of ways an event will occur. Although it is quite feasible to do this for a small number of tosses of the coin, what would happen if you tossed the coin 10, 20 or even 50 times? Fortunately, this series is the same as finding the number of ways of choosing r items from n (see Chapter 6 (page 137)) and is given by:

$$^nC_r = \frac{n!}{r!(n-r)!}$$

activity 7.3

How many ways are there of getting 4 heads from 10 tosses of a coin?

Using the formula we get:

$$^{10}C_4 = \frac{10!}{4! \times (10-4)!}$$
$$= 210$$

This is fine for a coin where the probability of each event is 0.5, but what about more general problems? Where an item can be in one of two states and the probability of both states is known and constant, the ideas just discussed can be used. For example, about 5% of people are in blood type AB, so the probability that any one person has this blood type is 0.05. What is the probability that in a group of 10 people, 4 will have this blood type? This is a binomial problem because a person either does or does not have this blood type. The probability that a person doesn't is $0.95(1 - 0.05)$. If 4 people have this blood type then it follows that 6 do not, so the probability of a route of the probability tree giving this combination is:

$$(0.05)^4 \times (0.95)^6 = 0.00000459$$

Since there are 210 ways of getting this combination ($^{10}C_4$, see above), the probability of 4 people out of 10 with blood type AB is:

$$210 \times 0.00000459 = 0.00096$$

In general if p is the probability of a 'success', where success is defined as a person or item being in a particular state, then the binomial distribution can be defined as follows:

$$P(r) = {}^nC_r\, p^r (1 - p)^{n-r}$$

where n is the number of trials and r the number of successes. To use this formula you simply need to know the values of p, n and r. For example, suppose that you wanted to find the probability that 2 or more people in the group of 10 had blood of type AB. You could find the probability of 2, 3, 4, and so on, and then add the probabilities together. However, there is an easier way – this is to use the fact that the probabilities must sum to 1, so $P(r \geq 2) = 1 - (P(0) + P(1))$. This reduces the number of calculations from 9 to 2. (With larger values of n, the saving is even more pronounced.)

$\left(\begin{array}{c} \textit{activity} \\ \textbf{7.4} \end{array}\right)$ Calculate the probability of $P(r \geq 2)$ for the example above.

The calculation of $P(0)$ is easy since there is only one route in this case and $^{10}C_0 = 1$. So:

$$P(0) = (0.5)^0 \times (0.95)^{10}$$
$$= 0.59874$$

(Note: anything raised to the power of 0 is 1.)
For the calculation of $P(1)$, $^{10}C_1 = 10$, so:

$$P(1) = 10 \times (0.5)^1 \times (0.95)^9$$
$$= 0.31512$$

and

$$P(r \geq 2) = 1 - (0.59874 + 0.31512)$$

$$= 0.08614, \text{ or about } 8.6\%$$

An easier method is to use the cumulative binomial function in Excel. The function name is

```
BINOMDIST(number_s,trials,probability_s, Cumulative)
```

where:

```
Number_s
```
 is the number of successes in trials [that is, r]
```
Trials
```
 is the number of independent trials [that is, n]
```
Probability_s
```
 is the probability of success on each trial [that is, p]
```
Cumulative
```
 is a logical value that determines the form of the function. If cumulative is `true`, then `BINOMDIST` returns the cumulative distribution function, which is the probability that there are at most `number_s` successes; if `false`, it returns the probability mass function, which is the probability that there are `number_s` successes. (*Taken from the Help facility in Excel.*)

By setting `Cumulative` as `true` we get the cumulative probability of r successes or less in n trials. So, in the above example, to find the probability that 2 or more had blood group AB you would first need to use the `BINOMDIST` function to find the probability of 1 or less. The function would therefore be:

```
BINOMDIST(1,10,0.05,true)
```

Excel returns a probability of 0.9139, so if we subtract this from 1 we get 0.0861, which is the same as we got above. To avoid using Excel repeatedly, a table for selected values of n, r and p is provided in the Appendix. This table gives you the probability of r successes or less, so to find the probability for $n = 10$ and $r = 1$ you would need to subtract the probability from 1 as before. Part of the binomial table is shown in Table 7.3 where the probability of 0.9139 has been highlighted.

Table 7.3 Part of the binomial table, giving the probability for different values of n, r and p (see Appendix)

		p		
n	r	0.01	0.05	0.1
10	0	0.9044	0.5987	0.3487
10	1	0.9957	**0.9139**	0.7361
10	2	0.9999	0.9885	0.9298

activity 7.5

The UK government's guideline is that hospital death rates that are 60% above the norm are unacceptable. Say a hospital performs 100 operations and the chance of dying in any one of these operations is 5%, which also happens to be the government's norm for this particular operation. Find the probability that the government's guidelines are exceeded.

Either a patient dies or lives so this is a binomial problem. The mean number of deaths in 100 operations will be 5, so 60% above the norm is 8 (that is, $5 + 5 \times .6$). You need to find the probability of 0 up to 7 deaths and subtract the sum from 1. Using Excel you should get the probability of 7 or less as 0.87. Therefore there is a chance of 0.13 that the hospital death rate will be unacceptable even if it appears to meet the norm. This means that 13% of hospitals will fail the government's guideline by chance.

activity 7.6

Use Excel to find the probability of P(0), P(1), P(2), P(3), P(4) and P(5) when $n = 5$ and $p = 0.2$. Plot these values in the form of a bar chart. How would you describe the shape of the distribution?

We would now set `Cumulative` as `false`, and the results using Excel are:

```
BINOMDIST(0,5,0.2.false) = 0.32768
BINOMDIST(1,5,0.2.false) = 0.40960
BINOMDIST(2,5,0.2.false) = 0.20480
BINOMDIST(3,5,0.2.false) = 0.05120
BINOMDIST(4,5,0.2.false) = 0.00640
BINOMDIST(5,5,0.2.false) = 0.00032
```

The chart in Figure 7.6 shows that the distribution is *right skewed*.

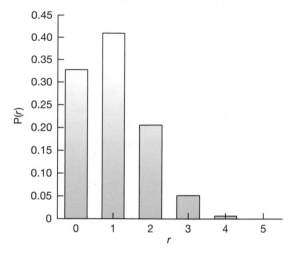

Figure 7.6 Bar chart for Activity 7.6

activity
7.7

Repeat Activity 7.6 for $n = 20$ and $p = 0.2$ (stop when P(r) is zero to 4 decimal places).

You should have obtained a chart similar to the one in Figure 7.7. Notice that the distribution is now much less skewed. (We shall return to the shape of the binomial distribution later.)

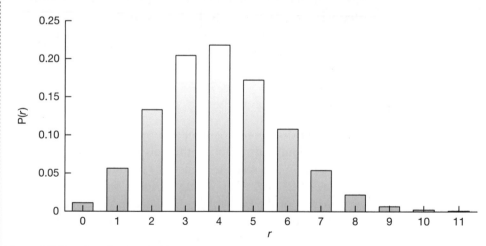

Figure 7.7 Bar chart for Activity 7.7

The mean and standard deviation of the binomial distribution

The mean of a binomial distribution is np.

The standard deviation is given by the formula:

$$\sigma = \sqrt{np(1 - p)}$$

activity 7.8

What is the mean and standard deviation of the binomial distribution with $n = 5$ and $p = 0.2$? (That is, for Activity 7.6.)

The mean is $5 \times 0.2 = 1.0$.
The standard deviation is $\sqrt{5 \times 0.2 \times 0.8} = 0.894$.
As the standard deviation is a measure of spread it would be interesting to see how many standard deviations would be needed to cover the distribution. One standard deviation would give a range of $1.0 \pm 0.894 = 0.106$ to 1.894. Looking at Figure 7.6 we can see that this includes $r = 1$ only. The probability for $r = 1$ is 0.4096
So about 41% of the distribution is covered by one standard deviation.

activity 7.9

What proportion of the distribution is covered by two standard deviations?

In this case we have $1.0 \pm 2 \times 0.894 = -0.788$ to 2.788
This covers the first 3 values of r and the probabilities add to 0.94208. So about 94% is covered by two standard deviations, which is a high proportion of the distribution.

activity 7.10

Repeat Activity 7.9 for the case where $n = 20$ and $p = 0.2$ (that is, Activity 7.7).

The mean is $20 \times 0.2 = 4$
The standard deviation is $\sqrt{20 \times 0.2 \times 0.8} = 1.789$
For two standard deviations we get a range of $4 \pm 2 \times 1.789 = 0.422$ to 7.589
This covers the distribution from $r = 1$ to $r = 7$ and adding the probabilities for these values of r we get 0.9563, which is almost 96%.

You will find that most observations rarely fall outside the range of the mean plus or minus two standard deviations. You will meet this idea again when we look at the normal distribution.

The Poisson distribution

The Poisson distribution is another example of a discrete probability distribution. Like the binomial distribution the Poisson distribution again models the either/or situation but in this case the chance of a particular event occurring is very small. That is, the event is 'rare'. Also, we are normally only given the mean occurrence of the event instead of the probability. The Poisson distribution is often used in situations where the event is unlikely (accidents, machine failures) or where the event occurs at random (arrivals of calls at a switchboard, for example).

The formula for the Poisson is less complicated than the binomial, and the probability of r events in a given unit (of time or length, and so on) is as follows:

$$P(r) = \frac{e^{-m}m^r}{r!}$$

where m is the mean number of events in the same unit and e is the constant $2.7182818 \ldots$ and can be found on many scientific calculators (usually in the form e^x).

A typical example of the Poisson distribution is as follows. The number of calls to a switchboard is random, with a mean of 1.5 per minute. What is the probability that there are no calls in any one minute?

All we need to do is to substitute $r = 0$ and $m = 1.5$ into the equation. That is:

$$P(0) = \frac{e^{-1.5}(1.5)^0}{0!} = 0.2231$$

(because $e^{-1.5} = 0.2231$, $1.5^0 = 1$ and $0! = 1$).

DID YOU KNOW?

Simeon Denis Poisson was born in 1781 in France. He was a gifted mathematician and the first mention of the Poisson distribution was in his paper titled 'Researches on the probability of criminal and civil verdicts' in 1837. His distribution has been used in many fields, particularly the military, and in the Second World War it was used to see whether the pattern of bombs landing on London was random or not. (If it was not random that would have suggested that the Germans had a sophisticated targeting mechanism in the bombs.)

(activity 7.11) Using a mean of 1.5 calls a minute, what is the probability that:

(a) There are more than 2 calls in any one minute?
(b) There are less than 6 calls in a 5-minute period?

It is not possible to calculate the answer to (a) directly since the maximum number of calls that could be received is not specified (in fact there is no maximum). However, as in the binomial distribution the probability can be found by noting that the sum of the probabilities must equal 1.

So, $P(r > 2) = 1 - (P(0) + P(1) + P(2))$

That is, $P(r > 2) = 1 - (0.2231 + 0.3347 + 0.2510) = 0.1912$

Question (b) is a little more difficult since the time period has been changed from a minute to 5 minutes. However, all that needs to be done is to work out the average rate over 5 minutes, which is 7.5 (5×1.5), and then continue as before. That is:

$$P(r < 6) = P(0) + P(1) + P(2) + P(3) + P(4) + P(5)$$

To make this calculation easier we could use Excel. The function for the Poisson distribution is:

```
POISSON(x,mean,cumulative)
```

where:

x is the number of events [that is, r]
Mean is the expected numeric value [that is, m]
Cumulative is a logical value that determines the form of the probability distribution returned. If Cumulative is true, POISSON returns the cumulative Poisson probability that the number of random events occurring will be between zero and x inclusive; if false, it returns the Poisson probability mass function that the number of events occurring will be exactly x.
(*Taken from the Help facility in Excel.*)

Using Excel we get:

$$POISSON(5,7.5,true) = 0.2414$$

So $P(r < 6) = 0.2414$

Table 7.4 Part of the Poisson table, giving the probability for different values of the mean and r (see Appendix)

mean	r	
	5	6
0.1	1.0000	1.0000
7.2	0.2759	0.4204
7.3	0.2640	0.4060
7.4	0.2526	0.3920
7.5	**0.2414**	0.3782
7.6	0.2307	0.3646

An alternative to using Excel is to refer to the cumulative Poisson probability table in the Appendix. This table gives you the probability of r or less events. Part of the Poisson table is shown in Table 7.4, where the probability of 0.2414 has been highlighted.

activity **7.12** In the *Quantitative methods in action* case at the start of this chapter we looked at the number of goals scored in each match of the 2014 World Cup. Use the Poisson distribution to calculate the expected frequency that 0, 1, 2... goals are scored and compare with the actual.

The mean number of goals per match was 2.65 and we can use the Poisson distribution to calculate the probability of 0, 1, 2... goals. The Excel function is

$Poisson(x,2.65,false)$ where x takes on the values 0, 1, 2...

The Excel screen print can be seen in Figure 7.8.

	A	B	C	D	E
		B11	f_x	=1-SUM(B2:B10)	
1	Goals	Probability	Expected	Actual	
2	0	0.0707	4.5	7	
3	1	0.1872	12.0	12	
4	2	0.2481	15.9	9	
5	3	0.2191	14.0	19	
6	4	0.1452	9.3	9	
7	5	0.0769	4.9	4	
8	6	0.0340	2.2	2	
9	7	0.0129	0.8	1	
10	8	0.0043	0.3	1	
11	9 or more	0.0017	0.1	0	
12		Sum	64.0	64	

Notice that the probability of 9 or more is 1 – probability of 8 or less

Figure 7.8 Use of Excel for Activity 7.12
Used with permission from Microsoft.

The second column gives the probability using the Poisson function. These probabilities are then multiplied by 64 (the number of matches played) to give the expected

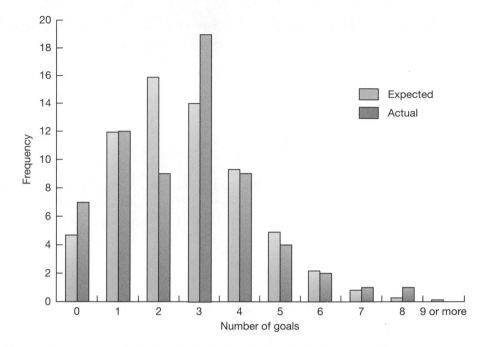

Figure 7.9 Comparison of actual and expected goals scored in the 2014 World Cup

frequency that this number of goals was scored. So we can see that the expected number of times a match would have one goal is 12, which is exactly what happened. The largest discrepancy is for 2 goals where there is a difference of 6.9. You will also notice that to ensure that the expected values added to 64 we had a category of 9 or more goals.

A chart would give a better comparison and Figure 7.9 uses a multiple bar chart to compare the actual and expected frequencies.

The chart indicates that there is some agreement between the actual and expected frequencies, but there are some cases of quite poor agreement, particularly for two and three goals. We cannot, at this stage, really say whether the goal scoring is a random event. In Chapter 9 we will see how we can do a more formal test on how close the two distributions are.

The use of the Poisson distribution as an approximation to the binomial distribution

As you will probably have noticed it is a little easier to calculate probabilities using the Poisson distribution than it is using the binomial distribution. In some circumstances it is possible to use the Poisson distribution instead of the binomial distribution. The error you will get as a result will be quite small providing the following conditions are met:

- The number of trials, n, is large (greater than 30)
- The probability of a success, p, is small (less than 0.1)
- The mean number of successes, $n \times p$, is less than 5.

<table>
<tr><td>

activity
7.13

</td><td>

A batch contains 1% defective items and a sample of size 40 is chosen. What is the probability that there are exactly 2 defective items? Are the conditions for using the Poisson distribution instead of the binomial met for this problem?

</td></tr>
</table>

This is a binomial problem and the answer using the binomial distribution is:

$$P(2) = 40C_2 \times (0.01)^2 \times (1 - 0.01)^{38}$$

$$= 780 \times 0.00006826$$

$$= 0.0532$$

However, we can also use the Poisson to solve this problem because n is large, p is small and the mean number of defects is $0.4(40 \times 0.01)$ which is less than 5.

Using the Poisson distribution for $r = 2$, we get:

$$P(2) = \frac{e^{-0.4} \times (0.4)^2}{2!}$$

$$= 0.0536$$

which is an error of less than 1%.

The mean and standard deviation of the Poisson distribution

The *variance* of the Poisson distribution is equal to the mean. So the standard deviation, which is the square root of the variance, is equal to the square root of the mean. In symbols this becomes:

$$\sigma = \sqrt{m}$$

For example, if the mean is 1.5 then the standard deviation will be $\sqrt{1.5} = 1.225$.

The normal distribution

Many observations that are obtained from measurements follow the normal distribution. For example, the heights of people and the weights of loaves of bread are approximately normally distributed. The normal distribution is completely symmetrical or bell shaped. The mean, mode and median of this distribution all lie at the centre of the bell, as you can see in Figure 7.10.

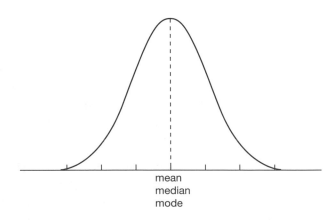

Figure 7.10 The normal distribution

mean
median
mode

The normal curve has the following properties:

1 The curve is symmetrical about the mean.

2 The total area under the curve is equal to 1 or 100%. This means that probability can be equated to area (which is also true for other distributions).

3 The horizontal axis represents a continuous variable such as weight.

4 The area under the curve between two points on the horizontal axis represents the probability that the value of the variable lies between these two points.

5 As the distance between two points gets less, the area between the two points must get less. Taking this to its logical conclusion, the probability of a specific value is zero. It is therefore only meaningful to talk about ranges, such as 800 g to 810 g.

6 The position and shape of the curve depends on the mean and standard deviation of the distribution. As the standard deviation gets larger, the curve will get flatter and extend further on either side of the mean.

DID YOU KNOW?

The normal distribution was first derived mathematically by DeMoivre in 1733. Laplace used the curve in 1783 to describe the distribution of errors and in 1809 Gauss used the curve to analyze astronomical data. (This is the reason it is often called the Gaussian curve.) The normal distribution is now the most commonly used distribution in statistics.

activity **7.14**

The average weight of a 'standard' loaf of bread is 800 g and the weights are normally distributed. If a loaf is selected at random, what is the probability that it will weigh less than 800 g?

Property 1 above says that the normal curve is symmetrical about the mean, so that 50% of the loaves will be below the mean weight of 800 g and 50% will be above. Hence the probability will be 0.5 or 50%.

activity **7.15**

What proportion of loaves weigh more than 815 g?

This problem has been illustrated diagrammatically in Figure 7.11, where the area representing all loaves with a weight exceeding 815 g has been shaded.

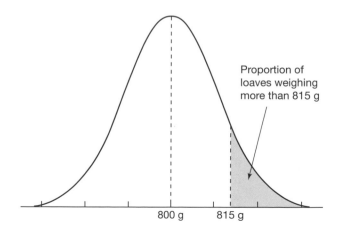

Proportion of loaves weighing more than 815 g

Figure 7.11 Distribution of the weight of a loaf of bread

800 g   815 g

This shaded area is clearly a small proportion of the total area, but it would be difficult to estimate the actual figure from the diagram alone. Tables are used to obtain this area but, before you can do this, you need to understand the properties of the *standard normal distribution.*

The standard normal distribution

The standard normal distribution has a mean of zero and a standard deviation of 1. This is illustrated in Figure 7.12. The figures along the horizontal axis are the number of standard deviations and are called the Z values. You will see from the diagram that the majority of the distribution is covered within 3 standard deviations either side of the mean.

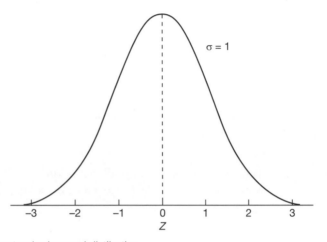

Figure 7.12 The standard normal distibution

To demonstrate the use of the normal table you should now refer to the table provided in the Appendix. The table provided in this book gives you the area in the *right hand tail* of the distribution, but other tables may give the area in a different way. (Once you have used one table you should find it a simple matter to use a different type.)

The first column gives the Z value to one decimal place and the first row gives the second place of decimals. For example, for a Z value of 0.55, you would look down the first column until you found 0.5 and then across until you were directly under 0.05. The area is 0.2912, or 29.12%. This is the area in the tail for Z being greater than 0.55. Since the distribution is symmetrical, the area being less than $Z = -0.55$ is also 29.12%. You will see these areas shaded in Figure 7.13.

activity
7.16

What is the area between a Z value of 1 and -1?

The area of the curve for Z greater than 1 is 0.1587 or 15.87%. To find the area from the mean ($Z = 0$) to any Z value you need to use the fact that half the distribution has an area of 0.5. So to find the area from $Z = 0$ to $Z = 1$ you would subtract this from 0.5. That is, $0.5 - 0.1587 = 0.3413$. Since the distribution is symmetrical, the area from 0.0 to -1.0 is also 0.3413. The area from -1 to $+1$ is therefore 0.6826. In other words, 68.26% of the normal curve is covered by ± 1 standard deviations. This area can be seen in Figure 7.14.

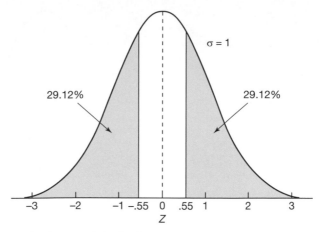

Figure 7.13 Areas under the normal distribution

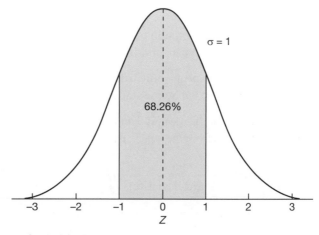

Figure 7.14 Diagram for Activity 7.16

If you repeat this for $Z = 2$ and $Z = 3$, you should find that just over 95% (95.44%) of the normal distribution is covered by ±2 standard deviations, and almost 100% (99.73%) is covered by ±3 standard deviations.

activity
7.17

What is the value of Z if the area of the upper tail is 5%?

This problem is illustrated in Figure 7.15. To solve this problem the normal table is used in reverse. That is, the table is inspected to find the area of 0.05. This figure does not exist, but you should find that a Z value of 1.64 gives an area of 0.0505, while a Z value of 1.65 gives an area of 0.0495. The most accurate value of Z would be the average of these two values, which is 1.645.

Standardizing normal distributions

Unfortunately, most normal distribution problems do not have a mean of zero or a standard deviation of 1, so the normal table cannot be used directly to solve general

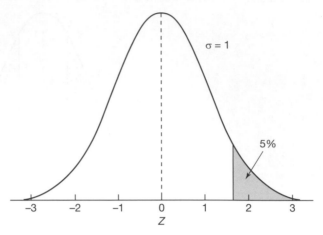

Figure 7.15 Diagram for Activity 7.17

problems. However, all you have to do is to calculate the number of standard deviations from the mean, and this can be done quite easily, as follows:

■ subtract the mean value from the particular value (*x*) that you are interested in
■ divide this value by the standard deviation.

For example, if the mean is 5 and the standard deviation is 2, then a value of 9 is two standard deviations from the mean. This calculation is called the *Z transformation* and is given by:

$$Z = \frac{x - \text{mean}}{\text{standard deviation}}$$

If *x* is less than the mean, the value of *Z* will be negative. This negative value simply indicates that *x* is to the left of the mean. Since the distribution is symmetrical about the mean, you can ignore the sign when using the table.

activity **7.18**

A batch of loaves is baked. The weight of the loaves is normally distributed with a mean of 800 g and a standard deviation of 10 g. What proportion of loaves will weigh more than 815 g?

This is the same problem that you met in Activity 7.15 (see Figure 7.11), but you now should be able to solve this using the normal table. However, you first have to transform the problem using the *Z* formula. You should first note that:

$$Z = \frac{815 - 800}{10} = 1.5$$

That is, 815 g is 1.5 standard deviations away from the mean.

It is now a simple matter of looking up *Z* = 1.5 in the normal table. If you do this you should get an area of 0.0668 or 6.68%, which means that 6.68% of all loaves weigh more than 815 g. This is represented in Figure 7.16.

The problem can become slightly more difficult, as illustrated in the next activity.

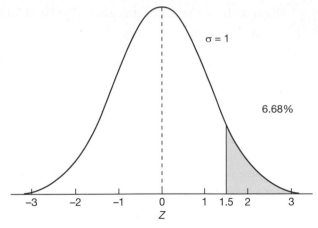

Figure 7.16 Diagram for Activity 7.18

---

activity
7.19

A loaf is chosen at random. What is the probability that the weight will lie between 810 g and 812 g?

To find the probability it is necessary to find the shaded area in Figure 7.17. This area cannot be found directly, but it can be found by *subtracting* the area greater than 812 from the area greater than 810. To do this it is necessary to calculate two Z values as follows:

$$\frac{810 - 800}{10} = 1.0$$

and

$$\frac{812 - 800}{12} = 1.2$$

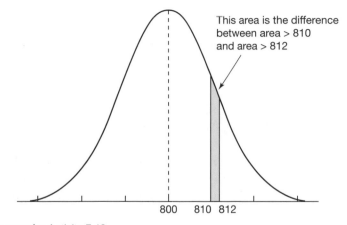

Figure 7.17 Diagram for Activity 7.19

The areas from the normal table are 0.1587 and 0.1157 and the required area is:

$$0.1587 - 0.1151 = 0.0436$$

The probability that the weight will be between 810 g and 812 g is therefore 0.0436 or 4.36%. Alternatively you could say that 4.36% of all loaves weigh between 810 g and 812 g.

activity
7.20

What proportion of loaves weigh between 790 g and 805.5 g?

To solve this problem you should note that the required area is the *sum* of the two areas A and B in Figure 7.18.

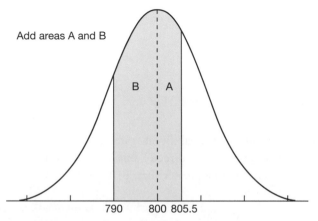

Add areas A and B

B A

790   800 805.5

Figure 7.18 Diagram for Activity 7.20

To calculate area A it is necessary to find the area greater than 805.5 and then subtract this from 0.5. (Don't forget that the tables used in this book give the area in the *right hand* tail of the distribution.) The calculation is as follows:

$$Z = \frac{805.5 - 800}{10} = 0.55$$

This gives an area of 0.2912 and area A is therefore $0.5 - 0.2912 = 0.2088$.

Area B is found in a similar manner.

$$Z = \frac{790 - 800}{10} = -1.0$$

The negative sign indicates that the area is to the left of the mean and can be ignored for the purposes of obtaining the area from the normal table. Area B is therefore $0.5 - 0.1587 = 0.3413$.

The combined area is $0.2088 + 0.3413 = 0.5501$ or 55.01%, which is the proportion of loaves with weights between 790 g and 805.5 g.

In addition to calculating the probability or proportion of a variable having a value between specified limits, it is possible to carry out the reverse process. This is illustrated in the next activity.

activity
7.21

The baker wishes to ensure that no more than 5% of loaves are less than a certain weight. What is this weight?

The diagram for this problem can be seen in Figure 7.19.

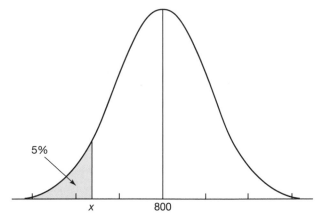

5%

x 800

Figure 7.19 Diagram for Activity 7.21

It is necessary to calculate the value x, but first the Z value corresponding to an area of 5% must be found. Although this area is in the lower tail, the method is identical to that used when the area in the upper tail has been given. (Don't forget that the distribution is symmetrical about the mean.) The value of Z for an area of 5% is 1.645, but because it is to the left of the mean, the value is negative; that is, -1.645. Substituting this value into the formula gives:

$$-1.645 = \frac{x - 800}{10}$$

Multiplying both sides by 10 gives:

$$-16.45 = x - 800$$

Then adding 800 to both sides:

$$x = 800 - 16.45$$

$$= 783.6 \text{ g}$$

So no more than 5% of the batch should weigh less than 783.6 g.

Although the preceding activities cover the most common applications, it is possible to use the Z formula to calculate either the mean or the standard deviation. This is demonstrated next.

activity
7.22

A large number of loaves were weighed and it was found that 8% weighed less than 783.6 g. Assuming that the standard deviation hasn't changed, what has happened?

This problem is illustrated in Figure 7.20. If the standard deviation hasn't changed, then the only explanations are that the mean has changed or that it is not what it was

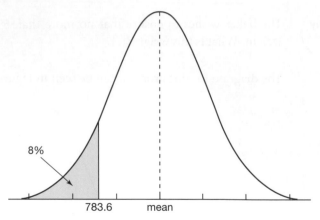

Figure 7.20 Diagram for Activity 7.22

thought to be. Again, it is necessary to work backwards. The Z value corresponding to a proportion of 8% is 1.405, which will again be negative. The value of x is 783.6 and it is required to find the value of the mean.

$$-1.405 = \frac{783.6 - \text{mean}}{10}$$

Multiplying both sides by 10 gives:

$$-14.05 = 783.6 - \text{mean}$$

Then adding 14.05 to both sides:

$$0 = 797.7 - \text{mean}$$

that is: mean $= 797.7$ g

The normal distribution as an approximation to the binomial distribution

If a particular binomial distribution is symmetrical it is possible to use the normal distribution to solve binomial problems. The conditions that make the binomial distribution symmetrical are that both $n \times p$ and $n \times (1 - p)$ are greater than 5. This means that p needs to be near to 0.5 and n should be large.

activity **7.23**   Use Excel to plot the binomial distribution for $n = 30$ and $p = 0.3$.

You should have obtained Figure 7.21 and you should notice that the distribution is approximately symmetrical.

The next activity will show you how to use the normal distribution as an approximation to the binomial.

activity **7.24**   The probability of a defective item is 0.3. If a sample of 30 were taken, what is the probability that at least 5 were defective?

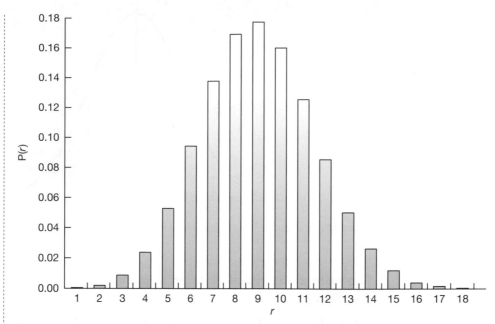

Figure 7.21 Binomial distribution with $n = 30$ and $p = 0.3$

Using the binomial table in the Appendix we would find the probability of 4 or fewer defectives, which is 0.0302.

The probability of at least 5 defectives is then:

$$P(r \geq 5) = 1 - 0.0302$$
$$= 0.9698$$

To solve this problem by the normal distribution it is first necessary to calculate the mean and standard deviation. The mean is $n \times p = 30 \times 0.3 = 9.0$ and the standard deviation is:

$$\sqrt{30 \times 0.3 \times 0.7} = 2.51$$

It is then necessary to make a *continuity correction*. This is because the binomial distribution is a discrete probability distribution whereas the normal distribution is a continuous one. To get around this problem it is assumed that the discrete value 5 is a continuous variable in the range 4.5 to 5.5. To find the probability greater than 4, the value 4.5 is used, as you can see in Figure 7.22.

This problem now becomes one of finding $P(r > 4.5)$, which is $1 - P(r < 4.5)$, and

$$Z = \frac{4.5 - 9}{2.51}$$
$$= -1.79$$

$$P(Z < -1.79) = P(Z > 1.79)$$

and from the normal table the probability is 0.0367, so the required probability is: $1 - 0.0367 = 0.9633$, which compares well with the correct value of 0.9698.

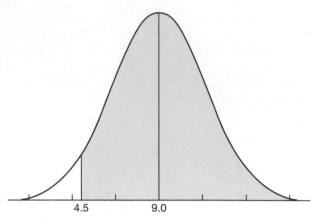

Figure 7.22 Normal approximation to the binomial for Activity 7.24

The normal distribution as an approximation to the Poisson distribution

The normal distribution can also be used to solve Poisson problems. This is valid provided the mean is greater than about 10.

<table>
<tr><td>activity
7.25</td><td>The number of calls to a switchboard is random, with a mean of 1.5 per minute. What is the probability that there are fewer than 6 calls in a 5-minute period?</td></tr>
</table>

We looked at this problem in Activity 7.11 where we calculated the probability to be 0.2414. To solve this problem using the normal distribution you would note that the mean is 7.5 calls in a 5-minute period. (The mean of 7.5 is less than the recommended level, so it will be interesting to see how good the approximation will be in this case.)

To use the normal distribution, the continuity correction again needs to be applied. In this case the probability of less than 5.5 calls needs to be found. The standard deviation is the square root of the mean (7.5), which equals 2.739.

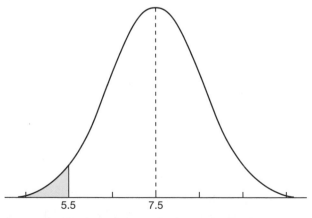

Figure 7.23 Normal approximation to the Poisson distribution for Activity 7.25

The calculation is straightforward using the normal distribution:

$$Z = \frac{5.5 - 7.5}{2.739} = -0.7302$$

$P((r < 5.5)) = P((Z < -0.7302) = P((Z > 0.7302) = 0.2327$ (from the normal table)

This represents an error of under 4% (the difference between 0.2414 and 0.2327 as a percentage of 0.2414).

Reflection

We have looked at only a few probability distributions: there are many, many more. Some are quite simple, such as the uniform distribution which can be used when values between the smallest and largest are constant. Other distributions are quite complex, however, and their shape may depend on two or more parameters.

Because it is so much easier to work with a mathematical distribution than with raw data, we often need to 'fit' a distribution to a set of data. We must remember, however, that mathematical distributions are usually only approximations. Further, some sets of data cannot be represented by a mathematical distribution - an example is data that is bimodal.

The World Cup example illustrated that probability distributions can be used for quite ordinary situations. You can also use the Poisson distibution to calculate the expected number of goals scored if goal scoring was a random event (see Activity 7.12). However the most useful distribution is the normal as it can be used for such a wide range of situations. It is used in quality control, weights of animals and the distribution of errors to name just a few examples. It is also believed that the distribution of death rates amongst doctor's patients is also normal and it has been proposed that, if this analysis had been conducted during the 1980s and 1990s, the Shipman tragedy, in which a family doctor killed at least 250 of his patients over a 23-year period, might have been avoided (The *Lancet*, vol. 362, August 2003). The analysis required some transformation of the data as there were many non-random factors involved (for example, age). The resulting transformed data had a mean of 0 and a standard deviation of 1 and, as we know, we expect almost the entire distribution to be covered by ±3 standard deviations. When researchers analyzed the Shipman data they found that in 1998 his mean death rate corresponded to a Z value of 6.6 which is well above what could have occurred by chance.

An important use of the normal distribution is in sampling and we will come back to this in Chapters 8 and 9.

Key points

- Data can be plotted in the form of a *histogram* to give us a picture of how the data is distributed from the smallest to the largest value.
- Distributions can be either *discrete* or *continuous*.
- The shapes of many naturally occurring datasets appear to be very close to shapes defined by mathematical distributions.
- Examples of these distributions include the *binomial distribution* and the *Poisson distribution*, which are discrete distributions, and the normal distribution, which is a continuous distribution.
- The binomial distribution is used when an event can either happen or not happen.
- The Poisson distribution is used when the chance of an event happening is very small (it is a rare event). It is used where events occur at random such as arrivals to a queue.

■ The normal distribution is the most widely used distribution in statistics. Before a normal distribution problem can be solved it needs to be transformed into the standard normal form which has a mean of zero and a standard deviation of 1.

Further reading

Like probability there are a large number of texts on probability distributions, ranging from introductory level to more advanced texts. Morris (2011) gives a good general description of the common distributions (binomial, Poisson and normal) without using many equations. Most other texts aimed at the business student such as Curwin and Slater (2013) give a similar treatment to this text.

http://www.**palgrave.com**/oakshott-eqm6

Practice questions

Solutions to all questions are freely available

1 If a coin is tossed 5 times, how many ways are there of getting 3 heads?

2 What is the probability of getting 3 heads if a coin is tossed 5 times?

3 A job hunter is applying for nine jobs and believes that she has in each of the nine jobs a constant and independent 0.48 probability of getting an offer.
   (a) What might make you think that you are dealing with a binomial situation?
   (b) What is the probability that she will get at least three job offers?

4 The sex ratio of newborn infants is about 105 males to 100 females. If 4 infants are chosen at random, what is the probability that:
   (a) All four are males?
   (b) Exactly three are male?
   (c) Two are male and two are female?

5 The quality control manager of a company is concerned at the level of defective items being produced. Out of a batch of 20 items, 2 were found to be defective. Should the quality control manager be concerned given that in the past the defective rate has been 3%?

6 A shopkeeper finds that 20% of the cartons containing 6 eggs he receives are damaged. A carton is picked at random, checked and returned to the consignment. The procedure is repeated a further 3 times. What is the probability that out of the 4 cartons inspected
   (a) none were undamaged?
   (b) at least 3 were undamaged?

7 Calls arrive at a switchboard according to the Poisson distribution. If the average number of calls received in a 5-minute period is 6.7, find the probability that:
   (a) There are fewer than 4 calls received in a 5-minute period.
   (b) There are more than 7 calls received during a 5-minute period.
   (c) There are no calls received in a 1-minute period.

8 Several lengths of plastic tubing are examined for the number of flaws in intervals of given length. If 1500 flaws are found in 1000 intervals each of 1 mm, find the probability, assuming a Poisson distribution of
   (a) at least 2 flaws in an interval of 1 mm
   (b) an interval between two consecutive flaws being greater than 5 mm.

9 A coffee shop has an average arrival rate of 3.2 customers every 4 minutes. These random arrivals are Poisson distributed. What is the probability of getting
   (a) no customers in a 4 minute interval?
   (b) at least 3 customers in a 4 minute interval?
   (c) less than 5 customers in an 8 minute interval?

10 What is the area in the tail of the distribution for a Z value of 1.25?

11 What is area between the Z values of 1.45 and 2.45?

12 What is the area between Z values of -0.67 and 1.05?

13 A particular normal distribution has a mean of 5 and a standard deviation of 1.5. What is the area corresponding to a value:

 (a) greater than 6?

 (b) less than 4?

 (c) between 4 and 6?

 (d) between 6.5 and 7.5?

14 The daily demand for petrol at a garage is normally distributed with a mean of 20 000 litres and a standard deviation of 7200 litres. What is the probability that the demand in any one day is:

 (a) greater than 25 000 litres?

 (b) greater than 17 000 litres?

 (c) between 20 000 and 25 000 litres?

 (d) between 30 000 and 35 000 litres?

15 A recent large survey found that the average annual salary in the banking industry was £45,121 with a standard deviation of £24,246. If an employee is chosen at random what is the probability that he will earn more than £80,000? If there are 500,000 people working in the banking industry how many of them will earn more than £100,000?

16 Suppose that the time taken by a switchboard to answer a call is normally distributed with a mean of 48 seconds and a standard deviation of 10 seconds. What is the probability that a call will be answered within one minute?

17 The length of a special type of bolt is normally distributed with a mean diameter of 5.5 mm and a standard deviation of 0.4 mm. Bolts are only acceptable if their diameter is between 4.5 and 6 mm. What proportion of bolts will be accepted?

18 The specification for the length of an engine part is a minimum of 50 mm and a maximum of 55 mm. A batch of parts is produced that is normally distributed with a mean of 54 mm and a standard deviation of 2 mm. Parts cost £10 to make. Those that are too short have to be scrapped; those that are too long are shortened at a further cost of £8.

 (a) Find the percentage of parts that are

  (i) undersize

  (ii) oversize

 (b) Find the expected cost of producing 1000 usable parts.

19 As an incentive for customers to spend more money on its credit card a bank has decided to award high spending customers with a free gift. However, it doesn't want to give gifts to more than 5% of customers. If the mean spend per customer is £135 with a standard deviation of £55, what balance should the company specify? However, at the end of the first month it was found that 8% of customers qualified for the free gift. What has happened? Assuming that the standard deviation hasn't changed, calculate the new mean spend per customer.

20 Crumbly Biscuits produces golden cream biscuits which are sold in notional 300 g packets. The weights of these packets are normally distributed with a mean of 320 g and a standard deviation of 10.4 g.

(a) What is the probability that if you select a packet at random it will weigh:
  (i)   less than 300 g?
  (ii) more than 325 g?
  (iii) between 318 and 325 g?
(b) Out of a batch of 500 packets, how many would weigh less than 300 g?
(c) It has been decided to reduce the mean weight to 310 g. What would the standard deviation need to be if no more than 3% of packets must weigh less than 300 g?

21 A company that is considering the launch of a new product estimates that the possible demand for the product, in its first year, will be approximately normally distributed with a mean of 2000 units and a standard deviation of 500 units. What is the probability that the first-year demand will be:
(a) over 2500 units?
(b) over 2800 units?
(c) less than 1600 units?

22 A large departmental store has analyzed the monthly amount spent by its credit card customers and found that it is normally distributed with a mean of £100 and a standard deviation of £15. What percentage of people will spend:
(a) over £130?
(b) over £120?
(c) below £70?
(d) between £100 and £130?
(e) between £115 and £130?

What is the minimum amount spent of:
(f) the top 10%?
(g) the top 3% of customers?

23 If IQ scores for a certain test are approximately normally distributed with a mean of 100 and a standard deviation of 15, find the probability of a randomly selected individual scoring:
(a) 115 or more
(b) 130 or more
(c) between 115 and 130

24 The weekly demand for a liquid oil-based product that is marketed by a company is normally distributed with a mean of 2000 gallons and a standard deviation of 500 gallons. How many gallons of the product must the company have in stock at the start of the week to have only a 0.06 probability of running out of stock, assuming that no further supplies of the product are available during the week?

25 The weights of articles produced by a machine are normally distributed with a mean of 16g and a standard deviation of 0.5g. Only articles that have weights in the range 15.75 g to 16.75 g are acceptable and the remainder must be scrapped.
(a) What percentage of output will be scrapped?
(b) If an average of 10 000 units are produced per week and each scrapped unit costs £7, what will be the average weekly cost of scrapped units?
(c) A new machine can be hired at a cost of £10 000 per week. This would also produce articles with a mean of 16 g, but the standard deviation of the weights would be only 0.2 g. Is it worth hiring the new machine? (Assume that the old machine would have no scrap value.)

26 A company has to decide which of two possible new products, A or B, it should launch. A computer risk analysis package suggests that the profit that will result if A is developed is normally distributed with a mean of £15 million and a standard deviation of

£9 million. The profit that would be generated by developing product B is also normally distributed, with a mean of £10 million and a standard deviation of £5 million. Which product should the company launch to minimize its chances of incurring a loss?

27   Solve Activity 7.5 using both the Poisson and the normal approximation to the binomial. Comment on the suitability of both approximations.

28   Assuming that the event 'goals scored' is random and the mean number of goals scored per game is 2.65, use the Poisson distribution to calculate the probability of getting eight goals in a game (the Brazil versus Germany match). Comment on the chance of this score line occurring in a future World Cup event.

Assignment

Goodtaste Ltd, a coffee manufacturer, has recently been prosecuted for selling an underweight 100 g jar of coffee. You have been asked to give assistance to the quality control manager who is investigating the problem.

Jars are filled automatically and the filling machine can be preset to any desired weight. For the 100 g jars of coffee a weight of 101 g is set. There is no subsequent checking of the weight of individual jars, although samples are occasionally taken to check for quality. The standard deviation will depend to a certain extent on the mean weight, but for weights between 90 g and 110 g it is virtually constant at 1.5 g.

You have been asked to apply your knowledge of the normal distribution to the problem. In particular you have been told that prosecution only occurs when the product is underweight by more than 2%, so you need to find the probability that such a weight could happen by chance.

(a) Assuming that the mean weight is 101 g, what proportion of jars are:
  (i)   under 100 g in weight?
  (ii) under 98 g in weight?
  (iii) under 97 g in weight?
  (iv) over 100 g?
  (v)   within 2 g of the marked weight?

(b) What should the mean weight be set to in order that the probability of a jar weighing less than 98 g is less than 0.1%?

(c) Write a short note to the quality control manager summarizing your results.

8 INTERPRETING WITH CONFIDENCE: ANALYSIS OF SAMPLE DATA

PREREQUISITES

In order to fully understand this chapter you should have read through Chapter 3 (*Collecting data: surveys and samples*) and Chapter 7 (*The shape of data: probability distributions*).

OBJECTIVES

- To be able to calculate best estimates of the mean and standard deviation of a population
- To be able to calculate confidence intervals for a population mean
- To be able to calculate confidence intervals for a population percentage

INTRODUCTION

You were introduced to the idea of sampling in Chapter 3, where the problems of recording information about the whole 'population' were discussed and the need for sampling became apparent. Information from a sample is subject to *error*, and the purpose of this chapter is to be able to *quantify* this error. This is achieved by stating the margin of error that accompanies the sample estimate of a given population parameter. Thus it would be possible to calculate the margin of error for opinion polls for example.

QUANTITATIVE METHODS IN ACTION

Using statistics to identify benefit fraud

The Department for Work and Pensions (DWP) has estimated that in 2012–13 the total value of overpayments amounted to £3.5bn. This is made up of

- 0.7%, or £1.2bn, of total benefit expenditure is overpaid due to fraud;
- 1.0%, or £1.6bn, of total benefit expenditure is overpaid due to claimant error;
- 0.5%, or £0.8bn, of total benefit expenditure is overpaid due to official error.

Note: Figures do not add to £3.5bn due to rounding errors in the estimates.

Because of the huge number of claims, it is not possible to scrutinise every one, so a sampling system is used. Table 8.1 gives the sample sizes for each of the six main benefits. As you will see, the sample size for each benefit is a tiny proportion of the claimant population.

Each case is checked in detail, and from the analysis it is possible to provide national estimates for the

i. Percentage of cases that is incorrect; and
ii. Percentage of expenditure overpaid
iii. Value of the overpayments (the percentage in (ii)) is applied to the total benefit expenditure.

As we are dealing with samples from a very large population it is necessary to provide confidence intervals for the true mean overpayment. Figure 8.1 shows 95% confidence intervals for four benefits in 2012–13. As you see the benefit with the largest range is housing benefit.

Table 8.1 The number of benefit claims that were sampled and reviewed during 2012–13

Benefit	Sample size	Percentage of total claimant population reviewed
Housing benefit	12100	0.2%
Income support	4400	0.4%
Jobseekers allowance	4700	0.3%
Pension credit	5000	0.2%
Employment and support allowance (official error only)	3100	0.2%
State pension (official error only)	2000	0.1%
Total DWP claims (for benefits outlined above)	31300	0.2%

Source: 'Fraud and error in the benefit system: 2012–13 estimates (Great Britain)', p. 10, Department of Work and Pensions. Contains public sector information licensed under the Open Government Licence v3.0.

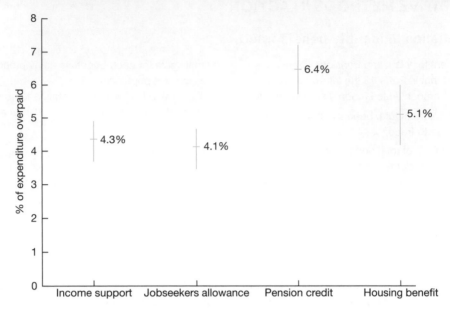

Figure 8.1 95% confidence intervals for four benefits

Samples and sampling

Sampling is an extensive and in many cases controversial technique. Whenever there is a general election in the UK the question of sampling accuracy is raised and this was most evident in the 1992 election where the polls incorrectly forecast a Labour majority. However, sampling people's views and intentions is notoriously difficult and even the best sampling plan can fail in these circumstances. Fortunately, when sampling is done by measurement, the results tend to be much more reliable. Sampling in industry and business tends to be of the measurement kind, and it will be this aspect of sampling that will be emphasized here.

activity 8.1

Why is it necessary to take samples?

The alternative to taking samples is to measure or test every member of the population. (The word 'population' in this context doesn't necessarily mean people; it is used to define all the items or things that are of interest, such as all television sets produced by a company in a day.) It is impractical to measure or test every member of the population for the following reasons:

- *It would take too long.* Measuring or testing can be time consuming and it is simply not always feasible to find the necessary time.
- *It might be too expensive.* Testing costs money as inspectors need to be employed and goods that are to be tested take up space and cannot be sold until the testing is complete.
- *Some tests are destructive.* Sometimes goods have to be tested to destruction, and if all the goods were tested there would be nothing left to sell!
- *The total population is unknown.* There are occasions when the size of the population is so large as to be considered infinite (without limit). In other cases the size of the population is simply unknown.

activity 8.2

You work for a company that manufactures plastic containers. The raw material is supplied in granular form and is delivered in 100 kg bags. The granules have to be tested for fire resistance and you are given the job of selecting the material for testing. How would you go about this task?

Since this is likely to be destructive testing, the only option available to you is to test a sample from each consignment. It is important that more than one bag is tested, since one particular bag may not be typical of the rest of the batch. Perhaps this bag happens to be old stock, or is different in some way. Whenever you take samples you must ensure that the samples are selected at *random*; that is, every member of the population must have an equal chance of being selected. (See Chapter 3.) In this case you would need to randomly select a number of bags and then test a small quantity from each of the bags selected. The number of bags chosen and the amount of material tested from each bag would depend on the specific requirements of the test.

Point estimates

The whole purpose of obtaining a sample from a population is to obtain estimates of various population *parameters*, such as the mean, the standard deviation or percentage.

These parameters can also be obtained for the sample, and it is the purpose of this section to show how the population parameters and the sample *statistics* are related. However, before continuing, it is necessary to define the symbols that are to be used throughout this (and the next) chapter.

The convention is to use Greek letters for the population parameters and normal letters for the sample statistics. The various symbols used are given below.

Parameter	Population	Sample
Mean	μ	$\bar{x}$
Standard deviation	σ	s
Percentage (or proportion)	π	P

The one exception to this rule is that the size of the population is usually referred to as N and the sample size as n.

example 8.1

10 samples of plastic granules were tested for fire resistance and the combustion temperatures (in C) are as follows:

Sample no.	1	2	3	4	5	6	7	8	9	10
Temperature	510	535	498	450	491	505	487	500	501	469

activity 8.3

What are the mean and standard deviation of the figures in Example 8.1, and what can you conclude about the whole batch?

You should have found the mean to be 494.6C, with a standard deviation of 23.03C. (See Chapter 5 if you are not sure about these calculations.) These figures are *best estimates* of the population mean and standard deviation. At this point it would be worth reminding ourselves of the reason why the variance and standard deviation are calculated using $n - 1$ instead of n.

The population of temperatures will follow some distribution. This distribution will probably have a few extreme values, but most of them will be clustered around the mean. The standard deviation of the population is a measure of spread; and all values, including the extreme ones, contribute to this value. However, if a sample is chosen at random, the sample is most unlikely to include any of the extreme values, so the spread of the sample will be less than that of the population. It has been found that dividing by $n - 1$ instead of n will compensate for this. As the sample gets larger, of course, the difference between the results of dividing by n or $n - 1$ diminishes; when n is greater than 30, the difference is very small.

The bigger the sample size n, the more accurate we would expect the sample mean to become as an estimate for the population mean. But how is information about the sample size taken into consideration in estimating the population parameters? Read on to find out.

Sampling distribution of the mean

Suppose you were sampling from a skewed distribution such as the number of goals scored (assuming this is a random event – see *Quantitative methods in action*, page 144). The chart for this random (Poisson) distribution is shown in Figure 8.2. This distribution has a mean of 2.65. If you took several small samples (say of size 2) of matches played and then plotted the distribution of the mean, you would get something like the chart in Figure 8.3. The distribution still has a skewness about it, and the mean varies from 0.5 to 6, which is quite a large spread. The mean of this distribution is 2.71. Figure 8.4 shows what happens when you increase the sample size to 30. Now the distribution is looking less skewed, and the range of the means is from 2.2 to 3.4; a much reduced spread. The mean of this distribution is 2.66, which is very close to the actual mean of 2.65.

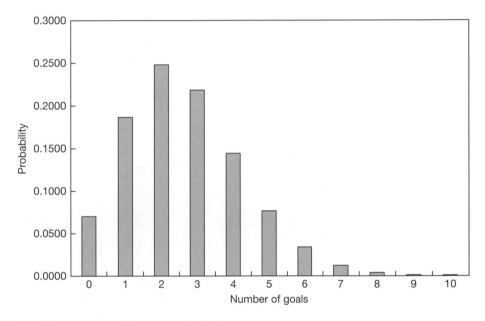

Figure 8.2 An example of a skewed distribution

The reason why a larger sample size reduces the spread and gives you a more accurate mean is that any high values are compensated for by low values. As the sample size gets larger, this 'distribution of the means' starts to look normal in shape. If your distribution is symmetrical, such as the weight of loaves baked (see Figure 7.3 page 146), you would find that the distribution of the means is itself normal in shape with a much smaller sample size. This is because there is a high probability that each sample will contain values close to the actual mean and a low probability that values will be in the tails of the distribution.

So to summarise, if you took repeated samples from a distribution, the 'sampling distribution of the means' would tend to follow the normal distribution. The degree of agreement with the normal curve depends on two factors:

- The distribution of the population values
- The sample size

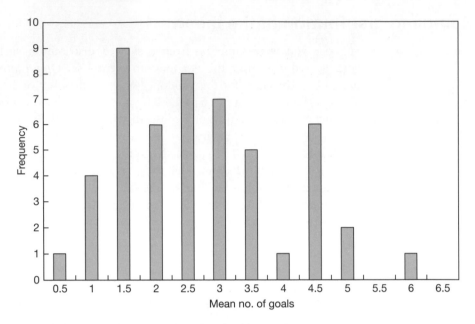

Figure 8.3 Distribution of mean number of goals when $n = 2$

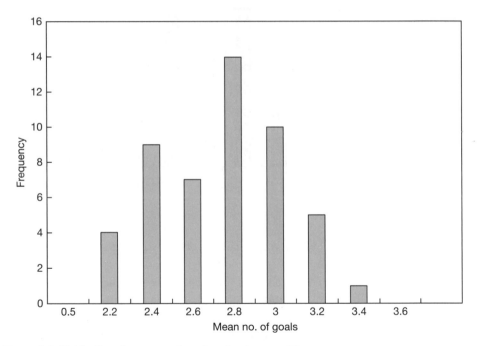

Figure 8.4 Distribution of mean number of goals when $n = 30$

If the population values were normally distributed, the 'sampling distribution of the means' would also be normal. If the population is not normally distributed, the agreement with the normal distribution depends on the sample size; the larger the sample size, the closer the agreement. This very important result is known as the *central limit theorem*.

In addition, the spread of this sampling distribution depends on the sample size; the larger the sample size, the smaller the spread (that is, the standard deviation). The standard deviation of the sampling distribution is called the *standard error*, as it measures the error that could arise in your estimate due to the spread of the sampling distribution. To avoid confusion with the standard error of the sampling distribution of a percentage, which will be discussed later, the standard error of the sampling distribution of the means will be referred to as SEM (the standard error of the mean). Is it necessary to collect many samples in order to calculate the value of SEM? Fortunately not, as there is a relationship between σ and SEM. This relationship is as follows:

$$SEM = \frac{\sigma}{\sqrt{n}}$$

So the larger the sample size (n), the smaller the value of SEM, which makes sense.

These ideas are illustrated in Figure 8.5. Two sampling distributions are shown: one for a sample size of 4 and one for a sample size of 16. The population distribution (assumed normal in this case) has been superimposed on to the diagram.

You will see that the mean of each sampling distribution is the same and equal to the population value. You would normally only take one sample, and from Figure 8.5 you can see that the mean of a sample can lie anywhere within the relevant sampling distribution, although it is more likely to be near the centre than in the tails. This variation depends on the value of SEM, so the smaller this figure, the more reliable your estimate of the population mean will be.

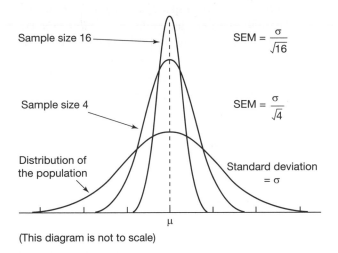

(This diagram is not to scale)

Figure 8.5 Sampling distribution of the means

activity
8.4

The standard deviation of the population of combustion temperatures for the plastic granules is known to be 23.75C. What is the value of SEM for a sample of size 10 and for a sample of size 40?

The value of SEM when $n = 10$ is:

$$\text{SEM} = \frac{23.75}{\sqrt{10}}$$

$$= \frac{23.75}{3.1623}$$

$$= 7.510$$

That is, 7.510C.

When $n = 40$, SEM becomes:

$$\text{SEM} = \frac{23.75}{\sqrt{40}}$$

$$= \frac{23.75}{6.3246}$$

$$= 3.755$$

That is, 3.755C. Notice that to halve the value of SEM, the sample size was increased fourfold. Calculation of the sample size necessary to give a prescribed level of accuracy will be discussed later.

Confidence intervals for a population mean for large samples

Rather than simply quote the value of SEM, a much better idea of the reliability of your estimate is to specify some limits within which the true mean is expected to lie. These limits are called *confidence limits* or *intervals*.

When calculating confidence intervals it is necessary to decide what level of confidence you wish to use. The most common level is 95%, which means that you are 95% confident that the true mean lies within the calculated limits. Or, put another way, there is a 5% chance that the true mean doesn't lie within these limits. Other limits are frequently used, such as 90%, 99% and 99.9%; but remember that as the confidence level gets closer to 100%, the interval gets larger and larger (at 100% it would be infinitely large).

The *normal distribution* (see Chapter 7, page 156) can be used to calculate these limits when the sample size is large as, according to the central limit theorem, the sampling distribution of the sample mean will be approximately normal. A large sample is generally considered to be 30 or over.

Figure 8.6 illustrates the Z values that enclose 95% of the standard normal distribution. The values ± 1.96 have been found from the normal table (Appendix) by noting that the area (or probability) in either tail is 0.025 ($= 0.05/2$).

From your knowledge of the normal distribution, you will know that any normal distribution can be transformed into the standard normal distribution using the formula:

$$Z = \frac{x - \mu}{\sigma}$$

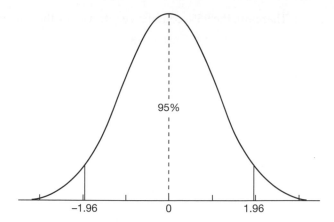

Figure 8.6 95% confidence interval for the standard normal distribution

However, this formula is for individual x values. For a sampling distribution of the means, the x needs to be replaced by $\bar{x}$ and σ needs to be replaced by SEM. The formula then becomes:

$$Z = \frac{\bar{x} - \mu}{\text{SEM}}$$

If you rearrange this formula to make μ the subject, you will get:

$$\mu = \bar{x} \pm Z \times \text{SEM}$$

This is the equation you would use to calculate confidence intervals using the normal distribution. For 95% confidence intervals, the Z value is 1.96 and the formula becomes:

$$\mu = \bar{x} \pm 1.96 \times \text{SEM}$$

How would you use this formula? The next example should help you.

example
8.2

Imagine that you work for the quality control unit of a sugar producer. One of your tasks is to weigh samples of 1 kg bags of sugar, and from a sample of 36 bags you obtain a mean weight of 0.985 kg and a standard deviation of 0.056 kg.

activity
8.5

What is the 95% confidence interval for the true mean weight of bags of sugar?

From the discussion on point estimates, you know that the best estimate of the true mean is 0.985 kg. That is:

$$\bar{x} = 0.985 \text{ kg}$$

As we have a large sample the population standard deviation can be approximated by the sample standard deviation(s), and so the value of SEM is:

$$\frac{s}{\sqrt{n}} = \frac{0.056}{\sqrt{36}}$$

$$= 0.00933$$

Therefore the 95% confidence interval for the true mean is:

$0.985 \pm 1.96 \times 0.00933$

$= 0.985 \pm 0.018$

$= 0.985 - 0.018$ and $0.985 + 0.018$

$= 0.967$ and $1.003\,\text{kg}$

The 0.967 kg is the *lower* limit and 1.003 kg is the *upper* limit. The ±0.018 is often called the *half width* of the confidence interval. It is usual to write this confidence interval as:

$0.967, 1.003\,\text{kg}$ (or 0.967 to 1.003 kg)

If you took another 36 bags you would get a slightly different sample mean and therefore the confidence interval would be different. It is likely that both these confidence intervals would contain the true mean, but if you took 20 different samples you would expect that *one* of these intervals would *not* contain the true mean. That is, there is a 1 in 20 or 5% chance that your confidence interval would not contain the true mean. This is illustrated in Figure 8.7, where confidence intervals for 5 sample means have been drawn, two of which do not contain the true mean.

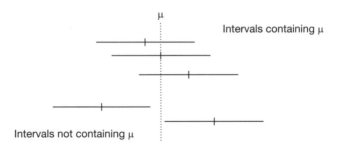

Figure 8.7 Diagram to illustrate confidence intervals

If you wanted to reduce the chance of the interval not containing the true mean you could calculate 99% confidence intervals. From the normal table, the value of Z for 0.005 (1% divided by 2) is 2.58, so the 99% confidence interval is:

$0.985 \pm 2.58 \times 0.00933$

$= 0.985 \pm 0.024$

$= 0.961, 1.009\,\text{kg}$

The interval is wider, which was expected. Now there is only a 1% chance that the true mean will be outside these limits. If these limits are too wide, the only way to reduce them (for the same confidence level) is to increase the sample size.

Confidence intervals for a population mean for small samples

For large samples we were able to make use of the central limit theorem in our assumption that the sampling distribution of the sample mean will be normal no

DID YOU KNOW?

There are many graphical ways of representing uncertainty in an estimate. The Bank of England uses a fan chart to represent uncertainty in its forecasts. In Figure 8.8 the forecast of CPI is quite uncertain and gets larger with time. The CPI is expected to lie somewhere within the fan 90% of the time, and the remaining 10% of occasions they can fall anywhere outside the coloured area of the fan chart.

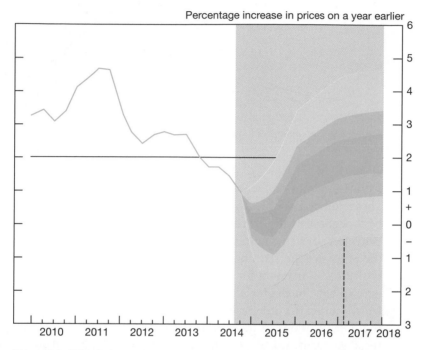

Figure 8.8 CPI inflation projection

Source: Bank of England Inflation Report, February 2015-http://www.bankofengland.co.uk/publications/Documents/inflationreport/2015/febfc.pdf.

matter what the shape of the distribution of the population. We were also justified in using the sample standard deviation in place of the population standard deviation in the calculation of SEM. However, for small samples neither of these assumptions holds, so even if we assume that the population is normal we have a problem with the standard deviation. The reason for this is that the uncertainty generated by estimating σ decreases the reliability of the confidence interval. To overcome this problem a different distribution is used, called the '*t-distribution*'. This distribution is symmetrical like the normal, but it is flatter. This 'flatness' increases the percentage of the distribution in the 'tails' and this means that the confidence interval, for the same confidence level, is wider. The amount of 'flatness' decreases with increase in *n*, the sample size. When *n* is 50 there is virtually no difference between the two distributions, and even for a sample size of 30 the difference is quite small.

Figure 8.9 shows the *t*-distribution for a sample size of 6, together with the normal distribution for comparison.

The *t*-table is given in the Appendix. If you compare this table with the normal table, you will see two important differences. First, the numbers within the table are

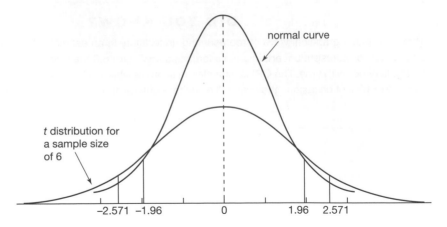

Figure 8.9 Comparison of the normal and *t*-distributions

t-values and not probabilities; second, the numbers in the first column are different. These numbers are the *degrees of freedom* (*v*) of the sample. Degrees of freedom can be thought of as the 'freedom' that you have in choosing the values of the sample. If you were given the mean of the sample of 6 values, you would be free to choose 5 of the 6 but not the sixth one. Therefore there are 5 degrees of freedom. The number of degrees of freedom for a single sample of size *n* is *n* − 1. For a very large sample (shown as ∞ in the table) the *t* and *Z* distributions are exactly the same. Since the *t*-distribution is a little easier to use, you might prefer to use this table when you want the *Z* value of one of the 'standard' probabilities. In the table supplied in this book these 'standard' probabilities are 0.2, 0.1, 0.05, 0.025, 0.01, 0.005, 0.001 and 0.0001.

To use this table you would first decide on the probability level. For a 95% confidence interval you would choose the 0.025 level, since this represents 2.5% in each tail. For a sample size of 6, the degrees of freedom is 5, so the *t*-value for 5 degrees of freedom at 95% confidence level is 2.571. This value has been shown in Figure 8.9. (Remember that the *t*-distribution is symmetrical about the mean of zero, so the equivalent value in the left hand side of the distribution is −2.571.)

The formula for calculating confidence intervals using this distribution is the same as when the normal distribution was used, except that *Z* is replaced by *t*, and is therefore:

$$\mu = \bar{x} \pm t \times \text{SEM}$$

activity **8.6**

In Activity 8.3 you calculated the mean and standard deviation of the combustion temperatures of a sample of size 10 to be 494.6C and 23.03C respectively. Calculate the 95% confidence intervals for the true mean combustion temperature of the entire batch.

The best estimate of σ is 23.03C, so the value of SEM is:

$$\frac{23.03}{\sqrt{10}} = 7.283$$

To find the 95% confidence interval for the true mean, you would use the t-table in the Appendix to find the appropriate value of t. The value of t for 9 degrees of freedom, with a probability of 0.025, is 2.262. Substituting this value into the equation for μ gives you:

$$494.6 \pm 2.262 \times 7.283$$

$$= 494.6 \pm 16.5$$

$$= 478.1, \quad 511.1\,\text{degC}$$

So the true mean combustion temperature of the whole consignment lies between 478.1C and 511.1C at the 95% level of confidence.

Confidence interval of a percentage

Percentages occur quite frequently in the analysis of survey results; for example, the percentage of people who like a particular product, or the percentage of students over the age of 25. Provided n is large and the percentage is not too small or too large, the sampling distribution of a percentage can be approximated by the normal distribution.

The standard error of the sampling distribution of percentages (SEP) is:

$$\text{SEP} = \sqrt{\frac{P(100 - P)}{n}}$$

where P is the sample percentage.

The calculation of a confidence interval for a percentage is similar to that of the mean, that is:

$$\pi = P \pm Z \times \text{SEP}$$

(activity 8.7) A survey among 250 students revealed that 147 were female. What is the 95% confidence interval for the true percentage of female students?

The value of P is $\dfrac{147}{250} \times 100 = 58.8\%$

That is, the survey suggested that 58.8% of the student population is female. The value of SEP for this problem is:

$$\sqrt{\frac{58.8 \times (100 - 58.8)}{250}}$$

$$= 3.113$$

The value of Z for 95% confidence is 1.96, so the confidence interval becomes:

$$58.8 \pm 1.96 \times 3.113$$

$$= 58.8 \pm 6.1$$

$$= 52.7, 64.9$$

That is, the true percentage lies somewhere between 52.7% and 64.9%.

Calculation of sample size

Since the value of both SEM and SEP depend on the sample size, the width of the confidence interval for the same confidence level can be reduced by increasing the value of n. For the sugar example (Activity 8.5) the half width of the interval – that is, the difference between the lower or upper limit and the sample mean – is 0.018 kg for a confidence level of 95%. This was obtained by multiplying SEM by 1.96; that is:

$$\text{Half width of confidence interval} = 1.96 \times \text{SEM}$$

$$= 1.96 \times \frac{\sigma}{\sqrt{n}}$$

If you wanted to reduce this half width to, say, 0.015 kg, then you would need to calculate the value of n required to achieve this reduction. That is:

$$1.96 \times \frac{0.056}{\sqrt{n}} = 0.015$$

since the best estimate of $\sigma = 0.056$ (see Example 8.2).

Rearranging this equation gives:

$$\sqrt{n} = \frac{1.96 \times 0.056}{0.015}$$

$$= 7.3173$$

so $n = 53.5$.

So a sample size of about 54 would be required to achieve an accuracy of ± 0.015 kg.

(**activity 8.8**) What sample size would be required to reduce the half width for the percentage of female students from 6.1% to 1%?

The calculation is similar to that for the mean. That is:

$$1.96 \times \text{SEP} = 1.0$$

The value of P is 58.8%, so:

$$1.96 \times \sqrt{\frac{58.8 \times (100 - 58.8)}{n}} = 1.0$$

Dividing both sides by 1.96 and squaring gives:

$$\frac{58.8 \times 41.2}{n} = 0.2603$$

Therefore:

$$n = \frac{58.8 \times 41.2}{0.2603}$$

$$= 9306.8$$

That is, a sample of about 9000 students would need to be selected to ensure this level of accuracy!

Finite populations

The assumption that has implicitly been made in this chapter is that the population is infinitely large, or at least much larger than the sample. The reason for this is that all sampling is done *without* replacement. That is, you would not measure or test the same person or item twice. This has no effect when the population is large, but for small populations, the probability that an item will be selected will change as soon as one item has been selected. (See Chapter 6.) To overcome this problem, the standard error (either SEM or SEP) is modified. This is achieved by multiplying the value by the *Finite Population Correction Factor*, which is:

$$\sqrt{\frac{(N-n)}{(N-1)}}$$

where N is the size of the population.

$\left(\begin{array}{c}\textit{activity}\\ \textbf{8.9}\end{array}\right)$ In the sugar example (Example 8.2) SEM was 0.00933. What is the value of SEM if the size of the population is 100?

The value of SEM is multiplied by the correction factor, that is:

$$0.00933 \times \sqrt{\frac{(100-36)}{(100-1)}}$$

$$= 0.00933 \times 0.8040$$

$$= 0.00750$$

This is a *reduction*. (Since SEM is reduced, confidence intervals will also be reduced.)

As N gets larger relative to n, the correction factor approaches 1 and can therefore be ignored. For example, if you try $N = 10\,000$ and $n = 10$, you should get a value of 0.9995.

Reflection

As a society we are always hungry for information. Whether it is a business that wants to find out how consumers are rating its product, or a newspaper that wants to find out how we are going to vote, the key issue is how to obtain *reliable* information. Although most serious surveys are conducted scientifically, any information obtained from a sample is subject to sampling error. Being able to quantify this error is one of the most important contributions of statistics.

Even the most carefully conducted survey can give erroneous results, however. The classic case of this was during the General Election in 1992 in the UK, when the five main opinion polls predicted a Labour lead of 0.8%. The exit polls conducted by the BBC and ITV suggested a Conservative lead of 4%, but when the actual result was declared the Conservatives won by 7.5%. The error in the opinion polls was more than 8% – far higher than the expected 2% or 3% margin of error. An enquiry afterwards put the error down to three main factors: a late swing, wrong quotas, and a high refusal rate (polled voters who declined to say how they would vote). Later investigation showed that Conservative voters were more likely to give a 'don't know' than Labour voters. Various methods have been used since to compensate for this problem, including the assumption that 60% of those who say that they don't know will in fact vote for the same party that they voted for in the previous election. (See www.alba.org.uk/polls)

Key points

- A sample can be used to provide estimates of population parameters such as the mean, proportion and standard deviation.
- Every estimate of these parameters will have a sampling error associated with it. We can reduce this error by taking a larger sample but we can never eliminate the error entirely.
- The central limit theorem allows us to calculate this error because we can assume that the sample mean (or proportion) comes from a normal distribution.
- We normally express this error in the form of a confidence interval. The confidence is expressed in percentages and the common values are 95% and 99%.
- We can calculate the sample size required to give a specific minimum error.
- For small samples we use the *t*-distribution because for the same confidence level we get a slightly wider interval.
- We usually assume an infinitely large population but when this is not true we can make a simple adjustment.

Further reading

All statistical texts and many quantitative methods texts will have a chapter on confidence intervals. Texts aimed at the business student will treat the material in a similar way to this text while those texts aimed at maths or stats students will be much more mathematical and probably beyond the ability of most business students. Morris (2011) is very descriptive and uses few equations.

http://www.**palgrave.com**/oakshott-eqm6

Solutions to all questions are freely available

Practice questions

1   A university contains 16 000 students and it is required to find out how many students have part-time jobs. 50 students are selected at random and of these, 20 admitted to working during term time. What is the value of:
   (a) the size of the population?
   (b) the sample size?

(c) the sample percentage?

(d) the estimate of the true percentage?

(e) the 95% confidence interval of the true percentage?

2   A sample of six packets of tea is selected from a production line. The contents of these packets are 9.4, 9.1, 10.2, 8.9, 10.9 and 9.2 g respectively. Obtain the 95% confidence interval estimate of the mean net weight of a packet, if the weights are normally distributed.

3   A random sample of 100 adult females from the population of a large town has a mean height of 169.5 cm with a standard deviation of 2.6 cm. Construct a 95% confidence interval for the mean height of all adult females in the town.

4   A sample of 60 people was asked if they thought that if children watched video 'nasties' they were more likely to commit a crime. Out of the sample, 45 thought that they would. Calculate the 95% confidence interval for the true percentage.

5   The weight of each of 10 specimens of carbon paper was found to be (in grams):
7.4, 8.3, 10.9, 6.9, 7.9, 8.2, 8.6, 9.1, 9.9, 10.0
Given that the weights are normally distributed, construct (a) 95% and (b) 99% confidence intervals for the true mean of the population weights.

6   A credit card company wants to determine the mean income of its card holders. A random sample of 225 card holders was drawn and the sample average income was £16 450 with a standard deviation of £3675.

(a) Construct a 99% confidence interval for the true mean income.

(b) Management decided that the confidence interval in (a) was too large to be useful. In particular, the management wanted to estimate the mean income to within £200, with a confidence level of 99%. How large a sample should be selected?

7   From a population of 200, a sample of 40 people were asked for their views on capital punishment. 12 people thought that hanging should be imposed for certain crimes. Estimate the 95% confidence interval for the true percentage.

8   A company involved in a market research survey takes a random sample of 800 orders which were delivered in a given month. Of these orders, 320 went to customers aged under 21. Estimate the percentage of all the company's orders which went to this age group during the month in question, with 95% confidence.

9   In a sample of 200 of a company's business customers, 160 say that they are likely to make a further purchase within the next 12 months. Estimate the percentage of all the company's customers who will make a further purchase within the next year with 95% confidence.

10   An insurance company is concerned about the size of claims being made by its policy holders. A random sample of 400 claims had a mean value of £230 and a standard deviation of £42.
Estimate the mean size of all claims received by the company:

(a) with 95% confidence

(b) with 99% confidence

11   A quality control inspector wishes to estimate the mean weight of bags of cement leaving a production line on a particular day to within 2 g at the 95% level of confidence. It is known that the standard deviation of the weights remains fairly constant at 60 g. How large a sample should the inspector take?

12   A company wants to estimate, with 95% confidence, the percentage of people in a town who have seen its press advertisements. The company would like its estimate to have a margin of error of ±4%. How large a sample of people will they need to take if:

(a) a preliminary estimate suggests that the true percentage is about 10%?

(b) no preliminary estimate is available?

13 A survey of 16 houses in a particular district found the mean value to be £129 500 with a standard deviation of £55 524.

(a) Give a 95% confidence interval for the average value of all properties in the district.

(b) If it is required to halve the confidence interval for the same confidence level, what sample size would be required?

(c) If it is known that there are only 200 houses in the district how will this affect your answer to part (a)?

14 A national survey of 1975 adults in the UK found that 51% were in favour of leaving the EU. Find the 95% confidence interval for the percentage of all adults in the UK that favour leaving the EU. Does your analysis suggest that a majority of UK adults wish to leave the EU? (*Source:* Opinium Research [http://www.opinium.co.uk], online poll conducted between 17 and 20 January 2015)

Assignment

The latest internal accounts for an off-licence chain showed that the annual sales of wines and spirits had fallen by more than 30%. This fall has been blamed on the relaxation of the limits of duty free goods that can be brought into Britain from EU countries from 1993.

In order to test this theory it was decided to ask a random sample of shoppers if they intend to travel to France this year. Of the 75 shoppers questioned, 27 were certain to go to France at least once. It was also decided to ask a random sample of 60 returning holiday makers how much they had spent on duty free alcohol. Of these 60, 8 refused to answer, and for the remaining 52 people the average spend was found to be £37.26, with a standard deviation of £35.97.

(a) What is the percentage of shoppers who said they were definitely making at least one trip to France this year?

(b) Calculate the 95% confidence interval for the true percentage of shoppers who intend to travel to France this year. Interpret this interval.

(c) Calculate the 95% confidence interval for the true mean amount spent on duty free alcohol for all holiday makers returning from France.

(d) Calculate the number of shoppers to be questioned so that the half width of the confidence interval for the percentage of shoppers who intend to travel to France is no more than 3%.

(e) The half width of the confidence interval for the average spend on duty free alcohol must be reduced to £5. How many holiday makers need to be sampled?

(f) What reservations (if any) do you have about this kind of survey?

9 CHECKING IDEAS: TESTING A HYPOTHESIS

PREREQUISITES

To complete this chapter successfully you should have read through Chapter 8 (*Interpreting with confidence: analysis of sample data*)

OBJECTIVES

- To understand the ideas behind hypothesis testing
- To know how to perform tests of hypothesis on the mean of a population
- To know how to perform tests of hypothesis on a percentage
- To know how to perform a 'goodness-of-fit' test
- To be able to apply the chi-square test to categorical data
- To know how to use Excel and SPSS to perform tests of hypothesis

INTRODUCTION

In Chapter 8 you saw how to analyze a sample so that estimates of some population parameters, such as the mean or percentage, could be obtained. In this chapter the emphasis is slightly different in that you are told the value of the population parameter and then use the sample to confirm or disprove this figure. For example, you may want to determine the effect on fuel consumption of a particular make of car by modification to the carburation system, or you may want to determine if a trade union can be sure that, if a ballot was called, the majority of the membership would vote for strike action. In both these examples a *hypothesis* would be made concerning the population and this hypothesis tested using the sample data.

QUANTITATIVE METHODS IN ACTION

Are waiting times at A&E getting worse?

During recent winters the National Health Service (NHS) has struggled to meet the government target that 95% of patients should spend no longer than 4 hours in Accident and Emergency (A&E). Towards the end of 2014, waiting times rose to give the worst performance for a decade. During 2013–14, the median percentage of patients waiting more than 4 hours was between 5% and 7.5%. Total attendance has risen by 32% in 10 years, which has put a considerable strain on the NHS and explains some of the problems experienced in recent years.

This case looks at the year 2013–14, when there were 21.7 million attendances at A&E in England, of which 14.2 million were at Type 1 A&E departments (a Type 1 department is a major A&E department, which is a consultant-led 24-hour service with full resuscitation facilities). Figure 9.1 is a chart of total attendance at A&E and attendance at Type 1 departments during 2013–14.

July 8 to 14 was the busiest week, and this was 20% higher than the quietest week (23 to 29 December). One interesting statistic is the variance of demand. This can be represented by the coefficient of variation (see Chapter 5). This statistic varied between 3.7% and 4.7%, except for Devon, Cornwall and the Isles of Scilly, and also Leicestershire and Lincolnshire, where it was 7%. It is not clear why these two areas had such a high variance, although an increase in tourists during the summer months could be a factor for Devon and Cornwall.

As the number of attendances has risen, it would perhaps be expected that waiting times would increase. As we shall see in this chapter, we can use statistics to test these kinds of relationships. So the researchers would have applied a test of *significance* on the relationship between attendance and waiting times to see if there was evidence of an association between these two variables.

Surprisingly, there was no significant correlation between these two variables (see Chapter 10 for details about correlation). In fact in two areas (Lancashire and Durham, Darlington and Tees), there was a significant *negative* correlation; that is, the larger the attendance, the lower the waiting times. The reason for the negative correlations could be due to the fact that these regions anticipated higher demand and adjusted staffing levels accordingly.

Figure 9.1 Total attendance and attendance at major (Type 1) departments during 2013–14

Source for data: House of Commons Library, Accident & Emergency Performance, England 2013–14: national and regional data. RESEARCH PAPER 14/22 14 April 2014. Contains Parliamentary information licensed under the Open Parliament Licence v3.0: http://www.parliament.uk/site-information/copyright/open-parliament-licence/.

The purpose of hypothesis testing

activity 9.1

The light bulbs manufactured by Bright Lights are designed to last for 1000 hours on average. How can the company be sure that the average lifetime of a large batch of bulbs really is 1000 hours?

The mean lifetime could be found by testing a sample of bulbs and constructing a confidence interval within which the true mean is likely to lie. If the interval does contain 1000 hours, then you could assume that the true mean really is 1000 hours.

Alternatively, you could construct a confidence interval for the supposed true mean of 1000 hours and see if the sample mean was contained within this interval.

However, there is a third approach. This approach makes the *hypothesis* that any departure from the supposedly true mean by the sample mean is simply due to chance effects. It is then a matter of calculating the probability that this sample result could have occurred by chance. This is the general idea of hypothesis testing – it assumes that the hypothesis is true and then tries to disprove it. This hypothesis is known as the *null* hypothesis. If the null hypothesis is rejected, an *alternative* hypothesis is accepted. The null hypothesis is called H_0 and the alternative hypothesis H_1.

The null hypothesis is tested at a particular *significance level*. This level relates to the area (or probability) in the tail of the distribution being used for the test. This area is called the *critical region,* and if the *test statistic* lies in the critical region, you would infer that the result is unlikely to have occurred by chance. You would then reject the null hypothesis. For example, if the 5% level of significance was used and the null hypothesis was rejected, you would say that H_0 had been rejected at the 5% (or the 0.05) significance level, and the result was *significant*.

These ideas apply to all types of hypothesis tests. The precise form of each hypothesis and the calculations necessary to test H_0 depend on the test being carried out. There are very many tests that can be applied to samples. The most important group are *parametric* tests. These tests compare sample statistics with the population parameters and make assumptions about the form of the sampling distribution. *Non-parametric* (or distribution-free) tests are more general and do not insist on such stringent conditions. They can also be used where the data can only be ordered (ordinal data) rather than measured. However, non-parametric tests are less discriminating; that is, the results tend to be less reliable.

Whatever the test, the steps for checking the hypothesis are the same. This is:

Step 1   Set up the null and alternative hypotheses and determine (usually from tables) the boundaries of the critical region. These boundaries are called the *critical values.*

Step 2   Calculate the test statistic.

Step 3   Decide whether to accept or reject H_0.

Large sample test for a population mean

The normal distribution can be used to solve problems involving means if the population is normal *and* the standard deviation of the population (σ) is known. If normality cannot be assumed then a large sample size will ensure that the sampling distribution of the means is approximately normal.

However, as in the calculation of confidence intervals (see Chapter 8) the standard deviation may be unknown and has to be estimated from the sample. In these cases the normal distribution can be used as an approximation, provided the sample size is large.

The formula for Z is also the same as that used in the derivation of the formula for confidence intervals. That is:

$$Z = \frac{\bar{x} - \mu}{\text{SEM}}$$

where $\bar{x}$ is the mean of the sample, μ is the mean of the population, and SEM is the standard error of the sampling distribution of the means, and is given by:

$$\text{SEM} = \frac{s}{\sqrt{n}}$$

where n is the sample size and σ is the standard deviation.

$\left(\begin{array}{c}\textit{activity}\\ \textbf{9.2}\end{array}\right)$ The distribution of the lifetime of all bulbs made by Bright Lights is normal, and the standard deviation of the population is known to be 120 hours. A sample of 30 bulbs were tested and the mean lifetime was found to be 1100 hours. Is this consistent, at the 5% level of significance, with the supposed true mean of 1000 hours?

Step 1

Set up H_0 and H_1 and decide on the critical values.

The null hypothesis in this case is that the true mean lifetime is 1000 hours. The alternative hypothesis can be one of three statements. These are:

The true mean is *not* equal to 1000 hours

or   The true mean is greater than 1000 hours

or   The true mean is less than 1000 hours

Using symbols, the null and alternative hypotheses become:

$$H_0: \mu = 1000 \text{ hours} \quad H_1: \mu \neq 1000 \text{ hours}$$
$$or \quad H_1: \mu > 1000 \text{ hours}$$
$$or \quad H_1: \mu < 1000 \text{ hours}$$

(The ':' is the mathematical shorthand for 'such that')

The first form of the alternative hypothesis is used for a *two tailed* (or a two sided) test and the other two forms are used for *one tailed* tests. The two tailed test is used when you have no reason to suppose that the true mean could be either greater than or less than the value given by the null hypothesis. The one tailed test is used when you are more interested in one side of the supposed mean than the other. The golden rule when carrying out hypothesis tests is that H_0 and H_1 are set up *before* the test is carried out (and preferably before the data is collected). You may find the diagrams in Figure 9.2 and Figure 9.3 helpful in clarifying the situation.

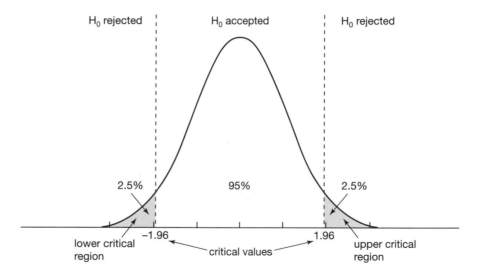

Figure 9.2 Two tailed test at the 5% significance level

In Figure 9.2 the critical values of ± 1.96 mark the boundaries of the two critical regions at the 5% significance level. These values are found from the normal table in the Appendix. If the test statistic (Z) is either greater than the right hand critical value or less than the left hand value, then H_0 is rejected. If Z lies in between the two critical values then H_0 is accepted – *or you should really say that you do not have sufficient information to reject H_0.*

The left hand diagram of Figure 9.3 illustrates the case where the alternative hypothesis is of the 'less than' kind. There is only one critical region in this case and you would reject H_0 if Z was *less* than the critical value of -1.645. The reason that the critical value is different than for the two tailed case is that the area in the one tail is now the full amount (5% in this example) and not half as it was before. The right

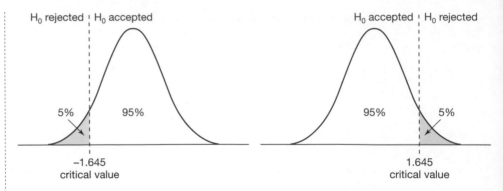

Figure 9.3 One tailed test at the 5% significance level

hand diagram is for the 'greater than' case, and the same reasoning applies here as in the left hand diagram. That is, H_0 would be rejected if Z was *greater* than 1.645.

The light bulb example would be a two tailed test because there is nothing in the wording of the problem that suggests that you are more interested in one side of the mean. So the null and alternative hypotheses for this example are:

$$H_0: \mu = 1000 \text{ hours} \qquad H_1: \mu \neq 1000 \text{ hours}$$

and the critical values are ± 1.96.

Step 2

Calculate the test statistic.

In this problem, $n = 30$, $\mu = 1000$, $\sigma = 120$, and $\bar{x} = 1100$. Therefore

$$\text{SEM} = \frac{\sigma}{\sqrt{n}} = \frac{120}{\sqrt{30}}$$

$$= 21.9089$$

and:

$$Z = \frac{\bar{x} - \mu}{\text{SEM}}$$

$$= \frac{1100 - 1000}{21.9089}$$

$$= \frac{100}{21.9089}$$

$$= 4.56$$

This is your test statistic.

Step 3

Decide whether to accept or reject H_0.

It is now necessary to decide if this value of Z could have happened by chance, or if it is indicative of a change in the population mean.

Since Z (4.56) is greater than 1.96 and is therefore in the critical region, you can reject H$_0$ at the 5% level of significance. This is shown clearly in Figure 9.4, where the 0.1% significance level ($Z = 3.3$) has also been added. The result is significant, and you would conclude that there has almost certainly been a change in the mean lifetime of light bulbs.

The following activity illustrates the use of one tailed tests.

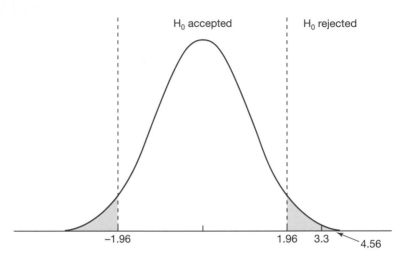

H$_0$ accepted   H$_0$ rejected

−1.96   1.96   3.3   4.56

Figure 9.4 Diagram for Activity 9.2

activity **9.3**

The mean fuel consumption for a particular make of car is known to be 33 mpg. A modification to this car has been made that should reduce fuel consumption. 35 cars are fitted with this device and their fuel consumption is recorded over 12 months. At the end of this period the mean fuel consumption of the 35 cars is found to be 34.8 mpg with a standard deviation of 5.7 mpg. Is there any evidence, at the 5% level of significance, that the fuel consumption has been improved?

This is a one tailed test since it is hoped that the modification will improve the fuel consumption – there is nothing to suggest that fuel consumption will be made worse. The Z-test can be used without assuming normality because the sample is 'large' (over 30).

The null and alternative hypotheses for this problem are:

$$H_0: \mu = 33 \text{ mpg} \quad H_1: \mu > 33 \text{ mpg}$$

and the critical value of Z at the 5% significance level is 1.645.

$$\sigma = 5.7 \text{ mpg}, \bar{x} = 34.8 \text{ and } n = 35$$

Therefore:

$$\text{SEM} = \frac{5.7}{\sqrt{35}}$$

$$= 0.9635$$

and the test statistic is: $Z = \dfrac{34.8 - 33.0}{0.9635}$

$$= 1.868$$

Since 1.868 is greater than the critical value of 1.645, you would reject the null hypothesis. That is, there is a *significant* difference between the mean fuel consumption before and after the modification has been fitted. You would conclude that the modification appears to have improved the fuel consumption of this particular make of car.

It is important to draw a diagram when carrying out hypothesis tests. The diagram for this problem is shown in Figure 9.5.

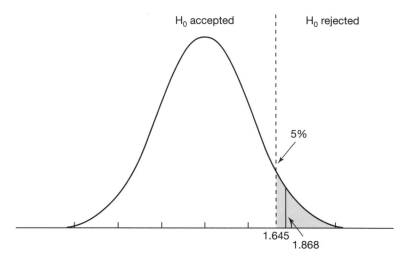

Figure 9.5 Diagram for Activity 9.3

This diagram clearly shows that the test statistic is in the critical region, and H_0 should therefore be rejected. You may have noticed that H_0 would *not* have been rejected if the test had been two tailed. (Compare this diagram with Figure 9.2.) This is why it is so important to ensure that you are justified in using a one tailed test, as the chance of rejecting H_0 is greater in the one tailed case.

Small sample test for a population mean

As in the case of confidence intervals, it is necessary to assume that the population is normal and to use the t -distribution instead of the normal distribution. The formula for the t -statistic is:

$$t = \frac{\bar{x} - \mu}{\text{SEM}}$$

which is identical to the expression for Z. The formula for SEM is also the same, except that the standard deviation used is the estimate obtained from the sample. That is:

$$\text{SEM} = \frac{s}{\sqrt{n}}$$

The same considerations apply concerning the critical region, except that the critical value is obtained from the t-distribution on $n - 1$ degrees of freedom (see Appendix). For example, the critical value on 7 degrees of freedom at the 5% significance level is ± 2.365 for a two tailed test, and ± 1.895 for a one tailed test.

The following activity may help you understand the differences between the Z- and t-tests.

activity 9.4

A tomato grower has developed a new variety of tomato. This variety is supposed to give good crops without the need for a greenhouse. One of the supposed attributes of this tomato is that the average yield per plant is at least 4 kg of fruit. A gardening magazine decides to test this claim and grows 8 plants in controlled conditions. The yield from each plant is carefully recorded and is as follows:

Plant	1	2	3	4	5	6	7	8
Yield	3.6	4.2	3.3	2.5	4.8	2.75	4.2	4.6

Does this data support the grower's claim at the 5% level of significance? (It can be assumed that the yield per plant is normally distributed.)

This is a one tailed test, since the claim is that the yield should be *at least* 4 kg. The null and alternative hypotheses are therefore:

$$H_0 : \mu = 4\text{kg} \quad H_1 : \mu < 4\text{kg}$$

(The alternative hypothesis is less than 4 kg because the gardening magazine is attempting to disprove the claim.)

The critical value on 7 degrees of freedom at a significance level of 5% for a one tailed test is -1.895. (This figure was obtained from the t-table in the Appendix.)

Estimates of the mean and standard deviation of the yield from this sample are:

$$\bar{x} = 3.74 \quad s = 0.8466$$

$$\text{and} \quad \text{SEM} = \frac{0.8466}{\sqrt{8}}$$

$$= 0.2993$$

The test statistic is therefore:

$$t = \frac{3.74 - 4}{0.2993}$$

$$= -0.869$$

Since -0.869 is *greater* than -1.895, you cannot reject H_0. (You may find it easier to ignore the negative signs and just compare 0.869 with 1.895, in which case 0.869 is *less* than 1.895.) Alternatively, you could draw a diagram as shown in Figure 9.6.

This diagram confirms that the test statistic is not in the critical region, and therefore it is not possible to reject H_0. That is, it hasn t been possible to disprove the grower's claim.

NOTE: In practice the *experimental design* for this example would be a little more involved than has been suggested here.

Figure 9.6 Diagram for Activity 9.4

The Z-test for a population percentage

Testing a sample percentage against some expected or hypothesized value (π) is another important test. The test given here is based on the assumption that n is large and π is not too large or too small.

The standard error of the sampling distribution of a percentage (SEP) was given in Chapter 8 as:

$$\sqrt{\frac{P(100 - P)}{n}}$$

where P is the sample percentage.

However, for hypothesis testing it is the population parameter, π, that must be used. With this substitution, the equation for STEP becomes:

$$\text{SEP} = \sqrt{\frac{\pi(100 - \pi)}{n}}$$

The Z statistic is similar to that used for the test on a mean and is:

$$Z = \frac{P - \pi}{\text{SEP}}$$

The following activity illustrates how the test would be carried out.

---

activity 9.5

A trade union is considering strike action and intends to ballot its large membership on the issue. In order to gauge the likely result of the ballot, a survey was conducted among a random sample of members. Of the 60 people surveyed, 36 were in favour of a strike. Would the ballot give the required simple majority for a strike?

For a strike to be called, at least 50% of the membership must agree. Anything less would not be good enough. The null and alternative hypotheses should therefore be:

$$H_0: \pi = 50\% \quad H_0: \pi > 50\%$$

The cut-off point for the decision is 50% and the test will determine whether the sample percentage (P) of $\dfrac{36}{60} \times 100 = 60\%$ is significantly *greater* than 50%.

The critical value for a one tailed test at the 5% level is 1.645.
So:

$$SEP = \sqrt{\dfrac{50 \times (100 - 50)}{60}}$$
$$= 6.455$$

and the test statistic is:

$$Z = \dfrac{60 - 50}{6.455}$$
$$= 1.549$$

Since 1.549 is less than 1.645, H_0 cannot be rejected. That is, it appears that there may not be a majority for strike action. However, the critical value and test statistic are quite close, and therefore the result is hardly conclusive. (Don't forget that the survey result is only a 'snapshot' of people's opinion at one instant in time. Some people may not have been entirely honest with their answers and others may change their opinion before the ballot.)

Figure 9.7 confirms that the test statistic is just inside the acceptance region.

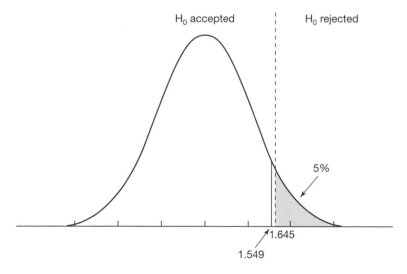

Figure 9.7 Diagram for Activity 9.5

Hypothesis tests involving two population means

The tests we have looked at so far are for a single sample. In many situations we may have collected two samples and we want to test to see if the two population means are the same. As in the single sample case we have different tests for large and small samples. We also have another factor to consider: are the samples independent of each other or not? Samples that are independent mean that the measurements of one sample are not influenced by the second sample. In some situations, once we have (randomly) chosen the members of the first sample the members of the second sample will not be independent. For example, you might want to compare the reading ability of children before and after following a reading programme. The reading scores of a group of children represent the first sample and the second sample is represented by the reading scores of the *same* children at the end of the reading programme. The second sample is therefore related to the first sample by the identity of the child. There are good reasons why you should use this *paired* approach but it requires a test that doesn't demand independence. The mathematics involved in applying all these tests are more complicated than for the single sample case and the use of statistical software such as SPSS is recommended. However, although SPSS is better, it is also possible to use Excel to carry out some of the tests.

Large sample tests for two independent population means

We normally wish to set up the null hypothesis that the difference in the means of the two populations will be zero; that is:

$$H_0 : \mu_1 - \mu_2 = 0$$

The alternative hypothesis can be either one or two tailed. That is:

$$H_1 : \mu_1 - \mu_2 \neq 0 \text{ for a two sided test, and}$$

$$H_1 : \mu_1 > \mu_2 \text{ or } \mu_1 < \mu_2 \text{ for a one sided test.}$$

For a large sample we can assume that the difference between the means of the two sampling distributions is normally distributed with a mean equal to the difference of the population means and a standard error of:

$$\sigma_{(\bar{x}_1 - \bar{x}_2)} = \sqrt{\left(\frac{\sigma_1^2}{n_1} + \frac{\sigma_2^2}{n_2} \right)}$$

As in the single sample case, the population standard deviations are required, but provided that each sample size (n_1 and n_2) is at least 30 we can use the estimate given by the samples as an approximation.

The test statistic will be

$$Z = \frac{(\bar{x}_1 - \bar{x}_2) - (\mu_1 - \mu_2)}{\sigma_{(\bar{x}_1 - \bar{x}_2)}}$$

activity
9.6

A high street store was interested in discovering whether credit card customers spent more or less than cash customers. A random sample of 50 credit card customers were found to have spent £55.30 on average with a standard deviation of £18.45, while a random sample of 40 cash customers were found to have spent £52.75 on average with a standard deviation of £17.22. Is there any evidence at the 5% significance level that there is any difference between the mean amounts spent by the two types of customers?

This is a two tailed test and the null and alternative hypotheses will be:

$$H_0 : \mu_1 - \mu_2 = 0 \quad H_1 : \mu_1 - \mu_2 \neq 0$$

The standard error will be $\sqrt{\left(\dfrac{18.45^2}{50} + \dfrac{17.22^2}{40}\right)} = 3.7711$

and the test statistic will be $\dfrac{(55.30 - 52.75) - 0}{3.7711} = 0.676$

Since this is less than 1.96 we cannot reject H_0 and must conclude that there is no evidence to suggest that credit card customers spend more or less than cash customers.

Small sample tests for two independent population means

Just as in the single sample case we need to use the t-distribution instead of the normal. Both populations from which the samples have been taken should be approximately normally distributed with equal variances (variance is the square of the standard deviation). If the conditions of normality cannot be met it is possible to use *non-parametric* tests, details of which can be found in McClave and Sincich (2013). A modified test is available if the equality of variance cannot be assumed. The standard error for the small sample case is slightly different from that for large samples. It is:

$$\sigma_{(x_1 - x_2)} = \hat{\sigma}\sqrt{\left(\frac{1}{n_1} + \frac{1}{n_2}\right)}$$

where $\hat{\sigma}$ is the estimate of the *pooled* standard deviation of the populations and is given by:

$$\hat{\sigma} = \sqrt{\frac{(n_1 - 1)s_1^2 + (n_2 - 1)s_2^2}{n_1 + n_2 - 2}}$$

The test statistic is given by:

$$t = \frac{(\bar{x}_1 - \bar{x}_2) - (\mu_1 - \mu_2)}{\sigma_{(\bar{x}_1 - \bar{x}_2)}}$$

The critical value at a particular significance level and $(n_1 + n_2 - 2)$ degrees of freedom can be found from t-tables (see Appendix).

activity
9.7

A health magazine has decided to test the claim of the makers of a new slimming pill that has just come on the market. The company claims that the pill will allow people to lose weight if taken daily. The health magazine obtained a sample of 14 people who agreed to take the pill for a month. This group was split into two, a sample of 8 who would be given the slimming pill and a control group of 6 who would (unknown to them) be given a placebo (a fake slimming pill). The weight change at the end of the month is given in Table 9.1 where a minus indicates a loss of weight and a positive figure indicates a gain in weight.

Table 9.1 Weight change (in lbs) data for Activity 9.7

Sample 1	Sample 2 (control group)
-2	-2
-6	5
3	-5
-10	8
0	4
2	0
-4	
-9	

It would of course be possible to apply the single sample test on the sample of 8 people to see if the mean weight change is different to zero. However, the use of a control group is quite common in medical research as it allows unknown factors such as people's 'belief' in a product to be taken into account.

If we assume that the health magazine is not biased in its opinion of the pill, this is a two tailed test and the null and alternative hypotheses will be:

$$H_0 : \mu_1 - \mu_2 = 0 \quad H_1 : \mu_1 - \mu_2 \neq 0$$

The mean and standard deviation for sample 1 are −3.25 and 4.862, respectively. The equivalent figures for the control group are 0.833 and 4.579, respectively. The pooled standard deviation is therefore:

$$\hat{\sigma} = \sqrt{\frac{(8-1)4.862^2 + (6-1)4.579^2}{8+6-2}}$$
$$= 4.746$$

and the standard error is

$$4.746\sqrt{\frac{1}{8} + \frac{1}{6}} = 2.563$$

The test statistic is:

$$t = \frac{(-3.25 - 0.833) - 0}{2.563}$$
$$= -1.593$$

The critical value on 12 degrees of freedom at 5% significance level is -2.179. As the test statistic is greater than this value we cannot reject H_0, so we conclude that there is no evidence that the slimming pill has any effect on weight change.

This test could be performed either in Excel or in SPSS, but SPSS is far superior to Excel when it comes to tests of hypotheses. To carry out the test you need to put your data in one column, which has been called 'Weight'. The next column, called 'Group', tells SPSS which group each of the weight values is in. Value 1 is for sample 1 and 2 for sample 2 (see Chapter 4 for the way that SPSS organizes data). The t-test can be found in the `Compare Means` under the `Analyze` main menu. The test you want is the `Independent Samples T-Test` (see Figure 9.8). Add 'Weight' as your test variable and `Group` as your grouping variable (see Figure 9.9). Then click `OK`. The output you get is shown in Figure 9.10.

SPSS first checks whether the variances of the two samples are equal. As they are, we only need look at the top row of the table. The t-value of -1.593 agrees with our calculated value. The `Sig (2-tailed)` is 0.137: this is the probability of obtaining a test statistic at least as extreme as the one obtained. It is the area in the tail or tails of the distribution for this value of the test statistic. This probability is often called the *observed significance level* or *p-value*. If we were testing at the 5% (0.05) level, then a *p*-value less than this figure would be significant and we would reject the null hypothesis. However, in our case 13.7% is greater than 5%, so we cannot reject H_0. The `Confidence Interval` of the difference is also given, and as this straddles zero it again confirms that there is no difference in means.

Figure 9.8 Independent samples *t*-test using SPSS

Grouping variable defines
the sample. Click Define
Groups to specify 1 or 2

Figure 9.9 Setting up the test in SPSS
Reprint courtesy of International Business Machines Corporation, © International Business Machines
Corporation.

Independent Samples Test

		Levene's Test for Equality of Variances		t-test for Equality of Means						
									95% Confidence Interval of the Difference	
		F	Sig.	t	df	Sig. (2-tailed)	Mean Difference	Std. Error Difference	Lower	Upper
Weight	Equal variances assumed	.178	.680	-1.593	12	.137	-4.083	2.563	-9.668	1.502
	Equal variances not assumed			-1.608	11.274	.135	-4.083	2.540	-9.657	1.490

Variances are equal   *t* value   Significance level is >0.05

Figure 9.10 SPSS output
Reprint courtesy of International Business Machines Corporation, © International Business Machines Corporation.

Paired samples

We have already mentioned that the two-sample t-test is only valid when the two samples are independent. In many cases this assumption is not valid as the data is *paired*; that is, each observation of one sample is paired with an observation in the other sample. This can occur if identical conditions apply to pairs of observations. The null hypothesis is that the *difference* of the population means, μ_d, is zero and the alternative hypothesis can be either one or two tailed, depending on whether we

DID YOU KNOW?

A statistical significant result does not always mean practical significance. For example in clinical trials a result may be significant because of the (large) size of the sample but from a clinical point of view it doesn't prove its clinical superiority over an existing drug or procedure. Conversely an insignificant result in a small sample might in fact be of clinical importance. It is important to consider the context in which a statistical test is carried out.

Source: 'Trial and Error. How to Avoid Commonly Encountered Limitations of Published Clinical Trials', Sanjay Kaul, MD, George A. Diamond, MD. *Journal of the American College of Cardiology*, Vol. 55, No. 5, 2010.

http://www.straightstatistics.org/article/trial-and-error-perils-p-value

believe the difference could be positive, negative or not equal to zero. The test statistic for this test is:

$$t = \frac{\overline{x}_d - \mu_d}{\sigma_{\overline{d}}}$$

where $\overline{x}_d$ is the sample mean of the n differences and μ_d is the population mean difference if the null hypothesis is correct (usually zero). $\sigma_{\overline{d}}$ is the standard error of the differences and is given by:

$$\sigma_d = \frac{s_d}{\sqrt{n}}$$

where s_d is the standard deviation of the differences.

(*activity* **9.8**) A publishing company has developed a new reading scheme that is supposed to improve the reading ability of children. In order to be able to justify its claim, 12 children were first given a standardized reading test before taking part in the programme. At the end of the programme they were tested again. The test scores before and after the programme can be found in Table 9.2. Does this data support the company's claim?

Table 9.2 Test scores for Activity 9.8

Child	Before	After	Difference
A	110	108	−2
B	121	122	1
C	95	98	3
D	80	90	10
E	130	132	2
F	100	105	5
G	105	105	0
H	85	90	5
I	95	96	1
J	100	98	−2
K	82	85	3
L	135	132	−3

The data are not independent because each member of the 'before' sample is related to a member of the 'after' sample by the attributes of the child. The advantage of this design is that it only looks at the differences between each child; it ignores the variation between children, which could be large. If the reading programme had had no effect you would expect the true average difference in test scores to be zero. The null hypothesis is therefore:

$$H_0 : \mu_d = 0$$

The alternative hypothesis is one tailed because we are testing to see if the programme improves reading ability (it is unlikely to make it worse), so:

$$H_1 : \mu_d > 0$$

The differences (after-before) can be found in Table 9.2, and the mean of the differences is 1.92 with a standard deviation of 3.655. The standard error of the differences is:

$$\sigma_{\bar{d}} = \frac{3.655}{\sqrt{12}}$$
$$= 1.055$$

and the test statistic is:

$$t = \frac{1.92 - 0}{1.055}$$
$$= 1.820$$

The critical value of t at the 5% significance level and on 11 (12 − 1) degrees of freedom is 1.796. We can therefore reject H_0 at the 5% significance level and conclude that there is some evidence that the new reading programme does increase reading ability as represented by the testing method. Of course, a child's reading ability may

Figure 9.11 Setting up the paired t-test in SPSS
Reprint courtesy of International Business Machines Corporation, © International Business Machines Corporation.

p value for two tailed test

		Mean	Std. Deviation	Std. Error Mean	95% Confidence Interval of the Difference Lower	95% Confidence Interval of the Difference Upper	t	df	Sig. (2-tailed)
Pair 1	Before - After	-1.917	3.655	1.055	-4.239	.405	-1.817	11	.097

Paired Samples Test / Paired Differences

Figure 9.12 Output for the paired *t*-test
Reprint courtesy of International Business Machines Corporation, © International Business Machines Corporation.

well have increased without following the programme, so in practice a control group would be involved in the *experimental design*.

The paired *t*-test can be performed using SPSS and again it can be found under `Compare Means (Paired Samples T-Test)`. Figures 9.11 and 9.12 give the relevant screen shots. The *p*-value for a two tailed test is 0.097, so for a one tailed test it will be half this, which is 0.048. As this is less than 0.05, H_0 is rejected. It is interesting to note here that had our alternative hypothesis been two sided ($\mu_d \neq 0$), then we would not have rejected H_0.

Hypothesis tests involving two population percentages

As well as conducting tests between two means it is possible to conduct tests between two percentages. Provided the sample sizes are large, the difference between the two percentages ($\pi_1 - \pi_2$) will be normally distributed. The null hypothesis will be:

$$H_0 : \pi_1 - \pi_2 = 0$$

and H_1 can be either one or two sided.

The standard error of the differences between the two percentages is:

$$\sigma_{(P_1 - P_2)} = \sqrt{\hat{P}(100 - \hat{P})\left(\frac{1}{n_1} + \frac{1}{n_2}\right)}$$

where $\hat{P}$ is the estimate of the population percentage and is given by:

$$\hat{P} = \frac{n_1 P_1 + n_2 P_2}{n_1 + n_2}$$

P_1 and P_2 refer to the two sample percentage.

The test statistic is:

$$Z = \frac{(P_1 - P_2) - (\pi_1 - \pi_2)}{\sigma_{(P_1 - P_2)}}$$

activity
9.9

A top hairdresser has just opened two hairdressing salons in a large town and he is interested in whether there are any differences in the type of customers who use these two salons. During one month a random sample of customers at both salons were asked to complete a questionnaire. From the analysis of the questionnaire it was discovered that out of 200 customers at Top Cuts, 56 were under the age of 25. At Smart Cuts, 54 out of 150 were in this age bracket. Is there any difference in the percentage of under 25s at the two salons?

This is a two tailed test and the null and alternative hypotheses are:

$$H_0: \pi_1 - \pi_2 = 0 \quad H_1: \pi_1 - \pi_2 \neq 0$$

$$P_1 = \frac{56}{200} \times 100 \quad P_2 = \frac{54}{150} \times 100$$

$$= 28\% \qquad\qquad = 36\%$$

So:

$$\hat{P} = \frac{200 \times 28 + 150 \times 36}{200 + 150}$$

$$= 31.4\%$$

The standard error of the differences is:

$$\sigma_{(P_1 - P_2)} = \sqrt{31.4(100 - 31.4)\left(\frac{1}{200} + \frac{1}{150}\right)}$$

$$= 5.013$$

The test statistic is:

$$Z = \frac{(28 - 36) - 0}{5.013}$$

$$= -1.596$$

As this is greater than -1.96 we cannot reject H_0 and therefore conclude that there is no evidence to suggest that the percentage of customers in the under 25 age group is different in the two salons.

The chi-square hypothesis test

All the tests discussed so far in this chapter are called *parametric* tests in that they are testing a parameter (either the mean or proportion). However, there are also *non-parametric* tests and the text by McClave and Sincich (2013) contains many tests in this category. Perhaps the most useful non-parametric test is the chi-square test and there are two forms of this test. The first form, called the '*goodness of fit test*', tests to see if the data fits some distribution. The second form of the test is called the *test of association* and tests to see if there is any association between categories in a two-way table. For both forms of the test you have to count the number of data items that are observed to be in a particular category. The test statistic is calculated using the following formula:

$$\sum \frac{(O - E)^2}{E}$$

where O represents the observed count and E represents the expected count. The formula simply says: 'Find the difference between the observed and expected frequency of one category, square this value to remove any negative signs and then divide by the expected frequency for that category. Repeat this for all categories and sum the individual answers.'

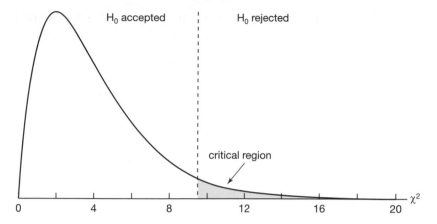

Figure 9.13 The chi-square distribution on 4 degrees of freedom

This test statistic follows the χ^2 distribution (pronounced *chi-square*). The shape of this distribution depends on the degrees of freedom of the data. For example, for 4 degrees of freedom you would get the shape shown in Figure 9.13.

The area under the curve is again 1, but only one tail is used for the critical region - the upper tail. The area representing 5% has been indicated, and H_0 would be rejected if the test statistic was in this region.

The critical value of χ^2 is found from the χ^2 table that you will find in the Appendix. For example, the critical value on 4 degrees of freedom at the 5% (0.05) significance level is 9.488. The test statistic follows the χ^2 distribution providing the expected values are not too small. We normally consider anything below 5 to be too small and if this occurs it is necessary to combine categories until this minimum number is achieved. We will meet this situation in Activity 9.11.

The 'goodness of fit' test

Suppose you threw a six-sided die 36 times. You would *expect* the faces numbered 1 to 6 to appear the same number of times; that is, 6. However, you might *observe* a rather different frequency.

> *activity*
> **9.10**

Try this experiment for yourself and record the number of times each face appeared.

Suppose you got the following:

Face	1	2	3	4	5	6
Frequency	4	6	9	5	4	8

Is your observed frequency due to chance effects or does it indicate that the die is biased in any way? (In this example, face 3 occurs most.) The null hypothesis is that the die is fair and the alternate hypothesis is that it is biased; that is:

H_0: die is fair H_1 : die is biased

Since the sum of the frequencies is fixed, you are 'free' to choose 5 of them; therefore the degrees of freedom is 5. From the χ^2 table, the critical value on 5 degrees of freedom and at the 5% significance level is 11.070. If the test statistic is greater than this value, H_0 will be rejected.

To calculate the χ^2 statistic you need to subtract the observed values from 6, square the result and then divide by 6. This calculation is shown in Table 9.3.

Table 9.3 Chi-square calculation for Activity 9.10

O	E	(O − E)	(O − E)²	$\dfrac{(O - E)^2}{E}$
4	6	−2	4	0.667
6	6	0	0	0.000
9	6	3	9	1.500
5	6	−1	1	0.167
4	6	−2	4	0.667
8	6	2	4	0.667
			Sum	3.668

The sum of these values is 3.668 and this is compared with the critical value of 11.070. H_0 cannot be rejected and you would have to assume that the die was fair. The diagram in Figure 9.14 demonstrates that the test statistic is not in the critical region.

Figure 9.14 Diagram for Activity 9.10

(activity 9.11) The *Quantitative methods in action* case in Chapter 7 used the goals scored in the 2014 football World Cup as an example of a Poisson distribution. In that chapter we used the Poisson distribution to calculate the expected number of times 0, 1, 2… goals were scored. The result of this calculation is repeated in Table 9.4. Use the chi-square test (at the 5% level of significance) to see if actual data does fit a Poisson distribution, that is goals scored are random.

Table 9.4 Using the Poisson distribution on goals scored

Goals	Probability	Expected	Actual
0	0.0707	4.52	7
1	0.1872	11.98	12
2	0.2481	15.88	9
3	0.2191	14.02	19
4	0.1452	9.29	9
5	0.0769	4.92	4
6	0.0340	2.17	2
7	0.0129	0.82	1
8	0.0043	0.27	1
9 or more	0.0017	0.11	0
Sum		64.0	64

Combine the last 5 goal categories as expected values are less than 5.

Our hypothesis is that the data follows a Poisson distribution, so H_0 and H_1 will be:

H_0: The goals scored follow a Poisson distribution.
H_1: The goals scored do not follow a Poisson distribution.

Before we set up the chi-square test, we should note that the expected values of 5, 6, 7, 8 and 9 or more goals are below 5, so we should combine these categories to give us an expected value of 8.29 (4.92 + 2.17 + 0.82 + 0.27 + 0.11) and actual of 8 (4 + 2 + 1 + 1 + 0). We set up the chi-square test in the normal way, and we get a test statistic of 0.807 (see Table 9.5).

Table 9.5 Chi Square calculation for Activity 9.11

Goals	O	E	(O − E)	(O − E)²	$\dfrac{(O - E)^2}{E}$
0	7	4.52	2.48	6.15	1.361
1	12	11.98	0.02	0.00	0.000
2	9	15.88	−6.88	47.33	2.980
3	19	14.02	4.98	24.80	1.769
4	9	9.29	−0.29	0.08	0.009
5 or more	8	8.29	−0.29	0.08	0.010
				Sum	6.129

As we have 6 categories and we have to estimate the mean for the Poisson distribution, the degrees of freedom is $6 - 1 - 1 = 4$. The critical value at a significance level of 5% with 4 degrees of freedom is 9.488, and as the test statistic is below this, we cannot reject the null hypothesis. We therefore conclude that the goals scored do follow a Poisson distribution and the number of goals scored is random.

The test of association

example 9.1

The Personnel Manager of a company believes that monthly paid staff take more time off work through sickness than those staff who are paid weekly (and do not belong to the company sickness scheme). To test this theory, the sickness records for 561 randomly selected employees who have been in continuous employment for the past year were analyzed. Table 9.6 was produced, which placed employees into 3 categories according to how many days they were off work through sickness during the past year. For example, 95 monthly paid employees were off sick for less than 5 days.

Table 9.6 Number of days off sick by type of employee

Type of employee	Number of days off sick		
	Less than 5 days	5 to 10 days	More than 10 days
Monthly paid	95	47	18
Weekly paid	143	146	112

activity **9.12**

Is there any association between type of employee and numbers of days off sick?

Table 9.6 is a *contingency table.* The null and alternative hypotheses are:

H_0 : There is no association between type of employee and number of days off sick.
H_1 : There is an association between type of employee and number of days off sick.

In order to calculate the χ^2 test statistic it is necessary to determine the expected values for each category. To do this you first have to work out the row and column totals, as shown in Table 9.7.

Table 9.7 Table for Activity 9.12

Type of employee	Number of days off sick			Total
	Less than 5 days	5 to 10 days	More than 10 days	
Monthly paid	95	47	18	160
Weekly paid	143	146	112	401
Total	238	193	130	561

You now need to apply some basic ideas of probability (see Chapter 6) to the problem. If an employee were chosen at random, the probability that he or she was monthly paid would be $\frac{160}{561}$ and the probability that he or she would have been off sick for less than 5 days is $\frac{238}{561}$. Therefore, using the multiplication rule for two probabilities, the probability that the person is both monthly paid *and* in the 'less than 5 days' category is $\frac{160}{561} \times \frac{238}{561}$. Since there are 561 employees in total, the *expected* number of employees with both these attributes is

$$\frac{160}{561} \times \frac{238}{561} \times 561$$

$$= \frac{160 \times 238}{561}$$

$$= 67.9$$

This could be written as:

$$\text{Expected value} = \frac{\text{Row Total} \times \text{Column Total}}{\text{Grand Total}}$$

and is applicable for all cells of a contingency table. The rest of the expected values can now be worked out and a table set up similar to the one used for the 'goodness of fit' test (Table 9.8).

Table 9.8 Calculation of the chi-square test statistics

O	E	(O – E)	(O – E)²	$\frac{(O - E)^2}{E}$
95	67.9	27.1	734.41	10.816
47	55.0	–8.0	64.00	1.164
18	37.1	–19.1	364.81	9.833
143	170.1	–27.1	734.41	4.318
146	138.0	8.0	64.00	0.464
112	92.9	19.1	364.81	3.927
			Sum	30.522

The sum of the χ^2 values is 30.522, and this is the test statistic for this problem. The critical value depends on the degrees of freedom of this table. As you know, degrees of freedom relates to the number of values that you are free to choose. If, for example, you chose the value for the top left hand cell in Table 9.7, the bottom left hand cell is determined since the two cells must add to 238. Likewise, you could choose the next cell along, but then all other cells are determined for you. So, for this problem, there are 2 degrees of freedom. Fortunately, there is a formula for calculating the degrees of freedom which is:

(number of columns − 1) × (number of rows − 1)

In Table 9.7, there are 3 columns (excluding the total column) and 2 rows, so the degrees of freedom are:

$(3 - 1) \times (2 - 1) = 2$

The critical value for 2 degrees of freedom at the 5% significance level is 5.991, and at the 0.1% significance level it is 13.815. Therefore, since the test statistic is greater than 13.815, H_0 can be rejected at the 0.1% significance level, and you could conclude that there does seem to be an association between staff category and the number of days off sick.

It is possible to be more specific about this association by looking at the individual χ^2 values and also the (O − E) column. The two largest χ^2 values are 10.816 and 9.883. These both relate to the monthly paid staff, which suggests that this group of employees has a higher frequency in the 'less than 5 days category' than expected, but a lower frequency in the 'more than 10 days' category.

(activity 9.13) A survey is regularly carried out on mobile phone usage and Table 9.9 is one example from Northern Ireland.

Is there any association between gender and whether a driver is using a mobile phone?

Table 9.9 The percentage of drivers observed using a mobile phone by gender

All cars	Type of phone			
	Hand-held	Hands-free	Neither	Total
Base = 100	%	%	%	Count
Male	1.3	0.4	98.3	10 068
Female	0.5	0.4	99.1	6 976
Total	1.0	0.4	98.6	17 044

Source: The Continuous Household Survey, Northern Ireland Statistics and Research Unit.

The null and alternative hypotheses are:

H_0: There is no association between gender and whether a driver uses a mobile phone.

H_1: There is an association between gender and whether a driver uses a mobile phone.

Rather than do another manual calculation, we will look at how we can use Excel to carry out the test. The first thing we must do is to convert the data to *counts* rather than *percentages*. This is easily done as the total counts are provided. However, because the percentages in the original table had been rounded, the counts might give fractional values. To prevent this happening, Excel's ROUND function is used. For example, the formula for 'male' and 'handheld' is =ROUND((C4*$F$4/100),0).

The spreadsheet containing the calculations is shown in Figures 9.15 and 9.16, and can also be found on the companion website.

The number of degrees of freedom is $(3 − 1) \times (2 − 1) = 2$.

The critical value for 2 degrees of freedom is 5.991 (as in the previous activity).

The test statistic of 27.31 is greater than the critical value, so the null hypothesis is rejected – the results show that there *is* an association between gender and whether drivers use a mobile phone. If you look at the table closely, in fact, you can see that females are much less likely than males to use a mobile phone while driving.

SPSS and the chi-square test

SPSS has a routine called Crosstabs which can create a contingency table from raw data and calculate various inferential test statistics, including the chi-square statistic. To demonstrate the use of Crosstabs we will use the samples of anonymized individual records (SARs) from the 2001 census (see census.ukdataservice.ac.uk). The census collects data on every individual in the UK: it asks questions on gender, health, employment, housing and ethic origin, to name just a few. Datasets from the census are extremely large (with millions of records) and are therefore difficult to handle.

▲	A	B	C	D	E	F	G
1							
2				Table of percentages			
3			Hand-held	Hands-free	Neither	Total	
4		Male	1.3	0.4	98.3	10068	
5		Female	0.5	0.4	99.1	6976	
6		Total	1	0.4	98.6	17044	
7							
8							
9				Counts			
10			Hand-held	Hands-free	Neither	Total	
11		Male	131	40	9897	10068	
12		Female	35	28	6913	6976	
13		Total	166	68	16810	17044	
14							
15							
16			Chi-Square calculations				
17		Observed	Expected	O-E	(O-E)^2	(O_E)^2/E	
18		131	98.06	32.94	1085.044	11.07	
19		40	40.17	-0.17	0.03	0.00	
20		9897	9929.77	-32.77	1074.18	0.11	
21		35	67.94	-32.94	1085.22	15.97	
22		28	27.83	0.17	0.03	0.00	
23		6913	6880.23	32.77	1074.18	0.16	
24					Total	27.31	
25							

Figure 9.15 Spreadsheet for Activity 9.13
Used with permission from Microsoft.

Table of percentages

	Hand-held	Hands-free	Neither	Total
Male	1.3	0.4	98.3	10068
Female	0.5	0.4	99.1	6976
Total	1	0.4	98.6	=SUM(F4:F5)

Counts

	Hand-held	Hands-free	Neither	Total
Male	=ROUND((C4*$F$4/100),0)	=ROUND((D4*$F$11/100),0)	=ROUND((E4*$F$11/100),0)	10068
Female	=ROUND((C5*$F$12/100),0)	=ROUND((D5*$F$12/100),0)	=ROUND((E5*$F$12/100),0)	6976
Total	=SUM(C11:C12)	=SUM(D11:D12)	=SUM(E11:E12)	=SUM(F11:F12)

Table of percentages

Observed	Expected	O-E	(O-E)^2	(O-E)^2/E
=C11	=$F11*C13/$F$13	=B18-C18	=D18^2	=E18/C18
=D11	=$F11*D13/$F$13	=B19-C19	=D19^2	=E19/C19
=E11	=$F11*E13/$F$13	=B20-C20	=D20^2	=E20/C20
=C12	=$F12*C13/$F$13	=B21-C21	=D21^2	=E21/C21
=D12	=$F12*D13/$F$13	=B22-C22	=D22^2	=E22/C22
=E12	=$F12*E13/$F$13	=B23-C23	=D23^2	=E23/C23

Figure 9.16 Excel formulae for Activity 9.13
Used with permission from Microsoft.

The SARS dataset is a sample from the census: while still very large (1 843 525 records), it can easily be handled with SPSS. To demonstrate the use of `Crosstabs` in SPSS we will attempt to see whether there is an association between distance to work and gender.

The null and alternative hypotheses are:

H_0: There is no association between distance to work and gender.
H_1: There is an association between distance to work and gender.

The `Crosstabs` routine is found within the `Analysis/Descriptive` statistics menu, as you can see in Figure 9.17. If you click on `Crosstabs` you get the dialog boxes shown in Figure 9.18 and Figure 9.19. In the `Cell display` we will request the observed and expected counts (frequencies), percentage by `Column`, and `Unstandardized` and `Adjusted standardized` residuals. The `Unstandardized` residuals are simply the difference between the observed and expected counts (O – E). The `Adjusted standardized` residuals are similar to the $(O – E)^2/E$ statistic we calculated before. This statistic is used when H_0 is rejected, as any cell with a value outside the range of −2 to 2 could be the possible reason for the rejection.

The `Statistic` dialog box allows you to request particular inferential statistics. The `Chi-square` is the obvious one, but the other statistic to request is `Phi and Cramer's V`. Statisticians prefer these other two statistics as the chi-square statistic is influenced by the sample size; as the sample size increases, so does the value of the chi-square statistic. The absolute value of both Phi and Cramer's V statistic varies between 0 and 1, with 0 representing no association and 1 perfect association.

Both the `Statistics` and `Cell Display` dialog boxes are closed by clicking on `Continue`. The `Crosstabs` routine is executed by clicking on `OK`. Part of the contingency table output is shown in Figure 9.20; the statistical output is shown in Figure 9.21.

Figure 9.17 The SARS data and the `Crosstabs` routine
Reprint courtesy of International Business Machines Corporation, © International Business Machines Corporation.

Click on Statistics and cells

Figure 9.18 Crosstabs routine with cell display
Reprint courtesy of International Business Machines Corporation, © International Business Machines Corporation.

Figure 9.19 Crosstabs routine with statistics display
Reprint courtesy of International Business Machines Corporation, © International Business Machines Corporation.

You will see from Figure 9.21 that all the significance levels (or *p*-values) are zero. In fact the zero really means 'less than 0.001', which is highly significant. H_0 is rejected and we conclude that there *is* an association between distance to work and gender. If you look at Figure 9.20, in fact, you will see that the largest adjusted standardized residuals are for less than 2 km and over 40 km. From this table you should be able

More women in this category

Distance to Work (including study in Scotland) * Sex Crosstabulation					
			Sex		
			Male	Female	Total
Distance to Work (including study in Scotland)	less than 2km	Count	79618	106159	185777
		Expected Count	100083.2	85693.8	185777.0
		% within Sex	17.2%	26.8%	21.7%
		Residual	-20465.2	20465.2	
		Adjusted Residual	-107.6	107.6	
	2km to less than 5km	Count	80343	88534	168877
		Expected Count	90978.7	77898.3	168877.0
		% within Sex	17.4%	22.4%	19.7%
		Residual	-10635.7	10635.7	
		Adjusted Residual	-57.9	57.9	
	5km to less than 10km	Count	78749	72892	151641
		Expected Count	81693.2	69947.8	151641.0
		% within Sex	17.0%	18.4%	17.7%
		Residual	-2944.2	2944.2	
		Adjusted Residual	-16.7	16.7	
	10km to less than 20km	Count	73130	54519	127649
		Expected Count	68768.0	58881.0	127649.0
		% within Sex	15.8%	13.8%	14.9%
		Residual	4362.0	-4362.0	
		Adjusted Residual	26.5	-26.5	
	20km to less than 40km	Count	42131	23850	65981
		Expected Count	35545.8	30435.2	65981.0
		% within Sex	9.1%	6.0%	7.7%
		Residual	6585.2	-6585.2	
		Adjusted Residual	53.5	-53.5	
	40km and over	Count	28202	11179	39381
		Expected Count	21215.6	18165.4	39381.0
		% within Sex	6.1%	2.8%	4.6%
		Residual	6986.4	-6986.4	
		Adjusted Residual	72.3	-72.3	
	at home	Count	45025	30624	75649

Observed frequency   Difference between observed and expected   Adjusted residual gives information on form of association   More men in this category

Figure 9.20 Part of the `Crosstabs output`
Reprint courtesy of International Business Machines Corporation, © International Business Machines Corporation.

to conclude that men travel further to work than women. However, both Phi and Cramer's V statistics are only 0.2, which does not suggest a very strong association.

The chi-square test for association is a very important and useful test in the area of statistics in particular, and decision-making in general. However, there are a couple of problems that you need to be aware of.

Two by two tables

The χ^2 distribution is a continuous distribution, whereas the sample data is discrete. Normally the sample size is sufficient to avoid making a continuity correction, but this will be needed for 2×2 tables. The correction required is to *subtract* 0.5 from the *absolute* value of the difference between the observed and expected values. For example, if the difference was −2.7, the corrected value would be −2.2 (not −3.2).

Chi-Square Tests

	Value	df	Asymp. Sig. (2-sided)
Pearson Chi-Square	34440.792[a]	10	.000
Likelihood Ratio	35964.794	10	.000
Linear-by-Linear Association	29350.732	1	.000
N of Valid Cases	857649		

a. 0 cells (0.0%) have expected count less than 5. The minimum expected count is 24.45.

p values

Symmetric Measures

		Value	Approx. Sig.
Nominal by Nominal	Phi	.200	.000
	Cramer's V	.200	.000
N of Valid Cases		857649	

Figure 9.21 Statistical output from `Crosstabs`
Reprint courtesy of International Business Machines Corporation, © International Business Machines Corporation.

Tables of percentages

The χ^2 test is applied to tables of frequencies, *not* percentages. If you are given a table of percentages you will need to convert it to frequencies by multiplying each percentage by the total frequency. If you are not given the total frequency then it is not possible to use this test.

Reflection

Hypothesis testing is another very important statistical concept. Without being able to test ideas in a scientific manner, we would never be confident, for example, that a new drug or procedure was a significant improvement on a previous one.

Hypothesis testing originated from work carried out in the 1930s and 1940s by three famous statisticians, R.A. Fisher, J. Neyman and E. Pearson. The approach by Fisher was different from those of Neyman and Pearson, and resulted in quite heated debates in academic journals. Even today argument still rages on the reliance on arbitrary significance levels, and a few statisticians believe that conventional hypothesis testing should be abandoned in favour of probability values based on some *a priori* expectation of results. Most statistical software, including SPSS, gives p-values, which can be more helpful than test statistics and critical values.

Whenever you do hypothesis tests, be careful about 'accepting' the null hypothesis. John Tukey (1991) gives the following good reason why it is dangerous to accept a null hypothesis:

> Statisticians classically asked the wrong questions – and were willing to answer with a lie, one that was often a downright lie. They asked 'Are the effects of A and B different?' and they were willing to answer 'no.'
>
> All we know about the world teaches us that the effects of A and B are always different – in some decimal place – for any A and B. Thus asking 'Are the effects different?' is foolish.
>
> What we should be answering first is 'Can we tell the direction in which the effects of A differ from the effects of B?' In other words, can we be confident about the direction from A to B? Is it 'up,' 'down' or 'uncertain'?
>
> If the third answer to this first question is that we are 'uncertain about the direction' – it is not, and never should be, that we 'accept the null hypothesis.'

Key points

- A *hypothesis* is formulated, and a *test* conducted on a sample of data in order to either accept or reject the hypothesis.
- The test can either be two sided or one sided. We only use a one sided test when we are only interested in one side of the mean or proportion.
- Apart from the chi-square test, the tests applied in this chapter are *parametric tests* – they test a parameter of a population.
- The *population parameters* tested in this chapter include the mean and percentage.
- For tests of percentages, the sample size must be large.
- For tests on the mean, a large sample allows the *Z-distribution* to be used; otherwise it is necessary to use the *t-distribution*.
- We can test a single mean or proportion or we can test two means or proportions. For a mean the test can either be two independent means or the samples can be paired.
- The *chi-square test* is used to test whether a frequency distribution follows some expected distribution, and can also be used to test whether there is an association between categories.
- Figure 9.22 summarizes the different tests applicable to means and proportions.

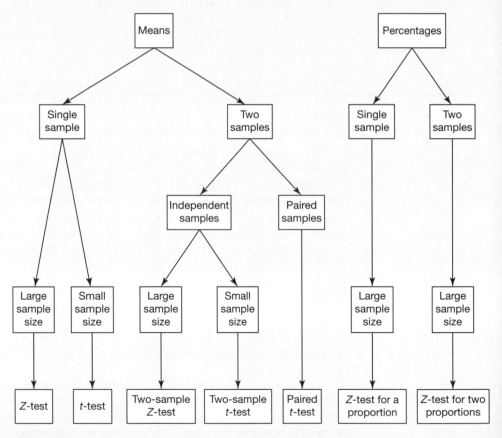

Figure 9.22 Summary of tests applicable to means and proportions

Further reading

As with confidence intervals there are a large number of texts aimed at the business student. However if you want to take the subject further McClave and Sincich (2013) is the 'gold standard' in this area. There is also an interesting article in *Statistical Science* by Tukey (1991).

http://www.**palgrave.com/oakshott-eqm6**

Solutions to all questions are freely available

Practice questions

1 What is the critical value for a two sided Z-test at 5% significance?

2 What is the one sided critical *t*-value at 1% significance for a sample size of 12?

3 What is the critical chi-square value for a contingency table of size 4×3 at 5% significance?

4 A company has analyzed the time its customers take to pay an invoice over the past few years and has found that the distribution is normal, with a mean of 5.8 weeks and a standard deviation of 2.3 weeks. In order to speed up payment the company threatened to charge interest if bills were not paid within 3 weeks. A sample of 10 customers was then analyzed and the mean time to pay had been reduced to 4.9 weeks. Is there any evidence that the mean time for *all* its customers had actually been reduced?

5 A motorcycle is claimed to have a fuel consumption which is normally distributed with mean 54 mpg and a standard deviation of 5 mpg. 12 motorcycles are tested and the mean value of their fuel consumption was found to be 50.5 mpg. Taking a 5% level of significance, test the hypothesis that the mean fuel consumption is 54 mpg.

6 The lifetime of electric light bulbs produced by a given process is normally distributed; the bulbs are claimed to have a mean lifetime of 1500 hours. A batch of 50 was taken, which showed a mean lifetime of 1410 hours. The standard deviation of the sample is 90 hours. Test the hypothesis that the mean lifetime of the electric light bulbs matches the claim.

7 A company has been accused of selling underweight products. This product is supposed to weigh 500 g; a sample of 6 was weighed and the results were:

495, 512, 480, 505, 490, 502

Is there any evidence that the mean weight is less than 500 g? (The weight of the product is known to be normally distributed.)

8 The Speedwell Building Society has claimed that there has been a significant increase in the percentage of its customers taking out fixed-rate mortgages. In the past, 30% of customers had this type of mortgage, but during the past week 60 out of 150 new mortgages have been at a fixed rate. Is the claim by the building society correct?

9 The number of accidents occurring at a large construction site during the past week has been as follows:

Mon	Tue	Wed	Thu	Fri
6	5	6	8	12

Is there any evidence that accidents are more likely on certain days of the week?

10 In Britain a survey was carried out of 171 radio listeners who were asked what radio station they listened to most during an average week. A summary of their replies is given in Table 9.10, together with their age range.

Table 9.10 Data for Question 10

	Age range		
	Less than 20	20 to 30	Over 30
BBC	22	16	50
Local radio	6	11	16
Commercial	35	3	12

(a) Is there any evidence that there is an association between age and radio station?

(b) By considering the contribution to the value of your test statistic from each cell and the relative sizes of the observed and expected frequencies in each cell, indicate the main source of the association, if any exists.

11 A component produced for the electricity industry is supposed to have a mean outside diameter of 10 cm. The mean diameter of a sample of 36 components taken from today's output is 9.94 cm with a standard deviation of 0.018 cm. Does this suggest that the production process is not meeting the specifications?

12 Before a special promotion, the percentage of customers who bought your product at a certain supermarket was 36%. After the promotion a random sample of 200 shoppers at the supermarket revealed that 80 of them had bought the product. Is there evidence of a significant change?

13 In the week before Christmas it was hoped that the mean takings of a shop's branches would be £40 000. However, 40 randomly sampled branches had mean takings of only £37 000 with a standard deviation of £6000. Does this suggest that the mean takings of all the branches were significantly different from the target figure?

14 A bank claims that 60% of people who apply for a personal loan will be granted it. However, a random sample of 500 loan applications contains only 250 which were successful. Does this suggest that the success rate is significantly different from 60%?

15 You are approached one day by a sales manager who has used a computer package to calculate the mean size of order placed by all the company's customers last year. His calculations show that the mean size of order placed was £36.90 with a standard deviation of £4.20. The manager wants advice on how to carry out a hypothesis test to see if the mean size of order placed last year was significantly different from the previous year's figure (this was £30.58). What would your advice be?

16 An inspection by the Environmental Health Department has recently taken place at a company that processes and packs cooked food. The inspectors expressed concern at the amount of dust that was detected in the air within the Cooked Meat department. Although the quantity of dust does not exceed the legal limit, the inspectors recommended that the extractor fans be replaced as soon as possible.

The company looked at various types of extractor fans on the market at the current time and reduced the choice to just two: the Ameba and the Bewax. In order to decide which one to purchase, the manufacturers have loaned the company one unit of each type so that a comparison can be made.

Ameba was installed first, and each week for the next six weeks the filters within the fan were weighed, cleaned and replaced. The Ameba unit was then removed and the Bewax unit placed in the same position and the experiment repeated. The amount of dust (in grams) collected by the two units was as follows:

| Ameba | 5.7 | 6.4 | 6.1 | 4.8 | 7.2 | 2.9 |
| Bewax | 2.9 | 4.7 | 6.3 | 3.0 | 7.0 | 3.5 |

Which extractor fan should the company purchase? (Use a 5% significance level.)

17 In an experiment, a sample of 400 consumers are simultaneously presented with four test packages.

Package A carries a competition offering the chance to win £10 000

Package B carries a token for a free gift

Package C simply carries a message '10% off normal price'

Package D carries a token offering 20 pence off the next purchase of the product

The consumers are then asked to choose the package which they find to be the most attractive. The results of the experiment are given below:

Package	No. of consumers selecting it
A	106
B	92
C	102
D	100

Are these results consistent with the hypothesis that consumers are equally likely to select each package?

18 In a market research survey 200 people are shown the proposed design of a new car and they are asked if they like the design. The responses, broken down by age groups, are shown in Table 9.11. Is there any evidence that age is associated with attitude to the proposed design?

Table 9.11 Data for Question 18

	Age		
	Under 21	21–35	Over 35
Liked design	20	40	80
Disliked design	30	20	10

19 A telephone company has found in the past that 60% of requests from business customers for new installations are for direct lines, 25% are for switchboard connections and 15% for fax machine and other connections. However, a random sample of 300 customers taken last month reveals that 120 are requesting direct lines, 80 are requesting switchboard connections and the remainder are requesting fax machine and other connections. Does this sample suggest that a significant change in the pattern of demand has occurred?

20 You have been asked to help in the design and analysis of a sales campaign involving a selected number of supermarkets. Janet Graves, the Marketing Manager, believes that it is the 'caring image' of the business that attracts customers rather than price cuts alone. To test this idea Janet obtained approval to invest in staff training and other expenditure to generate a friendly atmosphere within a supermarket. Advertising on television and local radio was also to be increased during the campaign. You randomly selected 8 supermarkets throughout the country representing different areas and spending patterns. Following staff training, the campaign was started and continued for a month.

The sales turnover (in £000s) for each supermarket for the month before and after the campaign was noted and is as follows:

Supermarket	A	B	C	D	E	F	G	H
Sales Before	150	75	110	300	120	560	350	185
After	178	50	150	400	180	540	350	235

Is there any evidence at the 5% significance level that sales have improved as a result of the sales campaign?

21 In 2003 an educational researcher sampled 250 students to find out how many hours a week they spent in paid employment. Out of this 250, 30 said that they worked for more than 20 hours a week. The researcher repeated this survey in the year 2008 with a group of 220 students and found that 40 worked for more than 20 hours a week. Is there any indication that students were spending more time working in 2008 than they did in 2003?

22 A company has just relocated to a new site and managers are interested in whether the new site has changed staff's lunch preferences. At the old site 39% said that they brought their own lunch to work, 12% said that they skip lunch altogether, 18% responded that they bought it from the local shop and 31% said they bought it from the staff canteen. After a survey of 227 staff at the new site into their lunch habits the following data was obtained (Table 9.12).

Table 9.12 Data for Question 22

Category	Observed frequency (new site)
Bring lunch to work	42
Skip lunch	95
Buy from local shop	27
Use canteen	63

Use the chi-square goodness of fit test at the 5% significance level to determine whether staff have changed their lunch habits since moving to the new site.

23 MyBook is a social networking website and the organizers of the site wish to discover if a recent advertising campaign has changed the demographic mix of its users. A survey was conducted among its current users and the results are shown in Table 9.13. This table also gives the previous percentage of people in each category.

Table 9.13 Data for Question 23

Age group	Before campaign	Number after campaign
Less than 18	2.7%	6
18–19	29.9%	118
20–24	53.4%	102
Older than 24	14.0%	26
Total	100%	252

Use the chi-square test at the 5% level to see if there has been a change in the demographic mix of the users.

Assignment

In order to assess the effectiveness of a company training programme, each employee was appraised before and after the training. Based on the comparisons of the two appraisals, each of the 110 production staff were classified according to how well they had benefited from the training. This classification ranged from 'worse', which means they now perform worse than they did before, to 'high', which means they perform much better than they did before the training. The results of this appraisal can be seen in Table 9.14, where you will notice that employees have been further classified by age.

Table 9.14 Data for the assignment

Age of employee	Level of improvement				Total
	Worse	None	Some	High	
Below 40	1	5	24	30	60
40+	4	5	31	10	50
Total	5	10	55	40	110

(a) Is there any association between level of improvement at the job and age?

(b) What is the 95% confidence interval for the percentage of employees who showed a high level of improvement at their job?

10 CAUSE AND EFFECT: CORRELATION AND REGRESSION

PREREQUISITES

Knowledge of hypothesis tests (Chapter 9: *Checking ideas: testing a hypothesis*) would be useful

OBJECTIVES

- To be able to draw and interpret scatter diagrams
- To be able to calculate Spearman's rank correlation coefficient
- To be able to calculate Pearson's product moment correlation coefficient
- To understand and know how to use the least squares regression line
- To understand the limitations of these techniques
- To know how to use SPSS to analyze multi-variate data

INTRODUCTION

The statistical analysis that you have covered so far has been concerned with the characteristics of a single variable. However, in some circumstances it might be of interest to look at two variables simultaneously – for instance, you might suspect that cost of production is dependent on the quantity produced, or that sales of a product are related to price. This chapter introduces two techniques: *correlation*, to measure the association between two variables, and *regression*, to obtain the relationship between the variables. It is also possible to develop relationships between several variables, as indicated in the *Quantitative methods in action* case study. This chapter will show how SPSS can be used for this technique, which is called *multiple regression*.

QUANTITATIVE METHODS IN ACTION

Predicting time that aircraft take to taxi to the terminal building or runway

Movement of aircraft within an airport is of vital importance. Not only should there be no conflicts between different aircraft, but also the time that an aircraft takes to taxi either to the terminal building or to the runway should be able to be predicted and preferably minimised. Airports employ either controllers or decision support systems to schedule the takeoff and landing of aircraft; an accurate prediction of taxi time is vital for this task.

This case examines the study carried out at two hub airports in Europe; these are Stockhold-Arlanda and Zurich airports. Both are large airports. Researchers collected data on each aircraft during a typical day and information on such factors as whether the aircraft was arriving or leaving, as well as the start and end of the taxi period.

The purpose of the study was to understand the factors that influence taxi times for a particular type of aircraft and whether an equation could be created, using regression analysis, to link these factors. When using a regression type model, it is necessary to decide on the dependent and independent variables to be used. It was discovered that taxi speed was a better dependent variable to use than taxi time, and to make the model linear, a log transformation was taken of the taxi speed. For the independent variables the obvious one was distance travelled, but others included:

- Angle of turning – The more turning the aircraft has to do, the longer it will take the aircraft to reach its destination.
- Departures versus arrivals – There can be a significant difference between the speed of departures and those of arrivals.
- Amount of traffic – This is the number of other aircraft manoeuvring in the airport.

Other possible variables were considered, including the number of engines an aircraft had, the type of runway and the standing areas for the aircraft.

There was a correlation between the log of the speed and the distance travelled, but this was non-linear (see Figure 10.1). Using a log transformation on both speed and distance gave a linear relationship with a value of 0.479 for the coefficient of determination (R^2). This means that nearly half the variation in speed can be explained by distance travelled. Another important factor was departures versus arrivals. A dummy variable with a value of 0 or 1 was used for this factor. The angle was also important, and again a log transformation was necessary. By including these factors the value of R^2 rose to 0.863 for the Stockholm airport and 0.878 for the Zurich one. This means that only around 13% of the variation was unexplained.

A series of validation tests were carried out on the model, with good results. In most cases the error

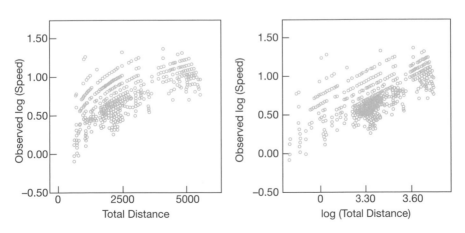

Figure 10.1 Scatterplots showing how distance and log (distance) varies with log (speed)

between predicted and actual taxi times was less than ±5 minutes. A plot of predicted taxi times minus the actual taxi times is shown in Figure 10.2. The results have been sorted by the error in prediction.

In conclusion the model showed that the average speed between the gate and runway (and vice versa) was highly correlated to the taxi distance, with higher speeds being expected for longer distances. Arrivals had higher average speeds than departures, due to aircraft waiting to takeoff. Other factors such as the turning angle had a significant effect on average speed.

Source: Journal of the Operational Research Society (2013) 64, 1347–60.

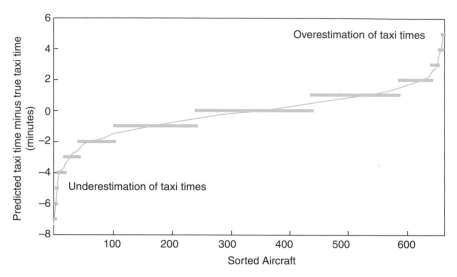

Figure 10.2 Comparison between predicted and actual taxi times

Scatter diagrams

A scatter diagram is simply a way of representing a set of bivariate data by a scatter of plots. One variable is plotted on the *x*-axis and the other on the *y*-axis. Normally the *x* variable (the *independent* variable) is the one that you believe influences the *y* variable (the *dependent* variable). That is *y depends on x*.

Examples of scatter diagrams are given in Figures 10.3 to 10.6. Figure 10.3 indicates a *positive correlation* because as the number of deliveries increases, so apparently does the delivery time. Figure 10.4 indicates a *negative correlation* because as the air temperature increases, the heating cost falls. Figure 10.5 suggests that no correlation exists between salary and age of employees. Figure 10.6 suggests that the quantity produced and the efficiency of a machine are correlated but not linearly.

When categorizing scatter diagrams you may find it easier to draw a closed loop around the points. This loop should be drawn so that it encloses all the points but at the same time makes the area within the loop as small as possible. If the loop looks like a circle, this suggests that there is little, if any, correlation, but if the loop

Figure 10.3 Positive correlation

Figure 10.4 Negative correlation

Figure 10.5 No correlation

Figure 10.6 Non-linear correlation

looks more like an ellipse then this suggests that there is some correlation present. An ellipse pointing upwards would represent a positive correlation and one pointing downwards would represent a negative correlation. If you try this with Figures 10.3 to 10.5 you will see that this agrees with the statements already made. A loop around the points in Figure 10.6 would clearly show the non-linear nature of the association.

The closer the ellipse becomes to a straight line, the stronger the correlation. If the ellipse became a straight line you would say that you have perfect correlation (unless the straight line was horizontal, in which case there can be no correlation since the dependent variable has a constant value).

example
10.1
The Production Manager at Lookwools Engineering suspects that there is an association between production volume and production cost. To prove this he obtained the total cost of production for different production volumes and the data are as follows:

Units produced (000s)	1	2	3	4	5	6
Production costs (£000s)	5.0	10.5	15.5	25.0	16.0	22.5

activity 10.1 Draw a scatter diagram for the data in Example 10.1 and comment on the association (if any).

Since production cost depends on volume, the horizontal (x) axis represents volume (units produced) and the vertical (y) axis represents cost. The scatter diagram for this data is shown in Figure 10.7.

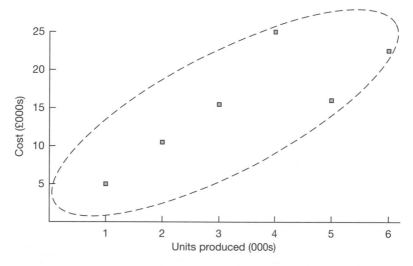

Figure 10.7 Scatter diagram for Activity 10.1

A closed loop has been drawn around the points and from this you should be able to make the following observations:

■ There is a positive correlation between volume and cost.
■ The loop is a fairly narrow ellipse shape suggesting that, for the range of data provided, the association is reasonably strong (but not perfect).
■ If the point representing 4000 units was omitted the ellipse would be narrower.
■ There is no evidence of non-linearity in the data.

Although these observations are valid, the sample size is rather small to make definite conclusions. In practice a larger sample size would be advisable (at least twelve pairs) and the cost of 4000 units would be checked. Sometimes these 'rogue' results suggest that other factors are influencing the dependent variable and further investigation is necessary.

Correlation

The technique of *correlation* measures the strength of the association between the variables. There are two widely used measures of correlation. These are *Spearman's rank correlation coefficient* and *Pearson's product moment correlation coefficient*. Both

Figure 10.8 Range of values of the correlation coefficient

give a value between -1 and 1 so that -1 indicates a perfect negative correlation, 1 a perfect positive correlation and zero indicates no correlation. This is illustrated in Figure 10.8.

Spearman's rank correlation coefficient (*R*)

This method involves ranking each value of x and y and using the following formula to calculate the coefficient R.

$$R = 1 - \frac{6 \sum d^2}{n(n^2 - 1)}$$

where d is the difference in rank between pairs and n is the number of pairs. The value of R lies between 1 and -1.

The procedure to calculate this coefficient is as follows:

1 Rank both variables so that either the largest is ranked 1 or alternatively the smallest is ranked 1.
2 For each pair obtain the difference between the rankings.
3 Square these differences and sum.
4 Substitute the sum of these differences into the formula.

If during Step 1 you find you have equal rankings for the same variable, it is the *mean* of the rankings that is used. For example, if rank 3 occurs twice then both should be given a ranking of 3.5. The next ranking is 5.

$\left(\begin{array}{c}\textit{activity}\\ \textbf{10.2}\end{array}\right)$ Calculate Spearman's rank correlation coefficient for the data given in Example 10.1.

Step 1

Rank both variables.

If you use rank 1 as being the lowest and rank 6 as the largest value, then the 'Units Produced' are already ranked for you. 'Production Costs' start at 5.0 (£000s) and this will have a rank 1, while 25.0 is the largest and will be given a rank of 6. This can be seen below.

Units produced (000s)	1	2	3	4	5	6
Rank	1	2	3	4	5	6
Production costs (£000s)	5.0	10.5	15.5	25.0	16.0	22.5
Rank	1	2	3	6	4	5

Steps 2 and 3

Calculate differences, then square and sum them. You will find it easier if you set out the calculations in a table similar to Table 10.1.

Table 10.1 Calculation of R for Activity 10.2

No. of units	Cost	Difference (*d*)	*d²*
1	1	0	0
2	2	0	0
3	3	0	0
4	6	−2	4
5	4	1	1
6	5	1	1
		Sum	6

Step 4

Substitute the sum of d^2 into the formula. The sum of d^2 is 6 and there are 6 pairs of values, so Spearman's rank correlation coefficient is:

$$R = 1 - \frac{6 \times 6}{6 \times (6^2 - 1)}$$

$$= 1 - \frac{36}{6 \times 35}$$

$$= 0.829$$

This value is close to 1 which supports the assessment made from the scatter diagram that there is a fairly strong positive relationship between cost of production and production volume.

Data do not always consist of actual measurements. For example, in market research, data may consist of opinions on a particular product. This kind of data is called *ordinal* data. Ordinal data has the property that although it does not have actual numerical values, it can be ranked.

The next example should help you understand how to apply Spearman's method to ordinal data.

example **10.2**

BSL Marketing has been asked to conduct a survey into the public's attitude to a new chocolate bar. A pilot survey was carried out by asking 5 people of different ages to try the product and give their reaction. The result of this survey is shown in Table 10.2.

Table 10.2 Survey results for Example 10.2

Person	Age range	Response
A	below 10	very good
B	15 to 20	fair
C	20 to 25	fair
D	10 to 15	excellent
E	over 25	disliked

activity
10.3

Is there any evidence of an association between age and preference for the product?

Both the age range and response can be ranked. It doesn't really matter how you rank them as long as you take your method into account when you come to interpret your coefficient. In the calculations that follow I have used low rankings for low age range and low rankings for the low response ratings (that is, 'disliked' has a ranking of 1). Using this method the rankings are as shown in Table 10.3.

Table 10.3 Rankings for data in Activity 10.3

Person	Age range	Rank	Response	Rank
A	below 10	1	very good	4
B	15 to 20	3	fair	2
C	20 to 25	4	fair	2
D	10 to 15	2	excellent	5
E	over 25	5	disliked	1

Notice that both B and C are ranked equal second in their responses. To compensate for the missing third rank a *mean* rank of 2.5 is used instead of rank 2. You can see this in Table 10.4.

Table 10.4 Calculation of *R* for Activity 10.3

Person	Age range	Response	Difference (d)	d²
A	1	4	−3	9
B	3	2.5	0.5	0.25
C	4	2.5	1.5	2.25
D	2	5	−3	9
E	5	1	4	16
			Sum	36.5

The sum of the square of the differences is 36.5, and substituting this value into the formula gives:

$$R = 1 - \frac{6 \times 36.5}{5 \times (5^2 - 1)}$$
$$= 1 - \frac{219}{120}$$
$$= -0.825$$

This value is fairly large, which suggests an association between age and response. Since the coefficient is negative, it would appear that younger people are more likely to react favourably to the product.

Pearson's product moment correlation coefficient (*r*)

This measure of correlation tends to be the most popular, but it can only be used when the data is on the interval scale of measurement, that is, when the data consists of actual measurements. The formula for *r* is:

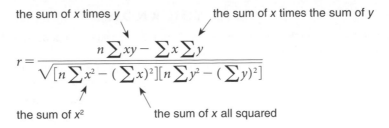

the sum of x times y   the sum of x times the sum of y

the sum of x^2 the sum of x all squared

$$r = \frac{n\sum xy - \sum x\sum y}{\sqrt{[n\sum x^2 - (\sum x)^2][n\sum y^2 - (\sum y)^2]}}$$

This formula looks daunting at first sight but it is quite straightforward to use, as you will see by attempting Activity 10.4.

*(**activity** **10.4**)*

Calculate the Pearson's product moment correlation coefficient for the data given in Example 10.1 (page 232).

To obtain this coefficient you are advised to set out the calculations in tabular form, as shown in Table 10.5.

Table 10.5 Calculation of r for Activity 10.4

Units produced x	Production cost y	xy	x^2	y^2
1	5.0	5.0	1	25.00
2	10.5	21.0	4	110.25
3	15.5	46.5	9	240.25
4	25.0	100.0	16	625.00
5	16.0	80.0	25	256.00
6	22.5	135.0	36	506.25
$\sum x = 21$	$\sum y = 94.5$	$\sum xy = 387.5$	$\sum x^2 = 91$	$\sum y^2 = 1762.75$

The summations can then be substituted into the formula for *r*:

$$r = \frac{6 \times 387.5 - 21 \times 94.5}{\sqrt{[6 \times 91 - (21)^2][6 \times 1762.75 - (94.5)^2]}}$$

$$= \frac{340.5}{\sqrt{(105 \times 1646.25)}}$$

$$= \frac{340.5}{415.7598} = 0.8190$$

This calculation agrees with Spearman's calculation (see Activity 10.2) in that there is a strong positive correlation between production volume and cost.

Pearson's product moment correlation coefficient is a more accurate measure of the correlation between two *numeric* variables. However, it cannot be applied to non-numeric data.

DID YOU KNOW?

Regression to the mean refers to the tendency of an average value in a population to move away from the extreme values towards the average value.

   If you take a sample from a population and find the average, this average value is likely to be some way from the true mean. Suppose you now take a second sample. If the first sample was some way from the mean (that is it was an extreme value), then the mean from the second sample is likely to be closer to the mean. The further away that the average of the first sample was from the true mean, the closer the mean of the second sample will be to the true mean. This tendency was called *regression to the mean* by Sir Francis Galton FRS (1822–1911) in a study of the average heights of sons of very tall and very short parents. He found that sons of very tall or very short parents tend to be tall or short, respectively, but not as tall or as short as their parents.

   The problem occurs when people mistake regression to the mean, which is a statistical phenomenon, for a causal relationship. When this occurs, we often talk about the *regression fallacy*. For example, people often believe that there is a causal relationship between herbal remedies and improvement in their condition. Someone suffering from arthritis might try a herbal remedy when the pain is at its worst and find that the pain reduces. Apart from the placebo effect, the pain would probably have diminished anyway due to the regression to the mean and not as a result of the medicine or treatment.

Source: Robert Todd Carroll, 'Regressive Fallacy', *The Skeptic's Dictionary*.

$\left(\begin{array}{c}\textit{activity}\\ \textbf{10.5}\end{array}\right)$ How large does Pearson's correlation coefficient have to be before we are convinced that there is real association between two variables?

There is no easy answer to this question as it depends on the number of data points. If we went to the extreme and only had 2 data points we would find that the correlation would be perfect as there is no scatter around the imaginary line between the two points. Conversely, the more data points we have the larger the scatter and therefore the smaller the value of r. In order to allow for the number of data points when assessing the value of r we can apply a *significance test* (see Chapter 9) to the result. The null hypothesis is that there is no association or the two variables are unrelated. That is:

$$H_0 : \rho = 0$$

and

$$H_1 : \rho \neq 0 \text{ where } \rho \text{ is the population coefficient}$$

The test is simple to apply. The *test statistic* is our calculated value of r and the *critical value* can be found from the table in the Appendix. These tables are based on v *degrees of freedom* and for bivariate data $v = n - 2$.

$\left(\begin{array}{c}\textit{activity}\\ \textbf{10.6}\end{array}\right)$ Carry out a test of significance on the value of r calculated in Activity 10.4.

The value of r was 0.8190, which is our test statistic. The critical value on 4 $(6-2)$ degrees of freedom at a 5% significance level is 0.8114. We can therefore reject H_0 (just) and conclude that there is a significant correlation between the number of units produced and the production cost.

Linear regression

The technique of *linear regression* attempts to define the relationship between the dependent and independent variables by the means of a linear equation. This is the simplest form of equation between two variables and, fortunately, many situations can at least be approximated by this type of relationship.

The scatter diagram for the production cost data of Example 10.1 has been reproduced in Figure 10.9. You will see that a line has been drawn through the data and this line represents the linear relationship between the two variables. However, since the relationship is not perfect it is possible to draw several different lines 'by eye' through the diagram, each of which would look reasonable. However, each line would represent a slightly different relationship as the gradient and/or intercept on the y-axis would be different. To decide how good a particular line is, you could find the difference between each point and the line. These differences are often referred to as the 'errors' between the actual value and that predicted by the line.

These errors have been represented by vertical lines on the diagram. Note that the errors below the line are negative and those above the line are positive. If you add these errors you will find that the total error is zero. Does this prove that the line is a good one? Unfortunately not, because the zero value is only obtained by adding positive and negative values. Many more lines could be found that also would give a total error of zero. The errors could be added, ignoring the sign, but it can be shown that the best line or the 'line of best fit' is obtained when the sum of the squares of the errors is minimized. Squaring the errors not only removes the minus sign, but also gives more emphasis to the large errors.

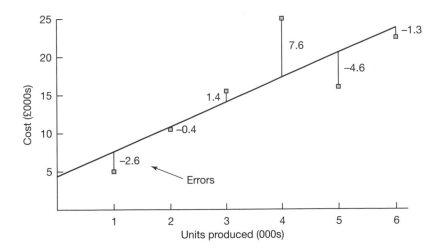

Figure 10.9 Line of best fit drawn through the data from Example 10.1

The method of least squares

Linear regression involves finding that line that minimizes the sum of squares of the errors. The theory behind the *method of least squares* is beyond the scope of this book, but the application of the theory is straightforward. The most important part is to ensure that the y variable is the dependent variable – so, for example, the production cost depends on the number of units produced.

The linear regression model is given in the form:

the dependent variable   the independent variable

$$y = a + bx$$

constants

The values of a and b that minimize the squared errors are given by the equations:

$$b = \frac{n \sum xy - \sum x \sum y}{n \sum x^2 - (\sum x)^2}$$

$$a = \frac{\sum y}{n} - b \frac{\sum x}{n}$$

You can think of b as the slope of the regression line and a as the value of the intercept on the y-axis (value of y when x is zero).

activity
10.7

Calculate the regression line for the production cost data given in Example 10.1 (page 232).

You will probably realize that there are many similarities between the formula for b and that for r, the product moment correlation coefficient. Since the correlation coefficient has already been calculated for this data (Activity 10.4), you can note that:

$$\sum x = 21, \quad \sum y = 94.5,$$

$$\sum xy = 387.5 \quad \text{and} \quad \sum x^2 = 91$$

Substituting these values into the equations for a and b gives:

$$b = \frac{6 \times 387.5 - 21 \times 94.5}{6 \times 91 - 21^2} = 3.2429$$

and

$$a = \frac{94.5}{6} - \frac{(3.2429 \times 21)}{6} = 4.3999$$

The regression equation for this data is therefore:

$$y = 4.4 + 3.24x$$

That is: cost $= 4.4 + 3.24 \times$ units. This suggests that for every 1 unit (1000) rise in production volume, the production cost would rise, on average, by 3.24 units (£3240), and that when nothing is produced ($x = 0$), the production cost would still be £4400. This probably can be explained by factory overhead costs that are incurred even when there is no production.

In order to estimate the value of y for a particular value of x, this x value is substituted into the above equation.

(activity)
10.8

Calculate the cost of production for production volumes of

(a) 2500 units
(b) 20 000 units

Have you any reservations regarding the costs obtained?

To obtain the cost of production for these two cases you would simply substitute the values of 2.5 and 20 into the equation $y = 4.4 + 3.24x$.

That is:

(a) $y = 4.4 + 3.24 \times 2.5 = 12.5$

So 2500 units would cost about £12 500 on average.

(b) $y = 4.4 + 3.24 \times 20 = 69.2$

and 20 000 units would cost £69 200 on average. However, 20 000 units is well outside the range of data used in the original analysis. You cannot be certain that the relationship between cost and volume will remain linear outside this range and so it would be unwise to place too much reliance on the predicted figure.

Coefficient of determination

Before a regression equation can be used effectively as a predictor for the dependent variable, it is necessary to decide how well it fits the data. One statistic that gives this information is the *coefficient of determination*. This measures the proportion of the variation in the dependent variable explained by the variation in the independent variable. It is given by r^2, which is the square of the product moment correlation coefficient.

---

activity 10.9

What is the value of r^2 for the production cost data of Example 10.1?

The value of r is 0.8190, so $r^2 = 0.671$, which means that 0.67 or 67% of the variation in production cost is explained by the production volume. Alternatively, 33% of the variation is *not* explained.

Using Excel to analyse bivariate data

Excel can easily plot scatter plots for you and obtain the statistics you have met so far in this chapter. It is recommended that you try out the next four activities yourself.

---

activity 10.10

Use a spreadsheet to draw a scatter chart of the data in Example 10.1.

Figure 10.10 is a screen shot of the first stage in creating a scatter chart in Excel 2013. The steps for creating a scatter chart in Excel are the same as for other charts (see *Creating charts with Excel 2013* in Chapter 4, page 70). The final scatter diagram has already been shown in Figure 10.7 (page 233).

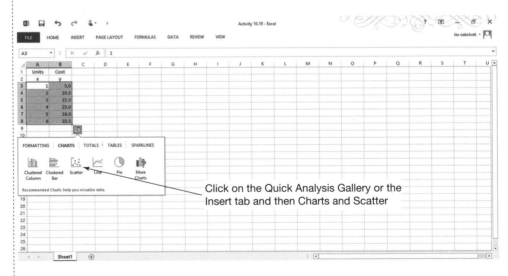

Figure 10.10 Using Excel 2013 to create a scatter chart
Used with permission from Microsoft.

As well as creating charts, Excel can also be used to calculate the regression and Pearson's correlation coefficients. In finding the correct function to use you may find Table 10.6 useful: it lists the most commonly used bivariate functions. Figure 10.11 shows how the functions have been applied to the data for Example 10.1.

Table 10.6 Commonly used bivariate functions in Excel

Function	Meaning
=CORREL (x-values, y-values) or	Calculates the Pearson product moment correlation
=PEARSON (x-values, y-values)	coefficient r
=SLOPE (y-values, x-values)	Calculates slope of regression line
=INTERCEPT (y-values, x-values)	Calculates intercept of regression line
=RSQ (x-values, y-values)	Calculates r^2
=FORECAST (8, y-values, x-values)	Predicts y for $x = 8$ from the linear regression equation

	A	B	C
1	Units	Cost	
2	1	5	
3	2	10.5	
4	3	15.5	
5	4	25	
6	5	16	
7	6	22.5	
8			
9	Pearsons correlation coefficient (using CORRELL)	=CORREL(A2:A7,B2:B7)	
10	Pearsons correlation coefficient (using PEARSON)	=PEARSON(A2:A7,B2:B7)	
11			
12	Slope of regression equation (b)	=SLOPE(B2:B7,A2:A7)	
13	Intercept of regression equation (a)	=INTERCEPT(B2:B7,A2:A7)	
14			
15	Coefficient of determination (r-square)	=RSQ(A2:A7,B2:B7)	
16			
17	Forecast for x=8	=FORECAST(8,B2:B7,A2:A7)	

Figure 10.11 Excel's bivariate functions applied to data from Example 10.1
Used with permission from Microsoft.

Notice that for the Slope, Intercept, RSQ and Forecast functions it is most important that you put the y values first. You might notice too that there is no function for Spearman's correlation coefficient in Excel.

(activity 10.11) Use the Forecast function in Excel to predict the production cost for a volume of 8000 units.

You should have got a value of £30 343.

(activity 10.12) Add the regression line (the line of best fit) to the scatter diagram.

It is possible to use Excel to calculate the predicted y values for given x values, and then this new data series could be plotted on the same chart as the original data. However, an easier method is to use the *Quick Layout tab*. Click on Design under Chart Tools and then Quick Layout. Select *Layout 3*, which automatically inserts the regression line, as can be seen in Figure 10.12.

Figure 10.12 Adding the regression equation to a scatter diagram
Used with permission from Microsoft.

It could be useful to extend the axes to enable the chart to be used for predictions. Right click on the horizontal axes, then `Format Axis` and change *Maximum* to 10. Repeat this for the vertical axis and make the maximum 40. Now right click the Trendline, select `Format Trendline` and add 4 units to the `Forecast Forward` box on the right of the screen (see Figure 10.13). This equates to a production volume of 10 000 units.

Change to 4 so as to increase trendline by 4 units

Figure 10.13 Using the Excel Trendline Options
Used with permission from Microsoft.

activity
10.13

Use your chart to predict the cost of production for a volume of 8000 units.

From Figure 10.14 you will see that the predicted volume is just over £30 000, which agrees with the value obtained in Activity 10.11. Of course extrapolating the regression line assumes that the line remains linear outside the range of collected data. This reservation has already been mentioned in the solution to Activity 10.8.

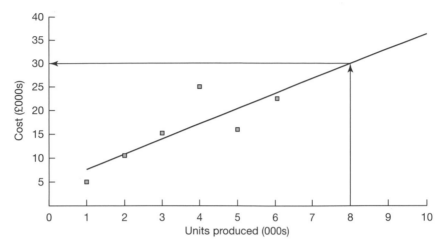

Figure 10.14 Using the regression line for forecasting

SPSS and scatter diagrams

SPSS can create a scatter diagram within the Graphs/Chart Builder menu. We will use the data from Example 10.1 to demonstrate the use of this routine. Click on Scatter/Dot and drag the Simple Scatter into the Gallery window. Now drag Units into the horizontal axis and Cost into the vertical axis (see Figure 10.15). Click on OK and you get the chart shown in Figure 10.16.

Figure 10.15 The Scatter routine in SPSS

Reprint courtesy of International Business Machines Corporation, © International Business Machines Corporation.

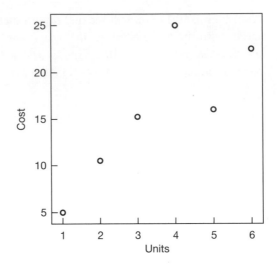

Figure 10.16 Scatter diagram from SPSS

SPSS and linear regression

Linear regression can be performed in SPSS using the regression routine under `Analysis` (see Figure 10.17). Add the two variables as before (Figure 10.18), and click `OK`. Part of the output is shown in Figure 10.19.

The coefficients agree with those that we calculated manually, and with those obtained from Excel.

Figure 10.17 Linear regression routine in SPSS

Figure 10.18 Setting SPSS for regression analysis
Reprint courtesy of International Business Machines Corporation, © International Business Machines Corporation.

Model Summary

Model	R	R Square	Adjusted R Square	Std. Error of the Estimate
1	.819ᵃ	.671	.588	4.7524

a. Predictors: (Constant), Units

Correlation coefficient

67.1% of the variation in cost is explained by the variation in units

Coefficientsᵃ

Model		Unstandardized Coefficients		Standardized Coefficients	t	Sig.
		B	Std. Error	Beta		
1	(Constant)	4.400	4.424		.995	.376
	Units	3.243	1.136	.819	2.854	.046

a. Dependent Variable: cost

The 'a' coefficient   The 'b' coefficient

Figure 10.19 Output from SPSS

Further topics in regression

The topics we have discussed so far in this chapter are the most important in terms of understanding the general principles of correlation and regression and will be sufficient for most courses. However there are a number of more advanced topics that might be included in some courses which we will cover here. These topics generally use ideas from earlier chapters (Analysis of sample data – Chapter 8 and Testing a hypothesis – Chapter 9) and so should be understandable by most students.

To make things more 'statistical' and to aid the introduction of multiple regression we are going to modify our formula for the equation of the regression line. So instead of using $y = a + bx$, as on page 240, we are going to use the equation in the form of

$$y_i = \beta_0 + \beta_1 x_i + e_i$$

where

y_i = the value of the dependent variable of the ith value
x_i = the value of the independent variable for the ith value
β_0 = the population intercept
β_1 = the population slope
e_i = the error of prediction for the ith value ($e_i = y_i - \hat{y}$)

The method of least squares (see page 240) minimizes the sum of the squared errors. In this calculation we are assuming that the errors are normally distributed with mean of zero and standard error of the estimate of

$$s_e = \sqrt{\frac{\sum_{i=1}^{n}(y_i - \hat{y})^2}{n-2}}$$

Hypothesis test for the slope, β_1

The parameter β_1 is only an estimate of the true population slope as it is derived from a sample. How do we know that the slope is not zero? We use the same idea as in Chapter 9 and set up the null and alternative hypotheses.

$H_0 : \beta_1 = 0$
$H_1 : \beta_1 \neq 0$

The test statistic follows a t-distribution and has value

$$t = \frac{b_1 - \beta_1}{s_b}$$

where b_1 is the sample regression slope and s_b is the standard deviation.
The formula for s_b is

$$s_b = \frac{s_e}{\sqrt{\sum_{i=1}^{n}(x_i - \bar{x})^2}}$$

$$= \frac{s_e}{\sqrt{\sum x_i^2 - \frac{(\sum x_i)^2}{n}}}$$

activity 10.14 Using Example 10.1 (page 232) test to see if the slope is significantly different from zero.

From Activity 10.7 we know that the regression equation is $y = 4.4 + 3.24x$ (see page 241), so $b_1 = 3.24$.

The standard error can be found from Table 10.7.

$$\text{So } s_e = \sqrt{\frac{90.3436}{4}}$$

$$= 4.7524$$

You will notice that this is the same value as obtained by SPSS (Figure 10.19).

Table 10.7 Calculation of s_e

Units produced	Production cost	Predicted $\hat{y}$	Residual $y - \hat{y}$	$(y - \hat{y})^2$
1	5.0	7.64	−2.6	6.9696
2	10.5	10.88	−0.4	0.1444
3	15.5	14.12	1.4	1.9044
4	25.0	17.36	7.6	58.3696
5	16.0	20.6	−4.6	21.16
6	22.5	23.84	−1.3	1.7956
			Sum	90.3436

Next we have to calculate the value of s_b. From Activity 10.7 (page 240) we know that $\sum x_i = 21$ and $\sum x_i^2 = 91$, so

$$s_b = \frac{4.7524}{\sqrt{91 - \dfrac{21^2}{6}}}$$

$$= 1.136$$

You will also see this figure in Figure 10.19 under 'Std Error' for Units.

We can now calculate the test statistic

$$t = \frac{3.240}{1.136}$$

$$= 2.852 \text{ (which again agrees with the } t \text{ value for Units given in Figure 10.19)}$$

The critical value on 4 (that is, $n - 2$) degrees of freedom is 2.776 at 5% significance level (2 tailed). As our test statistic is greater than this value we reject H_0 and conclude that $\beta_1 \neq 0$. (In Figure 10.19 the last column headed 'Sig.' gives a value of .046. This is the p-value which was discussed in Chapter 9 and since it is below .05 or 5% we again would reject H_0.)

Confidence intervals for the slope

As well as a significance test of the slope we can calculate 95% confidence limits within which the true regression line is expected to lie. The formula is

$$b_1 - t_{(n-2, \alpha/2)}s_b < \beta_1 < b_1 + t_{(n-2, \alpha/2)}s_b$$

Because $t_{(n-2, \alpha/2)} = 2.776$, $s_b = 1.136$ and $\alpha = .05$ our confidence intervals are

$$3.24 - 2.776 \times 1.136 \text{ and } 3.24 + 2.776 \times 1.136$$

$$= 0.086 \text{ and } 6.39$$

As this range does not include zero it reinforces our conclusion that $\beta_1 \neq 0$.

Multiple regression

So far we have only looked at one independent variable but it is possible to have several, as in the case of the hotel regression model discussed in the *Quantitative methods in action* case study at the start of this chapter.

The population multiple regression model is

$$y_i = \beta_0 + \beta_1 x_{1i} + \beta_2 x_{2i} + \cdots + \beta_k x_{ki} + e_i$$

The assumptions required (in addition to that mentioned for the simple two variable model) to use this model are:

1 The x_{ji} values are independent variables with fixed (i.e. non-stochastic) values.
2 The expected value of the random variable y_i is a *linear* function of the independent x_{ki} variables.
3 There is no significant linear relationship between the independent variables.

When the third assumption is violated we say that the data suffers from *multicollinearity*. Whenever there are a large number of independent variables it is very likely that some of the variables will be correlated with each other. The easiest way to check for multicollinearity is to produce a correlation matrix. This is quite easy with SPSS. The correlations between the independent variables should be low although there is no specific value at which we can say that multicollinearity is present. If correlations between two independent variables are high we may find that removing one of them is the easiest solution.

Activity 10.15 demonstrates the application of multiple regression analysis to a small problem with three independent variables.

Table 10.8 gives the top 15 medal-winning countries at the 2008 Olympics. Also provided is information on the country's population, its gross national income per capita (GNI) and the average life expectancy. Is there a relationship between any of these variables and the number of medals won?

Table 10.8 Data on Olympic medal-winning countries, 2008, in order of gold medals won

Country	Total medals won	Population (millions)	GNI ($ equivalent)	Life expectancy
China	100	1324.7	5 370	73
US	110	304.5	45 850	78
Russia	72	141.9	14 400	67
GB	47	61.3	34 370	79
Germany	40	82.2	33 820	79
Australia	45	21.3	33 340	81
South Korea	31	48.6	24 750	79
Japan	25	127.7	34 600	82
Italy	28	59.9	29 900	81
France	40	62.0	33 470	81
Ukraine	28	46.2	6 810	68

Netherlands	16	16.4	39 500	80
Jamaica	11	2.7	5 050	72
Spain	17	46.5	30 100	80
Kenya	14	38.0	1 540	53

Source: 2008 Population Reference Bureau and Wikipedia, the free encycopedia.

We first use SPSS to obtain the correlations between all the variables to see if any of the independent variables are correlated. As you can see in Figure 10.20 there is a correlation between GNI and life expectancy. This is to be expected as both variables measure a country's affluence.

We will now use SPSS to run a regression analysis on the other variables (omitting life expectancy). The results can be seen in Figure 10.21.

Correlations		Total medals won	Population in millions	Gross national income in $	Life expectancy
Total medals won	Pearson Correlation	1	.686**	.131	.052
	Sig. (2-tailed)		.005	.641	.853
	N	15	15	15	15
Population in millions	Pearson Correlation	.686**	1	-.281	-.068
	Sig. (2-tailed)	.005		.311	.810
	N	15	15	15	15
Gross national income in $	Pearson Correlation	.131	-.281	1	.796**
	Sig. (2-tailed)	.641	.311		.000
	N	15	15	15	15
Life expectancy	Pearson Correlation	.052	-.068	.796**	1
	Sig. (2-tailed)	.853	.810	.000	
	N	15	15	15	15
**. Correlation is significant at the 0.01 level (2-tailed).					

Life expectancy and Gross national income are correlated

Figure 10.20 Correlation matrix for the Olympic variables

A lot of information is provided in Figure 10.21. The *Model Summary* gives the R square value. The relevant figure to look at is the *Adjusted R Square* because this allows for the number of variables. The value of .514 means that the two independent variables, Population and GNI, account for just over half the variation in the dependent variable. The ANOVA table (this stands for *Analysis of Variance*) looks at the significance of the regression model. The F-statistic is used to measure this significance and a value of 8.411 is highly significant. The value of .005 is the p-value and is well below the 5% (.05) level normally accepted as significant. The final table gives the coefficients of the regression model which is described by:

Medals won $= 11.8 + .072 \times$ Pop $+ .001 \times$ GNI

Model Summary

Model	R	R Square	Adjusted R Square	Std. Error of the Estimate
1	.764[a]	.584	.514	21.053

a. Predictors: (Constant), Gross national income in $, Population in millions

The p-value

ANOVA[b]

Model		Sum of Squares	df	Mean Square	F	Sig.
1	Regression	7456.633	2	3728.317	8.411	.005[a]
	Residual	5318.967	12	443.247		
	Total	12775.600	14			

a. Predictors: (Constant), Gross national income in $, Population in millions
b. Dependent Variable: Total medals won

Coefficients[a]

Model		Unstandardized Coefficients		Standardized Coefficients	t	Sig.
		B	Std. Error	Beta		
1	(Constant)	11.794	12.536		.941	.365
	Population in millions	.072	.018	.784	4.041	.002
	Gross national income in $	.001	.000	.351	1.810	.095

a. Dependent Variable: Total medals won

Figure 10.21 Printout from SPSS on the Olympic regression results

How would we use this equation? If we take Great Britain as an example we have Pop = 61.3 and GNI = $34 370 so

$$\text{Medals won} = 11.8 + .072 \times 61.3 + .001 \times 34\,370$$
$$= 11.8 + 4.4 + 34.4$$
$$= 50.6$$

This is the predicted value and represents an error of 7.6% on the actual value.

activity **10.16** Use this equation to calculate the predicted medals won for Belarus whose population is 9.7 million and GNI is $10 740, and for Thailand whose population is 66.1 million and GNI is $7880.

Using the regression equation again we get for Belarus:

$$\text{Medals won} = 11.8 + .072 \times 9.7 + .001 \times 10\,740$$
$$= 11.8 + 0.7 + 10.7$$
$$= 23.2$$

This is not too far out from what they actually got (19).

For Thailand:

$$\text{Medals won} = 11.8 + .072 \times 66.1 + .001 \times 7880$$
$$= 11.8 + 4.8 + 7.8$$
$$= 24.4$$

This is very different from the total medals Thailand won (4).

activity 10.17 Can you think of reasons why the regression equation doesn't work very well for countries like Thailand?

I am sure that you can think of lots of reasons! The fact that we have a constant term of 11.8 means that we will only be able to use the model to predict the number of medals won by the top sporting nations. The reason that we were not far out in predicting Belarus is that they were 16th in the table. Statistically we didn't take a random sample. Instead we chose the top 15 countries on which to base our equation. Because we are only explaining around 50% of the variation in the medals won there are obviously other factors that could explain the other 50%. The countries that did well could have a culture of competing in sporting competitions, something which would be hard to model.

Reflection

As with all statistics, it is possible to draw misleading conclusions when using correlation and regression analysis. The biggest mistake is to assume that *association* means *causation*. This is certainly not the case as you can get spurious correlations, such as the study in San Francisco that showed that the more fire engines attend a fire, the worse the damage will be! The reason for this spurious correlation is that with large fires the two variables are correlated.

There are other cases that might seem quite reasonable, such as that students who do well at school also earn higher incomes later in life. This might be a valid cause and effect, but it might also be explained in other ways – for example, it might be that students who work hard at school also work hard at their job. This is called a *lurking variable* or *hidden variable*.

It is often quite difficult to differentiate real causation from spurious association. Take the example of shoe size and reading skills. It can be shown that there is a strong association between these – but this arises only because those with bigger feet also tend to be older! In this case age is called the *confounding factor*.

In other cases there may indeed be causation, without it being obvious which factor causes the other. For example, a study in America showed that students who smoked had worse grades that those who didn't. The conclusion drawn was that students would do better if they gave up smoking. In fact, of course, it might happen the other way round: perhaps students smoke because they don't do well academically – but this conclusion is not nearly so attractive!

Key points

- A *dependent variable* is a variable that depends on one or more other (*independent*) variables.
- The *correlation* between the dependent and an independent variable can be either *positive* or *negative*, depending on whether the dependent variable increases or decreases with an increase in the independent variable.

- Spearman's correlation coefficient can be calculated on any bivariate data but it is normally used for ordinal data.
- Pearson's product moment correlation coefficient can only be used on interval scale data.
- Given a value of the independent variable, a *linear regression model* allows the value of the dependent variable to be calculated.
- The method of least squares is used to calculate the parameters in a linear regression model.
- The *coefficient of determination* determines what proportion of the *variability* in the dependent variable is explained by the independent variable.
- A test on the significance of the regression slope can be calculated either by hand or by SPSS. The same is true for the confidence interval of the slope.
- A *multiple regression model* has more than one independent variable.

Further reading

There are a large number of texts on this topic at varying levels. Many texts such as Morris (2011), Curwin and Slater (2013) are aimed at the business student. Curwin and Slater has quite a good section on multiple regression as does Wisniewski (2010). A useful text for the student with good maths skills is the one by Anderson et al. (2010) but it goes way beyond what most business students need.

http://www.**palgrave**.com/oakshott-eqm6

Solutions to all questions are freely available

Practice questions

1 Suppose the correlation coefficient for age and earnings is 0.3. With the help of a sketch explain what this means. Define the age range to which this correlation might apply.

2 Suppose the correlation coefficient for age and alcohol consumption is -0.6. With the help of a sketch explain what this means.

3 Calculate Spearman's correlation coefficient for the following data.

x	1	2	3	4	5	6	7
y	9	6	7	9	5	2	1

4 A group of 6 students were monitored during their first year at university and their marks in Statistics and Management accounting were recorded. See below. Use Spearman's correlation coefficient to determine if there is any correlation between the scores in the two modules.

Student	Statistics	Management accounting
A	64%	77%
B	56%	52%
C	46%	66%
D	67%	67%
E	50%	62%
F	84%	87%

5 A regression line is $y = 3 + 5x$. What is the value of y if $x = 2$?

6 The data in Table 10.9 relates to the weight and height of a group of students.

(a) Draw a scatter diagram of weight against height for the whole data. Alongside each point write either 'm' or 'f' as appropriate.

Table 10.9 Weight and height data for Question 6

Height (in)	Weight (lb)	Sex
68	148	male
69	126	female
66	145	male
70	158	male
66	140	female
68	126	female
64	120	female
66	119	female
70	182	male
62	127	female
68	165	male
63	133	male
65	124	female
73	203	male

(b) Describe your scatter diagram. Try drawing an ellipse around
  (i) all the points
  (ii) the points relating to the male students
  (iii) the points relating to the female students.
  Is there any indication that the correlation is stronger for either group?
(c) Calculate Pearson's product moment correlation coefficient for the three sets of points identified in (b) above. Comment on the values obtained. (Collect data from a group of friends and repeat the analysis.)

7 A group of students compared the results they obtained in a quantitative methods assignment and a law assignment. The results by position in a group of 50 were as follows:

Student	A	B	C	D	E	F	G	H	I
Quants	5	8	45	2	9	5	15	20	3
Law	29	17	1	11	6	18	33	3	8

Use Spearman's rank correlation coefficient to discover whether there is any correlation between position in each subject.

8 A company is investigating the relationship between sales and advertising revenue. Data has been collected on these two variables and is shown below (all figures are in £000s):

Month	Jan	Feb	Mar	Apr	May	Jun	Jul	Aug	Sep	Oct	Nov	Dec
Sales	60	60	58	45	41	33	31	25	24	23	23	23
Adv.	6.0	6.0	6.0	5.8	4.5	4.1	3.3	3.1	2.5	2.4	2.3	2.3

(a) Plot a scatter diagram of the data given in the table above. Comment on the strength of the association between the two variables.
(b) Obtain the least squares regression line and comment on how well it fits the data.
(c) What would the expected sales be, given an advertising expenditure of £5000?

9   Consider the following pairs of variables and make an assessment of the likely correlation between them. Mark each pair to show whether you expect the correlation to be positive or negative (strong or weak), or close to zero:
  (a) Attendance totals and position in football league table
  (b) The age of a relatively new make of car and its value
  (c) The age of a vintage make of car and its value
  (d) Length of education and annual earnings
  (e) Level of unemployment and hire purchase sales over a period of 10 years.

10   The following data relate to the size of the electricity bill sent to 7 randomly selected customers and the time the customers took to pay the bills.

Customer no.	1	2	3	4	5	6	7
Size of bill	£100	£150	£200	£250	£330	£400	£480
Time to pay (days)	15	20	16	20	24	32	28

  (a) (i) Plot the data on a scatter graph.
     (ii) Use your calculator to find Pearson's correlation coefficient for the data.
  (b) Determine the least squares regression equation that can be used to predict how long a bill of a given size will take to pay.
  (c) Interpret your equation.
  (d) Draw the line on the scatter graph.
  (e) Use your equation to predict how long it will take a customer to pay:
     (i) a bill of £125, and
     (ii) a bill of £1000.
     What reservations do you have about these predictions?
  (f) The coefficient of determination for this data is 79.2%. Interpret this value.

11   A local government research unit is looking at the methods that councils use to collect rent from tenants living in houses and flats. In particular, it wants to know whether the relatively expensive door-to-door collection method is effective. A random sample of six local councils is selected and for each council the percentage of rent collected door-to-door and the percentage of total rent which is in arrears is recorded. The results are shown below.

% collected door-to-door	1	12	16	11	20	6
% of total rent in arrears	13	10	8	12	7	11

  (a) Plot the data for the two variables on a scatter graph.
  (b) Calculate Spearman's correlation coefficient for this data.

12   The personnel manager of a company is concerned with the high sickness records of its production staff. An analysis of its night shift revealed the figures shown in Table 10.10.
  (a) Plot a scatter graph of this data. What can you deduce about the association between number of days taken off sick last year and age?
  (b) Using your calculator's statistical mode or otherwise, calculate a correlation coefficient for this data.
  (c) Carry out a suitable test at the 5% level to see whether there is a significant correlation between days off work and age.
  (d) The least squares regression relationship between days off sick and age is:
     Days off sick $= 17.4 - 0.2118 \times$ Age
     (i) Plot this line on your scatter graph.

Table 10.10 Sickness records

Person	Age	Days off work last year
A	21	20
B	19	8
C	36	8
D	55	5
E	20	13
F	22	15
G	45	12
H	39	7
I	32	11
J	28	8

(ii) Do either of the numbers 17.4 or −0.2118 have a practical (*not* mathematical) meaning? If so, explain.

(iii) What prediction can you make about the days off sick for a person who is 65 years old and works on the night shift? Comment on your answer.

(iv) Calculate the coefficient of determination for this data and interpret its value.

(v) What other factors might affect days off sick?

13 A company believes that the monthly sales of one of its products are related to the amount spent on advertising during the previous month. It records monthly sales and advertising spend in the preceding month and obtains the data given below.

Sales (£m)	1.00	1.02	1.30	1.45	1.20	1.08	1.25
Advert. prev. month (£000s)	50	51	60	65	45	49	55

(a) Determine the regression equation for sales upon advertising.

(b) What value do you predict for next month's sales if advertising this month is
(i) £40 000 (ii) £80 000. Do you have any reservations with your answers?

14 A company is concerned at the variability in sales at its 10 stores. There are thoughts that this variability is to do with the size of the town in which the store is situated. It is also possible that the size of store might affect sales. Another thought is that the experience of the store manager (as measured by number of years working for the company) might have an influence. The data for the 10 stores is given below:

Sales (£000s)	Population of town (000s)	Size of store (000 m²)	Years' experience
67.0	20.0	4.3	12.0
89.0	30.0	6.4	5.0
90.0	25.0	2.1	6.0
154.0	36.0	3.5	3.0
102.0	34.5	5.0	5.0
75.0	15.0	1.7	2.0
250.0	65.0	12.1	1.0
87.0	31.0	7.6	4.0
54.5	24.9	4.4	3.0
69.0	18.6	4.7	1.0

    (a) Use SPSS or Excel to produce a scatter plot of sales against each of the other variables. What do you conclude from each plot?

    (b) Use SPSS or another statistical package to obtain the correlation coefficients of sales against each of the other variables. Do the correlations correspond to your conclusions in part (a)?

    (c) Use SPSS or another statistical package to obtain the regression equation with the largest R^2.

    (d) Use your equation to obtain the predicted sales for a 6000 m^2 store in a town with a population of 28 000 people and where the manager has 12 years' experience.

    (e) Comment on the data used for this investigation.

15 In Question 13 determine whether the regression slope is significant. Also, obtain the confidence interval for the slope.

Assignment

It seems reasonable to assume that the second hand price of a particular make of car is dependent on its age. Decide on a particular make and model of car and a suitable source for the data, such as your local newspaper. Collect data on the age and price of around 20 cars and use Excel to do the following:

    (a) Plot a scatter graph of the data. Does the scatter graph indicate that a linear relationship exists for all or part of the range of the data?

    (b) Obtain the regression equation that would enable the price of the car to be obtained given its age.

    (c) Using the equation obtained in (b) above and suitable examples, illustrate how the price of a car could be found if its age was known. Within what age range is your equation valid? Why is this so?

    (d) What proportion of the variability in price is explained by the age factor?

    (e) Investigate whether other factors, such as engine size, would improve the fit of the regression equation.

IV

DECISION-MAKING TECHNIQUES

HOW TO MAKE GOOD DECISIONS

PREREQUISITES

To complete this chapter successfully you should have worked through Chapter 6 (*Taking a chance: probability*).

OBJECTIVES

- To be able to use diagrams to represent a problem situation
- To understand how to make decisions using payoff tables
- To be able to calculate expected monetary values
- To know how to solve problems using decision trees
- To be able to use Bayes' theorem in decision-making
- To know how to use a spreadsheet to carry out sensitivity analysis on a decision tree
- To be able to calculate the expected value of perfect and imperfect information
- To understand the idea of utility
- To be able to apply the SMART technique to decisions involving multiple attributes
- To appreciate the use of Hiview3 MCDA software

INTRODUCTION

Everyone has to make decisions from time to time. These can vary from the simple, such as 'What should I have for breakfast this morning?', to the complex, such as deciding how to allocate spending on highway improvement projects. Many decisions have to be made with incomplete information, perhaps because the problem is unclear or the outcome of a decision is uncertain or because the outcome will occur at some time in the future. Many decisions involve more than one criterion, such as choosing which house to buy. Techniques have been developed that are able to take account of *uncertainty*, and these will be discussed in the first part of this chapter. The later part of the chapter will deal with one technique for handling problems in which we have more than one criterion to consider, such as the highway improvement problem described in *Quantitative methods in action*.

QUANTITATIVE METHODS IN ACTION

Highway improvement project selection in Louisiana, USA

In 2010 the US spent $155 billion on highways repairs and improvements (*The Tax Foundation*). Only 50% of this amount was paid for by drivers (motor vehicle licence, fuel duty, tolls, etc.). The rest was funded by $30 billion in general state and local revenues and $46 billion in federal aid.

Every year transportation departments have to screen thousands of road segments for road improvement and preselect a number of them for further evaluation. Finally, from this smaller subset, a number are selected that will meet budget constraints.

The normal method of how to select the final road improvement projects is by a cost-benefit analysis. The cost of each project is easy to measure, being the direct and indirect costs of labour and materials. The benefits have traditionally been measured through the reduction in accidents. In 2014 it was estimated that the annual cost to the country of automobile crashes was $871 billion in economic loss and societal harm (*National Highway Traffic Safety Administration*), which works out at $900 per person. So if a highway improvement reduces crashes, then this is a cost benefit. The trouble with this approach is that it favours highways with large volumes of traffic. Other highways with lower number of vehicles are excluded, even though the risk of an accident is higher.

Researchers at Louisiana State University looked at methods of project selection using the joint consideration of cost-benefit and risk criteria. They designed a two-step process. The first step was to measure risk (or hazard) by modelling the number of crashes over many locations using the negative binomial distribution. This is a similar distribution to the Poisson distribution that you met in Chapter 7.

They used the tail of the distribution to estimate the odds against observing a given crash count at a road segment. Using these odds and other crash statistics, they were able to preselect possible sites, thus eliminating thousands of potential sites. From this short list they used a method called data envelopment analysis (DEA) which is a form of multi-criteria decision-making to create a single *hazard efficiency* score for each site.

They then combined these hazard efficiency scores with the cost and benefit results to create a single *composite efficiency* score for each potential site. By using this composite score, the researchers were able to provide a compromise between obtaining a large benefit in crash reduction while including more sites classed as high risk.

The composite method generally gave a higher number of projects that could be selected compared to simply using a cost-benefit analysis. However, the benefits are lower in the composite method as there will be fewer sites with high traffic flows.

Sources: The Tax Foundation (taxfoundation.org)
National Highway Traffic Safety Administration (www.nhtsa.gov)

Table 11.1 A comparison of the number of projects selected given different budget constraints

Budget	$200m		$400m		$600m	
	Cost-benefit	Composite	Cost-benefit	Composite	Cost-benefit	Composite
No. Selected	11	17	22	27	30	36
Benefit ($m)	7.1	3.6	10.8	8.3	12.8	10.9

Source: 'Highway improvement project selection by the joint consideration of cost-benefit and risk criteria', *Journal of the Operational Research Society*, Vol. 64, 2013.

Problem formulation

Not all business problems are what they seem. Although in most text books (including this one) there is a tendency to portray a problem as well structured, this is far from the case in real life. In many cases it is not even obvious what the problem is and in these situations there is a danger that the wrong problem is solved. For example, one train company was disappointed in the sales of food and drink in its on-train buffet and thought that the reason was that items were overpriced. They therefore reduced the prices but all that they achieved was that the profit decreased - sales were exactly the same. In fact, on closer analysis they realized that the reason for the poor sales was that trains were over-crowded and passengers couldn't get to the buffet car! Whenever you are faced with a business problem you need to step back and take a holistic view. One of the best ways to do this is to draw diagrams of the problem situation. In this chapter we are going to look at several diagrams to help in identifying the problem and then more specialized diagrams to help solve a particular problem.

Mind maps

A mind map means what it says – it is simply a way of transferring your thoughts onto paper. There is no formal way of drawing a mind map and you can put things in any order. Where two things are related or causal it is a good idea to connect them up with a line or arrow. Mind maps are useful where you are trying to get a consensus among a group of people. In these situations it is usually a good idea to get each member of the group to write their thoughts on a 'post-it' note and stick it to a board or flipchart. You as facilitator can then arrange these notes into some logical sequence and from this some 'brain-storming' might be achieved.

(activity 11.1) Imagine that you are on a train and thinking about buying some food and drink from the buffet. Draw a mind map of the thoughts that might go through your mind before you make your decision.

Some ideas are shown in Figure 11.1 overleaf. These are only ideas and you may have got some better or different ones. Perhaps after drawing this map you realize that what perhaps is needed is more passenger information such as whether there is a trolley service, where the buffet car is and the prices.

Rich picture diagrams

Rich pictures were developed by Peter Checkland (1999) as part of his soft systems methodology. Instead of writing sentences as in mind maps you use cartoon-type symbols. There are some commonly used symbols (for example, 'stick men') but, generally, as long as it is clear to an observer what you are trying to say then almost anything is acceptable. (Words can also be added to make the meaning clear.) The diagrams can be drawn by commercial drawing programs such as *Microsoft Visio 2010* although hand-drawn diagrams are quite acceptable, fun to do and more spontaneous. Figure 11.2 gives a possible rich picture diagram for the buffet problem.

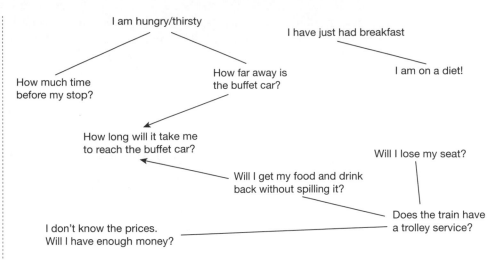

Figure 11.1 Mind map for the buffet decision

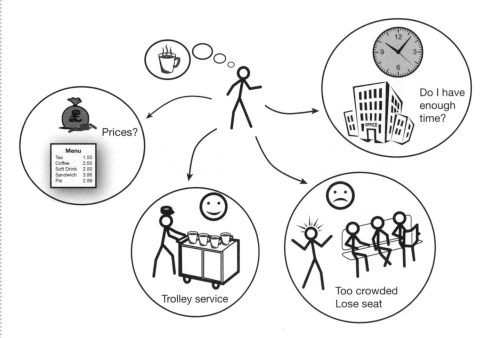

Figure 11.2 Rich picture for the buffet decision

Although rich pictures are a useful first step in structuring a problem they are rarely incorporated into a formal report. The next three types of diagram are more acceptable for publication.

Cognitive maps

These maps are similar to mind maps except they are more structured and attempt to explain the environment from a decision-maker's point of view. Cognitive maps or mapping began life in the field of psychology with Edward Tolman's work with rats.

They are now an essential part of a *soft systems analyst's* tool kit. A cognitive map makes use of *constructs* and links. These constructs are statements by the decision-maker which usually lead to possible outcomes or other constructs. The constructs are linked by arrows to show the direction of the connection. To demonstrate a simple application of cognitive maps the case of the buffet problem is expanded in Example 11.1 and given from the point of view of the rail manager who has to make the decision on what to do.

example
11.1

The manager of Avon railways is concerned at the poor sales of the buffet items [1] even after an attempt to boost sales by reducing prices [2]. Unless the buffet can produce a profit it will have to be withdrawn [3]. However this action might lose passengers to rival services [4] and therefore other solutions are being considered. It is clear that overcrowding [5] was preventing people from reaching the buffet car, and a customer survey showed that travellers were unhappy with the overcrowding in any case. Various solutions were proposed, including raising ticket prices [6] which would reduce demand [7] but this would upset passengers [8] and might cause problems with the rail regulator [9]. Another option was to increase the frequency of the service [10] or to add another coach to the trains [11]. Both these options would increase costs [12] although this cost should be offset by increased ticket and buffet sales [13]. Costs could also be reduced by having a trolley service instead of a buffet car [14]. A trolley service would also mean that the buffet car could be replaced by a passenger coach which would be a cheaper option.

Figure 11.3 shows the cognitive map drawn using these constructs. Each construct in the example is given a number so that the map is easier to follow.

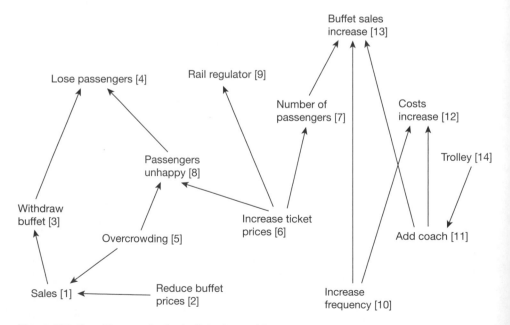

Figure 11.3 Cognitive map for the buffet sales problem

From this diagram the decision might be to investigate the option of replacing the buffet car with a passenger coach and using a trolley service instead. Of course a break-even analysis would be necessary to work out what trolley sales would be needed to pay for the passenger coach.

Causal loop diagrams

To take cognitive mapping one stage further we could show how one construct affects another by adding a '+' or '−' to an arrow head. An increase in ticket prices will reduce the number of passengers so a minus sign would be needed here, while an increase in frequency would increase costs so a plus sign would be needed at the arrow head. However the main use of causal loop diagrams is to identify *feedback loops*. A feedback loop is either reinforcing (positive) or balancing (negative). A reinforcing loop means that it is self-reinforcing and will continue to increase unless an external influence stops it. An example of a reinforcing loop is a population for which the birth rate is fixed. The population will continue to rise unless it is checked in some way. A balancing loop means that there is a dampening effect and a system will reach equilibrium. An example of a balancing loop is a central heating system which has a thermostat installed. Although the temperature may rise above the threshold it will gradually settle down to the pre-determined temperature. To find out if a loop is reinforcing or balancing you should count the number of negative signs. If this number is even you have a reinforcing loop, if odd you have a balancing loop (a zero is counted as even number).

An example of a causal loop diagram with feedback loops is the recruitment for a master's course at a university. In this diagram there are 3 factors that can be set by the university. These are the number of places available, the level of fees, and the quality of staff and the facilities. All the other factors are influenced by these. So, if the fees charged are high the level of student expectation will be high. The level of fees charged will also affect the income. This diagram is shown in Figure 11.4.

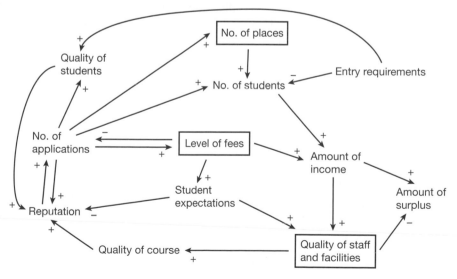

Figure 11.4 Example of a causal loop diagram for student recruitment
Source: Warwick Business School.

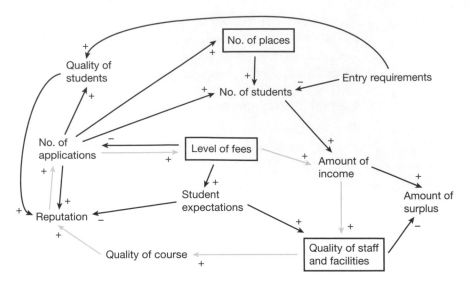

Figure 11.5 Causal loop diagram showing one feedback loop

There are several feedback loops in this diagram. One is shown in Figure 11.5. As this does not have any negative signs it is a reinforcing loop (of course this can be controlled by the level of fees set by the university).

activity
11.2

Identify some more loops in the diagram and decide whether they are reinforcing or balancing.

I am sure that you found several reinforcing loops. An example is: No. of places, No. of students, Amount of income, Quality of staff and facilities, Quality of course, Reputation, No. of applications and back to start. A balancing loop is: Level of fees, Student expectations, Reputation, No. of applications and back to start. The reason that this is a balancing loop (apart for the fact that it has an odd number of negative signs) is that when student expectation is high it is unlikely that the university will be able to meet this expectation and so the number of applications for the following year's course will be lower. The fees then will need to be lower to increase the number of applications. Students paying lower fees will have lower expectations and as these expectations will be exceeded the reputation of the course will go up Of course with so many feedback loops there will be interactions between them and it will not be easy to see the overall effect. However, the main purpose of a causal loop diagram is to give a picture of the situation so that managers can see the effect of changing the factors which they control. So reducing the quality of staff and facilities would have a detrimental effect on the course. It is possible to carry out a quantitative analysis of a causal loop diagram using a technique called *systems dynamics*. This technique is covered in Pidd (2010).

Influence diagrams

The final problem-identification diagram we will look at is an *influence diagram*. This diagram is often used where there is some uncertainty present. So the sales of a product or service could be affected by the demand as well as the price charged by a competitor, both of which are uncertain and which you have little control over. As well as an arrow to show a causal relationship, as we had in a causal loop diagram, four other symbols are used:

A cloud to represent an uncontrollable input

A rectangle to represent an input you have control over

An oval to represent an output

A circle to represent an intermediate result

Figure 11.6 is an influence diagram that shows how the marketing budget (advertising), price and a competitor's pricing influence the sales of a product and the eventual profit.

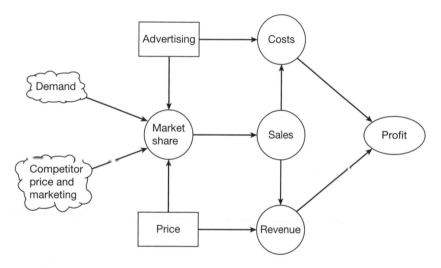

Figure 11.6 Example of an influence diagram

We will see later in this chapter how we can extend the idea of influence diagrams into *decision trees* which allow us to make decisions in conditions of uncertainty. Before then we are going to look at *payoff* tables so that numerical values can be put on some of the uncertain variables.

Payoff tables

A *payoff table* is simply a table that gives the outcome (for example, profits) of a decision under different conditions or *states of nature*. These states of nature may relate to possible demand for a product or they could be related to the national or global economy. The following are the most commonly used decision criteria.

- Maximax rule
- Maximin rule
- Minimax regret rule
- Hurwicz criterion

- Expected monetary value
- Expected opportunity loss

The *maximax* rule chooses the 'best of the best' and is a rule favoured by decision-makers who are *risk-seekers*. The *maximin* rule chooses the 'the best of the worst' and is a rule favoured by decision-makers who are *risk-averse*. The *minimax regret* rule minimizes the maximum *opportunity loss*. The opportunity loss is the loss that occurs through not taking the best option. To work out the opportunity loss you have to subtract each payoff for a particular state of nature from the best that could be achieved given that state. The *Hurwicz* criterion, like the minimax regret rule, attempts to give a compromise between the cautious maximin rule and the optimistic maximax rule. However, unlike the minimax regret rule, weights are assigned to the best and worst payoff for each decision option and the option with the highest weighted payoff is chosen.

The weighted payoff is calculated as:

$$\alpha \times \text{worst payoff} + (1 - \alpha) \times \text{best payoff}$$

The value of α (alpha) depends on the decision-maker's attitude to risk. The smaller the value, the bigger risk he is prepared to take; when $\alpha = 0$ the decision will be the same as for the maximax rule.

Expected monetary value or *EMV* is an expected value (see Chapter 7) in monetary terms. In this context it is a long-run average and is found by multiplying each payoff by the probability that this payoff will occur and adding. The option that maximizes the EMV is chosen.

Expected opportunity loss or *EOL* is essentially the same technique as the EMV method except that the probabilities are applied to the opportunity loss table and the option that *minimizes* the EOL is chosen.

example
11.2

A car accessory company, Marla plc, has developed a new car immobilizer and has to decide whether to market the product nationwide, to sell by mail order or to sell the patent to a large chain of motor accessory shops. The cost of distributing nationwide is very high but the potential profits could also be large. There is less risk with selling by mail order but the potential profits would also be less. The safe option is to sell the patent, but in this case the chance of making large profits would be lost. How does Marla make its decision given that it has limited knowledge of the likely demand for the product? The estimated profits for each decision depend on the state of the market, which has been defined as high, medium and low. The probability that the state of the market will be high, medium or low has been estimated as 0.25, 0.3 and 0.45, respectively. The expected profits (in £000s) are given in Table 11.2.

Table 11.2 Profits (£000s) for Marla plc

Decision	State of the market		
	High ($p = 0.25$)	Medium ($p = 0.3$)	Low ($p = 0.45$)
Nationwide	95	52	−26
Mail order	48	24	19
Sell patent	25	25	25

(*activity* 11.3) What are the best decisions using the maximax and maximin rules?

The largest payoff is 95 (£000s) for the 'sell nationwide' decision when the market is high. This is the decision that would be made using the maximax rule. The worst payoff for each decision is −26, 19, 25, and the highest of these is 25 so the decision under the maximin rule is to sell the patent.

(*activity* 11.4) What is the best decision using the minimax regret rule?

This rule requires you to create an opportunity loss table as described earlier. The largest payoff when the market is high is 95, so if the mail order option was taken instead this would mean that a 'loss' of 95 − 48 = 47 (£000s) would be made through not taking the best option. The complete opportunity loss table is shown in Table 11.3.

Table 11.3 Opportunity loss table (in £000s) for Example 11.2

Decision	State of the market		
	High	Medium	Low
Nationwide	0	0	51
Mail order	47	28	6
Sell patent	70	27	0

The largest loss for each decision is 51, 47 and 70. The smallest of these is 47, so the best decision under this rule is to sell by mail order.

(*activity* 11.5) What is the best decision using the Hurwicz criterion with an alpha of 0.6?

The weighted payoff is calculated from

$$\alpha \times \text{worst payoff} + (1 - \alpha) \times \text{best payoff}$$

For the decision to sell nationwide the worst payoff is −26 and the best is 95, so the weighted payoff is therefore

$$0.6 \times (-26) + 0.4 \times 95 = 22.4$$

Repeating this for the decisions to sell by mail order and to sell the patent we get:

Mail order: $0.6 \times 19 + 0.4 \times 48 = 30.6$

Sell patent: $0.6 \times 25 + 0.4 \times 25 = 25$

So under this criterion and using $\alpha = 0.6$, the decision is to go for the mail order option.

(*activity* 11.6) What is the best decision using the expected monetary value criterion?

Nationwide: $0.25 \times 95 + 0.3 \times 52 + 0.45 \times (-26) = 27.65$

Mail order: $0.25 \times 48 + 0.3 \times 24 + 0.45 \times 19 = 27.75$

Sell patent: $0.25 \times 25 + 0.3 \times 25 + 0.45 \times 25 = 25$

This suggests that, on average, choosing the 'mail order' option would give you a slightly higher payoff at £27 750.

activity 11.7

What is the best decision using the expected opportunity loss criterion?

The probabilities are applied to Table 11.2, and the result is:

Nationwide: $0.25 \times 0 + 0.3 \times 0 + 0.45 \times 51 = 22.95$

Mail order: $0.25 \times 47 + 0.3 \times 28 + 0.45 \times 6 = 22.85$

Sell patent: $0.25 \times 70 + 0.3 \times 27 + 0.45 \times 0 = 25.6$

The decision that would minimize the EOL is again the mail order option. (The EMV and EOL decision rules should always agree.)

The value of perfect information

Imagine that a market research company could forecast the demand for the new car immobilizer (Example 11.2) perfectly. How much would it be worth paying for this market research? If the market research company reported that demand would be low, the best option would be to sell the patent, whereas if it said that demand would be high, the option to sell nationwide would be chosen. Of course, high demand only occurs 25% of the time, medium demand 30% of the time and low demand 45% of the time. Therefore it is possible to work out the *expected* payoff if you had this perfect information. This is called the expected value *with* perfect information. The expected value *of* perfect information (EVPI) is simply the difference between the expected value with perfect information and the best EMV.

activity 11.8

What would be the expected value of perfect information for the payoff table given in Table 11.1?

The expected value with perfect information will be:

$0.25 \times 95 + 0.3 \times 52 + 0.45 \times 25 = 50.6$

The EVPI is therefore:

$50.6 - 27.75 = 22.85$, or £22 850

This is the maximum amount that a decision-maker would be prepared to pay for this information. (You should note that this is the same figure as the expected opportunity loss calculated in Activity 11.7.)

Decision trees

Payoff tables are useful when there is only one decision to make, but often a sequence of decisions are necessary. This is called *multiple-stage* decision-making and for these cases decision-makers generally prefer to use *decision trees*. Decision trees are similar to probability trees (see Chapter 6) except that as well as probabilistic (or chance) branches there are also decision branches. Decision branches allow the decision-maker to compare alternative options, while the chance branches handle the probabilistic nature of an outcome. The skeleton of a single-stage decision tree is shown in Figure 11.7.

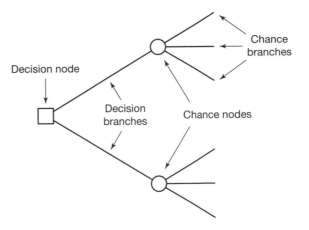

Figure 11.7 Decision tree

The square node represents the point where the decision is made, while the round nodes represent the point at which chance takes over. The decision tree is drawn from left to right, but to evaluate the tree you work from right to left. This is called the *roll back* method. You first evaluate the EMV at each chance node and then at the decision node you select the 'best' EMV (don't forget, 'best' can be lowest cost as well as largest profit).

Although a decision tree is not normally used for single-stage decision problems the next activity continues to use Example 11.2 since we know what the answer is using the EMV criterion.

(activity 11.9)   Use the decision tree approach to solve Example 11.2.

The decision tree for this problem has been drawn in Figure 11.8, and you will see that the outcomes for each decision and state of the market have been written at the end of each probabilistic branch. As before, the best decision is to sell by mail order.

The next problem illustrates a multi-stage decision problem.

Figure 11.8 Decision tree for Marla plc

(example 11.3)   The Delma Oil company has obtained government approval to drill for oil in the Baltic Sea. This area is known to contain oil deposits and industry sources believe that there is a 50% chance that oil will be found in a commercially viable quantity. The cost of the drilling programme is believed to be £30m but this could be more than offset by the potential revenue, which is put at £100m at today's prices.

The company could carry out test drillings at different sites, which would only cost £5m. From historical data, tests are likely to indicate a viable field 65% of the time. However, these tests are not completely reliable and the probability that they are correct is only 0.7. That is, if the tests are positive there is a 70% chance that a viable quantity of oil will be found, and if negative there is only a 30% (100 − 70) chance that oil will be found in a viable quantity.

The company could sell its rights to drill in the area, but the revenue obtained will depend on the outcome of the tests (if carried out) and are as follows:

Tests indicate oil	£35m
Tests don't indicate oil	£3m
No tests carried out	£10m

**activity
11.10**

What decisions should the company make given this information?

This problem involves two decisions. The first decision is whether to test drill and the second decision is whether to start a drilling programme. In order to solve this decision problem you would carry out the following three steps:

Step 1

Draw the decision tree. This is shown in Figure 11.9. You will see that the decision nodes have been numbered 1, 2 and 3 while the chance nodes have been labelled as a, b, c and d. The values at the end of each branch of the tree represent the *net* outcome. For instance, if drilling is carried out without any tests and oil is found, the net outcome is a profit of £100m − £30m = £70m, whereas if no oil is found a loss of £30m is made.

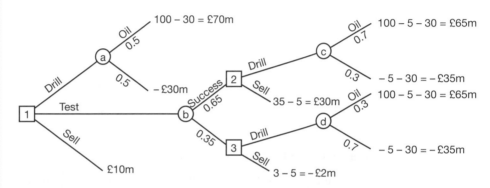

Figure 11.9 Decision tree for the Delma Oil company

Step 2

Working from the right, the EMV at the chance nodes a, c and d are calculated as follows:

Node	EMV
a	$0.5 \times 70 + 0.5 \times (-30) = £20m$
c	$0.7 \times 65 + 0.3 \times (-35) = £35m$
d	$0.3 \times 65 + 0.7 \times (-35) = -£5m$

(The EMV at node b cannot be calculated until Step 3.)

Step 3

The roll back technique is now employed. At decision node 2, the decision is to either drill or sell. Sell will give you £30m, whereas drilling will give you £35m. The option that gives the largest EMV is to drill, and so this is the option that would be taken. The value 35 is put above node 2 and the sell option is crossed out. If you repeat this for node 3 you should find that the best option here is to sell. The EMV at chance node b can now be calculated and you should find that this is £22.05m $(0.65 \times 35 + 0.35 \times (-2))$. You can now go to decision node 1 and compare the three decisions. You should find the following:

Drill: £20m

Test: £22.05m

Sell: £10m

The best decision is to test first. If the test gives successful results, only then should drilling start; *otherwise* the rights should be sold for £3m. You will see this analysis illustrated in Figure 11.10.

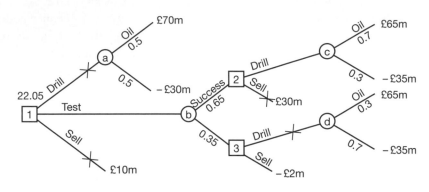

Figure 11.10 Completed decision tree for Delma Oil company

Decision trees and Bayes' theorem

In Example 11.3 you were given all the relevant probabilities, but in general you are more likely to be given just the *prior* probabilities and the *conditional* probabilities. You would then need to work out the relevant *posterior* probabilities using Bayes' theorem. You met Bayes' theorem in Chapter 6 where you used it to modify a prior probability given some new information. The next example requires you to use the same technique before you are able to solve the decision problem.

example
11.4

A small motor component company, CleanFuel, is trying to decide whether to market a fuel additive which it claims will improve fuel consumption. Unfortunately there are a number of competitors in the market who are also working on the same product and CleanFuel knows that if it decides to market the product it will face stiff competition from other companies.

Instead of marketing the product itself, it could sell the rights to it for £2m. However, if it goes ahead and markets the product itself, it estimates that the probability that sales will be high is only 0.2. The profit resulting from these high sales is put at £10m, but if the sales are low (with a probability of 0.8), the company will end up making a loss of £1m. An alternative is to commission a market research survey to see if motorists would purchase the product. This market research would indicate either high or low sales. From past experience CleanFuel knows that this particular market research company is better at predicting high rather than low sales. When sales have turned out to be high the company has been correct 75% of the time, but when sales have been low the company has only managed a 65% success rate.

The market research is confidential, so even if the results of the research indicate low sales it will still be possible to sell the rights for £2m. Of course, CleanFuel could also decide to market the product whatever the results of the survey.

(activity 11.11) Draw a decision tree for this problem.

The tree you should have obtained is shown in Figure 11.11.

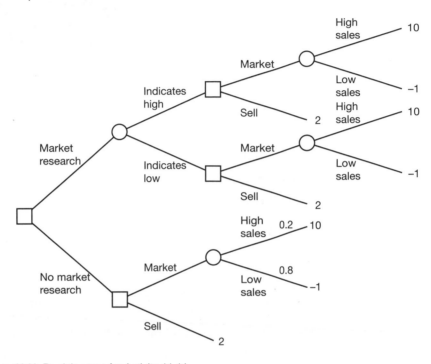

Figure 11.11 Decision tree for Activity 11.11

Notice that there are some probabilities that we don't appear to know. These are the probability of the market research giving a high and low forecast and the probability of high and low demand given the different outcomes of the market research. These probabilities can be obtained by the use of Bayes' theorem. The prior probabilities are 0.2 for high sales and 0.8 for low sales.

(activity 11.12) Draw a probability tree diagram and calculate using Bayes' theorem the following probabilities:

P(market research indicates high sales)
P(market research indicates low sales)
P(high sales | market research indicates high sales)
P(low sales | market research indicates high sales)
P(high sales | market research indicates low sales)
P(low sales | market research indicates low sales)

Note: For this activity you may find it helpful to refer back to page 133.

Figure 11.12 Probability tree diagram for Activity 11.12

Figure 11.12 gives the probability tree diagram, where you will see that the joint probabilities have been added to the end of each branch.

P(market research indicates high sales) $= 0.15 + 0.28 = 0.43$

P(market research indicates low sales) $= 1 - 0.43 = 0.57$

$$\text{P(high sales|market research indicates high sales)} = \frac{0.15}{0.43} = 0.349$$

P(low sales|market research indicates high sales) $= 1 - 0.349 = 0.651$

$$\text{P(high sales|market research indicates low sales)} = \frac{0.05}{0.57} = 0.088$$

P(low sales|market research indicates low sales) $= 1 - 0.088 = 0.912$

These probabilities can now be added to the decision tree and the tree rolled back to show that the best decision is to commission the market research and only to market the product if the research suggests that the sales will be high, and otherwise to sell the rights. You can see the final tree in Figure 11.13.

The preceding calculations did not make any reference to the cost of market research. It would be important for CleanFuel to know whether the cost of the market research was reasonable. An upper limit to how much to spend on market research is relatively easy to work out as it is the difference between the 'market research' and 'no market research branches' in Figure 11.13. The 'no market research' branch implies that the rights to the product will be sold for £2m.

activity
11.13

What is the maximum amount of money it would be worth CleanFuel paying for the market research?

The difference between the two branches is £0.36m (2.36 − 2). This is called the *expected value of imperfect information* (EVII) as it takes account of the fact that the market research is not completely reliable. CleanFuel should therefore not pay more than £0.36m for the market research.

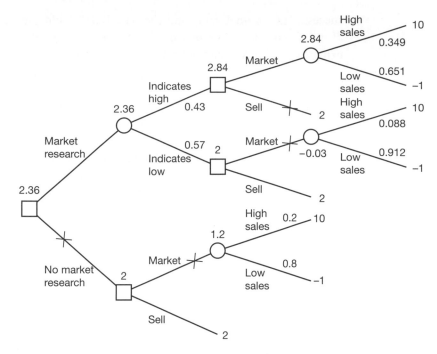

Figure 11.13 The completed decision tree for Example 11.4

Sensitivity analysis

The major difficulty with decision analysis is estimating the probabilities and the expected returns. In many cases the probabilities are simply best guesses. In decision analysis, the sensitivity of the recommended decision to changes in any of the estimated values should be investigated. The most effective way to look at how sensitive the final decision is to changes in the probabilities is to see how big a change in one of the probabilities is necessary for you to change your decision. If only a small change in probability is required then you would say that the decision is sensitive to the value of the probability. If it would take a large change in probability then you could say that the decision is insensitive to changes in the probability and that the decision is *robust*. To investigate the sensitivity of the decision it is normal to find the probability that makes you *indifferent* between two decisions.

activity
11.14

How much can the probability of a successful test in the Delma Oil company problem (Example 11.3) be allowed to vary before the decision changes from 'test first' to 'drill without test'?

You might have tried to solve this activity by trial and error, but this is not recommended as it can be tedious and there are better methods available. As the probability of success falls the EMV at node b will also fall. When this EMV becomes £20m we will be indifferent to 'test first' and 'drill without test'. To find this point of indifference we could calculate the EMV at node b using a different value of the probability of success. The original value and the new EMV could then be plotted and the point of indifference found graphically. To illustrate this method let us calculate the EMV using a probability of success of 0.4. The EMV at node b will then be:

$$0.4 \times 35 + 0.6 \times (-2) = £12.8m$$

This and the original value are plotted on the graph shown in Figure 11.14. The line between the two points intersects the £20m gridline at a probability of just under 0.6. From this we can deduce that the decision will change once the probability falls below this figure. Since the original probability was 0.65 this is a relatively small change in probability. We can therefore say that the decision whether to test drill or not is quite sensitive to the probability of a viable oil field.

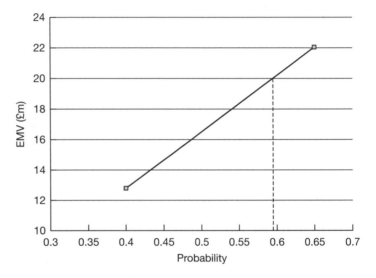

Figure 11.14 Graphical method for solving sensitivity analysis problems

An alternative algebraic method is to call the probability p and the EMV at node b then becomes:

$$35 \times p + (-2) \times (1 - p) = 35p - 2 + 2p$$
$$= 37p - 2$$

The decision will change when the value of this expression is less than £20m. That is:

$$37p - 2 < 20$$

that is, $37p < 22$

therefore, $p < 0.595$

which agrees with the answer found from the graphical method.

activity 11.15   Investigate the sensitivity of the decision on whether to carry out market research or not for the CleanFuel problem (Example 11.4) to changes in the probability of the market research company successfully predicting high sales.

When sales were high the success rate of the market research company was given as 75%; that is, the probability of success when sales were high was 0.75. To investigate changes in this probability we would need to determine what this probability would have to become for the decision to change from 'conduct market research' to 'don't conduct market research'. This problem is much more difficult to solve than for Activity 11.14 as any change in this probability makes many changes within the decision tree itself. The most effective method of carrying out sensitivity analysis on complex decision problems is to use the *goal seeking* routine in Excel. In fact, it is a good idea to use a spreadsheet for all decision tree problems as you can then see immediately the effects of changing any of the inputs, such as the probabilities or outcomes. To do this it is advisable to use the *drawing* toolbar in Excel to draw the tree diagram and enter the inputs as parameters at the top of the sheet. You can then enter formulae at appropriate points in the diagram. Figure 11.15 is a screen shot of the worksheet for the CleanFuel problem.

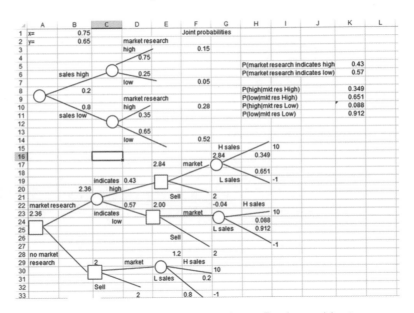

Figure 11.15 The decision tree for Example 11.4 added to an Excel spreadsheet
Used with permission from Microsoft.

The probabilities of the market research company making accurate forecasts when sales are high and low respectively can be seen in cells B1 and B2 and have been labelled as 'x' and 'y'. The value we are interested in is contained within cell B1. The Goal Seek routine can be found in the Data Tools group within the Data tab. Click on What-If Analysis and then Goal Seek. The Set cell is the cell that currently contains the value of 2.36, which we want to change to the value 2 (the EMV without market research). The By changing cell is cell B1, which currently contains the value 0.75. The dialog box for the Goal Seek routine can be seen in Figure 11.16.

The result of using Excel's Goal Seek can be seen in Figure 11.17, where you will see that the probability 'x' which is necessary to make you indifferent between market research and no market research is 0.525. This means that if the probability of successfully predicting high sales fell from 0.75 to below 0.525 the decision would

Figure 11.16 The Goal Seek dialog box
Used with permission from Microsoft.

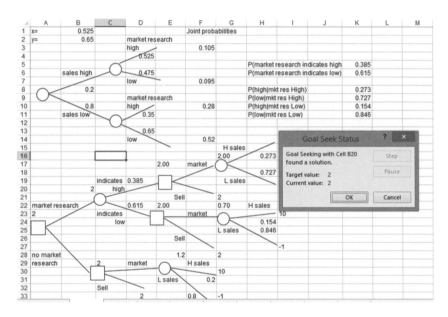

Figure 11.17 Result of using Goal Seek in Excel
Used with permission from Microsoft.

change from 'carry out market research' to 'don't carry out market research'. This is quite a large difference so we could say that the decision is fairly insensitive to changes in this probability.

activity 11.16

Investigate the sensitivity of the decision on whether to carry out market research or not for the CleanFuel problem (Example 11.4) to changes in the probability of the market research company successfully predicting low sales.

You should have found that the probability 'y' has now become 0.5, which is not such a large fall as in the probability of successfully predicting high sales. The decision is therefore more sensitive to changes in this probability.

Utility

The EMV criterion is a very useful and popular method for choosing between a number of alternatives. However, its main drawback is that it takes no account of the decision-maker's attitude to *risk*. Some decision-makers are *risk-seekers* – they are prepared to take the risk of making a loss if there is also a chance (even if this chance is small) of making large gains. Other decision-makers are *risk-averse* – they would always choose the safe option to avoid the risk of making a loss. One method of taking a decision-maker's attitude to risk into account is to evaluate their *utility* function. This converts monetary values into a scale between 0 and 1 in such a way that the change in the utility reflects changes in the decision-maker's preference for different amounts of money. In order to obtain this information, the decision-maker is asked a number of questions.

example
11.5

The owner of Marla plc (Example 11.2) has called in a firm of consultants to help her decide on the best decision for her company. Table 11.4 is a repeat of the data already provided earlier in this chapter.

Table 11.4 Profits (£000s) for Marla plc

Decision	State of the market		
	High ($p = 0.25$)	Medium ($p = 0.3$)	Low ($p = 0.45$)
Nationwide	95	52	−26
Mail order	48	24	19
Sell patent	25	25	25

To determine the owner's attitude to risk, the consultants asked the question:

'Would you prefer to accept a sum of £52 000 or to enter a lottery where the chance of winning £95 000 is 60% and the chance of losing £26 000 is 40%?'

The owner thought for a few seconds and decided that she would rather take the £52 000. The interviewer then kept raising the probability of winning the lottery until he reached the point where the owner could not make up her mind which option she would prefer; that is, she was indifferent between taking the £52 000 or entering the lottery. This occurred at a probability of 0.9. This procedure was repeated for the sum of £25 000 and £19 000, and the probability at which she was indifferent between the certain sum of money (£25 000 or £19 000) and entering the lottery was 0.7 and 0.65 respectively.

The approach to finding a decision-maker's utility function by the method described above is called the *probability-equivalence* approach. The largest of all the possible payoffs in the decision is given the utility of 1 and the smallest the utility of 0. In Table 11.4 we have the following values (in £000s) to consider: 95, 52, 48, 25, 24, 19, −26. The largest value, 95, is given the utility of 1 and the smallest value, −26, is given the utility of 0. From the answers to the owner's questions we are now able to work out her utility (u) for values of £52 000, £25 000 and £19 000 as follows.

$$u(52) = 0.9u(95) + 0.1u(-26)$$

$$= 0.9 \times 1 + 0.1 \times 0 = 0.9$$

So once the point of indifference has been established, the utility for a particular monetary value is simply the probability of the best outcome of the lottery.

activity **11.17**

Find the utility of the remaining monetary values.

$$u(25) = 0.7 \quad u(19) = 0.65$$

Unfortunately we do not have the utilities of either £48 000 or £24 000 (although as £24 000 is so close to £25 000 we could assume it is about 0.69). To find £48 000 we can draw a graph of utility against monetary value as shown in Figure 11.18. Interpolating this graph we can estimate the utility of £48 000 as about 0.87.

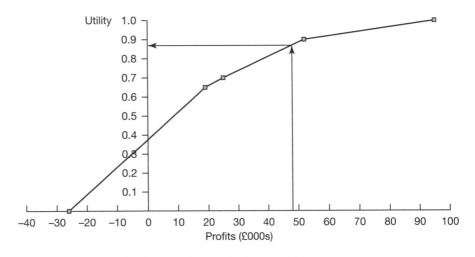

Figure 11.18 Graph showing the utility function for Example 11.5

The final step is to substitute the monetary values in Table 11.4 with the calculated utility values and find the decision that maximizes the expected utility.

activity **11.18**

Calculate the expected utilities for each decision and decide on the best option using this criterion.

Table 11.5 gives the utility values for each alternative and state of nature.

Table 11.5 Utility values for Marla plc

Decision	State of the market		
	High (p = 0.25)	Medium (p = 0.3)	Low (p = 0.45)
Nationwide	1	0.9	0
Mail order	0.87	0.69	0.65
Sell patent	0.7	0.7	0.7

The expected utilities are:

Nationwide: $0.25 \times 1 + 0.3 \times 0.9 + 0.45 \times 0 = 0.52$

Mail order: $0.25 \times 0.87 + 0.3 \times 0.69 + 0.45 \times 0.65 = 0.72$

Sell patent: $0.25 \times 0.7 + 0.3 \times 0.7 + 0.45 \times 0.7 = 0.7$

The decision has not changed – it is still 'sell by mail order' but there is now very little to choose between this and the risk-free option 'sell patent'. Notice too that there is now a bigger difference between 'sell nationwide' and the other two options. This reflects the fact that the owner is risk-averse – she doesn't want to risk the possible loss of £26 000.

Figure 11.18, which we drew previously, is a graph of the owner's utility function. You will notice that this has a concave shape. For a decision-maker who is a risk-seeker you would get a curve that is convex and for someone who is risk-neutral you would get a straight line. Figures 11.19 and 11.20 illustrate these different utility functions. Figure 11.21 is the utility function for someone who is risk-seeking at lower monetary levels but risk-averse at higher monetary levels.

Figure 11.19 A curve of the utility function for a decision-maker who is risk-seeking

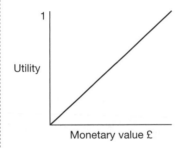

Figure 11.20 A curve of the utility function for a decision-maker who is risk-neutral

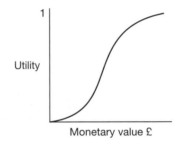

Figure 11.21 A curve of the utility function for a decision-maker who is both risk-seeking and risk-averse

DID YOU KNOW?

Peter Drucker (2003) wrote:

'A decision is a judgement. It is a choice between alternatives. It is rarely a choice between right and wrong. It is at best a choice between 'almost right' and 'probably wrong' – but much more often a choice between two courses of action neither of which is probably more right than the other.'

Multi-criteria decision-making (MCDA)

The techniques you have met so far have involved a single objective (for example, to maximize expected monetary value). However, in many real-life situations decision-makers have a number of conflicting objectives. In the *Quantitative methods in action*, for instance, highway improvement projects had to be selected based on a number of criteria including risk, traffic flows and cost. Similarly, in choosing a new house you might need to consider several criteria, including price, location, type and size. Clearly it is unlikely that you will get all the features you want, so you will have to decide which are most important. For personal choices such as choosing a house, it may not be necessary to use any formal techniques, but for larger problems it is important to use a formal method that can be documented. In this section you will meet a simple but powerful technique called *SMART* (Simple Multi-Attribute Rating Technique). This technique was developed by Edwards (1971) and has been applied to a wide range of situations.

The underlying method behind the SMART technique is quite simple. Decision-makers decide on a set of criteria that they feel are important to their problem. In simple cases there may be just a few criteria; in more complex cases there may be a hierarchy of criteria. In these cases it is useful to draw a *value tree* which shows the different levels of criteria in a tree structure. Once the criteria have been defined, it is necessary to score how well each option performs on each criterion. Important criteria will score more highly with some options than others, so it is necessary to devise some kind of scoring system. A percentage scoring system is normally used, whereby 0 represents the worst case and 100 the best. Once all the options have been scored for each criterion, the decision-makers weight each criterion according to its overall importance using *swing weights*. The way this is done is to imagine all the criteria are at their worst level and to consider the swing of each from the least preferred to the most preferred level. The decision-makers then choose the criteria that they consider to be the most important in terms of this swing. To be able to compare each option, the aggregate benefits across all criteria for each option are found, and the option with the highest aggregate benefit will be the most preferred. However, if we now take cost into consideration, there might be other options that, although they do not give such high benefits, do give much lower costs.

We will now demonstrate the method using the problem of choosing a house.

example
11.6

Suppose you have won £300 000 on the National Lottery and have decided to invest it in property. You have shortlisted five houses in your price range. You now have to decide which one of these houses to buy. To help you decide, you have made a list of the important attributes of each house. These attributes are:

■ Purchase cost.
■ Distance to rail station.
■ Location (the attractiveness of the neighbourhood).
■ Size of house (as measured by floor area).

The purchase cost of each house, together with its floor area and distance to the rail station, are shown in Table 11.6.

Table 11.6 Data for the house choice problem

House	Purchase cost	Floor area (square feet)	Distance to rail station (miles)
A	£275,000	1800	0.50
B	£260,000	1000	1.20
C	£240,000	800	0.25
D	£250,000	1200	2.50
E	£300,000	2000	0.75

activity
11.19

Draw a value tree for Example 11.6

The value tree is shown in Figure 11.22.

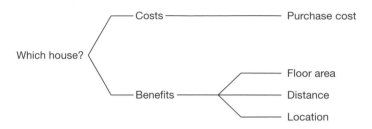

Figure 11.22 Value tree for the house purchase problem

It is now necessary to score each option on each criterion. Clearly if closeness to the rail station is important to you then you would score house C as 100 and house D as 0. For the other houses you might adopt a simple pro rata approach simply based on distance but for this exercise we will treat all criteria in the same way. The most effective means of doing this is shown below:

1 Draw a line and divide it into ten equal parts, labelling it as shown in Figure 11.23.

Figure 11.23 Assigning weights (1): dividing a line

2 Next, write your least preferred option at the zero point and your most preferred at the 100 point mark (Figure 11.24).

Figure 11.24 Assigning weights (2): marking least and most preferred options

3 Then, using your judgement, indicate the positions of the remaining options (Figure 11.25).

Figure 11.25 Assigning weights (3): marking remaining options

The diagram now reflects your feelings, not just about the order of the options but also their importance relative to each other. You have judged that based on distance houses A and E are similar and are not much below house C in preference but that house B being over a mile away is much less favourable. However house B still scores much higher than the worst choice, house D. Remember though that we are looking at just this one criterion which is independent of the other criteria.

You repeat this exercise for both the size of house and the location criteria (the location being qualitative will be much more subjective than the other two criteria) and you get the Table 11.7 showing the scores for all criteria.

Table 11.7 Scores for the three criteria

House	Floor area	Distance	Location
A	90	85	40
B	50	40	20
C	0	100	0
D	60	0	100
E	100	75	90

activity
11.20

Based on Table 11.7 which house would you choose to buy?

Based on total score we might choose house E as it has the highest total (265). However this assumes that all criteria are equally weighted which is unlikely to be the case. To decide on the weighting to apply we use swing weights. Let us suppose that you choose location as the most important criterion: this then has a weight of 100. Floor area is the next most important criteron, and you decide that the swing from the least preferred to the most preferred size of house is only 60% as important as the swing from the worst location to the best location. Similarly you decide that distance from the rail station has a weight of 40. Figure 11.26 illustrates this process.

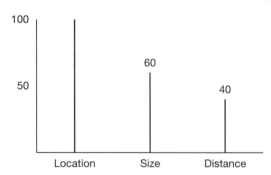

Figure 11.26 The swing weights method

The sum of these weights is 200 (100 + 60 + 40): to maintain consistency with the other weights you need to normalize them – to make the sum equal to 100 – which is easily done in this case simply by dividing by 2.

activity
11.21

Calculate the aggregate benefits for each house and decide on your preferred choice.

To calculate the aggregate measure of all these benefits for each house, we need to multiply the weight for each attribute by the normalized weight for that attribute, and add up the values. So for house A we would have:

$$(90 \times 30) + (85 \times 20) + (40 \times 50) = 6400$$

This figure should then be divided by 100 (the sum of the weights), giving 64.0. (Note: It is easier if this calculation is performed in Excel, and the function

$$= \text{SUMPRODUCT (B2:D2,\$B\$9:\$D\$9)/100}$$

can be used to calculate the aggregate benefit.) Table 11.8 shows the aggregate benefits.

Table 11.8 Aggregate benefits and costs for the house choice problem

House	Floor area	Distance	Location		Aggregate benefits	Cost (£000s)
A	90	85	40		64.0	275
B	50	40	20		33.0	260
C	0	100	0		20.0	240
D	60	0	100		68.0	250
E	100	75	90		90.0	300
Raw weights	60	40	100	Sum 200		
Normalized weights	30	20	50			

For this final table the costs, too, have been included. From this table you can see that – not surprisingly – house E has the highest aggregate benefits, but it also has the highest cost. House C has the smallest aggregate benefits and the lowest cost. However, house D has quite high benefits in comparison with its cost.

To see the relationship between benefits and cost, it is a good idea to create a chart in Excel (Figure 11.27). From this chart you can see that although house A is more expensive than house D, it does not have higher benefits. This is also true for houses B and D. From this it should be clear that only houses C, D and E are worth considering: the other two options are dominated by these three houses. In other words, neither house A nor house B has both higher benefits *and* lower costs than any of the properties C, D and E. If we draw a line connecting C, D and E, we get what is called the *efficient frontier*. You should note that the efficient frontier will always be on the outer boundary of the plot, reflecting our wish to minimize costs whilst maximizing benefits.

The efficient frontier allows us to reduce the number of options, and with a large number of options this can be a very useful device. However, it is still necessary to decide which house out of the three is best. If you want to spend all of the £200 000 win, then house E might be best; but you could save £50 000 by choosing house D, whose aggregate benefits are only 22 points below house E.

Sensitivity analysis and MCDA software

Although you may find the basic ideas behind the SMART technique simple the process of agreeing the relevant criteria and weights can be problematic. In many

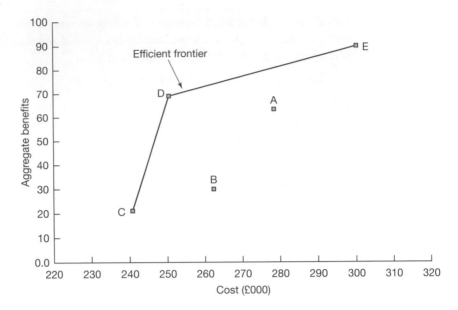

Figure 11.27 Chart of aggregate benefits versus cost

large-scale MCDA problems groups of stakeholders, experts and others get together and discuss and hopefully resolve the issues. This process is called a *decision conference*. The idea behind a decision conference is to agree a consensus but in many cases this is not possible. This is where sensitivity analysis can be useful as changes can be made to weights to see the effect on the overall results. In the case of the house purchase problem with only 3 criteria it would be quite simple to repeat the exercise several times. However with complex problems involving many options and criteria this is not a feasible approach. In these cases the use of software can be essential. One MCDA software is *Hiview3* produced by Catalyze. Not only does this software automate the process but it allows sensitivity analysis to be carried out easily.

Using Hiview3 you first create a value tree and add your decision criteria as you did in Activity 11.19. At the top of the tree is the *root* node which is the final decision you wish to make. This is 'Which house?' in Figure 11.22. The two main criteria are costs and benefits and beneath the benefits node are the three sub-criteria which we are to measure.

Once the criteria have been added you then score each option against each of the criteria. Hiview3 uses two types of score; constructed scales and natural scales. Constructed scales are the approach we used but you can also use natural scales for criteria that have a measurement, such as floor area. If you use a natural scale the software works out the score based on numerical values. A screen print of the criterion scores window for the location criterion is shown in Figure 11.28.

The next step is to apply the swing weighting method. To do this you click on `Benefits` on the tree and then choose `Weight Criteria Swings Below Selected Node`. You then add the agreed values as in Figure 11.29.

When all the data has been added you can get a summary by double-clicking `Benefits` (see Figure 11.30). This matches the figures we obtained in Table 11.8.

Figure 11.28 Scoring the location criterion in Hiview3

Figure 11.29 Applying swing weights to the Benefits node

Figure 11.30 Summary of the benefits data

You can then analyze the model and obtain the efficient frontier as we did manually. This is shown in Figure 11.31 where, although the cost scale is reversed and has been normalized to 100, the same three houses are on the frontier.

The next step in any MCDA analysis is to do a sensitivity analysis. This can be easily done in Hiview3 which allows you to either summarize the whole model using the `Sensitivity Down` window or to examine each criterion using the `Sensitivity Up` option. The latter option has been used on the distance criterion and is shown in Figure 11.32. The horizontal axis is the cumulative weight of the distance criterion (as shown in Figure 11.30) which is currently 20 and shown by a vertical line. The sloping lines show how the aggregate benefits for each house change as the weight on the distance criterion changes.

activity **11.22**

How sensitive is the overall solution to changes in the weight of the distance criterion?

At the current weight of 20 for the distance criterion, house E has the highest aggregate benefits. This will still be the highest option until the weight of the distance criterion reaches 80, at which point house C takes over. House E will also have the highest option even if the weight fell to zero. This analysis suggests that the solution is not sensitive to the weight of the distance criterion.

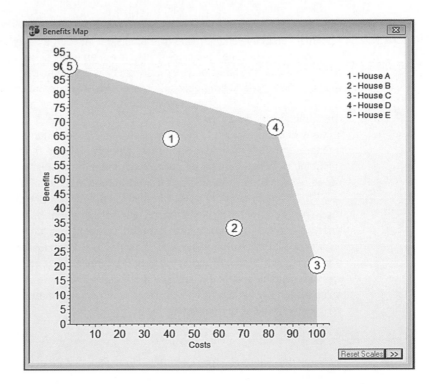

Figure 11.31 The efficient frontier

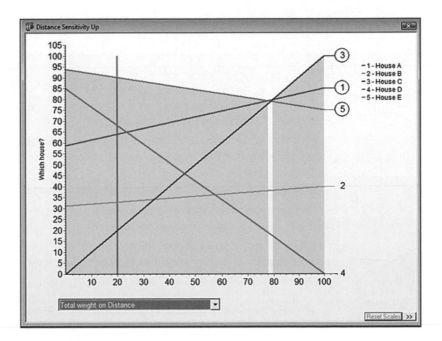

Figure 11.32 Sensitivity analysis on the distance criterion using Hiview3

Reflection

The intention of this chapter is to give an insight into some decision-making techniques available to businesses. Decision-making is not an exact science, and major decisions will not be made on the basis of quantitative techniques alone. Many decisions have to take into account the wishes of the public, the shareholders and many other stakeholders. In addition many problems are not clear or well structured and require some 'problem structuring' using diagrammatic methods first.

Many decision-making techniques have weaknesses and make many assumptions. For instance, the EMV method is a long-run average, so there must be some reservation about using the technique for one-off decisions. Another issue arises when we assume a discrete range of conditions. In Example 11.4 we assumed that the market would be either high or low. This is a very arbitrary range; there could be any number of market conditions between these two extremes. This is the reason why sensitivity analysis is so important, as such an analysis makes it possible to see how robust a solution is to changes in assumptions.

With all real decision-making, one challenge is that the issues are often complex and not easy to resolve. If we can split a problem into smaller parts (divide and conquer), we can often come to an acceptable solution more quickly and more easily than if we had tried to solve the larger problem. This is particularly the case with the SMART technique, in which we focus on the key attributes first.

Key points

- Many decision problems are poorly defined so the use of pictures and diagrams is often an essential first step in solving such a problem. These diagrams range from rich pictures which are hand-drawn to more formal causal loop diagrams which can show feedback loops.

- Once a decision problem is defined a number of more formal diagrams and techniques can be used.

- Many decision problems are made under conditions of uncertainty so probability plays an important part in these techniques.

- The simplest techniques are those involving payoff tables. These then lead on to decision trees. When the probability of an event (or state of nature) is known it is possible to use the technique of expected monetary value (EMV).

- Bayes' theorem is a powerful technique that can be used in conjunction with decision trees and allows probabilities to be adjusted when new information (such as market research) becomes available.

- Another application of decision trees is to calculate the value of information.

- All decisions involve risk so it is useful to ascertain a decision-maker's attitude to risk. This can be found using utility theory techniques.

- Where a decision involves several criteria, it is possible to use a multi-attribute technique such as SMART to find the option that gives maximum benefit at the lowest cost.

Further reading

There are very many decision-making techniques and this text has indentified some of the most useful ones. For a fuller explanation of the various techniques there are many texts available. One of the best is Goodwin and Wright (2014) which has a behavioural analysis slant to it. Daellenbach and McNickle (2012) is also very good and covers both problem structuring and management science techniques. Drucker (2007) is well known for his writings on management and is useful background reading. For specific techniques, Pidd (2010) is a good text on problem structuring methods in general and systems dynamics in particular. The most well known author on problem structuring methods is Checkland (2006), although this text is not for the casual reader.

http://www.**palgrave**.com/oakshott-eqm6

Solutions to all questions are freely available

Practice questions

1 A company intends to market a new product, and it estimates that there is a 20% chance that it will be first in the market and this will give it £2m revenue in the first year. However, if it is not first in the market the expected revenue will only be £0.5m. What is the EMV?

2 Please refer to Figure 11.33 for this question and note that the objective is to maximize EMV.
   (a) What is the value of x?
   (b) What is the EMV at probabilistic node B?
   (c) What is the EMV at probabilistic node C?
   (d) What should the decision be at decision node A?
   (e) What should the value of x be in order that you will be indifferent to choosing between decision 1 and decision 2?

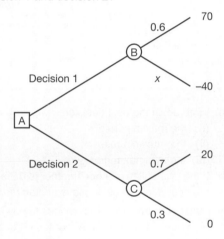

Figure 11.33 Diagram for Question 2

3 An inventor develops a new product. Having made the product he has three choices of what to do with it:

1 manufacture the product himself
2 allow someone else to make it and be paid on a royalty basis
3 sell the rights for a lump sum.

The profit which can be expected depends on the level of sales and is shown in Table 11.9 (in £000s).

Table 11.9 Payoff table for Question 3

	High sales	Medium sales	Low sales
Manufacture	80	40	−20
Royalties	50	30	10
Sell	20	20	20

The probabilities associated with the level of sales are 0.2, 0.5 and 0.3 for high, medium and low sales respectively.

(a) Write down the best decision using:
   (i)   the maximax rule
   (ii) the maximin rule
   (iii) the minimax regret rule
(b) Calculate the best decision using the expected monetary value.
(c) A survey might help to determine the likely level of sales. What is the maximum amount that the inventor should be prepared to pay for this survey?

4   An owner of a campsite is trying to decide whether to build a swimming pool, a tennis court or an indoor bar area. She can only afford to build one of these and she needs help in deciding which one to choose. The profitability of each will, to some extent, depend on the weather. If the weather if hot, campers would prefer the swimming pool, but if the summer is cool, an indoor bar will be more profitable. The owner has estimated the annual profitability (in £000s) of each option for three states of nature (the weather) as shown in Table 11.10.

Table 11.10 Payoff table for Question 4

	Weather		
	Hot	Average	Cool
Swimming pool	100	50	30
Tennis court	70	90	40
Bar	50	100	170

(a) Write down the best decision using:
   (i)   the maximax rule
   (ii) the maximin rule
   (iii) the minimax regret rule
(b) If the probability of a hot summer is 0.2 and that of a cool summer is 0.35, calculate the best decision using the expected monetary value.

5   An investment trust manager wishes to buy a portfolio of shares and he has sufficient funds to buy either portfolio A, portfolio B or portfolio C. The potential gains from the portfolio will depend upon the economy over the next 5 years and estimates (in £m) have been made as shown in Table 11.11.

Table 11.11 Payoff table for Question 5

	Growth	Stable	Recession
A	5	2	−2
B	4	7	−4
C	4	4	4

(a) Write down the best decision using:
   (i)   the maximax rule
   (ii) the maximin rule
   (iii) the minimax regret rule
(b) The manager estimates that the probability that the economy will grow over the next 5 years is 0.5, while the probability of a recession is put at 0.2. Calculate the best decision using the expected monetary value criterion.

(c) A leading economist is prepared to give more accurate estimates of these probabilities for a fee of £50 000. Would it be worthwhile employing the economist?

6 You have £1000 to invest for three months. A friend is offering you a car for £1000 which he says is half price. You believe that there is a 0.25 chance of selling it for £2000, a 0.50 chance that you could sell it for £1200 and a 0.25 that you would only get £500 for it. An alternative is to invest the £1000 in a savings account for 3 months where you would get £8.75 interest. Using the EMV criterion decide whether to buy the car or invest in a savings account.

7 A person is hard up and can't afford to pay for the car tax on his car. He needs to travel to a see his girl friend and could either get the train which would cost £50 or risk taking the car which would cost £10 in petrol. However if he risks driving without tax he believes that there is a 1 in 50 chance of being caught and fined £1000. Based on purely financial considerations what decision should he take? By how much would the chance of being caught have to change before his decision changes?

8 You are considering the purchase of some new computerized machinery for your factory, and have to decide between buying it immediately or waiting for a few months, since the price of the equipment has been falling steadily over the past year. You have been advised that, if you wait for six months, there is a 60% chance that the price will fall to £12 000; otherwise it will remain steady at £16 000.

If you buy now, the £16 000 cost can be reduced by the £2000 saving which you expect will result from the increased efficiency due to the new machine being operative over the 6-month period.

(a) Assuming that your objective is to minimize expected costs, what course of action should you take?

(b) The estimate that there is a 60% chance that the price will fall is only very rough. By how much must this probability decrease before you would be indifferent between buying the equipment now and delaying the purchase?

9 A department store has to decide whether to expand on its existing site in the town centre or to move to a new site on the outskirts. There is a possibility that a rival store may open a branch in the town centre in the near future. If this new branch does open, the first store's total profits over the next 5 years will be £10m if it does not move, as against £16m if it does.

If the rival branch does not open, total profits for the town centre site are estimated at £40m, and for the new site at £32m. The probability of the rival branch opening is estimated to be about 70%. Which decision would maximize expected profit? (For simplicity, you should ignore factors like the time value of money.)

10 Cast Iron Construction plc (CIC) is a company specializing in high-rise office blocks. They have recently decided to consider building in third world countries and they have a choice of 2 sites. One is in the earthquake prone island of Tutamolia and the other is in the politically unstable country of Flesomnial.

The building cost of £5m is the same for both countries and it is estimated that that the return over 10 years for each country will also be the same at £20m. However, in Tutamolia, CIC have a choice of strengthening the building at a further cost of £5m. If they do this the probability that the building will collapse if an earthquake occurs is only 0.01, whereas if no strengthening work is done the probability that the building would collapse is 0.7.

The probability that an earthquake will occur in the next 10 years is put at 0.1. If an earthquake does occur any time during the 10 years and the building collapses the company will forfeit the return of £20m, and in addition they will have to pay compensation to the government of £10m.

If CIC decides to build in Flesomnial there is a 20% chance that the country will be taken over by a dictator and the company will not receive any return on its investment.

(a) Draw a decision tree for this problem and use this decision tree to determine the decision that will maximize CIC'c expected return.

(b) The probability that an earthquake will occur is really only a guess. What should this probability become before the decision found in part (a) changes?

11   At its latest meeting, an investment club is trying to decide which investment out of 3 possible ones to buy this month.

A member has estimated the potential returns on these investments over the next 6 months given 3 different scenarios relating to the movement of the stock market (Table 11.12).

Table 11.12 Payoff table for Question 11

Investment	Stock market movement (in £00)		
	Rising	Stable	Falling
A	150	25	−100
B	90	50	0
C	−10	10	50

(a) Write down the best decision if:
  (i)   the club was risk-seeking
  (ii) the club was risk-averse.
(b) Write down the opportunity loss table and obtain the best decision using the minimax regret criterion.
(c) If the probability of the stock market rising is 0.2 and 0.6 for a fall, calculate the best decision using the EMV criterion.
(d) What is the expected value of perfect information (EVPI)?
(e) To decide the club's attitude to risk, each member took part in an exercise designed to evaluate their utility function. The result of one member's answers are as follows:

'I am indifferent between investing in a share that would give me a return of £9000 for certain or entering a lottery that will give me a 0.5 probability of a £15 000 return and a 0.5 probability of a −£10 000 return.'

'I am indifferent between investing in a share that would give me a return of £2500 for certain or entering a lottery that will give me a 0.3 probability of a £15 000 return and a 0.7 probability of a −£10 000 return.'

  (i)   Sketch the member's utility function and comment on what it shows.
  (ii) From your sketch estimate the utilities for returns of £5000, £1000, £0 and −£1000. What is the best decision for the club that would maximize the expected utility?

12   Pizza Classic is a family-run pizza delivery company that has been in the Bristol area for over 20 years. In its current 3-year business plan it has estimated the probability of high and low demand for its pizzas as 0.55 and 0.45 respectively. It has also estimated that the net present value (using a discount rate of 10%) of income will be £750 000 if the demand is high and £375 000 if the demand is low. (The company assumed that the demand will either be high or low for all 3 years.)

The company is now considering setting up an internet site where customers could order their pizzas. The start-up costs of this venture would be £20 000 (payable now).

It is believed that an internet site would increase the amount spent per customer and therefore that net income from both high and low demand would increase, as shown in the following table.

Year (end)	1	2	3
High demand	£300 000	£400 000	£400 000
Low demand	£150 000	£250 000	£200 000

If the company decides to go ahead with the plan it could employ consultants to conduct a marketing campaign. The consultants would charge £30 000 and they believe that there is an 80% chance that their campaign would be a success and customers would approve the plan. If the campaign were a success it is believed the probability of high demand would increase to 0.65. If the consultants concluded that customers would not be likely to use the site, the company would abandon the idea of an internet site.

(a) Using a discount rate of 10%, calculate the net present value for both high and low demand over the next 3 years (assume that income occurs at the end of each year and that the discount factors for years 1 to 3 are 0.9090, 0.8264 and 0.7513, respectively).

(b) Draw a decision tree for the problem.

(c) Determine the optimal decision for the company.

(d) What is the maximum amount that you would be prepared to pay the consultants?

(e) The probabilities used by Pizza Classic are really only guesses. How might you test the sensitivity of the outcome to changes in these probabilities?

13 Jayes Pharmaceutical has a number of high earning products, including the new A1 asthma spray. Preliminary sales of this product suggest that profits per unit sold amount to £10.

However, a recent report in an American journal suggests that A1 can cause an allergic reaction in up to 1% of people using the spray. The company now has a dilemma: should it continue selling the spray, knowing that there is this risk, or should it abandon it and re-market an older, less effective spray?

If it continues to sell this product and allergies develop, the company will have to compensate the buyer and the loss in profits will cost the company £20 per unit.

If the company decides to abandon the product and sell the older version it would expect to earn a profit of £1.50 per unit.

An alternative is to supply a free allergy testing kit worth £1 with each product sold. If the test is positive, the customer will get a full refund. This test is not perfectly reliable, however: the probability that the test will correctly indicate that someone will be allergic is only 0.9 and the probability that it will give a false positive reading is 0.3. The company would not be able to recover the costs of supplying this kit, so the company would effectively make a loss of £11.

(a) Draw a probability tree diagram showing the prior and conditional probabilities.

(b) Calculate the probability that the test will be positive.

(c) Calculate the following posterior probabilities:
   (i)   probability that a person is allergic if the test is positive.
   (ii) probability that a person is allergic if the test is negative.

(d) Draw a decision tree to determine the best course of action.

(e) If the company expected to sell 500 000 of these units per year, write down the annual profits from all three courses of action.

14 A simple screening test can be conducted to indicate if someone has a particular medical condition or not. However the test sometimes gives incorrect results. A false

positive result (when the person does not have the condition) occurs 5% of the time and a false negative result (when the person has the condition) occurs 10% of the time. It is estimated that 2% of the population have the condition.

It is possible to screen everyone at a cost of £50 per test. Those testing positive are then given treatment costing £300. Those testing negative are not given treatment but if they subsequently turn out to have the condition, treatment is expensive at £1000 per person. An alternative course of action would be to abandon the screening procedure and immunize everyone against the condition at a cost of £65 per person. No treatment costs are subsequently incurred.

Draw a decision tree for the problem and determine the most cost effective course of action.

15 A person is trying to decide between what car to buy. She has narrowed the choice down to 5 models, each costing a similar amount. Her criteria for choice of car include fuel consumption, top speed and environmental considerations. The 5 cars and the score for each criterion on each car are shown in Table 11.13.

Table 11.13 Scores for Question 15

Car	Consumption (miles/gallon)	Top speed (mph)	Environmental
A	45	90	50
B	15	140	0
C	60	80	100
D	35	100	60
E	55	110	30

She has also used swing weights on the criteria and decided that consumption is the most important criterion. Environmental considerations would have a swing weight of 60 and top speed a swing weight of 30.

(a) Convert the consumption figures and top speed into a score out of 100 by making the top value in each case 100 and the bottom one 0.

(b) Based on the aggregate benefits which car should she buy?

16 The lease on a shop is due to expire and the shop owner is trying to decide which of 8 vacant premises he should rent. List possible criteria he should consider in trying to make his decision. Table 11.14 gives the scores for each criteria against each option and also the swing weights of each attribute. Plot the efficient frontier and decide which shop(s) he should consider.

Table 11.14 Data for Question 16

Shop	Criterion X	Criterion Y	Criterion Z	Rental cost (£000s)
A	100	80	0	15
B	50	60	10	8
C	50	100	100	20
D	0	55	20	10
E	30	30	80	12
F	60	0	70	16
G	75	40	30	9
H	50	90	90	18

17 Chix Laboratory has recently come up with a method of producing joints of 'chicken' from non-animal products. The process is quite revolutionary and the taste and texture of the 'meat' is believed to be indistinguishable from the real thing. The product should also have an advantage in terms of price and shelf life (the product need not be stored in a refrigerator and will stay in good condition for up to two weeks).

However, the cost of setting up production is very high at £1m and it is not at all certain that consumers will accept the product. The marketing department has assessed the risk and believe that there is only a 30% chance that consumers will approve of the product. If consumers do approve then sales are estimated to be around £2.5m p.a., but if the reaction is negative then sales will amount to no more than £0.7m p.a. (the catering market is virtually guaranteed to want the product).

The risk could be reduced by carrying out a survey to gauge public reaction to the product. From past experience this kind of survey produces accurate results 85% of the time. (That is, if the survey indicates a favourable response, the probability that a favourable response occurs is 0.85; and similarly, if the survey suggests a negative response, the probability that a negative response occurs is 0.85.) The cost of this survey would be £100 000.

The product manager assigned to this new product line is Graham Green and he has requested your help in deciding whether to commission a survey or to proceed immediately with full production. You explain that the decision is perhaps more complicated than he thinks and the following options are available to him:

1 Proceed with full production.

2 Commission a survey. Whatever the results of the survey there are two further options: to proceed with full production or abandon the project.

3 Abandon the project.

Following discussions with the marketing department, you decide that carrying out the marketing survey before going into full production will not affect the expected sales revenue. You have also assumed that the probability that the survey will indicate a favourable response is 0.3.

(a) Draw a decision tree for the problem and decide what the correct decisions should be.

(b) Investigate the sensitivity of your answer to changes in the probability of a favourable response.

Assignment Since the catastrophe at the Fukushima nuclear plant in Japan following the tsunami in March 2011, Germany has decided to end the generation of electricity using nuclear energy by 2030. Use various diagrams to represent the situation and the choices open to countries for the generation of electricity. You should take into account factors such as global warming, peak oil and safety records of the electricity generation industry. (You will need to do some research into these and other factors.) Try and summarize the real problem and the choices open to governments.

CHOOSING WISELY: INVESTMENT APPRAISAL

OBJECTIVES

- To understand the reasons for investment appraisal
- To know how to select projects on the basis of their payback periods
- To be able to calculate the accounting rate of return
- To be able to discount a future sum of money
- To know how to select projects on the basis of their net present value
- To be able to calculate the internal rate of return for a project
- To understand the limitations of each method

INTRODUCTION

Companies are frequently faced with the need to decide between a number of investment opportunities. As capital is usually limited, a company will want to choose the 'best' project or projects. But what do we mean by 'best', and how can we differentiate between different projects that may look equally attractive?

The projects considered in this chapter are those that require an initial capital outlay and then generate income over several years. The life of a project is of paramount importance as a sum of money that will be generated in the future will not be so attractive as money that is available in the present. This chapter looks at several methods that can be used to determine the worth of an investment.

QUANTITATIVE METHODS IN ACTION

EU banks stress test

The period from 2007 to 2011 was a difficult time for the world economy. First there was the financial crisis caused by the bursting of the United States housing bubble and the subsequent rescue of banks in the USA and Europe. Then, just as economies were starting to recover from the recession, there was a crisis in the Eurozone, with first the 110bn-euro rescue package for Greece and then the 85bn-euro rescue for Ireland, followed by a €10 billion bailout for Cyprus. Since then Greece has secured a further €130 billion rescue package and has had a change of government that wants to renegotiate their austerity package. Even with these huge rescue packages, there are still worries over the health of the European banking system. The markets do not believe that the European banks are strong enough to withstand a second recession, and they think that many large investors are too exposed to countries such as Greece and Portugal, which have large debts.

In order to allay these fears, in 2009 the EU devised the *stress tests*. These tests were designed to see which European banks, if any, might fail given certain scenarios. The scenarios that were tested were:

- A baseline scenario that assumed a continuing recovery
- A double-dip recession that lasted two years
- A double-dip recession and another financial crisis for some European countries.

The purpose of these scenarios was to see whether banks had enough capital to survive these events. So, for instance, if house prices fell by half, then mortgages made by banks would be at risk. If the bank had insufficient capital to cover these losses, it would become insolvent.

The first tests took place in 2010, and in the UK these included HSBC, RBS, Lloyds and Barclays. In other countries many smaller banks were also tested; in Spain they tested 27 banks, as these banks have a large exposure to the collapsed property market. In total 91 banks were tested, of which 7 failed (5 Spanish banks, 1 German bank and 1 Greek bank).

In 2014 there were 123 banks tested. In the UK The Co-operative Bank, Nationwide, Santander and Standard Chartered were added to the 4 tested in 2010. One of the outcomes of the stress test was projected capital ratios. This ratio measures the amount of equity (capital and reserves) the bank has as a percentage of risk-weighted assets. The higher this ratio is, the better, and it should not be less than 8% under normal conditions and 4.5% in the stress scenario. Of the 8 UK banks tested, The Co-operative Bank, The Royal Bank of Scotland and Lloyds all had ratios of close to or less than 4.5% under the stress conditions. These banks had to make further provisions to improve their capital position, and all had shown improvements by the end of 2014.

Sources: 'Aggregate outcome of the 2010 EU wide stress test exercise coordinated by CEBS in cooperation with the ECB', CEBS, July 2010.

'Q&A: What are the European bank stress tests for?', BBC, July 2010, http://www.bbc.co.uk/news/business-10711590.

Bank of England. 'Stress testing the UK banking system: 2014 results', http://www.bankofengland.co.uk/financialstability/Documents/fpc/results161214.pdf.

Measures of investment worth

You may think that it should be easy to judge the worth of an investment. Surely the larger the profit that will be generated, the better? Unfortunately it is not so simple as this because two projects could generate the same total profit but be quite different in the pattern of cash flows. Example 12.1 illustrates a typical case.

example 12.1

BAS Holdings specializes in the development of out-of-town shopping centres. It is currently investigating three possible projects and these are located at Andover (A), Bristol (B) and Carlisle (C). The sites at Andover and Bristol require an investment of £4m each while the site at Carlisle requires an investment of £5m. Income from rents is guaranteed for up to 5 years, after which time BAS Holdings will transfer owner-ship to the local council. The net cash flows are given in Table 12.1, where year 0 refers to 'now'.

Table 12.1 Cash flows for Example 12.1

Year	Andover (£m)	Bristol (£m)	Carlisle (£m)
0	−4.0	−4.0	−5.0
1	1.0	1.5	0.0
2	1.0	2.5	0.5
3	1.0	0.5	1.5
4	1.0	0.5	2.0
5	1.0	0.0	3.0

In Example 12.1 the company has to decide which, if any, of the projects to accept. Even if all projects are profitable the company may not have the resources to proceed with them all. Perhaps it should compare each project in terms of the profit made at the end of the 5 years (4 years in the case of Bristol).

activity 12.1

What is the total profit for each project?

The profit is simply the sum of the cash flows over the life of each project and they are shown in Table 12.2.

Table 12.2 Calculation of total profits

Year	Andover (£m)	Bristol (£m)	Carlisle (£m)
0	−4.0	−4.0	−5.0
1	1.0	1.5	0.0
2	1.0	2.5	0.5
3	1.0	0.5	1.5
4	1.0	0.5	2.0
5	1.0	0.0	3.0
Profit	1.0	1.0	2.0

On the basis of total profit the Carlisle project is best, but this project also has the largest initial investment and income is not generated until year 2. Andover and

Bristol give the same profit, but notice how differently the earnings are generated. Bristol gives larger cash flows at the start, but no earnings are received in year 5, whereas Andover gives a constant flow of earnings for the full 5 years.

You should now appreciate that deciding on the best project is not a simple matter. There are several methods that can be used to compare projects and these fall into two categories. The first category is often termed 'traditional' and involves accounting procedures that do not take into account the time value of money. The second method involves procedures that *discount* future sums of money.

DID YOU KNOW?

The International Monetary Fund (IMF) estimate of the total cost of the global financial crisis is $2.3 trillion (£1.5 trillion) (*Source:* BBC 20 April 2010). In comparison, the GDP of the USA in 2010 was $14.7 trillion (*Source:* US Department of Commerce, Bureau of Economic Analysis).

Traditional methods for comparing projects

There are two main methods in this category. These are the *payback* method and the *accounting rate of return* (ARR). The payback method simply tells you how long it takes for the original investment to be repaid.

(activity 12.2) What are the payback periods for the three projects given in Example 12.1?

You should have obtained 4 years for Project A, 2 years for Project B and 4 years for Project C. This indicates that the Bristol project is to be preferred since it takes less time for the original investment to be repaid.

The payback method is an easily understood method and favours projects that generate large cash flows early. This is an advantage since early cash flows will help a company's liquidity and also minimize risks of unforeseen problems in the future. However, this method ignores cash flows that are generated after the payback period. For example, with Project C large cash flows are generated in years 4 and 5 and this is not taken into account with the payback method.

The accounting rate of return (sometimes called the return on capital employed) is the ratio of average net income to the capital employed. The capital employed sometimes refers to initial capital and sometimes to average capital. There are also variations concerning what constitutes capital and what constitutes income. The definition used here refers to initial capital and can be expressed as follows:

$$\text{ARR} = \frac{\text{Average income (per year)}}{\text{Initial capital}} \times 100\%$$

(activity 12.3) Calculate the ARR for all three projects given in the example.

For Project A the average income is £5m/5 = £1m and the initial capital employed is £4m so the ARR is:

$$\text{ARR} = \frac{1}{4} \times 100 = 25\%$$

For Project B the average income will again be £1m (the total adds up to £5m – the same as Project A). Since the capital employed is £4m, the ARR is again 25%.

For Project C the average income is:

$$\frac{(0 + 0.5 + 1.5 + 2.0 + 3.0)}{5} = 1.4$$

Since the initial capital is £5m, the ARR is:

$$\text{ARR} = \frac{1.4}{5} \times 100$$
$$= 28\%$$

On the basis of the ARR, Project C is the better project.

The ARR is easy to calculate but it has many disadvantages, such as not allowing for timing of the cash flows. For example, Project A and Project B are ranked equal even though Project B generates larger cash flows in the first two years.

Discounted cash flow techniques

The disadvantages of the payback and the ARR methods are that they do not take into account the time value of money. If you were offered £1000 now or £1000 in a year's time, which would you take? I am sure that you would take £1000 now! However, what would be your decision if you were offered £1000 now or £2000 in a year's time? Unless you were desperate for money, you would probably prefer to wait a year and get the £2000. These two cases are clear cut. But what would be your decision if you were offered £1000 now or £1100 in a year's time? If you could put the money to good use so that after a year you would have more than £1100, then your decision should be to take the £1000 now.

It is clear from this that money in the future is not worth as much as money now, so we need some method of *discounting* future sums of money. In order to understand the idea of discounting, it is first necessary to revise the idea of *simple* and *compound* interest. Simple interest is the expression used when interest on a sum of money is calculated on the principal only. This situation occurs when the interest is withdrawn as it is earned.

activity
12.4

You decide to invest £8500 in an investment account paying an interest rate of 5% p.a. The interest is paid out to you as it is earned. What interest would you receive at the end of each year?

The answer to this activity is 5% of £8500, which is £425.

Normally the interest is reinvested so that the interest also earns interest. In this case you would use the expression 'compound interest'.

> **activity 12.5**
>
> You again decide to invest £8500 in an investment account paying an interest rate of 5% p.a. This time, however, all interest is reinvested. How much would the £8500 have grown to at the end of the 10th year?

The principal at the end of the first year is simply the original principal plus the interest earned. That is:

$$8500 + \frac{5}{100} \times 8500 = 8500\left(1 + \frac{5}{100}\right)$$

This is £8500 + £425 = £8925.

The principal at the end of year 2 =

    the principal at the start of year 2+

    the amount of interest received during the year.

That is:

$$8500\left(1 + \frac{5}{100}\right) + 8500\left(1 + \frac{5}{100}\right) \times \frac{5}{100}$$

This can be simplified by noting that the expression $8500\left(1 + \frac{5}{100}\right)$ is common to both terms. The equation can therefore be factorized as follows:

$$8500\left(1 + \frac{5}{100}\right)\left(1 + \frac{5}{100}\right) = 8500\left(1 + \frac{5}{100}\right)^2$$

In general if you invest an initial principal P_0 for n years at an interest rate of r per cent, the principal at the *end* of the nth year is:

Interest rate   No. of years

$$P_n = P_0\left(1 + \frac{r}{100}\right)^n$$

Initial principal

This is called the *compound interest* formula.

So for $P_0 = 8500$, $r = 5$ and $n = 10$,

the principal at the end of the 10th year $= 8500\left(1 + \frac{5}{100}\right)^{10} = £13\,846$.

Another way of expressing this is that £13 846 in 10 years' time at an interest rate of 5% is equivalent to £8500 now. This is quite a useful idea as it allows you to make a judgement on the value of some future sum of money.

> **activity 12.6**
>
> You have been promised £10 000 in 5 years' time. What would this amount be worth now, assuming an interest rate of 6%?

To solve this problem the compound interest formula can be used in reverse. That is, P_n is known and you have to calculate P_0. In this case, $n = 5$, $r = 6\%$ and $P_n = 10\,000$, and the equation becomes:

$$10\ 000 = P_0\left(1 + \frac{6}{100}\right)^5$$

$$= 1.3382 \times P_0$$

Therefore

$$P_0 = \frac{10\ 000}{1.3382}$$

$$= £7473$$

Since this calculation will be repeated many times, you will find it easier to rearrange the compound interest formula to make P_0 the subject of the formula. That is:

$$P_0 = P_n \times \frac{1}{\left(1 + \dfrac{r}{100}\right)^n}$$

The expression $\dfrac{1}{\left(1 + \dfrac{r}{100}\right)^n}$ is called the *discount factor*.

For example, for $r = 6\%$ and $n = 5$, the discount factor is $\dfrac{1}{1.3382} = 0.7473$, so

$$P_0 = 10\ 000 \times 0.7473$$

$$= £7473.$$

activity **12.7** Discount the sum of £30 000 that is to be received in 4 years' time using an interest rate of (a) 2% and (b) 10%.

You should have found that the discount factors for 2% and 10% are 0.9238 and 0.6830 respectively. Therefore the discounted value of £30 000 is:

30 000 × 0.9238 = £27 714 at an interest rate of 2%

30 000 × 0.6830 = £20 490 at an interest rate of 10%

Net present value

activity **12.8** You have been offered either £5000 in 2 years' time or £6000 in 3 years' time. Which would you accept, assuming an interest rate of 5.5%?

This is a slightly different problem in that you are asked to compare a sum of money in 2 years' time with a sum of money in 3 years' time. In order to compare the two amounts you need to have a common base. The easiest method is to find the value now of both amounts. The diagram in Figure 12.1 explains this more clearly.

The discount factors are given on top of each arrow and the value at the point of the arrow is the value now of each sum of money. This shows you that £6000 in 3 years' time is the better choice since the *present value* of £6000 is worth more than the present value of £5000 due in 2 years' time. This idea of calculating the present value of a sum of money can be extended to the case where a project generates a series of cash flows and the present value of the sum of these cash flows is required. The interest rate that is used is usually called the *discount rate* and is the *cost of capital* for the company.

Figure 12.1 Present value of a sum of money

activity **12.9**

In the case of BAS Holdings, the company's discount rate is 8%. Calculate the present value for each of the three projects given in Example 12.1.

The calculations are best set out in a table similar to Table 12.3.

From this table you should see that the largest present value is Project C with a total cash flow of £5.13m. However, to achieve this, a capital investment of £5m was required, whereas the other two projects only required an investment of £4m. To obtain the net profit, the investment should be deducted from the present value and, when this is done, the result is called the *net present value* or NPV.

Table 12.3 Calculation of present value

Year	Discount factor	Andover Cash flow (£m)	Andover Present value (£m)	Bristol Cash flow (£m)	Bristol Present value (£m)	Carlisle Cash flow (£m)	Carlisle Present value (£m)
0		−4.0		−4.0		−5.0	
1	0.9259	1.0	0.9259	1.5	1.3889	0.0	0.0
2	0.8573	1.0	0.8573	2.5	2.1433	0.5	0.4287
3	0.7938	1.0	0.7938	0.5	0.3969	1.5	1.1907
4	0.7350	1.0	0.7350	0.5	0.3675	2.0	1.4700
5	0.6806	1.0	0.6806	0.0	0.0	3.0	2.0418
			3.9926		4.2966		5.1312

activity **12.10**

What is the NPV for each of the three projects?

The calculations are:

£3.9926m − £4m = −£0.0074m or a loss of £7400 for Project A

£4.2966m − £4m = £0.2966m or a gain of £296,600 for Project B

£5.1312m − £5m = £0.1312m or a gain of £131,200 for Project C

On the basis of the NPV, Project A would result in a loss and is therefore not a profitable investment, while Project B is the most profitable investment.

When you use NPV to select one project out of many, you simply choose the project with the highest figure. You can also use NPV to make a decision about one project. In this case your decision should be as summarized in Table 12.4.

Table 12.4 Decision criterion when using NPV

NPV	Decision
Negative	Reject project
Zero	Indifferent
Positive	Accept project

Internal rate of return

The NPV method is a very useful method as it takes into account the timing of a series of cash flows. However, the decision is dependent on the discount rate used – a larger rate will reduce the NPV and could change the decision from accept to reject. An alternative approach is to calculate the discount rate that will give the NPV of zero. This is called the *Internal Rate of Return* or IRR. If the IRR for a project is greater than or equal to the cost of capital for a company, the project would be acceptable; if not, the project should be rejected. In the case of BAS Holdings, the cost of capital is 8% and any project with an IRR of at least this figure will be acceptable. Calculation of the IRR is not straightforward but an approximate value can be obtained using either a graphical approach or a linear interpolation. For both methods you need to calculate the NPV for two different discount rates. For the greatest accuracy the NPVs should be small, and preferably one should be positive and one negative. For the graphical method these points are plotted on a graph of NPV against discount rate and a line drawn between them. The point where the line crosses the horizontal axis (which represents zero NPV) can then be read from the graph.

activity **12.11**

Find the IRR for Project A.

For Project A, a discount rate of 8% gave an NPV of −£0.0074m. For most practical purposes this is virtually zero, so the IRR is about 8%. However, to get a more accurate answer you could try another discount rate, say 7.5%. The calculations for this discount rate are shown in Table 12.5.

Table 12.5 NPV calculations for a discount rate of 7.5%

Year	Discount factor	Cash flow (£m)	Present value (£m)
0		−4.0	
1	0.9302	1.0	0.9302
2	0.8653	1.0	0.8653
3	0.8050	1.0	0.8050
4	0.7488	1.0	0.7488
5	0.6966	1.0	0.6966
			4.0459

The NPV is 4.0459 − 4 = £0.0459m. These two values have been plotted in Figure 12.2.

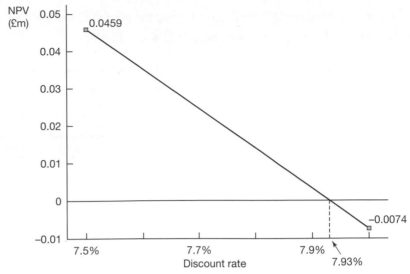

Figure 12.2 Graphical method for finding the IRR for the Andover project

You should find that the line cuts the horizontal axis at 7.93% and this is the value of the IRR for this project. To use the interpolation method the following formula can be used:

$$IRR = \frac{N_1 r_2 - N_2 r_1}{N_1 - N_2}$$

where an NPV of N_1 was obtained using a discount rate of r_1 and an NPV of N_2 was obtained using a discount rate of r_2.

So for $N_1 = 0.0459$, $r_1 = 7.5\%$, $N_2 = -0.0074$ and $r_2 = 8\%$, the IRR is:

$$IRR = \frac{0.0459 \times 8 - (-0.0074) \times 7.5}{0.0459 - (-0.0074)}$$

$$= \frac{0.42195}{0.0532}$$

$$= 7.93\%$$

This is the same as the value obtained from the graph.

DID YOU KNOW?

The *Daily Express* reported on 21 March 2011 that 120 millionaires were being created every day as Britain recovered from recession. The basis of the story was research carried out by Barclays Wealth. They found that there were a total of 619 000 millionaires in the UK in 2010, up from 528 000 at the end of 2008, which gives the figure of 120 per day. However the report also states that at the end of 2008 the number of millionaires had fallen by 15%, which means that the real starting point of the calculation should have been about 621 000. In reality, the number of millionaires had actually fallen since the start of the recession! When to start counting is important for investment managers, although there are rules they have to abide by when selling investment products to the public.

Source: http://www.straightstatistics.org/article/britains-missing-millionaires

activity 12.12

Find the IRR for Project B using the graphical method.

(Hint – try discount rates of 11% and 13%.)

The NPV values calculated in Table 12.6 have been plotted in Figure 12.3 where you will see that the line joining the two points cuts the axis at a discount rate of about 12.1%.

Table 12.6 Calculations for the NPV using discount rates of 11% and 13%

Year	Discount factor @ 11%	Cash flow (£m)	Present value (£m)	Discount factor @ 13%	Present value (£m)
0		−4.0	−4.0		−4.0
1	0.9009	1.5	1.3514	0.8850	1.3275
2	0.8116	2.5	2.0290	0.7831	1.9578
3	0.7312	0.5	0.3656	0.6931	0.3466
4	0.6587	0.5	0.3294	0.6133	0.3067
5	0.5935	0.0	0.0000	0.5428	0.0000
NPV			0.0754		−0.0614

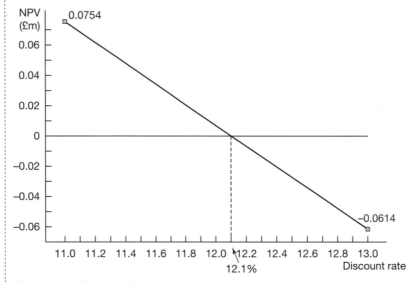

Figure 12.3 IRR for the Bristol project

activity 12.13

Find the IRR for Project C using the formula.

Two rates have been tried: one at 6% which gave an NPV of £0.5305m and one at 8% which gave an NPV of £0.1312m. (You are recommended to do these calculations yourself.) Substituting these values into the formula gives:

$$\frac{0.5305 \times 8 - 0.1312 \times 6}{0.5305 - 0.1312} = \frac{3.4568}{0.3993}$$
$$= 8.66\%$$

The results of the IRR calculations agree with the NPV method; that is, Project A is not profitable, while Project B appears to be more profitable than Project C. The advantage of the IRR method is that it allows you to have a benchmark against which projects can be measured, and a rate of return is something that management understand. The disadvantages are that it is more difficult to calculate and does not take into account the absolute value of the cash flows. So, on the basis of IRR, a project giving an NPV of £100 might look better than a project with an NPV of £1m. There is also the problem that in certain circumstances it is possible for the IRR method to give multiple solutions or no solution at all! It is possible to use Goal Seek in Excel to find the IRR. See Activity 11.15 (page 278) for details on using Goal Seek.

Other applications of the compound interest formula

Sinking funds

A firm wishes to purchase a machine costing £800 in 3 years' time by making 4 equal instalments (the first now, the second at the end of the first year, the third at the end of the second year and the fourth at the end of the third year – that is, when they purchase the machine) in a savings plan paying 5.2% net per annum. How much should each instalment be?

If we assume that the price of the machine will not increase then the investment plan must realize £800 at the end of the third year. If each instalment was for £200 the total amount saved would exceed £800 as a result of the interest received. If you look at Figure 12.4 you will see that the first payment will earn interest for 3 years, the second payment will earn interest for 2 years and the third payment will earn interest for just 1 year. The final payment will be made at the end of the third year and we can assume that the machine will be purchased immediately afterwards. So how would you find the correct amount to save? You could do it by trial and error but a little mathematics would be much more effective! If we call the unknown instalment x, then:

the first instalment will grow to $£x(1.052)^3$ at the end of the plan
the second instalment will grow to $£x(1.052)^2$ at the end of the plan
the third instalment will grow to $£x(1.052)$ at the end of the plan
the fourth instalment will stay at $£x$

Total amount accumulated $= x(1.052)^3 + x(1.052)^2 + x(1.052) + x$

This must equal £800. So:

$$x(1.052)^3 + x(1.052)^2 + x(1.052) + x = 800$$

Factorizing we get:

$$x[(1.052)^3 + (1.052)^2 + 1.052 + 1] = 800$$
$$x(1.1643 + 1.1067 + 1.052 + 1) = 800$$

So $4.323x = 800$ and

$$x = 800/4.323$$
$$= 185.06$$

Therefore each instalment should be £185.06.

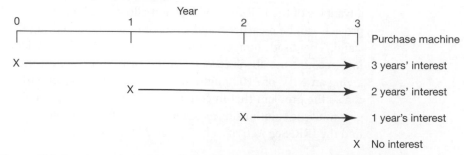

Figure 12.4 Regular savings plan

This type of savings plan is called a *sinking fund*. The method in Activity 12.14 will work for any number of years but it is possible to derive a formula (using the sum of a geometric series) that makes the calculation quicker. The formula is:

$$\frac{x\left[\left(1 + \dfrac{r}{100}\right)^{n+1} - 1\right]}{\dfrac{r}{100}}$$

The meaning of the symbols x, r and n is the same as before. (*Note:* Before using this formula make sure that the timings of the regular payments x correspond to those given in Activity 12.14.)

---

activity 12.15

Solve the problem in Activity 12.14 using the sinking fund formula.

We again need to find x, so:

$$\frac{x\left[\left(1 + \dfrac{5.2}{100}\right)^{4} - 1\right]}{\dfrac{5.2}{100}} = 800$$

$$x[(1.052)^4 - 1] = 800 \times 0.052$$

$$0.2248x = 41.6$$

$$x = \frac{41.6}{0.2248}$$

$$= 185.05$$

which is the same as before (apart from the small rounding error).

Constant repayments

This sinking fund formula is a special case of the situation where an amount P_0 is invested followed by regular amounts x. The formula is:

$$P_n = P_0\left(1 + \frac{r}{100}\right)^n + \frac{x\left[\left(1 + \dfrac{r}{100}\right)^{n} - 1\right]}{\dfrac{r}{100}}$$

activity
12.16

You take out a 25-year repayment mortgage for £50 000 at a fixed interest rate of 8%. Repayments are made at the end of each year and will consist of part interest and part capital. Calculate the amount of the annual repayments.

Since you want the amount owed at the end of the 25-year period to be zero, then $P_{25} = 0$ and $P_0 = -50000$ (note: P_0 is negative because you owe £50 000).

Substituting these values together with $r = 8$, you get:

$$0 = -50\,000 \times \left(1 + \frac{8}{100}\right)^{25} + \frac{x\left[\left(1 + \frac{8}{100}\right)^{25} - 1\right]}{\frac{8}{100}}$$

$$0 = -50\,000 \times (1.08)^{25} + \frac{x\left[(1.08)^{25} - 1\right]}{0.08}$$

$$0 = -50\,000 \times 6.8485 + \frac{x\left[5.8485\right]}{0.08}$$

$$0 = -342\,425 + 73.106x$$

$$73.106x = 342\,425$$

$$x = 4684$$

So the annual repayment should be £4684.

If you multiply this amount by 25 you will get £117 100, which is the amount you would pay back over the life of the loan; that is, over double the amount you borrowed!

activity
12.17

You can only afford to pay back £4500 per year. How long would it take you to pay back the original loan?

This time you know x but not n, so:

$$0 = -50\,000 \times \left(1 + \frac{8}{100}\right)^{n} + \frac{4500\left[\left(1 + \frac{8}{100}\right)^{n} - 1\right]}{\frac{8}{100}}$$

$$0 = -50\,000 \times (1.08)^{n} + \frac{4500\left[(1.08)^{n} - 1\right]}{0.08}$$

$$0 = -50\,000 \times (1.08)^{n} + 56\,250 \times (1.08)^{n} - 56\,250$$

$$0 = 6250 \times (1.08)^{n} - 56\,250$$

$$6250 \times (1.08)^{n} = 56\,250$$

$$(1.08)^{n} = \frac{56\,250}{6250} = 9$$

To make n the subject of the formula we can take logs of both sides:

$$\log(1.08)^n = \log(9)$$

Using laws of logs (see Chapter 1):

$$n \times \log(1.08) = \log(9)$$

$$n = \frac{\log(9)}{\log(1.08)}$$

$$= \frac{0.9542}{0.03342}$$

$$= 28.55$$

So a total of 29 years would be required to pay off the loan for an annual payment of £4500.

Depreciation

Many investments such as consumer items and machinery depreciate so that after a few years the item is worth less than it was when it was first bought. One way of depreciating an item is the *reducing balance* method. This method assumes that a fixed percentage of the initial capital value of the item is written off each year. It results in a larger depreciation in the early years, which is what you would normally expect for these types of goods. To solve these problems we can use the compound interest formula, but in this case the interest rate r is the *rate of depreciation*.

activity 12.18

An item of machinery is bought for £30 000 and after 10 years its scrap value is £1000. Find (a) the rate of depreciation and (b) its book value after 5 years.

To solve this problem you would use the compound interest formula:

$$P_n = P_0\left(1 + \frac{r}{100}\right)^n$$

For $P_0 = 30000$, $P_{10} = 1000$ and $n = 10$ you get:

$$1000 = 30000 \times \left(1 + \frac{r}{100}\right)^{10}$$

$$\left(1 + \frac{r}{100}\right)^{10} = \frac{1000}{30000}$$

$$= 0.033\dot{3}$$

$$\text{So}\left(1 + \frac{r}{100}\right) = (0.033\dot{3})^{\frac{1}{10}}$$

$$= 0.7117$$

$$\frac{r}{100} = 0.7117 - 1$$

$$= -0.2883$$

$$r = -28.83\%$$

r is negative since the capital is decreasing in value. So the depreciation rate is 28.83%.

The *book value* is the value of the asset at a particular point in time. To calculate the book value after 5 years we simply use the calculated value of r in the formula, that is:

$$P_5 = 30\,000 \times \left(1 - \frac{28.83}{100}\right)^5$$

$$= 30\,000 \times 0.1826$$

$$= £5478$$

Compound interest with continuous compounding

The sum of £5000 is invested at 6% per annum compound interest. Find the value of the investment at the end of 5 years if interest is compounded (a) annually, (b) monthly, and (c) daily.

For the annual case you would use the compound interest formula with $r = 6\%$. That is:

$$P_5 = 5000 \times \left(1 + \frac{6}{100}\right)^5$$

$$= 5000 \times 1.3382$$

$$= £6691$$

If compounded monthly, the interest rate would be 0.5% per month (6/12) and the time period would be 60 (5 × 12 months). So the value of the investment at the end of 5 years would be:

$$P_5 = 5000 \times \left(1 + \frac{0.5}{100}\right)^{60}$$

$$= 5000 \times 1.3489$$

$$= £6744.50$$

If compounded daily, the interest rate would now be 0.01644% per day (6/365) and the time period would be 1825 (5 × 365).

$$P_5 = 5000 \times \left(1 + \frac{0.01644}{100}\right)^{1825}$$

$$= 5000 \times 1.3499$$

$$= £6749.33$$

As you can see the amounts are gradually increasing as the time period gets less. In the limit (that is, when the interest is continuously compounded), the value of an investment after n years is given by:

$$P_n = P_0 e^{\frac{r \times n}{100}}$$

where r is the annual interest rate and e is the exponential function (and can be found on all scientific calculators).

$$P_5 = 5000e^{\frac{6 \times 5}{100}}$$

$$= 5000 \times 1.3499$$

$$= £6749.50$$

Reflection

Throughout our lives we are faced with financial decisions. As children we must decide whether to spend our pocket money or save it and as we get older these decisions become more complex and more frequent. So we have to decide whether to borrow money to buy a house or car and where to invest our savings. There are a large number of institutions that want our money and until the financial crisis of the late 2000s we assumed that our money would be safe and earn a good return. We certainly didn't expect that some of the major banks such as Halifax would need huge amounts of taxpayer's money to remain solvent. Nor did we realize that the financial instruments the bank use to invest our money was so complicated and risky that only analysts really understood them. The methods used in this chapter, although relatively simple, are fundamental when making decisions on where to invest money. Hopefully the financial sector will go back to some of the tried and tested methods rather than risk another potential financial meltdown!

Key points

- Traditional accounting procedures do not take time into account. Examples of such methods are the *payback method* and the *accounting rate of return*.
- Compound interest is normally applied to an investment as this means that the interest also gains interest.
- The compound interest formula can be re-arranged so that you can work out the amount of money you need to invest now that will give you a desired sum of money in *n* years time.
- Put another way this means that you can calculate what a sum of money in *n* years time is worth at today's prices. This is called the *discounted cash flow technique* and allows investments that mature at different times to be compared more easily.
- When we subtract the initial investment we get the *net present value*.
- A net present value greater than zero means that a project is worthwhile.
- The *internal rate of return* gives the discount rate that makes the net present value zero.
- The compound interest formula also allows us to calculate sinking funds, constant repayments (mortgages) and depreciation of an asset.
- It is possible to modify the compound interest formula to allow for continuous compounding.
- Table 12.7 summarizes the four different methods of investment appraisal for Example 12.1.

Table 12.7 Summary of the different methods of investment appraisal for Example 12.1

Method	Project			Decision
	A	B	C	
Payback	4 years	2 years	4 years	B
ARR	25%	25%	28%	C
NPV	−£0.0074m	£0.2966m	£0.1312m	B
IRR	7.93%	12.1%	8.66%	B

Further reading

Investment appraisal is a huge subject and is treated differently depending on the background of the authors. So an accountant would look at the subject differently from an economist and a tax expert would also have a different approach. However, for a general text that covers the material in this chapter and extends it further, but in a non-mathematical manner, the one by Lumby and Jones (2000) is a good choice.

http://www.**palgrave**.com/oakshott-eqm6

Solutions to all questions are freely available

Practice questions

1 The following cash flows occur with 3 different investment opportunities. Use the payback method and the accounting rate of return to decide which is the best investment opportunity.

Year	Investment A	Investment B	Investment C
0	−20	−15	−5
1	12	0	3
2	10	10	3
3	5	5	3
4	3	5	3
5	0	5	3

2 One project involves an outlay of £2.5m and gets an annual net income of £1m for 5 years. Another project involves an outlay of £10m but gets no income until year 5 when the capital is repaid plus interest of £5m. Using the payback and accounting rate of return methods decide which is the most attractive project.

3 A buy-to-let investor is trying to decide between three properties. The first property costs £200 000 and he believes that after mortgage interest payments and expenses he will be able to get a net income of £400 per month. The second property costs £300 000 and the net income should be £500 per month while the third property costs £400 000 with a net income of £800 per month. Using the payback and accounting rate of return methods decide which property the landlord should buy. (Assume that the landlord does not sell the property and the rent does not increase.)

4 £10 000 is invested in a one-year fixed rate account paying 6%. What interest is payable at the end of the term?

5 £20 000 is invested in a 5-year fixed interest rate account paying 5%. Interest is paid out each year. What interest do you receive each year?

6 £20 000 is invested in a 5-year fixed interest bond paying 5% p.a. If interest is reinvested in the account how much will the bond be worth at the end of the 5 years?

7 £50 000 is invested at 5.5% for 6 years. If all interest is reinvested:
   (a) What would be the amount accumulated at the end of the 6 years?
   (b) How much interest would have been received during the 6 years?

8 A car is purchased for a £3000 deposit and 5 annual payments of £1000. What is the cost of the car at today's prices if a discount rate of 8% is assumed?

9 What is the present value of £50 000 that is payable in 5 years' time if interest rates are expected to be constant at 6% during this period?

10 You have been offered £20 000 in 1 year's time or £25 000 in two years' time. Which should you accept based on present values?

11   An annuity is a guaranteed annual income for life that is purchased through a pension plan. A particular annuity is bought with a pension pot of £50 000. If the annuity pays out £3500 p.a. for life what is the present value of this annuity assuming a life expectancy of 10 years and interest rate of 5%?

12   An investment costs £2m to set up and then gives an income of £0.6m p.a. for 5 years. Use the net present value method with a discount rate of 6% to decide if this investment is worthwhile.

13   Using the cash flows given in Question 1 and the NPV method of investment appraisal, decide which (if any) of the three investment opportunities should be undertaken. Assume a discount rate of 6%.

14   A project involves an investment of £2m and is guaranteed to produce an income of £0.5m each year for the next 5 years. Compare and contrast different methods for evaluating the worth of this project. Assume that the income occurs at the end of each year and that the discount rate is 7%.

15   A project costs £5m to set up, and a return of £2m p.a. for the next 3 years is guaranteed. A project will only be accepted if the internal rate of return is greater than 14%. Should the project be accepted?

16   On 1 January 2015 you invested £1000 in a building society's 5-year fixed rate account paying 5.4% net per annum. How much will be in the account on 1 January 2020 if no funds or interest are withdrawn throughout the period of the investment?

17   A car dealer is considering leasing some vehicles as an alternative to outright sales. The scheme she has devised requires the customer to pay an annual premium over a fixed period. If the dealer wants to accumulate £20 000 over a 3 year period what annual premium should she charge assuming an interest rate of 5.75%?

18   A car is purchased for a £4500 deposit and 5 annual payments of £1000. What is the cost of the car at today's prices if a discount rate of 7.5% is assumed?

19   A firm is considering the purchase of one of two machines. The first (machine A), costing £4000, is expected to bring in revenues of £2000, £2500 and £1500 respectively in the 3 years for which it will be operative; while the second (machine B), which costs £3900, will produce revenues of £1500, £2500 and £2000, and has the same lifetime. Neither machine will have any appreciable scrap value at the end of its life. Assuming a discount rate of 8%, compare and contrast different methods for evaluating which machine should be purchased. (Hint to calculating IRRs: a discount rate of 25% gave NPVs of −£32 and −£76 for machines A and B respectively.)

20   A company has the choice of two investments, both costing an initial £15 000. The first will yield cash flows of £6000 per year for 3 years (the first payment receivable 1 year after investment), while the second will yield a lump sum of £19 000 at the end of the 3 year period. Assuming a discount rate of 5%, which investment should be chosen? (Hint to calculating IRRs: a discount rate of 10% gave NPVs of −£79.20 and −£725.30 for investments 1 and 2 respectively.)

21   A machine which currently costs £800 will increase in price by 4% per year as a result of inflation.
    (a) What will the machine cost in 3 years' time?
    (b) If a firm wishes to purchase this machine in 3 years' time by making 3 equal instalments (the first now, the second in one year's time and the third in two years – that is, one year before the purchase), in a savings plan paying 5.2% net p.a., how much should each investment be?

22 A machine is purchased for £3750 and generates a revenue of £1310 per year for 5 years. After this time, it ceases to be productive and has no scrap value.
   (a) Assuming a discount rate of 11.2%, calculate its net present value.
   (b) Find a discount rate at which the net present value becomes negative, and use it to estimate the internal rate of return.

23 A firm wishes to provide a sinking fund in order to replace equipment that has a life span of 10 years. If the cost of the equipment will be £1m in 10 years' time, what annual amount does it need to put aside in an account paying 7% p.a.?

24 You decide to take out a 20-year mortgage for £65 000 at an annual interest rate of 7.5%.
   (a) What would be the annual repayment?
   (b) If you could increase the annual amount paid to £7000, how much money would you save over the life of the mortgage?

25 What would the annual payments be on a 25-year repayment mortgage for £150 000 at a fixed interest rate of 7%?

26 An item of machinery is purchased for £50 000 and after 5 years will have a scrap value of £5000. What is the rate of depreciation?

27 You have just bought a car for £12 000 from a garage that promises to buy the car back from you for £5000 in 3 years' time.
   (a) What is the rate of depreciation?
   (b) Given this rate of depreciation, what will the car be worth at the end of the first year?

28 Which is better: a savings account paying 7% p.a. where interest is compounded annually, or an account which pays an annual rate of 5% but where the interested is compounded continuously?

Assignment

MOS plc is a computer software company and its main business is the development of payroll systems. Recently it has also developed a number of specialized machine control systems and the company is keen to expand into this area. However, the risks in developing these types of systems are much greater than for payroll systems. This is partly to do with the fact that there is a risk that the software will not work, but also to do with the fact that it takes much longer for the project to be completed. A payroll system can be developed in under a year, while for control systems the development time can be 2 to 3 years. The policy of the company is to lease the software for a fixed period of time and during this period the client pays an annual rental that diminishes with time.

When MOS receives a request for a piece of software, a valuation exercise takes place. This valuation exercise looks at the financial implications as well as any technical problems. For payroll systems the market is very competitive and there is very little room for manoeuvre. However, for control systems there is much more flexibility in pricing. As with any small company, MOS has a limited amount of capital available, which currently amounts to £500 000 obtained through bank loans. MOS currently pays interest at a rate of 8.5% p.a.

MOS has options on three projects. Project A and Project B are payroll systems and both involve an expenditure of less than £100 000, while Project C is a specialized control system that involves an expenditure of £500 000. Details of the expenditure and leasing rental are shown in Table 12.8.

Use investment appraisal techniques to decide which (if any) of the projects should be accepted. Write a note to the Project Manager of MOS plc explaining your results and recommendations.

Table 12.8 Information for the assignment

Year	Project A (£000s)	Project B (£000s)	Project C (£000s)
0	−60	−80	−500
1	30	40	0
2	30	20	0
3	20	20	0
4	10	20	500
5	10	5	300
6			200
7			100

FORECASTING: TIME SERIES ANALYSIS

PREREQUISITES
There are no prerequisites for this chapter apart from a basic knowledge of Excel.

OBJECTIVES
- To be able to apply the technique of moving averages to isolate the trend in a time series
- To understand the circumstances in which the additive and multiplicative models should be used
- To be able to calculate the seasonal component for both the additive and multiplicative models
- To be able to calculate the seasonally adjusted series
- To know how to apply the technique of exponential smoothing in appropriate circumstances
- To be able to make forecasts, and to understand the limitations of these forecasts
- To know how to use Excel in time series analysis

INTRODUCTION
Many variables have values that change with time, such as the weekly sales of ice cream, visits abroad by UK residents, or the daily production rates for a factory. The changing value of such variables over a period of time is called a *time series*. The analysis of time series data is very important both for industry and for government, and a large number of people are employed to do this analysis. This chapter will look at the main features of a time series, and demonstrate some popular techniques.

QUANTITATIVE METHODS IN ACTION

The Ebola epidemic

The first case of Ebola in West Africa occurred in March 2014. This outbreak has since killed more than all other known Ebola outbreaks combined. Up to June 2015 there were an estimated 11 173 deaths. However the true number of deaths is probably much greater than this as not all deaths were reported. Some researchers believe that this figure should be multiplied by a correction factor of 2.5, which would put the number of deaths at 27 932.

The Centers for Disease Control and Prevention in the USA has developed a model* to forecast the number of Ebola cases in a community given various scenarios. The model requires inputs for:

- The population
- Number of people initially infected
- The number of days that people are infectious for
- The incubation distribution, which was assumed to be log normal with a mean of 6.3 days and a standard deviation of 3.31 days and which, along with its parameters, was determined by analyzing previous Ebola epidemics.

The researchers applied their model to both Liberia and Sierra Leone. They first fitted the model to the data from 26 March to 23 August 2014. They then used the model to test various scenarios. In particular they looked at the effect of the delay in delivering measures to prevent infection, such as hospitalization or treatment in Ebola treatment units

(ETUs) of 70% of infected patients. Figure 13.1 shows what effect these delays would have on the number of new Ebola patients in Liberia. This chart has been corrected for under-reporting of Ebola cases. The numbers (3408, 10 646 and 25 847) shown on the chart represent new Ebola patients at the peak of each start date. This chart predicts that early intervention is effective in controlling the disease.

In August 2014 the World Health Organization (WHO) finally declared the epidemic an international health emergency, and governments and international organizations started to provide the necessary resources and expertise to try to stop the spread of the disease.

By January 2015 new cases of Ebola fell rapidly, and by March 4 2015 only 132 new cases were reported in the whole of West Africa, with no new cases reported in Liberia. These figures demonstrate how accurate the model was in predicting the effectiveness of early intervention. Had these measures been started much earlier, there would have undoubtedly been a much smaller death toll.

Sources: 'Estimating the future number of cases in the Ebola epidemic – Liberia and Sierra Leone, 2014–15', *MMWR*, Vol. 63, No. 13, 2013. US Department of Health and Human Service, Centers for Disease Control and Prevention. World Health Organization (WHO) (http://apps.who.int/ebola/).
* The Excel model can be downloaded from http://dx.doi.org/10.15620/cdc.24900.

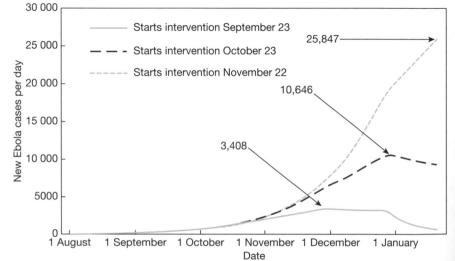

Figure 13.1 Predicted new Ebola patients given different start dates of intervention

Source: 'Estimating the future number of cases in the Ebola epidemic – Liberia and Sierra Leone, 2014–15', *MMWR*, Vol. 63, No. 13, 2013, Figure 3. US Department of Health and Human Services, Centers for Disease Control and Prevention.

The decomposition model

This model assumes that a time series is made up of several components. These components are:

- Trend
- Seasonality
- Cyclic behaviour
- Randomness

The trend represents the long-run behaviour of the data and can be increasing, decreasing or constant. Seasonality relates to periodic fluctuations that repeat themselves at fixed intervals of time. Cyclic behaviour represents the ups and downs of the economy or of a specific industry. It is a long-term fluctuation and for practical purposes is usually ignored. Randomness is always present in a time series and represents variation that cannot be explained. Some time series (for example, share prices) have a very high random component and the forecasts of these series will be subject to a high degree of error.

example 13.1

Table 13.1 consists of data relating to the sales of petrol at the Star petrol station for 3 weeks while Table 13.2 consists of the sales of sun cream by Mace Skin Care plc.

Table 13.1 Sales of petrol at the Star petrol station

Week	Day	Litres (000s)
1	Monday	28
	Tuesday	16
	Wednesday	24
	Thursday	44
	Friday	65
	Saturday	82
	Sunday	30
2	Monday	33
	Tuesday	21
	Wednesday	29
	Thursday	49
	Friday	70
	Saturday	87
	Sunday	35
3	Monday	35
	Tuesday	23
	Wednesday	31
	Thursday	51
	Friday	72
	Saturday	89
	Sunday	37

Table 13.2 Sales of sun cream by Mace Skin Care plc

Year	Quarter	Sales (£000s)
2012	1	6.00
	2	9.00
	3	12.00
	4	8.00
2013	1	8.00
	2	13.50
	3	17.00
	4	13.00
2014	1	12.00
	2	20.25
	3	30.00
	4	19.50
2015	1	18.00

activity
13.1

Plot the two series represented by Tables 13.1 and 13.2 on graph paper (or use a spreadsheet) and compare and contrast the important features of each.

You can check your graph with the ones in Figures 13.2 and 13.3. What can you say about these graphs? You should notice that both series show a marked seasonal component since the patterns repeat themselves at regular intervals. In the case of the Star petrol station, the highest sales always occurs on a Saturday and the lowest on a Monday. The time series for the quarterly sales of sun cream by Mace Skin Care plc shows a peak in quarter 3 and a trough in quarter 1. You should also notice that the sales of sun cream appear to have increased rapidly during the 3-year period.

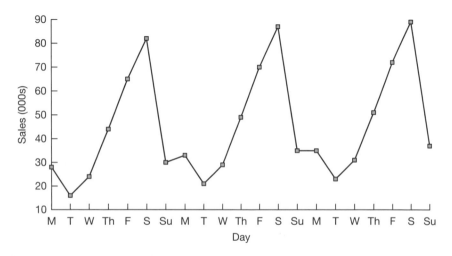

Figure 13.2 Sales of petrol at the Star service station

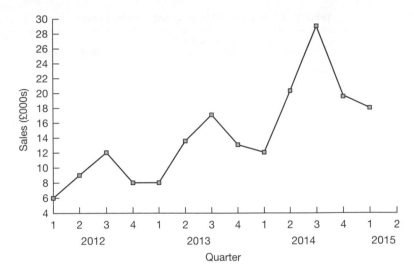

Figure 13.3 Sales of sun cream by Mace Skin Care plc

Isolating the trend

To isolate the trend you need to remove the seasonal fluctuations. In the case of the petrol sales the pattern repeats itself every week, so perhaps the average sales each week might be a useful calculation.

> *activity*
> **13.2**
>
> Calculate the average petrol sales for weeks 1, 2 and 3. Does this help remove the seasonal fluctuations?

The values you should have got are 41.3, 46.3 and 48.3 for weeks 1, 2 and 3 respectively. The seasonal fluctuations have certainly been removed, but then so has most of the data! This is therefore not the best of methods. However, why use Monday to Sunday as a week? Why not Tuesday to Monday or Wednesday to Tuesday? If you think along these lines you will see that many more than 3 averages can be obtained. This process is called *moving averages* since the average is moved by one time period each time. Since there are 7 days or periods in this example, you have to calculate a 7-point moving average.

The calculations for the first 3 averages are shown in Table 13.3 overleaf. Notice that the first average has been placed alongside Thursday: this is because Thursday is the middle of the week that starts on Monday.

> *activity*
> **13.3**
>
> Calculate the remaining moving averages and plot these figures on the same graph as you plotted the original series.

The complete table is shown in Table 13.4.

Table 13.3 Calculation of moving averages for petrol sales

Day	Petrol sales (000s litres)	Weekly total	7-point moving average
Monday	28		
Tuesday	16		
Wednesday	24		
Thursday	44	$28 + 16 + 24 + 44 + 65 + 82 + 30 = 289$	$289/7 = 41.3$
Friday	65	$16 + 24 + 44 + 65 + 82 + 30 + 33 = 294$	$294/7 = 42.0$
Saturday	82	$24 + 44 + 65 + 82 + 30 + 33 + 21 = 299$	$299/7 = 42.7$
Sunday	30		
Monday	33		
Tuesday	21		

NOTE: A shortcut is to notice that as you move down the table, you are simply dropping one period and adding another. That is, the total for Friday is $289 - 28 + 33 = 294$. This is particularly useful for large cycle lengths, such as 12- or 52-point moving averages.

Table 13.4 Moving averages for Activity 13.3

Day	Litres (000s)	Moving average
Monday	28	
Tuesday	16	
Wednesday	24	
Thursday	44	41.3
Friday	65	42.0
Saturday	82	42.7
Sunday	30	43.4
Monday	33	44.1
Tuesday	21	44.9
Wednesday	29	45.6
Thursday	49	46.3
Friday	70	46.6
Saturday	87	46.9
Sunday	35	47.1
Monday	35	47.4
Tuesday	23	47.7
Wednesday	31	48.0
Thursday	51	48.3
Friday	72	
Saturday	89	
Sunday	37	

The moving average figures have been superimposed on the original time series graph and are shown in Figure 13.4.

There is no doubt that the moving average has smoothed the data and therefore this second series should represent the trend. You can see from the graph that there is a slight upward movement to this trend.

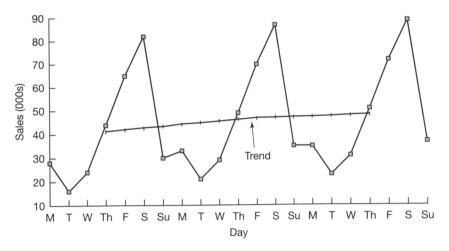

Figure 13.4 Time series graph of petrol sales with the moving averages plotted

The Star petrol station example illustrated the case where the moving average was based on an odd number of periods (7 days). However, with the sun cream series there is an even number of periods (4 quarters). The problem with this is that the middle of the year falls between quarters 2 and 3. This would not be very helpful since the original data relate to a specific quarter. (How would you plot a value between 2 quarters and what would this value mean?) To get round this problem, *centred moving averages* are used. The moving averages are worked out as before, placing the averages between periods. Pairs of averages are then taken and the average of the averages can be written down alongside a specific period. Table 13.5 illustrates the calculations for the first 2 centred moving averages.

Table 13.5 Calculation of moving averages for sun cream

Year	Quarter	Sales (£000s)	Moving average	Centred moving average
2012	1	6.0		
	2	9.0		
			8.75	
	3	12.0		$(8.75 + 9.25)/2 = 9.00$
			9.25	
	4	8.0		$(9.25 + 10.38)/2 = 9.81$
			10.38	
2013	1	8.0		
	2	13.5		

(activity
13.4*)* Calculate the remaining centred moving average figures for the sales of sun cream and plot these figures on the same graph as you plotted the original series.

You should have obtained Table 13.6. The centred moving averages can then be plotted, as in Figure 13.5. Notice the rapidly rising trend values.

Table 13.6 Centred moving averages for Activity 13.4

Year	Quarter	Sales (£000s)	Centred moving average
2012	1	6.00	
	2	9.00	
	3	12.00	9.00
	4	8.00	9.81
2013	1	8.00	11.00
	2	13.50	12.25
	3	17.00	13.38
	4	13.00	14.72
2014	1	12.00	17.19
	2	20.25	19.63
	3	30.00	21.19
	4	19.50	
2015	1	18.00	

NOTE: Figures have been rounded to 2 decimal places in this and subsequent tables. The figures will therefore not agree exactly to those obtained using a spreadsheet.

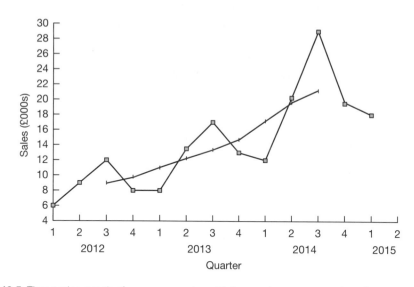

Figure 13.5 Time series graph of sun cream sales with the moving averages plotted

Isolating the seasonal component

There are two models that will allow you to isolate the seasonal component. The first is the *additive* model and is applicable if the seasonal swings are a constant difference from the trend. This means that the *difference* between the trend and a particular period remains approximately constant throughout the entire time series. The second model is the *multiplicative* model and is applicable if the seasonal swings are a constant percentage of the trend; that is, the seasonal swing will depend on the value of the trend at that point.

In equation form the additive model is:

$$Y = T + S + C + R$$

and the multiplicative model is:

$$Y = T \times S \times C \times R$$

where Y is the variable of interest, T is the trend, S is the seasonal component, C is the cyclic component and R is the random element.

(activity 13.5) By examining Figure 13.4, decide whether the additive or multiplicative model is more appropriate for the petrol sales series. Repeat this exercise for the sales of sun cream, using Figure 13.5.

You should have found that the seasonal swings about the trend for the petrol sales series appear reasonably constant, so an additive model is probably appropriate here. In the sun cream example the seasonal swings about the trend are increasing, so the multiplicative model is probably better. However, it is not always so clear cut and sometimes both models are tried and the results compared. To show this, both models will now be applied to the sun cream example.

To obtain the seasonal differences, the additive model can be rearranged as:

$$S + C + R = Y - T$$

So the value of the variable minus the trend value at that point will give you the seasonal difference plus the cyclic and random components. The cyclic component can only be isolated when values of the variable Y are available over many years (at least 20), which is rare. Usually the cyclic component is ignored, and its effect (if any) forms part of the random element.

For quarter 3 of 2012 the estimate of the seasonal difference is $12 - 9 = 3$. This tells you that sales for quarter 3 in 2012 are 3 units (£3000) above the trend. For quarter 4 of 2012 the seasonal difference is -1.81 ($8 - 9.81$), which means the sales are 1.81 below the trend.

(activity 13.6) Calculate the seasonal differences for the remainder of the data.

You should have obtained the seasonal differences shown in Table 13.7 overleaf.

If you look at these figures you will notice that for the same quarter number the seasonal difference varies. This is due to the random element. This variation can best be observed in Table 13.8, which also allows the average seasonal difference to be calculated.

The use of an average value helps to remove some of the random component. These averages should sum to zero since they should cancel out over the year. In the example above you will see that $-4.095 + 0.935 + 5.147 - 1.765 = 0.222$, which is clearly not zero. If each average is reduced by 0.056 $\left(\dfrac{0.222}{4} \right)$ then you will get the

Table 13.7 Seasonal differences for the sales of sun cream

Year	Quarter	Sales (£000s)	Centred moving average	Seasonal difference
2012	1	6.00		
	2	9.00		
	3	12.00	9.00	3.00
	4	8.00	9.81	−1.81
2013	1	8.00	11.00	−3.00
	2	13.50	12.25	1.25
	3	17.00	13.38	3.63
	4	13.00	14.72	−1.72
2014	1	12.00	17.19	−5.19
	2	20.25	19.63	0.62
	3	30.00	21.19	8.81
	4	19.50		
2015	1	18.00		

Table 13.8 Average seasonal differences for the sales of sun cream

Quarter	1	2	3	4	
2012			3.00	−1.81	
2013	−3.00	1.25	3.63	−1.72	
2014	−5.19	0.62	8.81		
Average	−4.095	0.935	5.147	−1.765	Sum = 0.222
Adjusted	−4.15	0.88	5.09	−1.82	Sum = 0.00

adjusted figures (rounded to 2 decimal places) shown in Table 13.8 and you should check that their sum is now zero.

The calculations for the multiplicative model are similar except that S is called the seasonal factor and is worked out by dividing Y by T. These factors are often expressed in percentage form by multiplying by 100. For example, the seasonal factor for quarter 3 in 2012 is:

$$\frac{12}{9} \times 100 = 133.3\%$$

DID YOU KNOW?

The ability to monitor and forecast the onset of infectious diseases is important in the fight to control their speed. Current methods using biological approaches are expensive and slow. Researchers have found that it is possible to monitor and forecast diseases anywhere in the world by analysing the access logs from online Wikipedia. This is because people tend to search for disease-related information before seeking medical attention (see http://journals.plos.org/ploscompbiol/article?id=10.1371/journal.pcbi.1003892).

Source: N. Generous, G. Fairchild, A. Deshpande, S.Y. Del Valle, R. Priedhorsky, 'Global Disease Monitoring and Forecasting with Wikipedia', *PLoS Comput Biol*, Vol. 10, No. 11, 2014: e1003892. doi:10.1371/journal.pcbi.1003892.

activity
13.7 Obtain the average percentage seasonal factors for the sales of sun cream by Mace Skin Care plc.

In this model a seasonal factor above 100% represents sales above the trend, and a value below 100% represents sales below the trend. The seasonal factors and average seasonal factors are shown in Tables 13.9 and 13.10 respectively.

Table 13.9 Seasonal factors for the sales of sun cream

Year	Quarter	Sales (£000s)	Centred moving average	Seasonal factor (%)
2012	1	6.00		
	2	9.00		
	3	12.00	9.00	133.3
	4	8.00	9.81	81.5
2013	1	8.00	11.00	72.7
	2	13.50	12.25	110.2
	3	17.00	13.38	127.1
	4	13.00	14.72	88.3
2014	1	12.00	17.19	69.8
	2	20.25	19.63	103.2
	3	30.00	21.19	141.6
	4	19.50		
2015	1	18.00		

Table 13.10 Calculation of average seasonal factors for the sales of sun cream

Quarter	1	2	3	4	
2012			133.3	81.5	
2013	72.7	110.2	127.1	88.3	
2014	69.8	103.2	141.6		
Average	71.3	106.7	134.0	84.9	Sum = 396.9
Adjusted	71.9	107.5	135.0	85.6	Sum = 400.0

Each average was adjusted by multiplying its value by $1.00781 \left(\dfrac{400}{396.9} \right)$, since the sum of the averages should in this case be 400.

Analysis of errors

Once you have isolated the trend and seasonal components it is a good idea to see how well the model fits the data. This is particularly important when you are not sure whether the additive or multiplicative model is the correct model to use.

For the additive model $Y = T + S$, so the Y variable can be predicted by adding the trend to the relevant adjusted average seasonal difference. For the multiplicative model $Y = T \times S$, so the prediction is made by multiplying the trend and adjusted average seasonal factor. In both cases the difference between the actual value and the predicted value gives you the error in the prediction. For example, the predicted sales of sun cream for quarter 3 in 2012 using the additive model is $9.00 + 5.09 = 14.09$. Since the actual value is 12.00, this represents an error of $-2.09 (12 - 14.09)$. Using the multiplicative model the predicted value is $9.00 \times \dfrac{135.0}{100} = 12.15$ and the error is now -0.15.

activity **13.8**

Calculate the remaining errors using both the additive and multiplicative models.

The errors for both models are shown in Table 13.11 and Table 13.12. The errors should be small and show no pattern. Even with small quantities of data the easiest way to look at the errors is by means of a graph. Figures 13.6 and 13.7 show that the multiplicative model gives the smallest errors and is therefore the better model, which is what was expected.

Apart from a graphical display of the errors, it is possible to analyze them statistically. Two statistics are normally calculated, the mean absolute deviation (MAD) and the mean square error (MSE).

Table 13.11 Calculation of the errors for the additive model

Year	Quarter	Sales (£000s)	Trend	Average seasonal difference	Predicted sales (£000s)	Error
2012	1	6.00				
	2	9.00				
	3	12.00	9.00	5.09	14.09	−2.09
	4	8.00	9.81	−1.82	7.99	0.01
2013	1	8.00	11.00	−4.15	6.85	1.15
	2	13.50	12.25	0.88	13.13	0.37
	3	17.00	13.38	5.09	18.47	−1.47
	4	13.00	14.72	−1.82	12.90	0.10
2014	1	12.00	17.19	−4.15	13.04	−1.04
	2	20.25	19.63	0.88	20.51	−0.26
	3	30.00	21.19	5.09	26.28	3.72
	4	19.50				
2015	1	18.00				

Table 13.12 Calculation of the errors for the multiplicative model

Year	Quarter	Sales (£000s)	Trend	Average seasonal factor (%)	Predicted sales (£000s)	Error
2012	1	6.00				
	2	9.00				
	3	12.00	9.00	135.0	12.15	−0.15
	4	8.00	9.81	85.6	8.40	−0.40
2013	1	8.00	11.00	71.9	7.91	0.09
	2	13.50	12.25	107.5	13.17	0.33
	3	17.00	13.38	135.0	18.06	−1.06
	4	13.00	14.72	85.6	12.60	0.40

2014	1	12.00	17.19	71.9	12.36	−0.36
	2	20.25	19.63	107.5	21.10	−0.85
	3	30.00	21.19	135.0	28.61	1.39
	4	19.50				
2015	1	18.00				

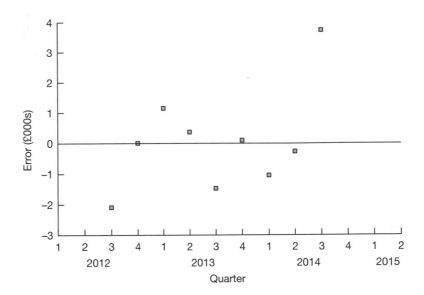

Figure 13.6 Errors for the additive model

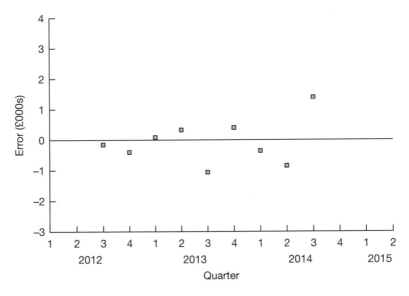

Figure 13.7 Errors for the multiplicative model

The formulae for these are:

sum the *absolute* values of the errors (ignore the sign)

sum the *square* of the errors

$$\text{MAD} = \frac{\sum |\text{errors}|}{n} \qquad \text{MSE} = \frac{\sum (\text{errors})^2}{n}$$

The MAD statistic is simply the mean of the absolute errors (or deviations), while MSE is the mean squared errors. Both statistics are valid, but you will find that many statisticians favour the MSE statistic. One reason for this is that squaring puts more emphasis on large errors. For the sun cream example, the calculation of MAD and MSE using the errors obtained from the additive model is shown in Table 13.13.

Table 13.13 Calculation of MAD and MSE for the additive model

Year	Quarter	Actual sales (£000s)	Predicted sales (£000s)	Error	Absolute error	Squared error
2012	3	12.00	14.09	−2.09	2.09	4.3681
	4	8.00	7.99	0.01	0.01	0.0001
2013	1	8.00	6.85	1.15	1.15	1.3225
	2	13.50	13.13	0.37	0.37	0.1369
	3	17.00	18.47	−1.47	1.47	2.1609
	4	13.00	12.90	0.10	0.10	0.0100
2014	1	12.00	13.04	−1.04	1.04	1.0816
	2	20.25	20.51	−0.26	0.26	0.0676
	3	30.00	26.28	3.72	3.72	13.8384
				Sum =	10.21	22.9861
				Mean	1.13	2.55

activity 13.9

Repeat the above calculation using the multiplicative model.

You should have obtained Table 13.14.

Table 13.14 Calculation of MAD and MSE for the multiplicative model

Year	Quarter	Actual sales (£000s)	Predicted sales (£000s)	Error	Absolute error	Squared error
2012	3	12.00	12.15	−0.15	0.15	0.0225
	4	8.00	8.40	−0.40	0.40	0.1600
2013	1	8.00	7.91	0.09	0.09	0.0081
	2	13.50	13.17	0.33	0.33	0.1089
	3	17.00	18.06	−1.06	1.06	1.1236
	4	13.00	12.60	0.40	0.40	0.1600
2014	1	12.00	12.36	−0.36	0.36	0.1296
	2	20.25	21.10	−0.85	0.85	0.7225
	3	30.00	28.61	1.39	1.39	1.9321
				Sum =	5.03	4.3673
				Mean	0.56	0.49

Both these statistics are smaller than that obtained with the additive model, demonstrating once again that the multiplicative model is better for this example.

Seasonally adjusted series

I am sure that you have heard the phrase 'seasonally adjusted' when economic time series are mentioned by the media. A common example is unemployment. If a series is seasonally adjusted it means that the seasonal component has been removed, leaving the trend component. By seasonally adjusting unemployment figures, for example, it is easy to tell what is happening to this important economic variable.

For the additive model a time series is seasonally adjusted by *subtracting* the seasonal difference, while for the multiplicative model the operation is one of *division*.

Normally this procedure is used when new data arrives and you want to see if there is any change in the trend of the series. So if you wanted to seasonally adjust the sales of sun cream in quarter 2 of 2015 you would need to divide the sales by the appropriate seasonal factor since the multiplicative model was shown to be the best model.

(activity
13.10)

The sales of sun cream by Mace Skin Care plc for quarter 2 of 2015 are £28 500. Seasonally adjust this figure.

The average seasonal factor for quarter 2 is 107.5% (see Activity 13.7), so the seasonally adjusted sales are $\dfrac{28\,500}{1.075} = £26\,512$.

Forecasting using the decomposition model

One purpose of time series analysis is to use the results to forecast future values of the series. The procedure for this is to extrapolate the trend into the future and then apply the seasonal component to the forecast trend. There are various methods of extrapolating the trend. If the trend is approximately linear then linear regression could be used by assigning numerical values to time. For example, using the sun cream series, quarter 1 of 2012 would have a value 1 and quarter 1 of 2015 would have a value 13. This is explained in more detail on page 341. However, you will often find it easier to extrapolate by eye ('eyeballing') since other factors can then be considered, if necessary. If there is doubt about the future behaviour of the trend, you could make two or three different extrapolations to give different forecasts (say, an optimistic and a pessimistic one).

For the sun cream example, a possible extrapolation of the trend has been made and can be seen in Figure 13.8. The forecast trend values for the remainder of 2015 have been read off this graph and are shown below:

Quarter	2	3	4
Trend forecast	25.5	27.0	28.5

To calculate the forecast for each quarter using the multiplicative model, these trend forecasts need to be *multiplied* by the appropriate seasonal factor. For example, for quarter 2 the average seasonal factor is 107.5%, so the forecast value is $25.5 \times 1.075 = 27.41$, or approximately £27 400. For the additive model the average

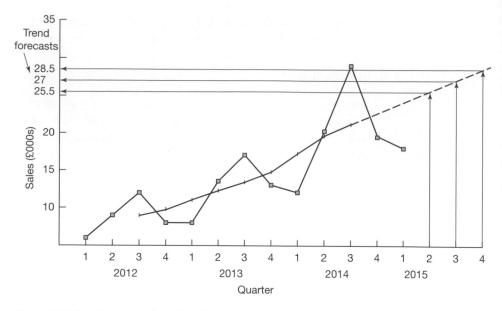

Figure 13.8 Trend forecasts for sales of sun cream

seasonal difference of 0.88 is *added* to 25.5; that is, 26.38, or approximately £26 400. The result using the multiplicative model is likely to be more accurate since the model had smaller errors. However, any forecasts are subject to considerable uncertainty and all forecasts should be treated with caution.

activity **13.11**   Use the multiplicative model to obtain forecasts for quarters 3 and 4 of 2015.

The seasonal factors for quarters 3 and 4 are 135.0% and 85.6%, so the forecasts will be:

$$27 \times 1.350 = 36.450 \text{ (approximately £36 500)}$$

and $28.5 \times 0.856 = 24.396$ (approximately £24 400)

DID YOU KNOW?

While statistical forecasting using time series analysis is very important many managers and analysts like to incorporate judgement into their forecasts. This is called *judgemental forecasting* and is a particularly useful method when the time series does not have a steady seasonal or trend pattern. The Bank of England uses its judgement when making forecasts about important economic indicators. (See Bank of England Inflation report February 2011, www.bankofengland.co.uk/publications/inflationreport/ir11feb.pdf)

Exponential smoothing

The technique of exponential smoothing is often used where a short-term forecast is required (that is, the next period). The formula for this technique is very simple:

Next forecast $=$ Last forecast $+ \alpha \times$ error in last forecast where α (alpha) is a smoothing constant. This constant takes a value between 0 and 1, so that the next forecast will simply be the last forecast plus a fraction of the last error. The error in the last forecast is the actual value minus the forecast.

To illustrate this technique, imagine that you are responsible for ensuring that the Small Brewery company has sufficient barrels available to store its beer. Full barrels are sent out and empty ones returned. You need to know how many barrels will be returned the next day to plan production. If insufficient barrels are available, beer is wasted, whereas if more barrels than expected are returned, you may have lost sales.

There are two problems with exponential smoothing. The first is what value of α to use. This can only be found by trial and error, and you may even have to change the value in the light of experience. It is usually found that a value between 0.05 and 0.3 gives the smallest values of MAD or MSE. For the Small Brewery company, a value of 0.1 has been chosen.

The second problem is how to get the first forecast, since a last forecast is required. Some people choose a suitable value while others prefer a warm-up period. Once several forecasts have been made, the starting value becomes less important anyway, but let us suppose that you have decided to use the warm-up method. You are to use the last 10 days for this purpose, and therefore your first proper forecast will be for day 11. The number of barrels returned over the last 10 days are:

Day	1	2	3	4	5	6	7	8	9	10
No. of barrels	20	13	19	19	25	17	15	13	22	20

If you take the forecast for day 2 as the actual for day 1, then the error is $-7 (13 - 20)$ and the forecast for day 3 becomes:

$$20 + (0.1 \times -7) = 19.3$$

The forecast for day 4 is now:

$$19.3 + (0.1 \times -0.3) = 19.27$$

and so on.

activity
13.12

Continue this process to achieve a forecast for day 11.

You will probably find it easier if you use a table similar to Table 13.15. As you can see, the forecast for day 11 is 18.95 (that is, 19 barrels).

Table 13.15 Forecasts using exponential smoothing and a smoothing constant of 0.1

Day	No. barrels	Forecast	Error	$\alpha \times$ error	Next forecast
1	20				
2	13	20.00	−7.00	−0.70	19.30
3	19	19.30	−0.30	−0.03	19.27
4	19	19.27	−0.27	−0.03	19.24
5	25	19.24	5.76	0.58	19.82
6	17	19.82	−2.82	−0.28	19.54

(continued)

Table 13.15 (*continued*)

Day	No. barrels	Forecast	Error	$\alpha \times$ error	Next forecast
7	15	19.54	−4.54	−0.45	19.09
8	13	19.09	−6.09	−0.61	18.48
9	22	18.48	3.52	0.35	18.83
10	20	18.83	1.17	0.12	18.95
11		18.95			

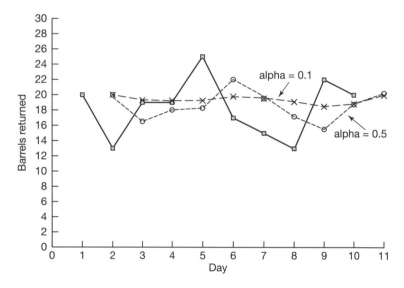

Figure 13.9 Numbers of returned barrels and forecasts using exponential smoothing

The time series of the original data and of the forecast values are shown in Figure 13.9. Also shown is the forecast using an α of 0.5, and you will see that a value of 0.1 gives a smoother series. This is generally true: the smaller the value of α, the greater the smoothing effect.

In terms of accuracy the errors can again be analyzed and MAD and MSE calculated. Using an α of 0.1, an MSE of 17.97 is obtained.

activity 13.13

Calculate the MSE statistic using an alpha of 0.5.

By using an α of 0.5 you should have found that the MSE statistic has increased to 23.21.

Simple exponential smoothing is a very useful and easy-to-use short-term forecasting technique. However, it will lag behind a series that is undergoing a sharp change, such as a series that has a seasonal component or a steep trend. If you want to use it on seasonal data you must seasonally adjust the series first.

Using spreadsheets in time series analysis

Time series calculations can be performed using standard Excel arithmetic formula commands. The line graphs can also be created using Excel's charting tools. Both the use of formulae and charting have been met in previous chapters, so the instructions given in this section have assumed that you are reasonably proficient in these skills.

(activity
13.14) Use Excel to carry out a time series analysis (using the multiplicative model) on the data relating to the sales of sun cream (Table 13.2, page 324).

The only formula you need to create the worksheet shown in Figure 13.10 is `Average`. When calculating the moving average for an even period by hand it is often recommended that you leave a blank line between successive figures of the main table. This is to allow you to place the moving average in between periods. However, this is not a good idea with a spreadsheet, as you would have to leave a blank row between the data. A better method is to place the moving average in the same row as the centred moving average. So in the sun cream data the moving average would start in the third row down. You can see this in Figure 13.10. Transferring the seasonal component to the summary table is another source of error for novice spreadsheet analysts. Don't be tempted to type the figures into the table. If you do this and the data changes, your summary table will not be updated. The only data that should be typed in is the original series itself. All other figures should be formulae, as you will see in Figure 13.10.

	A	B	C	D	E	F	G
1			Sales of sun cream				
2							
3		Year	Quarter	Sales	Moving	Centred moving	Seasonal
4					average	average	factor (%)
5		2012	1	6			
6			2	9			
7			3	12	=AVERAGE(D5:D8)	=AVERAGE(E7:E8)	=D7/F7*100
8			4	8	=AVERAGE(D6:D9)	=AVERAGE(E8:E9)	=D8/F8*100
9		2013	1	8	=AVERAGE(D7:D10)	=AVERAGE(E9:E10)	=D9/F9*100
10			2	13.5	=AVERAGE(D8:D11)	=AVERAGE(E10:E11)	=D10/F10*100
11			3	17	=AVERAGE(D9:D12)	=AVERAGE(E11:E12)	=D11/F11*100
12			4	13	=AVERAGE(D10:D13)	=AVERAGE(E12:E13)	=D12/F12*100
13		2014	1	12	=AVERAGE(D11:D14)	=AVERAGE(E13:E14)	=D13/F13*100
14			2	20.25	=AVERAGE(D12:D15)	=AVERAGE(E14:E15)	=D14/F14*100
15			3	30	=AVERAGE(D13:D16)	=AVERAGE(E15:E16)	=D15/F15*100
16			4	19.5	=AVERAGE(D14:D17)		
17		2015	1	18			
18							
19							
20		Quarter	1	2	3	4	
21		=B5			=G7	=G8	
22		=B9	=G9	=G10	=G11	=G12	
23		=B13	=G13	=G14	=G15		Sum
24		Average	=AVERAGE(C21:C23)	=AVERAGE(D21:D23)	=AVERAGE(E21:E23)	=AVERAGE(F21:F23)	=SUM(C24:F24)
25		Adjusted	=C24*400/$G$24	=D24*400/$G$24	=E24*400/$G$24	=F24*400/$G$24	=SUM(C25:F25)
26							

Figure 13.10 Excel worksheet showing the time series formulae for the multiplicative model
Used with permission from Microsoft.

You should have also added a chart to your spreadsheet. This chart should contain the original series and the trend. You can create this chart on a separate sheet or incorporate it as an object in the same sheet. The chart you should have used is a line graph and the instructions for creating a line chart are:

1 Highlight cells D5 to D17 and then, with the `Ctrl` key held down, highlight cells F5 to F17.

2 Click on the `Insert` tab then `Line` in `charts` group.

3 Choose `Line with Markers`.

4 Move chart to new sheet.

5 Now to get the year and quarter added to the horizontal axis first make sure that you are in the `Design` tab. Then click on `Select Data` in `Data` group and click `Edit` in `Horizontal (Category) Axis Labels` (see Figure 13.11).

6 Highlight cells B5 to C17 and click `OK`.

7 While you are still in the `Select Data Source` you can change the name for Series1 and Series2 (see Figure 13.11).

8 You can now add titles to each axis.

9 Click on `Design` in chart tools then on `Add Chart Element` then `Axis Titles`. For both horizontal and vertical axes click on required title format.

10 Double click on each title to edit.

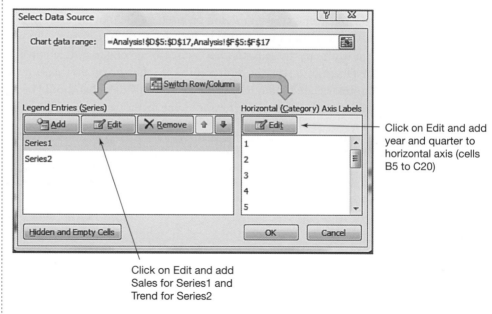

Click on Edit and add Sales for Series1 and Trend for Series2

Figure 13.11 Step 2 of the Chart Wizard in Excel
Used with permission from Microsoft.

The chart in Figure 13.12 is similar to Figure 13.8 which we produced earlier. The difference is that a smooth line has been drawn through the centred moving average points and extended to the end of 2015. This line has been produced using linear regression and to do this in Excel you do the following:

1 Right click on the centred moving averages (trend) as the series you want to create the trendline. Select `Add Trendline`

2 Now right-click on the trendline and select `Format Trendline`.

3 On the right-hand side of the screen `Forecast Forwards` by 3 units

4 To obtain the linear regression equation, you need to check `Display Equation on chart`.

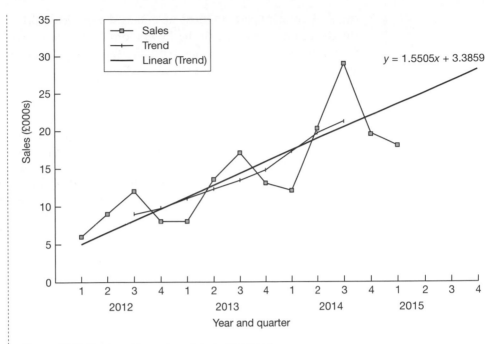

Figure 13.12 The trend line extrapolated using Excel

As you will see the trend equation is $Y = 1.5505x + 3.3859$. The Y variable is the trend values and the x variable are the period number on the time axis, starting from 1 for quarter 1 of 2012 and ending with 13 for quarter 1 of 2015. Trend forecasts will therefore be based on period numbers of 14, 15 and 16 and these can be substituted into the regression equation. For example, the trend forecast for quarter 2 of 2015 is:

$$Y = 1.5505 \times 14 + 3.3859$$

$$= 25.09 \ (£000s)$$

To arrive at the sales forecasts we need to multiply this value by the seasonal factor for quarter 2 which is 1.075 (see page 331). So the sales forecast for quarter 2 is $25.09 \times 1.075 = 26.97 \,(£000s)$.

activity **13.15** Calculate the trend and sales forecasts for quarters 3 and 4 of 2015.

Table 13.16 gives the figures you should have obtained for both the trend and sales forecasts.

Table 13.16 Forecasts for quarters 3 and 4 of 2015

Quarter	x	y	Seasonal factor	Sales (£000s)
3	15	26.64	1.350	35.96
4	16	28.19	0.856	24.13

These are similar figures to those we obtained in Activity 13.11.

The disadvantage with using the Excel's forecast is that we are assuming that the trend is linear, which may not be true. *Eyeballing* has the advantage that external factors can be taken into account when arriving at forecasts.

Reflection

There are many forecasting techniques; some are quite simple, such as the ones looked at in this chapter, whereas others are more complex, such as the one used to predict the number of Ebola cases during the epidemic in West Africa in 2014. The technique used for these forecasts applied something called the *Markov chain model*. However, the choice of forecasting method depends on the use to which the forecasts will be put and whether it is essential that staff within an organization know how the forecasts are made. Utility companies need very accurate forecasts if they are to maintain low levels of reserves, so quite complex forecasting techniques are used. Many businesses also operate very low stock levels because stock is an expensive commodity. In manufacturing, most companies operate a 'lean' manufacturing policy, which entails stock and parts arriving 'just in time' (JIT). To ensure that they don't run out of stock, some form of forecasting is needed.

Short-range forecasts are generally reasonably accurate, except perhaps for a series in which there is a great deal of variability, such as stock or commodity prices. Long-range forecasts, in contrast, which often use regression-type methods, can be horribly wrong. In 1952 IBM predicted that the total market for computers would be 52! Thirty years later, with the advent of the personal computer, IBM raised this figure to 200 000. Today IBM ships about this number every week. Alexander Bell once said that one day every city would have a telephone! Even Bill Gates is reported to have said once that '640k [memory] ought to be enough for anyone.' (See www.economicsuk.com/blog/000166.html)

Long-range forecasts are often more like star-gazing, but all businesses and governments do need to look into the future to some extent. The act of preparing forecasts helps to make an organization aware of the challenges it might one day face. There are also some engineering projects, such as a nuclear power station, that rely on forecasts because they take many years to build.

Key points

- A time series can consist of a seasonal component, a trend, a long-term cycle and randomness. Unless we have over 20 years of data we normally ignore the long-term cycle.
- To isolate the trend of a time series we take a moving average.
- To isolate the seasonality we can either use the additive or multiplicative models. The additive model is used when the seasonal fluctuations are a constant difference from the trend. The multiplicative model is used when the seasonal fluctuations are a constant proportion of the trend.
- We can sometimes tell by looking at the time series chart which is the most appropriate model to use. If not, we can use both models and calculate the mean square error (MSE). The model with the lowest MSE is the best.
- To obtain forecasts we extrapolate the trend and then apply the seasonal difference or factor.
- For short-term forecasts, exponential smoothing is a good method.

Further reading

This text is only an introduction to the huge subject of time series and forecasting. There are a large number of more advanced models that can be used. If you have an interest in the subject and are good at maths then the text by Makridakis et al. (2008) gives a thorough coverage but is quite technical. Forecasting techniques are used in sports and the text by Eastaway and Haigh (2014) is worth reading. The Operational Research (OR) Society has published an article on 50 years of OR in sport (Wright, 2009) and part of this publication discusses forecasting models used in sport.

http://www.**palgrave**.com/oakshott-eqm6

Solutions to all questions are freely available

Practice questions

1 You have just completed an analysis into the sales of a computer game over the past 3 years and the result is shown in Table 13.17.

   (a) Plot this series on graph paper.
   (b) From the raw data, calculate the centred moving average series and plot this on the graph. Comment on both series of data.
   (c) Use the additive decomposition model to obtain average seasonal differences for each period.
   (d) Obtain rough forecasts for 2015.

Table 13.17 Sales for Question 1

Year	Period	Sales (000s)	Year	Period	Sales (000s)	Year	Period	Sales (000s)
2012	1	30	2013	1	30	2014	1	35
	2	35		2	40		2	33
	3	35		3	38		3	37
	4	40		4	35		4	43
	5	50		5	52		5	50
	6	60		6	60		6	65

2 The personnel department of BBS plc, a large food processing company, is concerned about absenteeism among its shop floor workforce. There is a general feeling that the underlying trend has been rising, but nobody has yet analyzed the figures. The total number of shop floor employees has remained virtually unchanged over the last few years.

   The mean number of absentees per day is given in Table 13.18 for each quarter of the years 2012 to 2014 and quarter 1 of 2015.

Table 13.18 Mean number of absentees for Question 2

	Q1	Q2	Q3	Q4
2012	25.1	14.4	9.5	23.7
2013	27.9	16.9	12.4	26.1
2014	31.4	19.7	15.9	29.9
2015	34.5			

(a) Plot the data on a graph (leave space for the remaining 2009 figures).
(b) Use the method of moving averages to determine the trend in the series and superimpose this on your graph. Interpret your graph.
(c) Use an appropriate method to measure the seasonal pattern in the data. Briefly give reasons for your choice of method.
(d) Use your analysis to produce rough forecasts of the mean number of absentees there will be in the remaining quarters of 2015.

3 The manager of the electrical department at a high street store has asked you to perform a time series analysis on the quarterly sales figures of the numbers of TVs sold over the past 3 years (see Table 13.19). It is advised that you use Excel for this question.

Table 13.19 Sales for Question 3

Year	Quarter	No. of sales
2012	2	100
	3	125
	4	127
2013	1	102
	2	104
	3	128
	4	130
2014	1	107
	2	110
	3	131
	4	133
2015	1	107

(a) Produce a line graph of the number of sales. (Extend your time axes up to quarter 4 of 2015.) Describe the pattern exhibited by the data.
(b) Use moving averages to calculate the trend in your data and add this to your chart.
(c) What would be the best decomposition model, the additive or multiplicative? (Hint – calculate the MSE statistic for both models.)
(d) Extrapolate the trend and using your chosen model forecast the sales for the rest of 2015.

4 The following data refers to the daily end-of-business share prices for a particular company:

112, 111, 113, 115, 114, 112, 115, 111, 111, 112, 113

Use exponential smoothing with a smoothing constant of 0.1 to forecast the price on day 12.

5 Top Cycles is a small supplier of cycling equipment to the general public. In 2011 it started to sell a lightweight cycle which was an instant success; annual sales have risen from 633 units in 2011 to 765 units in 2014. However one of the problems has been in sourcing sufficient titanium for the frame. Top Cycles' manager is particularly concerned about whether the company will be able to handle demand during the last two quarters of 2015 as they have budgeted for an increase in demand of no more than 5%.

The sales by quarter for the past 4 years are shown in Table 13.20. Use these figures to forecast demand for each quarter during 2015. Will the company be able to meet demand?

Table 13.20 Sales data for Question 5

Year	Quarter	Sales
2011	1	55
	2	122
	3	315
	4	141
2012	1	61
	2	127
	3	342
	4	148
2013	1	60
	2	136
	3	366
	4	157
2014	1	66
	2	144
	3	382
	4	173

6 The chart in Figure 13.13 shows the turnover (in £000s) of Eat Well restaurant since
   2011. Superimposed on the chart is the trend line.
   (a) It has been suggested that a straight line could be used on the trend line. Comment
   on this proposal.
   (b) To analyze this time series a decomposition model could be used. For the additive
   model the mean square error (MSE) is 69.04 while for the multiplicative model it
   is 5.33. Based on these figures which is the best model? Explain how the chart
   reinforces your decision.

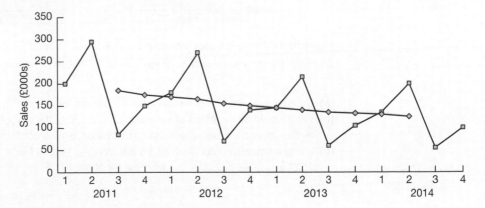

Figure 13.13 Chart for Question 6

(c) The seasonally adjusted figures for part of this series are given below. Use exponential smoothing with a smoothing constant of 0.2 to forecast the first period of 2015. Start the process in quarter 2 of 2013 using the actual 2013 quarter 1 figure as the forecast.

Year	Quarter	Seasonally adjusted turnover
2013	1	138.0
	2	134.6
	3	129.5
	4	124.6
2014	1	127.6
	2	125.8
	3	125.3
	4	117.7

(d) Calculate the MSE for the exponential smoothing process in (c)

7 The chart in Figure 13.14 shows the average daily oil consumption (in 000s barrels) from 1984 to 2007. Superimposed on this chart is an exponential forecasting line using a smoothing constant of 0.1.

Figure 13.14 Oil consumption chart for Question 7

Source: BP Statistical Review of World Energy

(a) Comment on the use of exponential smoothing for this series.
(b) What would be the effect of increasing the value of the smoothing constant? Would a higher value be more or less useful in forecasting the consumption for 2008?
(c) Using a smoothing constant of 0.5 the forecast for 2007 was 1777. If the actual for 2007 was 1696 calculate the forecast for 2008.

8 The sales figures represent the number of guitars sold each quarter for the years 2011–2014.

Year	Quarter	Sales
2011	1	101
	2	125
	3	129
	4	103
2012	1	107
	2	127
	3	135
	4	108
2013	1	112
	2	131
	3	135
	4	108
2014	1	114
	2	132
	3	138
	4	120

(a) Plot a chart of this time series.

(b) Calculate an appropriate moving average of the date and add this to your chart. What does this trend line tell you about the sales of guitars? Which decomposition model is likely to be the most appropriate? Why?

(c) Use both the additive and multiplicative models to isolate the seasonal component. Calculate the MSE (mean square error) for each model to determine which model is best. Is this consistent with your answer to (b)?

(d) Using your chosen model and the average seasonal component, deseasonalize the series and superimpose this on your chart. The actual sales for quarters 1 and 2 for 2015 turned out to be 115 and 132 respectively. Deseasonalize these figures and comment on whether these latest figures are consistent with the past trend.

(e) Use your trend line and the model identified in (c) to provide forecasts for quarters 3 and 4 of 2015. (It is suggested that you extrapolate the trend line by eye although you can get Excel to do it for you.)

Assignment

Obtain the latest data for the overseas travel and tourism case presented in the companion website. Carry out a time series analysis of the 'all visits' data' and see if the downward trend suggested by the Office of National Statistics (ONS) is true. Obtain forecasts for quarter 3 of the year following the last quarter of your new data.

14 MAKING THE MOST OF THINGS: LINEAR PROGRAMMING

PREREQUISITES
There are no prerequisites for this chapter apart from a basic knowledge of Excel.

OBJECTIVES
- To be able to formulate linear programming models for both maximizing and minimizing problems
- To know how to apply a graphical method to solve two-variable problems
- To understand the concept of shadow prices, and to be able to calculate their value
- To be able to carry out a sensitivity analysis on the problem
- To know how to use Excel to solve linear programming problems
- To be able to apply linear programming to transportation problems and to multi-objective problems

INTRODUCTION
Industry, and business in general, operates with limited resources. Frequently money, material and space are scarce, and companies attempt to utilize their resources as efficiently as is possible. The technique of *linear programming* is a procedure that can provide the best solution to many problems that involve an *objective*, such as profit maximization, and a *series of linear constraints*, such as time, labour and cost. This chapter introduces the technique and applies it to simple problems that can be solved either graphically or using Excel. The technique is also extended to problems where there is more than one objective, and for transportation problems.

QUANTITATIVE METHODS IN ACTION

Optimizing the maintenance and repair of salmon farming nets in Chile

Salmon farming first appeared in Chile in the early 1980s, and by 1985 there were 36 Chilean farm centres producing a total of about 2100 tonnes annually. By 2008 salmon farming was Chile's fourth largest export industry and the world's second largest salmon producer, with sales of over 2.3 billion annually. In 2008 the industry was hit by the ISA virus which affected Chile's production of salmon and demonstrated that the industry needed to modernise its operating procedures.

Salmon are reared from eggs and then kept in cages that are open to the sea. These net cages are made of nylon or polyester, which makes handling and maintenance easier than traditional metal ones. However, these cages still need maintenance, such as cleaning and repair. They also deteriorate over time and need replacing. If a net ruptures, there will be a large escape of fish, and it has been estimated that the economic cost of this escape could be as much as $200 000. To prevent ruptures, nets need to be inspected regularly, but this costs money as boats and divers are required. Nets are regularly removed for a thorough clean and coated with antifoulant to reduce algae.

The cost for one salmon farm operator in maintaining the fish cages is of the order of $10m p.a., so it is essential to try to optimise the maintenance and repair of the nets. The decisions that the fish farm operators need to make include:

- When to remove a net and change it for a new one
- When to replace a net for a bigger one (due to growth in fish size)
- Whether a net sent for repair should be treated with antifoulant
- How many nets to buy and when to buy them
- How many net boats are required and how to operate them.

The researchers developed a prototype *integer linear programming* model based on one fish farm which operates over a long stretch of coastline in southern Chile. This farm is divided up into several geographical areas. Each area is further subdivided into four to six centres which share rented net boats and the services of one net maintenance facility. You will see how to develop a linear programming model in this chapter. An integer linear programming model is similar except that the decision variables must be integers because, for example, you must have an integer number of net boats.

The model's input includes the type of net used, including the size and weight; the number of cages in each centre; the distance to the nearest port; the characteristics of the net boats, including their capacity, fuel consumption and the centres that the boats may sail to; the time taken to service a net; and all the various costs involved. The final model had 32 000 variables and 2100 constraints – so quite a large model!

The model demonstrated that a reduction in net maintenance costs of almost 18% is possible if the results obtained were applied on an annual basis. An important aspect of this model is that it can be used in day-to-day planning. An important part of any linear programming exercise is the results obtained from a sensitivity analysis, as you will see later in this chapter. A sensitivity analysis of this model indicated that:

- Two net boats are required but no more.
- The results are sensitive to any delay in maintenance repair time or transport times.
- Nets should be left in the water for longer before removal.
- Treatment with antifoulant is only minimally justified in the summer months and not at all during the winter.

Source: F. Cisternas, D. Delle Donne, G. Durán, C. Polgatiz and A. Weintraub, 'Optimizing salmon farm cage net management using integer programming', *Journal of the Operational Research Society*, Vol. 64, 2013, pp. 735–47.

Basics of linear programming

Linear programming (or LP) is concerned with the management of scarce resources. It is particularly applicable where two or more activities are competing for these limited resources. For example, a company might want to make several different products, each of which makes different demands on the limited resources available. How many of each product should be made so that contribution to profits is *maximized*? Or perhaps you want to determine the quantities of raw materials necessary for a particular blend of oil that will *minimize* the cost of production.

Before these and other problems can be solved you have to *formulate* the problem in linear programming terms. This involves expressing the problem as a series of *inequations* and finding solutions to these inequations that optimize some objective. This may sound very difficult but for *two-variable* problems (for example, two products) the problem can be solved using a graphical technique. For larger problems computer software is normally used.

Linear programming requires a knowledge of elementary algebra and the drawing of straight lines. If you are a little rusty in these areas you are advised to work through appropriate sections (*Elementary algebra*, *Graphs and straight lines* and *Solving linear equations graphically*) of Chapter 1.

DID YOU KNOW?

Linear programming was developed in 1940 by George B. Dantzig who came up with the *Simplex* method. This is an algorithm for finding the best solution to problems where there are many hundreds or thousands of possible solutions. It was used extensively in the Second World War where it made a significant contribution to the war effort. For this reason it was kept a secret until 1947.

Model formulation

Before a problem can be solved by the linear programming method, a model needs to be developed. The model consists of a description of the problem in mathematical terms. In particular, the variables of the problem need to be defined and the objective decided. In addition, the *constraints* need to be expressed as *inequations*.

The next few activities will take you through the procedure using the following example.

example
14.1

The company Just Shirts has been formed to make high quality shirts and is planning to make two types – the 'Regular Fit' and the 'Deluxe Fit'. The contribution to profits for each shirt is £5 for each Regular Fit shirt made and £8 for each Deluxe Fit shirt. To make each shirt requires cotton, of which 600 square metres is available each day, and machinists to cut and stitch the shirts. Twenty machinists are employed by the company and they each work an 8-hour day, giving 160 hours of labour in total. Each Regular Fit shirt requires 5 square metres of cotton and takes 1 hour to make, while each Deluxe Fit shirt takes 6 square metres of cotton and 2 hours to make. The company wishes to maximize contribution to profits, so how many of each type of shirt should be made on a daily basis?

activity 14.1

Define the variables for this problem.

You are required to determine the number of each type of shirt to produce. Let R represent the number of Regular Fit shirts that are to be made each day and D represent the number of Deluxe Fit shirts.

activity 14.2

It is required to maximize contribution to profits. How would you express this in equation form?

If you made just one of each type of shirt, you would make a profit of £5 + £8. However, you are making R Regular Fit and D Deluxe Fit shirts, so the total profit will be $5R + 8D$. The maximum profit can be written as:

Max. $5R + 8D$

activity 14.3

There is a limit of 600 square metres of cotton available each day. How would you express this as a constraint to production, given that each Regular Fit shirt requires 5 square metres and each Deluxe Fit shirt requires 6 square metres?

If you make R Regular Fit shirts then you will use $5R$ metres of cotton. Similarly you will use $6D$ metres of cotton to make D Deluxe Fit shirts. The sum of these two must be less than or equal to 600 square metres, so this can be written as:

$5R + 6D \leq 600$

activity 14.4

Repeat Activity 14.3 for the labour resource.

You will use R hours for the Regular Fit shirt and $2D$ hours for the Deluxe Fit shirt and 160 hours are available each day, so the *constraint* can be written as:

$R + 2D \leq 160$

You have now formulated the problem, although you should indicate that you are only interested in positive values of R and D, and the two constraints $R \geq 0$ and $D \geq 0$ will do this for you.

To summarize, the LP formulation for this problem is:

Max. $5R + 8D$

subject to:

$$5R + 6D \leq 600$$
$$R + 2D \leq 160$$
$$R, D \geq 0$$

There are many values of R and D that will satisfy these inequations. For instance, $R = 40$ and $D = 20$ would satisfy all the constraints, so this is a feasible combination. The problem is, which combination will give the largest profit?

Graphical solution of linear programming problems

The formulation of the problem is only the start (but for many students the hardest part). You now have to solve the problem. There are many computer packages on the market that will solve LP problems, but for two-variable problems it is possible to solve the problem graphically.

If, for the moment, you replace the inequality signs by equalities, the two main constraints become:

$$5R + 6D = 600 \text{ (cotton)}$$

and

$$R + 2D = 160 \text{ (labour)}$$

Since these equations contain only two variables, R and D, they can be represented as straight lines and plotted on a graph. Two points are required to plot a straight line and it is convenient to find where they cross the axes. To do this it is simply a matter of letting $R = 0$ and calculating D, and then letting $D = 0$ and calculating R.

(activity 14.5)　Plot the two equations, $5R + 6D = 600$ and $R + 2D = 160$ on graph paper.

The points where the two lines cross the axes are summarized in Table 14.1.

These two lines have been plotted on a graph (see Figure 14.1) and they mark the boundaries of the inequations. The *region* satisfying each inequation will be one side of the boundary. In this example the regions for both inequations are *below* the lines. To identify the required region it is normal to shade the *unwanted* region, that is the region *not* satisfying the inequality. The region that satisfies all inequalities is called the *feasible region*: any point within this region will satisfy all the constraints. From the graph for the Just Shirts example you should be able to identify the feasible region as 0ABC.

Table 14.1 Crossing points for Activity 14.5

Constraint	R	D
Cotton	0	100
	120	0
Labour	0	80
	160	0

Any point within the feasible region will satisfy all constraints, but which point or points give the largest profit? Fortunately, this can be found quite easily.

Finding the optimum – the isoprofit/cost method

The point p (40, 20) in Figure 14.1 is in the feasible region and the profit for this combination is:

$$5 \times 40 + 8 \times 20 = £360$$

However, there are other combinations of R and D that give the value of 360, since:

$$5R \times 8D = 360$$

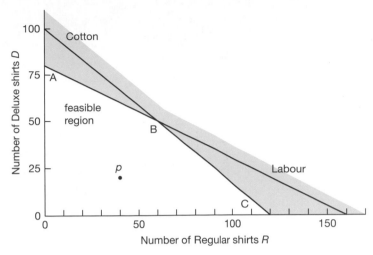

Figure 14.1 Graphical solution for the Just Shirts problem

Thus the profit equation is just another straight line and can be plotted in the same way as the constraints.

That is, if $R = 0$, then $D = 45$

and if $D = 0$, then $R = 72$

This line obviously passes through the point p (see Figure 14.2). Can this figure of 360 be increased? If you try, say, a value of 500 so that $5R + 8D = 500$, you will get another straight line that is parallel to the first one. The reason for this is that the gradient of the line stays the same – it is only the intercepts on the axes that change. Such lines are called *isoprofit* lines ('iso' means same).

(activity 14.6) Place a ruler on the isoprofit line and very carefully move it away from the origin and parallel to the line. What is happening to the profit as the isoprofit line moves away from the origin? At what point does it leave the feasible region completely?

You should have found that as the line moves away from the origin the profit increases and you will find that the point B is the point that is furthest away from the origin, yet still within the feasible region. The fact that the optimum point is at a corner point of the feasible region is not a coincidence – *the optimum value will always be found at a corner point of the feasible region.*

The values of R and D at point B can be read off the graph in Figure 14.2. You should find that $R = 60$ and $D = 50$ and this gives a profit of:

$5 \times 60 + 8 \times 50 = £700$

You may find it surprising that at the optimum solution more Regular Fit shirts are made than Deluxe Fit ones – this is because the Deluxe Fit version uses proportionately more resources.

You found the value of R and D from the graph, but for greater accuracy it is recommended that the relevant equations are solved algebraically. This is particularly

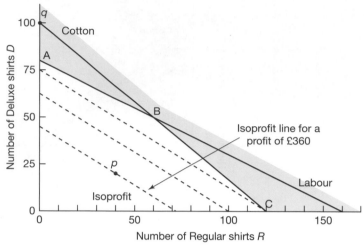

Figure 14.2 The isoprofit method

important when the graph shows that fractional values are involved or when it is difficult to decide which point is optimal. The method of simultaneous equations (see page 12) is used to solve for R and D and is as follows:

$R + 2D = 160$ equation (1)

$5R + 6D = 600$ equation (2)

Multiply (1) by 5 and subtract (2) from the result:

$5R + 10D = 800$

$5R + 6D = 600$

$4D = 200$

so: $D = 50$

If $D = 50$ is now substituted back into (1):

$R + 100 = 160$

$R = 60$

This is the solution found from the graph.

NOTE: A word of warning – even if you use simultaneous equations to solve for the two variables, you must still draw the graph first. Without drawing the graph you could quite easily solve pairs of equations outside the feasible region. Also, the optimum point could be on either axis (for example, point A or C in Figure 14.2).

Finding the optimum – an alternative method

Since you now know that the optimum point must be at a corner point of the feasible region, you could work out the value of the two variables at every corner point. For example, at point A the value of R is zero and D is 80, so the profit must be $8 \times 80 = £640$.

activity **14.7** Calculate the profits at the other corner points.

The profit for each corner point is shown in Table 14.2. These figures confirm that point B gives the greatest profit.

Table 14.2 Profit at each corner point of the feasible region

	R	D	Profit
Point A	0	80	£640
Point B	60	50	£700
Point C	120	0	£600

For feasible regions that have few corner points, this method is probably the quickest. However, it is necessary for you to understand the idea of isoprofit lines as this concept is important when looking at sensitivity analysis.

Tight and slack constraints

If you substitute the optimal values of R (60) and D (50) back into the constraints you will get the following:

Labour: $60 + 2 \times 50 = 160$

Cotton: $5 \times 60 + 6 \times 50 = 600$

Since these values correspond to the maximum quantity of both resources available, the resources are *scarce* and are called *tight* or *binding* constraints. Where a constraint has not reached its limit it is referred to as a *slack* or *non-binding* constraint. For example, if it was not possible to make more than 70 Deluxe Fit shirts, the constraint would be written as $D \leq 70$. This constraint would be slack because the optimal solution has not reached this limit.

Sensitivity analysis

Linear programming is a deterministic model; that is, all variables are assumed to be known with certainty, so the quantity of cotton available each day was assumed to be exactly 600 square metres and the contribution to profits of the Regular Fit shirt was assumed to be exactly £5. Of course, in reality you will never be 100% certain about the value of many of the parameters in an LP model and the purpose of sensitivity analysis is to ask 'what if' questions about these parameters. For example, what if more cotton can be purchased, or what if the profit of a Regular Fit shirt increased to £6?

Sensitivity analysis in linear programming is concerned with the change in the right hand side of the constraints (normally the resources) and changes to the objective function coefficients (that is, the profit/costs of each variable).

Changes to the right hand side of a constraint

Both the labour and cotton resources are tight constraints, and an increase in either of these resources will increase the profit made. The reason for this is that as the right hand side of a tight constraint increases, the constraint *and* the optimum point move *away* from the origin.

This can be demonstrated by resolving the simultaneous equations with the right hand side of the labour constraint increased by 1 to 161. That is:

$$R + 2D = 161$$
$$5R + 6D = 600$$

Solving these two equations simultaneously as before gives:

$$R = 58.5 \text{ and } D = 51.25$$

(Don't worry about the fractional values for the time being.) The new profit will be £702.50, an increase of £2.50. This £2.50 is called the *shadow price* of the labour resource. It is defined as the change in the value of the objective function if the right hand side is increased (or decreased) by one unit.

---

activity
14.8

Calculate the shadow price of the cotton resource.

You should have found that the shadow price of the cotton resource is £0.50 per square metre. That is, an additional profit of 50p could be made for each extra square metre of cotton that could be obtained.

So if it were possible to increase labour hours (perhaps by working overtime) or to increase the supply of cotton, a potentially larger profit could be made. However, this assumes that the direct costs would not increase as well. If, for instance, overtime rates increase costs by more than £2.50 per hour, then it wouldn't be economic to increase production in this way. However, assuming it is worthwhile, how many more hours should be worked? As the labour constraint moves away from the origin, there comes a point where it moves outside the cotton constraint; this is at point q in Figure 14.2. This means that the labour resource ceases to be scarce and further increase of this resource will just add to the surplus of labour. At point q, $R = 0$ and $D = 100$, so if these values are substituted into the labour equation you get:

$$0 + 2 \times 100 = 200$$

So the labour resource can increase by 40 hours (200 − 160), which means that a possible 40 × 2.50 = £100 extra profit can be made each day.

---

activity
14.9

What additional quantity of cotton would it be worth purchasing and what additional profit would result?

You should have found that the supply of cotton can be increased to 800 square metres per day, which is an additional 200 square metres. The extra profit would be £100.

Changes to the objective function coefficients

The objective function for the Just Shirts example is:

$$\text{Max. } 5R + 8D$$

where 5 (in £) is the contribution to profits for each Regular Fit shirt made and 8 is the profit per Deluxe Fit shirt. If it were possible to reduce costs, then profits per shirt would rise, and vice versa, but would the production of 60 Regular Fit shirts and 50 Deluxe Fit shirts remain the optimal solution?

(activity **14.10***)* Assume that the profit on a Regular Fit shirt has decreased to £2. Redraw the isoprofit line to see if the optimum point has changed.

Figure 14.3 shows the effect on the isoprofit line of reducing the profit of a Regular Fit shirt to £2.

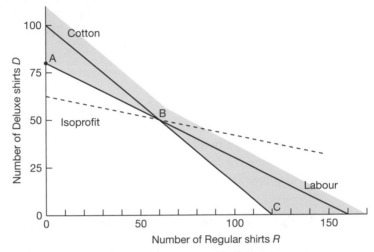

Figure 14.3 Effect on the optimum solution when the profit changes

The optimum solution has changed and is now at point A. In this solution you would make 80 Deluxe Fit shirts but no Regular Fit ones.

Although you could find the optimum point each time a change in the profit coefficient was made, it would be much easier if you knew the value of the profit that would cause a change in the optimal solution. If you let the profit be P, the isoprofit line has the equation:

$$P = 5R + 8D$$

Rearranging this equation into the form $y = mx + c$ gives:

$$D = -\frac{5}{8}R + \frac{P}{8}$$

The gradient of this line is $-\frac{5}{8}$. This gradient is simply the profit on a Regular Fit shirt divided by the profit on a Deluxe Fit shirt. If the profit on the Regular Fit shirt is £2 then the gradient of the isoprofit line becomes $-\frac{2}{8}$. Now consider what happens as the isoprofit line changes from a gradient of $-\frac{5}{8}$ to $-\frac{2}{8}$. At some point it must become parallel to the labour constraint line, and at this point the same profit will be obtained at both points A and B. (In fact all points along the line AB would give the same profit – this is known as *multiple optimal solutions*.)

To find the profit on the Regular Fit shirt that would make the isoprofit line parallel to the labour constraint, you need to work out the gradient of this line.

Rearranging the equation $R + 2D = 160$ into the standard $y = mx + c$ form will give you:

$$2D = 160 - R$$

that is, $D = 80 - \dfrac{1}{2}R$

or $\quad D = -\dfrac{1}{2}R + 80$

The gradient is therefore $-\dfrac{1}{2}$.

You now need to find the value of the profit on a Regular Fit shirt that will give you this gradient. This can be done with the help of some elementary algebra (see page 6).

Let x be the unknown value of the profit. Then the gradient of the isoprofit line is $-\dfrac{x}{8}$ and

$$-\dfrac{x}{8} = -\dfrac{1}{2}$$

This gives $x = 4$, so if the profit of a Regular Fit shirt falls below £4 the optimum solution changes to point A on the graph ($R = 0$ and $D = 80$). This is the *lower* limit for the profit of the Regular Fit shirt. There is also an *upper* limit and you are advised to tackle the next activity.

$\left(\begin{array}{c}\textit{activity}\\ 14.11\end{array}\right)$ Using the same procedure as above, calculate the *upper* value of the Regular Fit profit.

The upper limit can be found when the isoprofit line becomes parallel to BC, and since the gradient of the cotton line is $-\frac{5}{8}$ the equation becomes:

$$-\dfrac{x}{8} = -\dfrac{5}{6}$$

This gives $x = 6.67$, so if the profit on a Regular Fit shirt rises above £6.67, the optimum solution changes to point C on the graph ($R = 120$ and $D = 0$).

$\left(\begin{array}{c}\textit{activity}\\ 14.12\end{array}\right)$ Calculate the range of the profit of the Deluxe Fit shirt within which the optimal solution stays the same.

This again requires you to find the lower and upper values of the profit. You should have found that this profit range is from £6 to £10.

Minimization problems

The Just Shirts example was a *maximization* problem because a solution was required that maximized the contribution to profits. However, equally important are *minimization* problems in which some objective, for example cost, is to be minimized. The general procedure for dealing with minimization problems is no different from maximization problems. A feasible region will still be obtained, but instead of moving your *isocost* line *away* from the origin, you will be moving it *towards* the origin. There must be, of course, at least one 'greater than or equal to' constraint, otherwise you will arrive at the origin!

example 14.2

Ratkins, a local DIY store, has decided to advertise on television and radio but is unsure about the number of adverts it should place. It wishes to minimize the total cost of the campaign and has limited the total number of 'slots' to no more than 5. However, it wants to have at least one slot on both media. The company has been told that one TV slot will be seen by 1 million viewers, while a slot on local radio will only be heard by 100 000 listeners. The company wishes to reach an audience of at least 2 million people. If the cost of advertising is £5000 for each radio slot and £20 000 for each TV slot, how should it advertise?

This problem can be solved by the graphical method of linear programming because there are two variables: the number of radio adverts and the number of TV adverts.

activity 14.13

Formulate the problem given in Example 14.2.

The formulation for this problem is as follows:

Let R = no. of radio ads, and T = no. of TV ads:

Min. $5000R + 20000T$

Subject to: $0.1R + T \geq 2$ (Minimum audience in millions)

$$R + T \leq 5 \quad \text{(Maximum number of 'slots')}$$

$$\left.\begin{array}{l} R \geq 1 \\ T \geq 1 \end{array}\right\} \text{(At least one slot on each)}$$

activity 14.14

Solve this problem using the graphical method. Is the solution sensible?

The procedure for drawing the graph is the same as that for the maximizing case. That is, it is necessary to find the points at which the constraints cut the axes. Table 14.3 gives these values.

The graph for this problem is shown in Figure 14.4. You should confirm that the feasible region is given by the area enclosed by ABC. The optimum point will be at one of these corners, and this time it is necessary for you to find the point that gives the *minimum* value. You should have found that the coordinates and hence the cost at each of the corner points are as given in Table 14.4.

Table 14.3 Crossing points for Activity 14.14

Constraint	R	T
Audience	20	2
Total slots	5	5
Min. slots for radio	1	–
Min. slots for TV	–	1

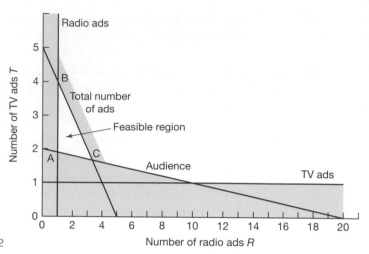

Figure 14.4 Graphical solution for Example 14.2

Table 14.4 Solution to Activity 14.14

	R	T	Cost
A	1	1.9	£43 000
B	1	4	£85 000
C	3.33	1.67	£50 050

Point A gives the minimum cost of £43 000. This solution implies that the company should buy 1 radio advert and 1.9 TV adverts, hardly a sensible solution. Unfortunately, linear programming will give fractional values, and if this is not sensible *integer linear programming* should be used as was discussed in the *quantitative methods in action* at the start of this chapter. This technique is not covered in this book, but for two variable problems a more realistic solution can often be found by inspecting the graph. In this particular case it is simply a matter of rounding the 1.9 to 2, which increases the cost to £45 000. However, do take care as rounding can often give you an *infeasible* solution. This can be avoided by checking to see that all constraints are still satisfied. In this example $R = 1$ and $T = 2$ does satisfy all 4 constraints.

Using Excel's 'Solver' to solve linear programming problems

Excel has an add-in called Solver that allows you to solve optimization problems. It may not be currently installed and if this is the case you will have to install it.

activity
14.15

Use Solver to solve Example 14.1 (the shirt problem).

The formulation for this problem was:

Max. $5R + 8D$

Subject to:

$5R + 6D \leq 600$ (cotton constraint)

$R + 2D \leq 160$ (labour constraint)

$R, D \geq 0$

where *R* was the number of Regular Fit shirts to make and *D* was the number of Deluxe Fit shirts to make.

Before using Solver you need to set up the relevant formulae and headings. The idea is to make the formulae general so that the worksheet can be used for other problems. Figure 14.5 shows one method of doing this.

Figure 14.5 Setting up the formulae for Solver

In this worksheet, cells `C10` and `D10` have been made the cells that will contain the optimal number of shirts. The total profit to be maximized is in cell `E10`. Cells `C6` to `D8` contain the coefficients of the constraints. Cells `E7` and `E8` represent the total resources used; to calculate these figures, you multiply the number made (currently zero) by the coefficients in the constraint equations. So $5R+6D$ becomes $C7 \times C10 + D7 \times D10$. (It is easier to use the $=$ `SUMPRODUCT` formula, as this allows you to use ranges: for several constraints this is much quicker.) Similarly, for the total profit you multiply the number made by the profit for each type of shirt. Again $=$ `SUMPRODUCT` simplifies this process.

The instructions for using Solver are as follows:

1 Click on the `Data` tab and then `Solver` in the `Analysis` group. (If it is not there, you will need to add it by clicking on `Add-Ins` in `Excel Options`.)
2 Set `Objective` to `E10`.
3 Click on `Max` in the dialog box.
4 `By Changing Variable Cells` becomes `C10:D10`.
5 For `Subject to the Constraints`, click on `Add`.
6 Add the constraints one at a time. (You can add them as ranges, as the inequality constraints are the same for both.)
7 Select `Simplex LP`. Tick `Make Unconstrained Variables Non-Negative`.

The Solver parameters should match those in Figure 14.6.

The solution to the problem can be seen in Figure 14.7. The values in cells `C10` and `D10` are 60 and 50 respectively, and the profit of 700 is shown in cell `E10`. These figures agree with those that we calculated manually.

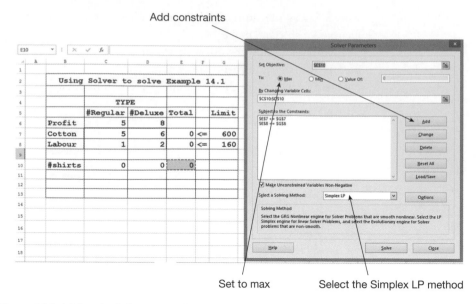

Figure 14.6 Adding the Solver constraints
Used with permission from Microsoft.

Figure 14.7 Solution found by Solver
Used with permission from Microsoft.

Solver can give you various sensitivity analysis reports, including changes to the objective function coefficients and changes to the right-hand side of the constraints. In the final dialog box, highlight the Sensitivity report.

From this report (Figure 14.8) you should be able to recognize the shadow prices and allowable changes in the objective function. For example, the profit of a Deluxe shirt can increase by £2 or decrease by £2, giving a range of £6 to £10 (the same range you found in Activity 14.12). You can also see that the right-hand side of the cotton constraint can increase by 200, which is what you found in Activity 14.8.

The advantage with using Solver is that you can easily make changes to the model and get updated results quickly. This is particularly true if you wanted to try adding other variables to the problem or new constraints. However it is often possible to use the sensitivity analysis report to decide if it is worthwhile adding a new product as the next Activity shows.

```
   A    B         C          D     E        F          G          H         I
1  Microsoft Excel 15.0 Sensitivity Report
2  Worksheet: [Activity 14.15.xlsx]Shirts
3  Report Created: 13/04/2015 12:32:44
4
5
6  Variable Cells
7                              Final Reduced  Objective   Allowable  Allowable
8     Cell         Name        Value  Cost   Coefficient  Increase   Decrease
9     $C$10 #shirts #Regular    60     0          5       1.666666667       1
10    $D$10 #shirts #Deluxe     50     0          8              2          2
11
12 Constraints
13                              Final Shadow  Constraint  Allowable  Allowable
14    Cell         Name         Value Price    R.H. Side  Increase   Decrease
15    $E$7   Cotton Total        600   0.5        600        200        120
16    $E$8   Labour Total        160   2.5        160         40         40
17
18
```

Figure 14.8 Sensitivity report from Solver
Used with permission from Microsoft.

activity **14.16**

In the Just Shirts problem (Example 14.1) consideration is being given to making a third shirt (European range). This new shirt will require 7 square meters of cotton and take 3 hours to make. If the expected contribution to profits of this new shirt would be £12 is it worthwhile making this new product? (Assume that you cannot increase either the supply of cotton or labour.)

As both cotton and labour are scarce resources then by making one European shirt you are losing profit from the other products as you will be making less of them. To solve this problem without re-running Solver you need to consider the opportunity cost involved in making one of the new shirts. The shadow price of the cotton resource is £0.50 per m² so as the new shirt requires 7m² the opportunity cost is 7 × 0.5 = £3.5. Similarly the shadow price for the labour resource is £2.50 an hour so the opportunity cost for making one European shirt is 3 × 2.5 = £7.5. The total opportunity cost is therefore £3.5 + 7.5 = £11.00. Table 14.5 summarizes these calculations.

Table 14.5 Opportunity cost of making one European shirt

Resource	Shadow price	Resource required	Opportunity cost
Cotton	£0.5 per m²	7 m²	£3.5
Labour	£2.5 per hour	3	£7.5
		Total	£11.00

As the expected contribution to profits of the new shirt is greater than £11 then it is financially worthwhile making this new shirt. However what this calculation doesn't tell you is how many of the new shirts should be made and what effect it has on the production of the other shirts. To discover this information it is necessary to amend the model and re-run Solver.

activity **14.17**

Amend your Excel model to allow for the third shirt and re-run Solver.

Letting E represent the number of European shirts to make, your new LP model should be

Max. $5R + 8D + 12E$

Subject to:

$5R + 6D + 7E \leq 600$

$R + 2D + 3E \leq 160$

$R, D, E \geq 0$

Figure 14.9 is a screen print of the results from Solver and Figure 14.10 shows the new sensitivity report.

	A	B	C	D	E	F	G	H	I
1									
2		Using Solver to solve Activity 14.17							
3									
4			TYPE						
5			#Regular	#Deluxe	#European	Total		Limit	
6		Profit	5	8	12				
7		Cotton	5	6	7	600	<=	600	
8		Labour	1	2	3	160	<=	160	
9									
10		#shirts	85	0	25	725			
11									
12									
13									
14									

Figure 14.9 Adding a new product
Used with permission from Microsoft.

	A	B	C	D	E	F	G	H	I
1		Microsoft Excel 12.0 Sensitivity Report							
2		Worksheet: [Activity 14.17.xls]Shirts							
3		Report Created: 19/11/2008 08:49:10							
4									
5									
6		Adjustable Cells							
7				Final	Reduced	Objective	Allowable	Allowable	
8		Cell	Name	Value	Cost	Coefficient	Increase	Decrease	
9		$C$10 #shirts	#Regular	85	0	5	3.571428571	1	
10		$D$10 #shirts	#Deluxe	0	-0.5	8	0.5	1E+30	
11		$E$10 #shirts	#European	25	0	12	3	1	
12									
13		Constraints							
14				Final	Shadow	Constraint	Allowable	Allowable	
15		Cell	Name	Value	Price	R.H. Side	Increase	Decrease	
16		$F$7	Cotton Total	600	0.375	600	200	226.6666667	
17		$F$8	Labour Total	160	3.125	160	97.14285713	40	
18									

Figure 14.10 The sensitivity report after adding a new product
Used with permission from Microsoft.

As you can see Solver has included the new product but at the expense of the existing Deluxe product. This is because relative to the amount of resources used the Deluxe shirt is contributing less profit than the other two products. You will also see that the profit on the European shirt can be reduced by £1 before it is not worth making - this reflects the difference between the opportunity cost calculated in Activity 14.16 and the profit of the shirt. You will also notice that the overall profit has increased from £700 to £725 even though the total number of shirts is unchanged at 110.

If you wanted to keep all three products then you would need to include a suitable constraint that specified this. This is left as an exercise for the reader.

DID YOU KNOW?

Linear programming has been used in almost all aspects of daily life from diet planning (e.g. finding the cheapest combination of foods that will satisfy nutritional requirement) to transportation of goods and to the economic impact of tourism development. It is possible to solve problems that require only integer solutions, as in the quantitative methods in action case at the start of this chapter. This method requires special algorithms which don't necessarily give optimal solutions. It is, however, a very useful technique and has been used in a wide range of problems where integer solutions are essential, such as crew rosters for airlines.

Applications of linear programming

Wherever it is required to maximize or minimize some function it is often possible to use linear programming to solve the problem. Linear programming has been used in such diverse areas as blending of oil products, inventory problems, cash flow, networks, transportation and allocation problems, cutting problems and multi-objective problems. We will look at two problems; these being transportation problems and problems involving more than one objective.

Transportation problems

example
14.3

The distribution manager of the BAZ oil company receives daily orders from his depots for bulk delivery of heating oil. On one particular day 4 depots request delivery of 24 500 litres in total and the 3 refineries have 40 500 litres available. Therefore there is no difficulty in meeting the order but the problem is deciding which refinery should supply which depot. The refineries are in different parts of the country and the cost of delivery from a refinery to a depot varies considerably. The cost in £ per litre from a refinery to a depot is given in Table 14.6 together with the availability (in 00s of litres) at each refinery and the requirement (again in 00s litres) at each depot.

Table 14.6 Transportation data for BAZ oil company

Depot \ Refinery	A	B	C	Required
P	5	13	7	60
Q	6	4	8	35
R	5	22	20	50
S	3	9	4	100
Available	175	80	150	

Cost per litre for delivery from refinery A to depot S

activity
14.18

What is the objective of this problem?

Clearly we want to transport the oil as cheaply as possible so the objective is to minimize the total cost. The cost function is simply the sum of the costs of transporting the oil from each refinery to each depot. If we use x_{ij} to represent the number of litres that need to be transported from refinery i to depot j then the objective will be as follows:

$$\text{Minimize cost} = 5x_{AP} + 13x_{BP} + 7x_{CP} + 6x_{AQ} + 4x_{BQ} + 8x_{CQ} + 5x_{AR} + 22x_{BR}$$
$$+ 20x_{CR} + 3x_{AS} + 9x_{BS} + 4x_{CS}$$

activity 14.19

What would be the constraints of the problem?

There will be 3 supply constraints. So for refinery A the sum of the amount delivered to each depot must be equal to or less than 175; that is:

$$x_{AP} + x_{AQ} + x_{AR} + x_{AS} \leq 175$$

and similarly for the other two refineries:

$$x_{BP} + x_{BQ} + x_{BR} + x_{BS} \leq 80$$
$$x_{CP} + x_{CQ} + x_{CR} + x_{CS} \leq 150$$

There will also be 4 demand constraints. So for depot A the amount delivered from each refinery is equal to or less than 60; that is

$$x_{AP} + x_{BP} + x_{CP} \leq 60$$

and similarly for the other 3 depots:

$$x_{AQ} + x_{BQ} + x_{CQ} \leq 35$$
$$x_{AR} + x_{BR} + x_{CR} \leq 50$$
$$x_{AS} + x_{BS} + x_{CS} \leq 100$$

So this small problem has $4 \times 3 = 12$ variables and $4 + 3 = 7$ constraints and could be solved using Solver. (This is left as an exercise for the reader – see Question 11 in the Practice questions section at the end of this chapter.) In real-life problems we could have hundreds of origins and destinations giving tens of thousands of variables and hundreds of constraints and special software would be required.

However because of the symmetry of the problem mathematicians have come up with an alternative method that for small problems can be solved without a computer. This is called the *Transportation algorithm*. The steps involved in using this algorithm are:

1 Find an initial feasible solution.
2 Test to see if the solution is optimal.
3 If not optimal, improve the solution and repeat step 2.

Step 1 Find an initial feasible solution

A feasible solution is one where all the requirements at the destinations are met and all supply at the origins is allocated. This means that:

Total supply = total requirements

In the BAZ case supply exceeds requirements by 160 units ($405 - 245$). However we can make this equation true by having a dummy destination or origin. In the case of

BAZ a dummy depot is required that will 'soak' up the excess capacity. The transportation cost for this dummy depot will be zero.

There are various methods of finding an initial feasible solution but the *least cost method* is probably a good compromise between a simple method that isn't very efficient (that is, takes longer to find the optimal solution) and a more complicated method that is more difficult to implement. The least cost method involves allocating as much as possible to the cheapest route (excluding the dummy route). In the BAZ case the cheapest *route* is A–S at £3 per litre. The requirement at S is 100 units and this can be met since 175 units are available at A.

activity **14.20**

Continue this process allocating as much as possible to the next cheapest route and so on.

The next cheapest route is B–Q is £4 (don't forget we have allocated the entire requirement for S so nothing can be added to route CS) and 35 units can be added to this route as 35 units are required and 80 units are available. For the next allocation you should have noted that there are two routes (AP and AR) which both cost £5. We can use either route but A–R is preferred as it avoids later having to use routes B–R and C–R which are the most expensive routes. We can now add 35 units to route C–P which completes the allocation for depot P. Finally we need to allocate 45 units and 115 units to the two dummy routes. Table 14.7 gives this feasible solution.

Table 14.7 An initial feasible solution

25 units delivered from A to P

The refinery costs used in step 2

Refinery / Depot	v_1 A		v_2 B		v_3 C		Required
u_1 P	(25)	5		13	(35)	7	60
u_2 Q	—	6	(35)	4	—	608	35
u_3 R	(50)	5	22			20	50
u_4 S	(100)	3	9			4	100
u_5 Dummy	—	0	(45)	0	(115)	0	
Available	175		80		150		60

The depot costs used in step 2

Lines help to show that no more can be added to a route

Quantity that won't be delivered

activity **14.21**

What is the cost of this initial solution?

You should have calculated the cost as follows:

$$(25 \times 5) + (35 \times 7) + (35 \times 4) + (50 \times 5) + (100 \times 3)$$
$$= £1060$$

Is this the best that can achieved; that is, is the solution optimal?

Step 2 Test to see if the solution is optimal

In order to decide if this is the optimal solution we need to calculate the *shadow prices*. If a shadow price is negative it means that for every unit that can be placed in the relevant route, this amount of money will be saved.

The way that shadow prices are calculated is as follows. Each route that is currently being used has a cost. This cost can be thought of as being made up of a cost at the depot (u) and a cost at the refinery (v). Each u and v is given a subscript (see Table 14.7) so for refinery A and depot P we have:

$$u_1 + v_1 = 5$$

activity 14.22

Write down the equations for the other 6 routes

You should have got the following equations:

$$u_1 + v_3 = 7$$
$$u_2 + v_2 = 4$$
$$u_3 + v_1 = 5$$
$$u_4 + v_1 = 3$$
$$u_5 + v_2 = 0$$
$$u_5 + v_3 = 0$$

In order to solve for 8 variables using only 7 equations it is necessary to allocate an arbitrary value of zero to one of the variables. If $u_1 = 0$ then it is possible to solve for the other variables.

activity 14.23

Solve for the other variables.

If $u_1 = 0$, then $v_1 = 5$ and $v_3 = 7$. We can now solve for other variables and $u_3 = 0$, $u_4 = -2$, $u_5 = -7$, $v_2 = 7$ and $u_2 = -3$.

We can now find the shadow prices of the unused routes by applying the following formula:

Actual cost − (cost at origin + cost at destination)

So for route B–P the shadow price is $13 - (0 + 7) = 6$.

activity 14.24

Find the shadow prices of the unused routes

The shadow price of route A–Q is

$$6 - (-3 + 5) = 4$$

The shadow prices of the other unused routes are:

$$B-P = 13 - (7 - 0) = 6; \quad B-R = 22 - (0 + 7) = 15;$$
$$B-S = 9 - (-2 + 7) = 4; \quad C-Q = 8 - (-3 + 7) = 4;$$
$$C-R = 20 - (0 + 7) = 13; \quad C-S = 4 - (-2 + 7) = -1$$

As we have one negative shadow price (route C–S) the solution is not optimal – we can reduce the cost by using this route.

Step 3 If not optimal, improve the solution and repeat Step 2

As much as possible should be sent via route C–S but care must be taken to ensure that the solution remains feasible. One method of achieving this is the *stepping stone* method.

The idea behind this method is that the rows and columns must remain balanced if the solution is to remain feasible. A '+' is added to route C–S to indicate that a quantity of oil should be added to this route. It is now necessary to add a '–' to a route in the same row or column that is currently being used. C–P is the only used route in the same column and a '–' has been added to this route (see Table 14.8). Another '+' is now added to route A–P to balance this row and a '–' has been added to route A–S for the same reason. A dotted line has been drawn round the diagram to show that the loop is closed. (The loop doesn't have to be rectangular – it just needs to arrive back at the starting point.)

Table 14.8 The stepping stone method

We now need to decide how much to add to route C–S. To avoid making any quantities negative you can only add the minimum quantity of the routes with '–' sign. The two routes with a '–' sign are C–P and A–S, and the smallest quantity is route C–P at 35 units. This quantity is now added or subtracted from each of the 4 'stepping stones' identified. This gives you your new table and you now have to repeat step 2 by recalculating the u s and v s.

activity
14.25

Repeat the process until the solution is optimal.

Table 14.9 shows the new table with the new u s and v s added and the shadow prices recalculated. As you will see all the shadow prices are non-negative so the solution is optimal.

Table 14.9 The optimal solution

Refinery / Depot	v_1 (5) A		v_2 (6) B		v_3 (6) C		Required
u_1 (0) P	(60)	[5] 7		[13] 1		[7]	60
u_2 (−2) Q	3	[6]	(35)	[4] 4		[8]	35
u_3 (0) R	(50)	[5] 16		[22] 14		[20]	50
u_4 (−2) S	(65)	3 5		[9]	(35)	[4]	100
u_5 (−6) Dummy	1	[0]	(45)	[0]	(115)	[0]	
Available	175		80		150		

The final solution is therefore:

Refinery A should deliver 6000 litres to depot P, 5000 litres to depot R and 6500 litres to depot S

Refinery B should deliver 3500 litres to depot Q only

Refinery C should deliver 3500 litres to depot S only

The total cost is £102 500, a saving of £3500 from the initial solution.

In some cases there will be alternative optimal solutions to a transportation problem. This occurs when one or more of the shadow prices is zero. By using the stepping stone method again it is possible to find this alternative solution(s) but the cost will of course be the same.

It is also possible to prevent certain routes from being used. This is easily achieved by giving this route a very high cost.

For the problem we looked at there were 3 origins and 5 destinations (including the dummy). If you look at any of the iterations you will see that there are 7 used routes which is $3 + 5 - 1$. It is generally true that the number of used routes is the number of origins + number of destinations −1. However in some cases the number of routes is less than this which will prevent you for calculating the u s and v s. This is called a *degenerate* solution. To get round this problem it is normal to pretend that a route is actually being used and add a zero quantity to it.

Finally remember, as in all linear programming problems, the use of the transportation algorithm is an approximation. In the case of BAZ oil we are assuming that the cost of transporting say 1000 litres of oil is equal to ten times the cost of transporting 100 litres. This of course is unlikely to be true.

The next application we will look at concerns the use of linear programming in problems where there is more than one objective or goal.

Multi-objective problems or goal programming

In the problems we have looked at so far there has been just one objective (e.g. maximize profit or minimize cost). However there are situations where there are conflicting objectives and we wish to get as close to each objective or *goal* as possible. This is called *goal programming* and is an important application of linear programming.

example
14.4

In Example 14.1 our objective was to maximize profits for Just Shirts. Instead we now have a number of goals which are (in order of priority):

Goal 1 (P_1) – to achieve a profit of at least £600
Goal 2 (P_2) – to use less than 150 hours of labour in total
Goal 3 (P_3) – to make at least 160 Regular shirts

In goal programming there are a number of goals which are desired although not all will be met. Each goal has a certain priority and the idea is to try and meet higher priority goals before attempting to meet lower priority ones. If we cannot meet a goal we try and get as close as possible to it. Goal programming models are all maximization problems.

The formulation of a goal programming model is slightly different to a normal LP one. In goal programming we define deviations from a goal as either + or −, so for Goal 1 we have

$$5R + 8D + d_1^- - d_1^+ = 600$$

where d_1^- = profit below £600 and d_1^+ = profit above £600. These deviations are called *deviational* variables. As we don't mind if the profit is above £600 we want to minimize d_1^- (the under-achievement of the £600 profit) and the objective we want to minimize is written as:

Minimize d_1^-

If we ignore the deviational variables and plot $5R + 8D = 600$ we get the graph shown in Figure 14.11. Any point above the line satisfies Goal 1.

activity
14.26

Now formulate the other two goals and plot the equations on the graph. Which goals can be met?

For Goal 2 we have:

$$R + 2D + d_2^- - d_2^+ = 150$$

Any combination of R and D on this side of the line meets Goal 1

Figure 14.11 Goal 1

where the deviational variables d_2^- and d_2^+ now refer to the over- and under-achievement of Goal 2. In this case we do not want to exceed 150 hours so we want to minimize d_2^+. Just taking the first two goals the objective function becomes:

Minimize $P_1 d_1^- + P_2 d_2^+$

P_1 and P_2 are labels showing the priority levels for the goals.

The line $R + 2D = 150$ has now been plotted and shown in Figure 14.12. As you can see we can meet the first two goals in the feasible area given by ABC.

Figure 14.12 Goals 1 and 2

The third goal is defined as:

$$R + d_3^- - d_3^+ = 160$$

We also want to minimize d_3^- as this represents the under-achievement of Goal 3. The total deviation we want to minimize is therefore:

Minimize $P_1 d_1^- + P_2 d_2^+ + P_3 d_3^-$

Again P_1, P_2 and P_3 remind us of the priority levels for each goal.

This is plotted in Figure 14.13 where you will see that Goal 3 cannot be met.

activity
14.27

What is your recommended solution and how far does this solution over- or under-achieve each goal?

Anywhere in the area ABC will meet the first two goals. The nearest point to Goal 3 is C which is $R = 150$ shirts and $D = 0$ shirts Substituting these values into each goal constraint we get:

Goal 1

$5 \times 150 + 8 \times 0 = £750$; so $d_1^- = £0$ and $d_1^+ = £150$

Goal 2

$150 + 2 \times 0 = 150$; so $d_2^+ = 0$ hours and $d_2^- = 0$ hours

Figure 14.13 Goals 1, 2 and 3

Goal 3

$$d_3^- = 160 - 150 = 10 \text{ shirts and } d_3^+ = 0 \text{ shirts}$$

So we under-achieve Goal 3 by 10 shirts

Use of Solver in goal programming

To use Solver we must include the deviational variables and solve in a sequential fashion, starting with the highest priority goal. The relevant deviational variable is minimized in each iteration and we continue until all goals are achieved or until a better solution cannot be found.

Figure 14.14 shows the Excel model for Example 14.4. Note that the left hand side (LHS) now contains both the original and deviational variables relevant to that constraint. Figure 14.15 shows the Solver parameters. In the first iteration we want to minimize d_1^-. As expected this gives us a value of d_1^- of zero (Figure 14.16). In the next iteration we want to minimize d_2^+ but we also want to keep $d_1^- = 0$ so we include this into the constraint

N4		fx							
	A	B	C	D	E	F	G	H	I	J
1										
2			Using Solver for Goal Programming							
3										
4			TYPE							
5			#Regular	#Deluxe	d–	d+	Total		Limit	
6										
7		Goal 1	5	8	0	0	0	=	600	
8		Goal 2	1	2	0	0	0	=	150	
9		Goal 3	1	0	0	0	0	=	160	
10		#shirts	0	0						
11										
12										
13										
14										

Figure 14.14 The Excel model for Example 14.4
Used with permission from Microsoft.

(Figure 14.17). Again we get the expected result of $d_2^+ = 0$ so in the final iteration we include this as a further constraint while minimizing d_3^- (Figure 14.18). The final result is shown in Figure 14.19 which you will see agrees with that produced manually.

Minimize d_1^-

Include all deviational variables

Figure 14.15 Setting up Solver for first iteration
Used with permission from Microsoft.

Figure 14.16 Solver results after first iteration
Used with permission from Microsoft.

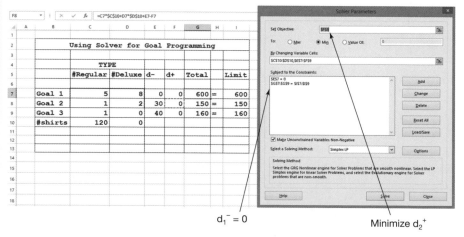

$d_1^- = 0$

Minimize d_2^+

Figure 14.17 Setting up second iteration of Solver
Used with permission from Microsoft.

$$d_2^+ = 0$$

Figure 14.18 Final iteration of Solver
Used with permission from Microsoft.

		#Regular	#Deluxe	d–	d+	Total		Limit
			TYPE					
Goal 1		5	8	0	150	600	=	600
Goal 2		1	2	0	0	150	=	150
Goal 3		1	0	10	0	160	=	160
#shirts		150	0					

$d_3^- > 0$ so Goal 3 cannot be met.
Best solution is to produce 150 Regular shirts

Figure 14.19 Final result of the Solver analysis
Used with permission from Microsoft.

Reflection

Solving an LP problem involves three phases. These are:

1 Formulate the problem so that it can be solved (matrix generator).

2 Solve it (optimizer).

3 Interpret the output (report-writing).

When using Solver, the first phase required the use of Excel to create the 'template' or matrix from which Solver could be used. Solver was then used to find the optimum solution. It also created reports, which it placed in a separate worksheet.

Although Solver can be used for problems with several variables and constraints, it is not very good for real-life problems where there are hundreds, if not thousands, of variables and constraints. In these cases specialist software is normally used, as Solver would be far too slow to set up and solve the problem.

Matrix-generation and report-writing software can be spreadsheet-based, or an algebraic MP language such as AMPL, MPL for Windows and XPRESS can be used. One of the most popular is MPL for Windows, as this allows you to input data in the same way for an LP formulation. For really large problems, however, AMPL or XPRESS are more powerful.

There are several optimizers on the market, including CPLEX, OSL, XPRESS and Lindo. All optimizers accept input from all matrix generators.

Many problems such as train scheduling are too complex for standard LP methods to be used. In these instances special algorithms or *heuristics* have to be used which, although they will not guarantee optimal solutions, do usually produce good solutions. However, since many millions of alternatives often have to be evaluated the algorithms need to be very efficient and powerful computers need to be used to arrive at a solution in a realistic time period.

Key points

- Linear programming is a method that finds the best solution amongst many possible solutions. It is an optimizing technique.
- The method requires an objective function, which can be either maximize or minimize, and a set of linear constraints.
- For two variable problems a graphical method can be used, but for more than two variables it is necessary to use *Solver* or a special purpose optimizer.
- One of the most important parts of a linear programming approach is the information obtained from a *sensitivity analysis*. This analysis gives the marginal value of a resource and the sensitivity of the solution to changes in the objective coefficients.
- There are many applications of linear programming including production problems, blending problems, capital rationing, transportation problems and problems involving more than one objective.
- Although transportation problems can be solved by the LP algorithm the *transportation algorithm* can be used to solve this type of problem.
- Goal programming is used to solve LP problems with more than one objective.

Further reading

Linear programming is an operational research (OR) technique and any text with OR or management science in the title will almost certainly include this technique. There is quite a lot of maths involved in the LP algorithm but fortunately it is not necessary for the business student to know details of how the algorithm works. In fact most students think that formulating the problem already contains too much maths! However for the student who wants to find out more about this important technique then the book by Anderson et al. (2014) is a good choice. For students who would like to read more about how OR in general and linear programming in particular are used to help businesses, the magazine *Impact*, produced by the OR Society, is a helpful resource and is freely available at www.theorsociety.com/impact.

http://www.**palgrave.com**/oakshott-eqm6

Solutions to all questions are freely available

Practice questions

1 A particular linear programming problem is formulated as follows:

Min. $Z = 2500x + 3500y$

Subject to:

$5x + 6y \geq 250$

$4x + 3y \geq 150$

$x + 2y \geq 70$

$x, y \geq 0$

Draw these constraints on graph paper and determine the optimum solution.

2 A manufacturer produces two products, P and Q, which when sold earn contributions of £600 and £400 per unit respectively. The manufacture of each product requires time on a lathe and a polishing machine. Each unit of P require 2 hours on the lathe and 1 hour on the polishing machine, while Q requires 1 hou on each machine. Each day, 10 hours are available on the lathe and 7 hours on the polishing machine. Determine the number of units of P and Q that should be produced per day to maximize contribution.

3 A manufacturer produces a component for diesel engines and a similar component for petrol engines. In the course of production, both components must pass through a machine centre and a testing centre. Diesel engine components spend 4 hours in the machine centre and 2 hours in the testing centre. Petrol engine components spend 2 hours in each centre. There are 16 hours available per day in the machine centre and 12 hours in the testing centre. A contract with a customer stipulates that at least 3 diesel engine components must be produced per day.

Each diesel component that is produced earns a contribution of £60 and each petrol component earns £45. How many units of each component should be manufactured each day in order to maximize contribution?

4 Bright Lights Ltd manufactures light bulbs for general household use. One design is used in microwave ovens and two types are produced: a low wattage and a high wattage version. The company obtains the glass shells from a supplier who can only supply a maximum of 1500 shells a day. The fitting and testing of the bulbs takes place on special machines of which there are one of each (for fitting and for testing) and both machines are available for 10 hours a day. The time to fit and test is different for the two bulbs, as shown in Table 14.10. Also shown is the contribution to profits for each bulb. The company's objective is to maximize contribution and they want to know how many bulbs of each type they should produce each day.

Table 14.10 Data for Question 4

	Low wattage	High wattage
Fitting (seconds)	20	30
Testing (seconds)	10	30
Contribution (pence)	5	7

(a) Formulate the problem as a linear programming model.
(b) Use Excel Solver to obtain the daily number of each bulb to produce so as to maximize contribution to profits.
(c) How much of each resource (glass shells, fitting time and testing time) are unused at the optimal solution? Would it be worth increasing any of these resources, and, if so, why?

5 A company has been set up in Bristol to manufacture rowing dinghies. Currently it has plans to produce a basic and a deluxe version. The two dinghies are similar and both take 1.5 days to manufacture. However, the deluxe version is much stronger and the profit is higher, as can be seen in Table 14.11.

Table 14.11 Details for Question 5

	Basic	Deluxe
Resin	10 kg	16 kg
Glass Fibre Mat	30 m	50 m
Profit	£50	£80

Due to safety regulations, the company is only allowed to store a limited amount of the raw material, which is 200 kg of resin and 900 m of mat. The required raw material is delivered on a daily basis.

The basic dinghy is likely to be a good seller, but it is assumed that the deluxe dinghy will be limited to a maximum of 9 per day. All boats produced by the end of the day are delivered to a distribution depot as there are no storage facilities available at the plant.

(a) If the current labour force is 27, use the graphical method of linear programming to demonstrate that there are multiple solutions to the problem. Hence suggest a sensible mix of dinghies to produce on a daily basis and show that this results in a profit of £1000 per day.

(b) **(i)** What is the shadow price of the resin resource?

(ii) As a result of improved storage facilities more resin can be held at the plant. What is the maximum amount of resin that would be worth storing, and how would this affect the profit calculated in (a)?

6 Revor plc has one production line for the manufacture of the ELEN PLUS and ELEN SUPER ignition systems. Both models use similar components in their manufacture but the SUPER model usually requires more of them and takes longer to produce. Relevant details are shown in Table 14.12.

There are supply problems for components A and B and daily usage is limited to 400 and 250 respectively. For component C, the company has entered into a contract with its supplier to take at least 150 per day.

It is also found that at least twice as many ELEN PLUS models are sold as ELEN SUPER, so production should reflect this fact.

The contribution to profits for the PLUS and SUPER models are £60 and £85 respectively.

You can assume that there are 60 employees engaged in the production of these ignition systems and that each employee works an 8-hour day.

(a) Formulate this as a linear programming problem, assuming that it is required to maximize profits.

(b) Use the graphical technique of linear programming to determine the optimal numbers of ELEN PLUS and ELEN SUPER models to produce each day. What is the daily profit associated with this production?

(c) Identify the scarce resources (tight constraints) for this problem. For each determine the shadow price. It is possible to purchase additional quantities of component A from an alternative supplier at a premium of £10 per component. Would it be worthwhile?

(d) The unit costs associated with the production of these systems is known to vary. However, the selling price is only changed annually. How much can the profit on the ELEN PLUS model be allowed to vary before the optimal solution found in (b) changes?

Table 14.12 Details for Question 6

	ELEN PLUS	ELEN SUPER
No. of component A	4	8
No. of component B	2	3
No. of component C	0	10
Manufacturing time (hours)	5	7

7   A company is planning a radio and TV advertising campaign and it has decided that it must use at least 60 adverts, have no more than 50 radio adverts, have at least as many radio as TV adverts and not exceed a budget of £34 000.

A radio advert is not as effective as a TV advertisement and the industry assigns a rating to each of the media to indicate their relative effectiveness. For radio the rating is 200 whereas TV gives a rating of 600.

(a) Assuming it is required to maximize the ratings, use the graphical technique of linear programming to find the number of each type of advertisement.

(b) What constraints are binding? What would happen to the overall rating if the maximum number of radio advertisements was increased to 100?

(c) How much could the rating on TV advertisements be reduced before the solution changes?

8   A wealthy investor has £550 000 in a bank account that she wishes to invest and is considering four general types of investment, which are: Government bonds, Corporate bonds, FTSE 100 stocks, Aim stocks

The goal of the investor is to maximize the rate of return on the money invested, where the annual expected return for each investment type is 4%, 5%, 6% and 8%, respectively. Any money not invested in one of these investment type remains in the bank where it earns interest at 3%.

The investor has decided to invest at least £50 000 on corporate bonds and that no more than £300 000 will be put into investments with an element of risk (i.e. corporate bonds and stocks). In addition she decides that at least one half of the money invested in the above 4 ways will go into stocks. Also no more than 25% of the money invested will go into the very risky Aim stocks.

(a) Formulate this problem as a four-variable linear programming problem.

(b) This problem was solved using Solver and part of the output from Solver is shown in Figure 14.20.

Adjustable Cells

Name	Final Value	Reduced Cost	Objective Coefficient	Allowable Increase	Allowable Decrease
Government bonds	200000	0		1E+30	0.015
Corporate bonds	50000	0		0.040	1E+30
FTSE 100 Stocks	125000	0		0.020	0.080
Aim Stocks	125000	0		1E+30	0.020

Constraints

Name	Final Value	Shadow Price	Constraint R.H. Side	Allowable Increase	Allowable Decrease
Constraint 1	500000	0	550000	1E+30	50000
Constraint 2	50000	-0.040	50000	100000	25000
Constraint 3	300000	0.050	300000	25000	200000
Constraint 4	0	0.015	0	50000	200000
Constraint 5	0	-0.005	0	500000	500000

Figure 14.20 Solver output for Question 8(b)

(i)   Use the output to describe the optimum investment plan, the amount of money left in the bank account and the annual yield from this plan in percentage terms.

(ii) It may be possible to relax the constraints regarding the minimum amount to invest in Corporate Bonds *or* the maximum amount to be invested in the riskier investments. Investigate both possibilities and make recommendations on which constraint should be relaxed, by how much and the resulting increase in return.

(iii) Use the printout to investigate the effect on the variables in solution of reductions in the rate of return of the four investments. Only consider one change at a time. Explain why the allowable decrease in the rate of return for Corporate Bonds is infinite.

9   Aquila is a specialist car manufacturer and currently it has two models; the LXT and HXT. The contribution to profits for the LXT is £580 and for the HXT it is £440.

During manufacture each product has to pass through 3 workshops: the Body shop, the Assembly shop and the Painting shop. LXT requires 5 hours in the Body shop, 9 hours in the Assembly shop and 7 hours in the Painting shop. The HXT model requires 10 hours in the Body shop, 2 hours in the Assembly shop and 5 hours in the Painting shop. Each shop works 40 hours per week. There is also a requirement that at least 60% of the total weekly output must be for the model LXT.

(a) Formulate this problem as an LP model (assuming that the objective is to maximize profit).

(b) Use the graphical technique of linear programming to determine how much of each model to make and the profit as a result of this production schedule.

(c) Which constraints are binding and how much slack (or surplus) do the non-binding constraints have?

(d) Solver shows that the range of the profit for the LXT for this solution to remain optimal is from £220 to £1980. Using your graph explain what will happen outside this range.

(e) The firm is considering the introduction of a new model ZXT which requires 4 hours in the Body shop, 2 hours in the Assembly shop and 1 hour in the Painting shop. If the shadow prices of the Body shop, Assemble shop and Painting shop are £35, £45 and £0 respectively determine the minimum contribution to profit that would be needed to make the production of the ZXT worthwhile.

(f) A major customer complains about the quality of the upholstery for the cars they receive. After investigating the issue, management decide that the interior of all cars should be cleaned as a separate process rather than in the Paint shop. LXT would require 5 hours for cleaning and HXT would require 4 hours. Management estimate that 30 hours could be made available for this new process without affecting the availability of resources in the other three shops. Would the introduction of the cleaning process change the optimal production plan already produced?

10   A baker wants to bake two types of family pie, Shepherd's Ecstasy and Lentil Puff. Both pies require two secret ingredients (A and B), both of which are in short supply. Shepherd's Ecstasy requires 0.5 kg of ingredient A and 0.25 kg of ingredient B, while Lentil Puff requires 0.4 kg of ingredient A and 0.7 kg of ingredient B. The maximum daily amount of ingredients A and B available is 6 kg and 14 kg respectively. The baker plans to sell each Shepherd's Ecstasy pie for £3 and each Lentil Puff pie for £2.50. The variable costs work out at £1.50 for each pie (any fixed costs are negligible).

Only one baking is done each day and the oven that is used to bake the pies can only hold 30 pies. A local restaurant has a daily order of 5 Lentil Puff pies which must be met.

(a) Formulate the problem assuming that the objective is to maximize profits.

(b) Use a graphical technique to determine how many of each pie that the baker should bake each day and the profit they will make.

(c) If a reduction of £0.25 was made to the selling price of Shepherd's Ecstasy how would your solution change?

(d) This problem was solved using Solver and the sensitivity analysis report is shown in Table 14.13.

Table 14.13 Data for Question 10

Constraints						
Cell	Name	Final value	Shadow price	Constraint RH side	Allowable increase	Allowable decrease
$D$6	A	6	3	6	8.5	4
$D$7	B	5.5	0	14	1E+30	8.5
$D$8	Oven	13	0	30	1E+30	17
$D$9	Restaurant	5	−0.2	5	10	5

(i) The restaurant has asked the baker to increase its order from 5 to 7 pies each day. What would be your response?

(ii) The baker could get hold of another 3 kg of ingredient A at an extra cost of £1 per kg. Would this be worthwhile and if so what would be the increase in profits?

(iii) The baker is considering making a 3rd type of pie which she has called the Corn Delight. This pie will use 0.6 kg of secret ingredient A and 0.1 kg of secret ingredient B. The profit on this pie would be £1.65. Should she go ahead with this new pie?

11 Solve the transportation problem in Example 14.3 (page 365) using Solver and the model developed in Activities 14.18 and 14.19.

12 The computer distributor Riglen owns 3 warehouses. These are at Watford, Bristol, and Birmingham. Goods are delivered to retail outlets in London, Wales, the North West (NW), the North East (NE) and the South West (SW).

Goods from the warehouses are delivered in standard size boxes. The requirements for one particular day last week are shown in Table 14.14.

Table 14.14 Delivery requirements for Question 12

Retail outlets	Number of boxes
London	530
Wales	350
NW	450
NE	500
SW	400

It is not always possible to fully meet demand and any shortfall is made up on the next delivery. This was the case for the day being considered and the following number of boxes were allocated for delivery to the 5 regions by the 3 warehouses:

Watford (Wat): 500 boxes; Birmingham (Birm): 900 boxes; Bristol (Bri): 500 boxes.

The average cost per box is shown in Table 14.15.

Table 14.15 Average cost per box for Question 12

Warehouse	Destination				
	London	Wales	NW	NE	SW
Wat	1.80	5.00	5.00	7.10	2.90
Birm	4.50	4.10	3.40	10.00	4.70
Bri	3.30	2.20	4.70	7.90	2.10

(a) Use the transportation algorithm to allocate the goods from each warehouse to each retail outlet as cheaply as possible. What is the cost of your allocation?

(b) Is there an alternative solution to the one found in part (a). What is it?

(c) What would be the additional cost per box of using the Bristol to London route.

(d) If more efficient vehicles could be used on the Birmingham to North East route the cost per box would be reduced. By how much does this cost have to fall before it becomes economic to use this route?

13   Revor plc, a car component manufacturer, has factories at Aberdeen, Bristol and Colchester. It sells its goods to a national distributor which owns 4 warehouses, located in different parts of the UK. Due to the recession, the quantity required by the supplier has fallen but Revor has not reduced its production capacity. Excess capacity is stored on the factory premises.

Goods purchased by the supplier are transported to its warehouse by container. The cost (in £00s per container) from each factory to each warehouse is shown in Table 14.16. Also shown is the normal weekly production at each factory and the requirements at each warehouse.

Table 14.16 Data for Question 13

Warehouse	Aberdeen	Bristol	Colchester	No. of containers required
P	5	13	7	60
Q	*	4	8	35
R	5	22	25	50
S	3	9	4	100
No. of containers available	175	80	150	

*For operational reasons it is not possible to deliver to warehouse Q from Aberdeen

(a) the current transport plan is as follows:

Aberdeen to warehouse	P	25 containers
Aberdeen to	R	50 containers
Aberdeen to	S	100 containers
Bristol to	Q	35 containers
Colchester to	P	35 containers

Calculate the cost of this plan and show that it is not the cheapest plan that could be achieved.

(b) Use the transportation algorithm to find the optimum solution. What is the cost of this solution?

14   The Global energy company produces two products; convection heaters and thermal heaters. Both products require a two step production process involving wiring and assembly. If X1 = numbers of convection heaters produced and X2 = number thermal heaters produced the LP model is given by:

Profit $= 7X1 + 6X2$
Subject to
$2X1 + 3X2 \leq 12$ (wiring hours)
$6X1 + 5X2 \leq 30$ (assembly hours)
$X1, X2 \geq 0$

(a) What is the optimal solution?

(b) The company now sets up the following goals:

Goal 1 to produce a profit of £30

Goal 2 to fully utilize the available wiring hours

Goal 3 to avoid overtime in the assembly department

Goal 4 to meet a contract to produce at least 7 convection heaters.

15   Question 4 referred to the Bright Lights company that manufactures light bulbs. For this question you are asked to consider 3 goals. These are (in this order) to use all 1500 bulb shells a day, to restrict the testing machine to 8 hours a day and to achieve a profit of at least £100. Can these goals be met?

Assignment

The food department at Riglen plc has brought out a new breakfast cereal called Hi-Fibre, which uses a concentrated form of fibre developed by Riglen's research laboratory. This product has been test marketed in a few selected areas and the consumer reaction has been favourable. However, several of the people questioned said that they would prefer a higher fibre content, so Dave Smith, the Product Manager, has decided to meet this demand with an additional product called Hi-Fibre Plus. This product will have double the fibre content of Hi-Fibre and will require additional cooking time. The selling price of Hi-Fibre Plus will be greater than for Hi-Fibre and the contribution to profits also will be higher. For Hi-Fibre the contribution will be 12p per 500g packet, and for Hi-Fibre Plus it will be 15p per 500g packet.

During the period of test marketing, 500 packets of the product were produced each day. However, from a commercial point of view at least 2500 packets of each product must be produced daily and it is expected that demand will soon exceed this figure. Dave's problem is that he is unsure of the quantities of each product to produce. Even if he assumes that he can sell all that he makes, the resources at his disposal are limited. The storage area can take a maximum of 12 000 packets, so total daily production of the cereal cannot exceed this figure. He has one oven and one packaging plant that operates for 12 hours a day and the supply of concentrated fibre is, for the moment, restricted to 120 kg per day. There is no practical limit to the other ingredients.

Dave Smith has asked you to use LP to solve his production problem and he has given you some additional information:

	Hi-Fibre	Hi-Fibre Plus
Cooking/packaging	3 seconds	5 seconds
Fibre content	5 g	10 g

All figures are based on 500 g of cereal.

(a) Formulate this problem in LP terms with the objective of maximizing contribution to profits.

(b) Use the graphical technique of linear programming to solve this problem.

(c) How much of each resource (that is fibre, storage space and the working day) is left after the optimal quantities of cereal are produced? Which resources are 'scarce' (that is, all used up)?

(d) Is it worthwhile increasing any of the scarce resources, and if so by how much? The additional cost of increasing fibre production is £20 per kg; storage space would work out at 20p per packet; and extending the working day would incur costs of £30 per hour.

(e) Would the optimal solution change if the profit contribution of either product changed?

(f) The sales department believes that the demand for Hi-fibre Plus will be greater than that for Hi-Fibre. If this is correct, production of Hi-Fibre Plus needs to be higher than Hi-Fibre. What increase in profit contribution of Hi-Fibre Plus will be necessary if the total profit is to remain the same?

15

PLANNING LARGE PROJECTS: NETWORK ANALYSIS

OBJECTIVES

- To know how to construct an activity-on-node network to represent a project
- To be able to calculate the earliest and latest start and finish times for each activity
- To be able to calculate the float for each activity, and to identify the critical path
- To be able to draw a Gantt chart and a resource histogram to smooth the use of resources required by a project
- To know how to apply the technique of crashing
- To apply the PERT technique when activity times are uncertain

INTRODUCTION

Network analysis is a branch of mathematics (combinatorial problems) that tries to optimize the flows in a network. This network could be the flow of goods or people between cities (the 'travelling salesmen problem') or it could be the scheduling of activities in a construction project. In Chapter 14 we showed how the *transportation algorithm* could be used to solve particular types of linear programming problems. The objective of the transportation algorithm was to minimize the cost of transporting goods from a set of origins to a set of destinations. In this chapter we will concentrate on a rather different type of network problem where the objective is to minimize the time taken to complete a project which consists of a set of interrelated activities. Although it is possible to use linear programming to solve this type of problem we will use a method often called *critical path analysis*, which for small problems can be solved by hand. This method identifies the activities that must start on time and cannot be delayed. These *critical* activities form a path (or paths) through the network and the time taken to complete this path gives the minimum time for the project to be completed. There are two different approaches to obtaining the critical path and in this chapter we will use the *Activity-on-node* method. We will also look at ways of scheduling resources in a project using a *Gantt* chart and resource histogram and we will look at a method for reducing the time of a project using a technique called *crashing*. Finally we will consider how uncertainty in activity times can be handled.

QUANTITATIVE METHODS IN ACTION

London's Crossrail project

In 2005 a bill was put before Parliament to construct and operate the Crossrail Railway. The bill went before both the House of Commons and the House of Lords and spelt out the route to be taken, the land to be acquired and the cost of construction.

By 22 July 2008 the bill had completed all Parliamentary stages and became known as The Crossrail Act (2008). This gave permission for the railway to be built, operated and maintained. It is intended that the main construction works will be complete in 2017, and trains should start operating in late 2018.

This project is the largest construction project in Europe, with a cost of £14.8bn. The route will run from Reading and Heathrow in the west, through new tunnels under central London, to Shenfield and Abbey Wood in the east.

A project of this size requires careful planning with hundreds of experts involved in very detailed analysis of works to be done and expected timescales for each operation. The tunnelling operation itself is massive, requiring eight tunnel-boring machines; each machine is 150m long and weighs 1000 tonnes. The 4.5 million tonnes of excavated material from the tunnels will be used to create a new 1500-acre RSPB nature reserve at Wallasea Island in Essex. As well as the tunnelling, there is the building of 10 new underground stations and the laying of track and signalling. Consideration also had to be given to routes that construction vehicles would take to go to and from a construction site. In addition it has become the largest archaeological site in Britain, and hundreds of archaeologists are involved in a race against time to map and preserve important historical artefacts. One site found was the Bedlam burial ground at Liverpool Street in the City of London where archaeologists discovered around 3000 skeletons from the 17th century.

When the first trains start running in 2018, it is believed that the capacity of London's rail network will have been increased by 10%, and parts of London will have been transformed.

Source: www.crossrail.co.uk

The activity-on-node method

This technique allows the time of the project and the slack (or *float*) of individual activities to be determined. If an activity has zero float you would say that it is *critical* because any delay in that activity would delay the entire project.

Before *critical path analysis* (or *CPA*) is used it is necessary to make a list of all the activities, their durations and which activities must immediately precede them.

Once this list has been completed, you should represent the project by the means of a diagram. The diagram used in this book uses the *activity-on-node* method. The basic diagram for this method is shown in Figure 15.1. The nodes represent the activity, and the lines the dependencies between activities.

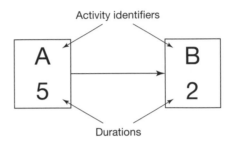

Figure 15.1 Activity-on-node

example 15.1

You have just obtained planning permission to build a garage and you are now in the process of planning the project. With a little help from a friendly builder you have made a list of activities that need to be completed, the durations of these activities and the order in which they can be tackled. This list is shown in Table 15.1.

Table 15.1 Details of the garage building project

Activity	Description	Immediate preceding activities	Duration (days)
A	Obtain bricklayer	–	10
B	Dig the foundations	–	8
C	Lay the base	B	1
D	Build the walls	A and C	8
E	Build the roof	D	3
F	Tile the roof	E	2
G	Make window frames	–	3
H	Fit the window frames	D and G	1
I	Fit glass to frames	H	1
J	Fit the door	E	1
K	Paint the door and window frames	I and J	2
L	Point the brickwork	D	2

Draw the network for the garage problem using the activity-on-node method.

The basic diagram for the garage problem is shown in Figure 15.2. You will see that the name of each activity is displayed in the box together with the duration. You will also see that there are start and end nodes. This is to ensure that every activity has at least one line entering and one line leaving its node.

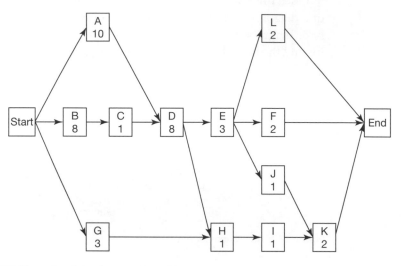

Figure 15.2 The network for the garage problem

For this method you need to display 4 additional pieces of information on each node: the earliest start time of the activity (EST), the latest start time (LST), the earliest finish time (EFT), and the latest finish time (LFT). This information should be displayed as in Figure 15.3.

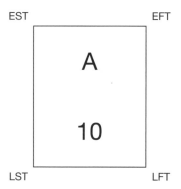

Figure 15.3 Information displayed on each node

In order to calculate the EST and EFT a *forward pass* is made through the network. If the start is at time zero, then the EST of activities A, B and G is zero and their EFT is 10, 8 and 3 respectively. The EST of activity C must be 8, since it can start as soon as B is completed. However, what about activity D? This activity cannot start until both A and C are completed, and as A is completed later than C, then activity A determines the EST of D, which must be 10. This is the general rule when calculating the EST – if there are two or more choices the EST is the *larger* of the EFTs of the preceding activities. From this you will see that the EST of K must be 22 and not 20.

activity **15.2**

Continue the forward pass through the network and add this information to your network. How long will it take you to complete the project?

You can now check your answers with Figure 15.4. From this diagram you will see that the project will take 24 days in total.

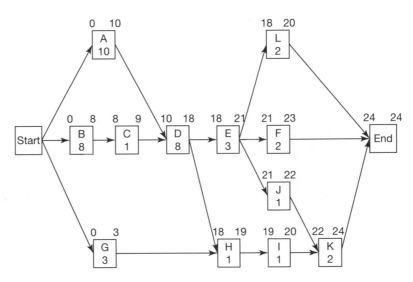

Figure 15.4 A forward pass through the network

To enable the LFT and LST to be calculated a *backward pass* is made through the network, starting at the END node. The LFT of activities F, K and L must be 24 since the project is only complete when all these activities have been completed. The LST of F, K and L must all be 22 days since the duration of all three activities is 2 days. To calculate the LFT of all other activities involves a process similar to that for the forward pass, with one difference, which is that when there is a choice, the *smallest* value is chosen.

activity **15.3**

Continue the backward pass through the network.

The completed network is shown in Figure 15.5 overleaf.

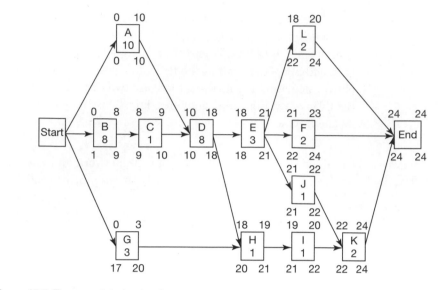

Figure 15.5 The completed network

The float of an activity

The float or slack of an activity is the difference between the EST and LST (or between the EFT and LFT) for each activity. For example, activity D has a zero float since the EST and LST are the same (10), while activity F has a float of 1 day (22 − 21).

(activity 15.4) Obtain the floats for the remainder of the activities. Which activities are 'critical'; that is, have no float?

You should have obtained the information shown in Table 15.2.

Table 15.2 Calculation of the floats

Activity	EST	LST	Float
A	0	0	0
B	0	1	1
C	8	9	1
D	10	10	0
E	18	18	0
F	21	22	1
G	0	17	17
H	18	20	2
I	19	21	2
J	21	21	0
K	22	22	0
L	18	22	4

From this you can see that activities A, D, E, J and K have zero floats and are therefore *critical*. Any delay in the start or finish times of these activities would delay the entire project by the same amount. The other activities could be delayed by up to their float without affecting the overall project time. For example, activity B (dig foundations) could be delayed by one day, but this activity would then become critical. You will notice that the critical activities form a path through the network – this is called the *critical path*. However, it is possible to have more than one critical path, as you will see in *Cost scheduling*, below.

DID YOU KNOW?

In its broader sense network analysis is being used in a wide range of fields. One such use is *social network analysis* where it is used to find links between people, groups, organizations, computers etc. It has been used in tracking the spread of diseases and in tracking people belonging to a terrorist organization. See www.orgnet.com

Resource scheduling

Activities of a project often involve resources of one kind or another. In the garage building example, labour is the obvious resource since each activity requires people to do the work. Perhaps you have asked a friend or neighbour to help and the two of you intend to help the bricklayer and do the less skilled jobs.

example **15.2**

For each activity in the garage building project you decide how many people are required to do these jobs, and you get the list shown in Table 15.3.

Table 15.3 Resource requirements for the garage project

Activity	No. of people required
A	0
B	2
C	2
D	1
E	1
F	2
G	1
H	1
I	1
J	2
K	1
L	1

Since some activities, such as digging the foundations and making the window frames, can take place at the same time, the number of people required at a particular time may be greater than the availability. However, it may be possible to delay non-critical activities, such as making the window frames, sufficiently to avoid this problem. The critical path network cannot easily solve this problem because this network is designed to show the *order* in which activities take place rather than *when* they take place. A better chart to use is the *Gantt* chart. A Gantt chart is like a bar chart that has been turned on its side. The horizontal axis is time and each activity is represented by a bar; the start of the bar is initially the EST and the end of the bar is the EFT. The float of an activity is represented by a dotted line.

activity 15.5

Draw the Gantt chart for the garage project.

This chart is shown in Figure 15.6.

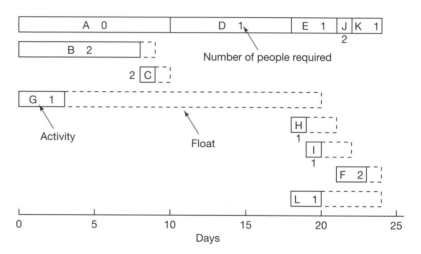

Figure 15.6 The Gantt chart

You will see that the bars representing the critical activities have all been placed on one line – this is because each activity follows one another on the critical path. The non-critical activities should, however, be placed on separate lines so that their floats can be clearly shown. The number of people required has been added to each bar. From this you can see that 3 people are required during the first 3 days $(0 + 2 + 1)$.

activity 15.6

Repeat this procedure for the entire project. When are more than 2 people required?

The figures are shown in Table 15.4. You can see that more than 2 people are required on several occasions. You might find this easier to see on the *resource histogram* in Figure 15.7.

Table 15.4 Daily resource requirement

Day	Number of people required
First 3 days	3
Next 6 days	2
Next day	0
Next 8 days	1
Next 2 days	3
Next day	1
Next day	4
Next day	3
Next day	1

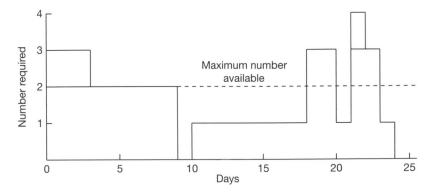

Figure 15.7 The resource histogram

From this histogram you will see clearly the peaks and troughs in the resource requirements. If a peak could be moved into a trough, the net result would be a smoother histogram. A perfectly smooth histogram would mean that the resource is being fully utilized and no further savings would be possible. In the case of the garage it would be possible to delay the start of activity G (make window frames) until day 9, since G has a float of 17 days. This would mean that from the start of the project until day 12, 2 people would be required all the time. The peaks at the end of the project are not so easy to solve. If the start of activity F (tile the roof) was delayed by its float of one day, the peak of 4 people during day 21 could be reduced by 1, so 3 people are required for much of the latter part of the project. The alternative to increasing the number of people is to extend the project. For example, if the critical activities J (fitting the door) and K (painting) were delayed until activity F had been completed, the completion of the project would be delayed by 2 days but only 2 people would be required for the entire time.

Cost scheduling

A very important resource in network analysis is money. This resource is usually so important that a separate technique has been devised to solve problems posed by financial considerations. This technique is called *crashing*.

It is usually desirable to reduce the time a project takes because there are often financial advantages in doing so. For example, the Department of Transport pays a bonus to contractors who complete a road building or repair project early (and a penalty is charged if the project time is overrun). It is often possible to speed up the completion of an activity at an extra cost. This cost may be incurred because a machine is hired or because more people are employed. The reduced duration is called the *crashed* duration, and the increased cost is called the *crashed* cost.

example
15.3

It is possible to reduce the time for completing activities B, D, E, F, G, K and L of the garage building project by employing additional labour. If this is done costs will increase for these activities. Table 15.5 gives you the durations and costs for all activities.

Table 15.5 Cost details for the garage project

Activity	Normal duration (days)	Crash duration (days)	Normal cost	Crash cost
A	10	10	£5	£5
B	8	2	£100	£700
C	1	1	£200	£200
D	8	5	£800	£1700
E	3	2	£500	£900
F	2	1	£200	£400
G	3	1	£150	£550
H	1	1	£50	£50
I	1	1	£20	£20
J	1	1	£20	£20
K	2	1	£30	£130
L	2	1	£100	£200

activity
15.7

What is the normal total cost of the project?

The total cost is simply the sum of *all* the activities, since all must be completed. This is £2175. If some of the activities are crashed this cost will increase. The question is which activities should be crashed in order to reduce the project time to a minimum but without incurring unnecessary costs.

activity
15.8

Would it be worth crashing all the activities identified above?

The answer to this question is no because not all the activities are on the critical path. Even if they were, some of the activities are more economic to crash than others. For instance, activity D costs £300 per day to crash (an extra cost of £900 and a time reduction of 3 days) while activity E costs £400 per day. The objective of crashing should be to find the minimum project duration at the minimum extra cost. In order to satisfy this objective it is first necessary to find the crash cost per day for each activity. This is necessary as the crashing can make non-critical activities become critical.

<table>
<tr><td>(*activity*
15.9)</td><td>Calculate the cost per day for activities B, D, E, F, G, K and L using the information given in Table 15.5.</td></tr>
</table>

This calculation is summarized in Table 15.6.

Table 15.6 Daily cost of crashing

Activity	Max. reduction by crashing (days)	Extra cost	Crash cost/ day
B	6	£600	£100
D	3	£900	£300
E	1	£400	£400
F	1	£200	£200
G	2	£400	£200
K	1	£100	£100
L	1	£100	£100

The next step is to write down all the paths through the network together with their durations. (Path GHIK can be ignored because it has a relatively short duration.)

<table>
<tr><td>(*activity*
15.10)</td><td>Make a list of all major paths through the network.</td></tr>
</table>

You should have found 8 major paths, which are shown in Table 15.7.

Table 15.7 Paths through the network

Path	Duration
ADEJK	24
BCDEJK	23
ADEF	23
ADHIK	22
BCDEF	22
BCDHIK	21
ADL	20
BCDL	19

<table>
<tr><td>(*activity*
15.11)</td><td>Which path should be reduced first and which activity should be crashed?</td></tr>
</table>

Path ADEJK should be reduced first as it the longest path through the network and therefore the critical path. Activities D, E and K can be crashed, but, of the 3, K is the cheapest. If K is crashed by 1 day then not only will the duration of path ADEJK be reduced by 1, but so will paths BCDEJK, ADHIK and BCDHIK. The project duration has now been reduced by 1 day at a cost of 100, but path ADEF is now critical, in addition to ADEJK.

activity
15.12

Continue to crash the network. What is the minimum project time and what activities should be crashed to keep the crashing cost to a minimum?

Both ADEF and ADEJK must now be crashed together as they are both critical. Both D and E are common to these 2 paths and, since D is the cheapest, this will be crashed by 3 days at a cost of £900. Finally, E is crashed by 1 day to reduce the project duration to 19 days at a cumulative extra cost of £1400. No further crashing is worthwhile because it is not possible to crash both critical paths (only F has any crashing capability left). You might find it easier to write the necessary steps in a table similar to the one shown in Table 15.8.

Table 15.8 Steps involved in crashing the network

Path	Duration	Step 1	Step 2	Step 3
ADEJK	24	23	20	19
BCDEJK	23	22	19	18
ADEF	23	23	20	19
ADHIK	22	21	18	18
BCDEF	22	22	19	18
BCDHIK	21	20	17	17
ADL	20	20	17	17
BCDL	19	19	16	16
Activities crashed		K − 1	D − 3	E − 1
Extra cost		£100	£900	£400
Cumulative extra cost		£100	£1000	£1400

activity
15.13

You are paying someone £150 per day to help you. How does this affect your recommended minimum project time?

It would be worthwhile crashing K because for an expenditure of £100 you would save £150; a net gain of £50. However, it wouldn't be worthwhile crashing D because for each day saved it has cost you £150 (£300 − £150). So minimum project time is 23 days.

activity
15.14

As well as the £150 daily overheads you have agreed to hire a cement mixer for 20 days at a fixed cost of £1000. If you keep this mixer for longer than 20 days you will pay an additional £100 per day but if you return it before the 20 days are up you will get a refund of £50 per day. How does this affect your crashing strategy?

Table 15.8 has been redrawn (Table 15.9) showing how the different costs are made up to give the total variable costs for a range of project times from 24 days to 19 days. These variable costs have then been plotted against project duration (Figure 15.8). From both table and chart you will see that the optimum project duration is 23 days as this gives the lowest cost of £3850.

Table 15.9 Total costs including penalty and bonus costs

Duration (days)	24	23	22	21	20	19
Crash cost (£)	0	100	300	300	300	400
Cumulative crash cost (£)		100	400	700	1000	1400
Overheads (£)	3600	3450	3300	3150	3000	2850
Penalty/bonus (+/−) (£)	400	300	200	100	0	−50
Total (£)	4000	3850	3900	3950	4000	4200

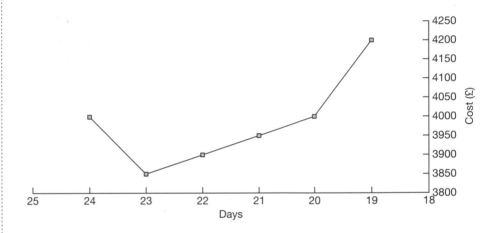

Figure 15.8 Chart showing cost function

Handling uncertainty in time estimates (the PERT method)

So far it has been assumed that all activity times are known with certainty. In practice most times will be an estimate and therefore the overall project time will be subject to error. Usually the best we can do is to have an optimistic time which would be fine if everything went according to plan, and a pessimistic time if the worst happened. You could of course analyze two networks; the first network using optimistic times and the second using the pessimistic times. You would then have a range of times within which the project would be expected to finish. An alternative is to use the PERT method (Programme Evaluation and Review Technique). This approach is useful where some or all of the activities have been carried out in the past and a good deal of information on their durations is available. In addition to being able to obtain an optimistic time (t_o) and a pessimistic time (t_p), a most likely time (t_m) is required. The most likely time is the time that occurs most frequently (the mode). The equations for calculating the mean activity time $(\bar{t})$ and the variance of the activity times (σ_t^2) are

$$\bar{t} = \frac{t_o + 4t_m + t_p}{6}$$

$$\sigma_t^2 = \left(\frac{t_p - t_o}{6}\right)^2$$

These calculations are repeated for each activity where uncertainty is present and the network analysis is then conducted in the normal way, but using the mean activity times.

Following the calculation of the project time and critical path the total variance in the project time can be found by adding the variances on the critical path. (If there are two or more critical paths the largest variance is used.) If it is now assumed that the project times are normally distributed the ideas of Chapter 7 can be applied. For example, we could calculate the probability that the project will exceed a certain time.

<table>
<tr><td>*activity*
15.15</td><td>In Table 15.10 the optimistic, pessimistic and most likely times have been added to the garage building project of Example 15.1 (see page 387). Calculate the expected times and variance for each activity.</td></tr>
</table>

The calculation of the expected time and variance for Activity A are:

$$\bar{t} = \frac{6 + 4 \times 9 + 14}{6}$$
$$= 9.33\,\text{days}$$

and

$$\sigma_t^2 = \left(\frac{14 - 6}{6}\right)^2$$
$$= 1.78$$

Table 15.10 Using PERT on the garage project

Activity	Optimistic time (days)	Pessimistic time (days)	Most likely time (days)
A	6	14	9
B	6	12	9
C	1	1	1
D	7	10	8
E	2	5	4
F	2	2	2
G	2	5	4
H	1	1	1
I	1	1	1
J	1	1	1
K	2	2	2
L	1	3	2

These calculations are repeated for each activity (a spreadsheet is recommended) and the following table should have been obtained.

Activity	Optimistic time	Pessimistic time	Most likely time	Expected time	Variance
A	6	14	9	9.33	1.78
B	6	12	9	9.00	1.00
C	1	1	1	1.00	0.00
D	7	10	8	8.17	0.25
E	2	5	4	3.83	0.25
F	2	2	2	2.00	0.00
G	2	5	4	3.83	0.25
H	1	1	1	1.00	0.00
I	1	1	1	1.00	0.00
J	1	1	1	1.00	0.00
K	2	2	2	2.00	0.00
L	1	3	2	2.00	0.11

Note that some variances are zero. This is because the three time estimates were identical, so there was no uncertainty with the times of these activities.

activity **15.16** Has the critical path changed? You will need to repeat Activities 15.2, 15.3 and 15.4 to check this. What is the expected time to complete the project now?

You should have found that the critical path is still A, D, E, J and K but the time has increased to 24.33 days.

activity **15.17** Find the probability that the project will take longer than 26 days.

To solve this activity it helps to draw a sketch of the normal distribution. This is done in Figure 15.9. As you see we need to calculate the area of the right hand tail.

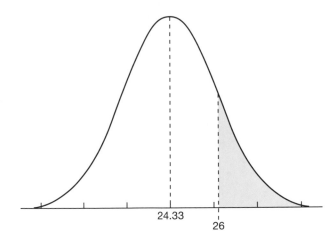

Figure 15.9 The normal distribution for Activity 15.17

To solve a normal distribution problem we need the standard deviation. To find the standard deviation we first add up the variance for each activity on the critical path:

$$1.78 + 0.25 + 0.25 + 0 + 0 = 2.28$$

and then square root this value to get 1.51 days.

Using the formula

$$Z = \frac{x - \text{mean}}{\text{standard deviation}} \quad (\text{see page 160})$$

we get

$$Z = \frac{26 - 24.33}{1.51}$$

$$= 1.11 \text{ standard deviations}$$

Looking this value up in the normal tables we find that the probability is 0.1335. So there is a 13.35% chance that the project will take longer than 26 days.

PERT makes assumptions about the form of the distribution of activity times and also the normality assumption of the project time. This normality assumption is quite important for working out the probability that a project will take more (or less) time than a specific time. For large projects with hundreds of activities this assumption is quite reasonable but for small projects like the garage one the assumption is probably doubtful.

DID YOU KNOW?

Did you get a ticket for the 2012 Olympics? There were 6.6 million tickets available and applications were received from 1.8 million people trying to buy 20 million tickets. A ballot was conducted to decide who was to get what tickets and how many. If you applied for tickets and were successful you had to buy them, so it was a gamble. Should you bid for more than you could afford or just go for the minimum you wanted? For some of the popular events less than half of the people who applied for tickets were successful. There was a lot of disquiet over the process and many people thought that a 'first come first served' basis would have been fairer. This method was tried in the 2008 Beijing Olympics but the system couldn't cope with the huge demand at the start of the process so the organizers reverted to a ballot. Some people have suggested other ideas, such as a true lottery in which you buy tickets for a pound and winners are then allowed to buy tickets for the Games. The method used by the 2012 organizers certainly achieved their goal of selling most of the tickets, and they have got an interest-free loan in the bargain because people had to buy tickets a year in advance!

Reflection

Critical path analysis is one of the most useful and easily understood techniques in the analyst's 'toolbox'. Software such as Microsoft Project™ is available and can help in applying this technique.

Even using the latest methods of project monitoring and control, many large projects have overrun in terms of time and cost. Berlin's Brandenburg airport was £3.2 billion over budget. The largest overrun to date is the tunnel under the English Channel, which was £21 billion over budget. In the UK the MOD major weapons project is £6.6 billion over budget, and the delivery time for 16 of its largest programmes are 39 years behind schedule (Mail Online)!

At the other extreme, the 2012 Olympic Park was completed ahead of schedule, although the final cost was a lot higher than the originally forecast £2.35bn.

Key points

- There are two main methods for planning and monitoring a project: the *activity-on-node* and the *activity-on-arrow* methods. In this chapter we have used the former procedure.
- *Critical path analysis* identifies the minimum time in which the project can be completed, together with the *critical activities* and the *float of the non-critical activities*.
- A *Gantt chart* is effective in showing when activities occur. By using such a chart it is often possible to reduce the *resources* required for a project.
- In some cases the total *duration* of a project can be reduced by reducing the duration of individual activities. The technique of *crashing* allows this reduction to be carried out at minimum additional cost.
- Activity times are rarely known with certainty and to allow for this a technique called PERT can be used. However, this technique makes assumptions which may not be valid for small projects.

Further reading

As mentioned at the start of this chapter there are two methods for constructing a network. The one used here and also by Anderson et al. (2014) is the activity-on-node method. Many texts such as Morris (2011) and Curwin and Slater (2013) use the activity-on-arrow method. Certainly the activity-on-arrow diagram looks neater but students usually find the activity-on-node method more logical. It is also the method used by Microsoft® Project and other project management software. For details of Microsoft® Project see www.microsoft.com/project/en/us/default.aspx.

http://www.**palgrave.com**/oakshott-eqm6

Solutions to all questions are freely available

Practice questions

1 Please refer to Figure 15.10 for this question.

Figure 15.10 Diagram for Question 1

(a) How long will the project take?
(b) How much float has activity D?
(c) How much float has activity F?
(d) If activity B takes 3 weeks longer than expected, will the project be delayed?
(e) If activity B requires 3 people continuously, D requires 2 people and C requires 1 person, how many people are required during week 6?

2 Yachtsteer manufactures a self-steering device for pleasure yachts and, as a result of increased competition from foreign manufacturers, it has decided to design and manufacture a new model in time for the next Boat Show. As a first step in planning the project, the major tasks and durations have been identified (Table 15.11). Draw a network to represent the logical sequence of tasks and determine how long it will be before the new product can be marketed.

Table 15.11 Details for Question 2

	Task	Time (weeks)	Preceding tasks
A	Design new product	8	–
B	Design electronics	4	–
C	Organize production facilities	4	A
D	Obtain production materials	2	A
E	Manufacture trial gear	3	C, D
F	Obtain electronic circuit boards	2	B
G	Decide on yacht for trials	1	–
H	Assemble trial gear and electronics	2	E, F
I	Test product in workshops	3	H, G
J	Test product at sea	4	I
K	Assess product's performance	3	J
L	Plan national marketing	4	K

3 Shipways boatyard undertakes spring refits on cabin cruisers and yachts, and in the past the company has received complaints from customers regarding the time taken to complete the job. As a consequence the Project Manager, Alan Waters, has decided to carry out a critical path analysis on the cabin cruiser refit. Table 15.12 gives, for each activity, the duration, immediate preceding activities and the number of yard assistants required.

Table 15.12 Details for Question 3

Activity	Description	Duration (days)	Immediate preceding activities	Yard assistants required
A	Bring craft up slipway	1	–	2
B	Check and overhaul seacocks, etc.	3	A	1
C	Scrape and prepare hull for painting	7	A	2
D	Paint hull	4	C	1
E	Remove engine	2	A	3
F	Overhaul engine	16	E	1
G	Clean and paint engine bilges	3	E	1
H	Refit engine	3	F and G	3
I	Apply antifoul paint to hull	2	D and H	2
J	Refloat	1	B and I	2

Note: The reason that I follows from both D and H is that a boat must be refloated no more than 48 hours after the antifouling paint has been applied. Antifouling should not therefore be started until the boat is ready for the water.

(a) Draw the network and determine how long the refit will take. What are the critical activities and how much float do the non-critical activities have?

(b) (i) Draw a Gantt chart and resource histogram for the refit. What is the maximum number of yard workers required and when is this required?

(ii) Unfortunately there are only 4 yard workers available during the period of the refit. Using your Gantt chart and/or histogram, reschedule the activities so that no more than 4 yard workers will be required.

4 Revor plc are urgently planning the production of their new lightweight car battery, the 'Epsilon'. They would like to exhibit their battery at a trade fair, which is to take place in 48 weeks' time. Various activities have to be completed before production can start, and these are shown in Table 15.13.

Table 15.13 Activities for Question 4

	Task	Preceding tasks	Duration (weeks)
A	Clear area	–	20
B	Commission consulting engineers to design equipment	–	2
C	Receive consultant's report	B	10
D	Place equipment out to tender	C	1
E	Obtain equipment	D	6
F	Install equipment	A, E	30
G	Recruit additional staff	C	6
H	Train new staff	G	4
I	Order and obtain materials	–	16
J	Pilot production run	F, H, I	3
K	Advertise new product	–	2

(a) Draw the network and show that it is not possible to start production within 48 weeks. What are the critical activities and how much total float do the non-critical activities have?

(b) It is possible to 'crash' (i.e., reduce the duration of) certain activities at increased cost. These activities are shown in Table 15.14.

Table 15.14 Crash and cost details for Question 4

Activity	Crashed duration (weeks)	Normal cost (£000s)	Crashed cost (£000s)
A	18	4	10
E	5	1	3
F	28	15	27
I	8	0.5	8.5
J	2	16	26

(i) Ron Smith, the Production Manager, suggests that only activity I need be crashed because this is the cheapest option and allows the greatest reduction in time to be made. Explain why this would not help the situation.

(ii) It has been estimated that for every week over 48 weeks that this project takes, a loss of £8000 is made as a result of lost profits. Decide on the strategy that will minimize the sum of crashed costs and loss of profits.

5 A painting and decorating firm has decided to use critical path analysis in order to plan its next job. The activities of this job are as shown in Table 15.15.

Table 15.15 Activities for Question 5

Activity	Description	Duration (days)	Preceding activities	Number of operatives
A	Order materials	3	None	0
B	Remove curtains and cover furniture	0.5	None	1
C	Wash interior woodwork	2	B	1
D	Sand exterior woodwork	1	None	2
E	Paint ceilings	2	A & C	2
F	Paint interior woodwork	4	E	3
G	Paint exterior woodwork	5	A & D	2
H	Hang wallpaper	2	F	4
I	Remove covers and replace curtains	0.5	H	1
J	Clean up and depart	0.5	G & I	4

(a) Draw a network representing the sequence of activities and the interdependencies between them.
(b) Determine how long it will take to complete the job and identify the critical activities.
(c) If it were to rain for 4 out of the 5 days allocated for painting the exterior woodwork, what effect would this have on the duration of the job? (Assume that it is dry for the remaining time.)
(d) It has now been decided to analyze the labour requirements for this job. Using graph paper, draw a Gantt chart for the job (assuming earliest start times apply). What is the maximum number of operatives required and when does this occur? Unfortunately, only 4 operatives are available. Explain how this will affect the time taken to complete the job.

6 A construction company is planning the building of a warehouse. The activities to complete the projects are shown in Table 15.16.

Table 15.16 Activities for Question 6

Activity	Duration (days)	Immediate predecessor
A	4	None
B	2	None
C	4	A, B
D	2	C
E	6	D
F	3	D
G	4	E
H	5	G, F

(a) Draw a suitable network diagram for this project.
(b) What is the project duration and what are the critical activities?

(c) On further discussion it is apparent that there is some uncertainty over the duration of Activity B. The project manager thinks that, although 2 days is the most likely time, it can be completed in as little as 1 day or if the weather is poor it can take as much as 7 days. Based on this information decide if the project duration and critical activities might be different from that found in part (b).

(d) For every day over 20 days the company will have to pay a penalty of £6500. There are also overheads of £1000 per day. What is the current total cost of the project?

(e) It is possible to reduce the time of (crash) some activities so as to reduce the project time. Table 15.17 gives the daily cost of crashing and the maximum time that the activities can be crashed. So for instance Activity A can be crashed by 1, 2 or 3 days at a daily crash cost of £5000. Which activities should be crashed so that the total cost of the project is minimized?

Table 15.17 Crash details for Question 6

Activity	Crash cost per day (£000s)	Maximum number of days that the activity can be crashed
A	5	3
B	3	1
C	15	1
E	7	1
H	20	2

Note: Activities not listed cannot be crashed.

7 A company has just won a contract to refurbish a hotel. The sequence of events from gaining the contract to completion is given in Table 15.18.

Table 15.18 Activity data for Question 7

Activity	Predecessor activities	Duration (weeks)
A	–	5
B	–	6
C	A	3
D	B	3
E	–	7
F	C, D, E	4

(a) Draw the network representing the sequence of activities and the inter-dependencies between them, identify the critical activities, the minimum time required to complete the project and the slack (float) of the non-critical activities.

(b) If activity A took 2 weeks longer than expected what increase in completion time would result and what activities are now critical?

(c) After some consultation with the hotel management it is decided to try and speed up the refurbishment by reducing (crashing) some activities. Table 15.19 gives the maximum crashing that can be achieved for each activity and the cost per week of this crashing.

Table 15.19 Crashing data for Question 7

Activity	Cost per week (£000s) of crashing	Maximum crashing available (weeks)
A	5	1
B	12	3
C	13	1
D	15	1
E	1	2
F	20	2

What activities would need to be crashed to reduce the project time to 11 weeks at minimum cost?

What is the maximum reduction at minimum cost that could be achieved?

8   TG UK services and repairs gaming machines and their agreement with Global Casino is that a fee and repair time for a particular job is agreed in advance. In addition, for every hour over the agreed repair time TG UK will pay Global £100, while for every hour below the time Global will pay them £100. For the latest contract a fee of £10 000 has been agreed with a repair time of 12 hours.

In the past TG UK have overrun repair times and have had to pay a penalty. For the latest contract TG UK have decided to apply some network planning to the activities and you have been given the task of recommending the appropriate course of action. After some investigation you have agreed the activities required in repairing this group of machines together with the expected durations and normal costs. This information is provided in Table 15.20. You also discover that it is possible to reduce some of these durations by 'crashing' activities. Table 15.20 also gives the maximum reduction possible and the hourly crash cost for each activity (note Activity A cannot be crashed).

There are also overhead costs to consider which total £100 per hour.

Table 15.20 Activity data for Question 8

Activity	Immediate predecessors	Normal duration (hours)	Normal cost	Crash cost per hour	Maximum reduction (hours)
A	–	3	£50	N/A	0
B	A	3	£200	£100	1
C	B	4	£500	£330	2
D	B	4	£100	£20	3
E	B	6	£300	£150	3
F	C, D, E	5	£500	£1000	1

(a) Using the normal durations draw a network representing the sequence of activities and the inter-dependencies between them.

(b) Identify the critical activities, the minimum time required to complete the project and the slack (float) of the non-critical activities.

(c) Taking into account the normal costs, overheads and penalty costs what would be the net profit if the project took the time found in part (b)?

(d) You now decide to see if crashing some of the activities reduces the company's costs and, therefore, make a larger profit. What strategy would you recommend in order to maximize the profit obtained from this contract? State clearly which activities should be crashed and by how much time. What would be the overall profit resulting from this strategy?

9 A market research agency has been engaged to carry out a customer survey following a promotional campaign for a company's range of products.

The conduct of the survey consists of the activities shown in Table 15.21.

Table 15.21 Activities for Question 9

Activity		Preceding activity	Duration (weeks)	No. of staff required
A	Draft the survey proposals	–	2	3
B	Obtain client's agreement	A	3	2
C	Recruit interviewers	A	2	2
D	Design and test questionnaire	B	1	1
E	Train interviewers	D, C	3	5
F	Order free gift samples	B	5	0
G	Select towns for use in survey	A	1	1
H	Set up a 'base' in each town	G	3	5
I	Carry out the survey	E, F, H	6	2
J	Analyze the results	I	5	2
K	Prepare report and make the presentation to the client	J	3	2

(a) Construct a network to illustrate the activities that have to be undertaken, and establish the earliest and latest start and finish times. Hence find the critical path and the total time taken to complete the survey.

(b) Draw a Gantt chart for this survey and determine how many staff are required during each day of the survey. (You can assume that the agency staff members are skilled in all tasks.)

(c) If other agency commitments restrict the number of persons that can be assigned to this survey to 7, can the project be completed without any delays?

10 A household products company has decided to launch a new 'greener' washing powder. After some discussion the marketing department has agreed on the ten activities that need to be done before the national campaign is launched. However there was some argument about how long three of the activities will take so three estimates were used for these activities: the optimistic time, the pessimistic time and the most likely time. Details of the activities and these time estimates are shown in Table 15.22.

It is imperative that the national campaign be launched within 32 days.

Table 15.22 Activities for Question 10

Activity	Description	Immediate predecessors	Optimistic time	Pessimistic time	Most likely time
A	Arrange meetings	None	2	2	2
B	Design publicity material	A	3	3	3
C	Design TV advertising	A	2	7	3
D	Design newspaper advertising	A	2	6	3

(continued)

Table 15.22 (continued)

Activity	Description	Immediate predecessors	Optimistic time	Pessimistic time	Most likely time
E	Specifications sent to ad agency	C and D	1	1	1
F	Preparation of TV and radio ads	E	10	10	10
G	Distribution of washing powder within trial area	None	3	3	3
H	Run campaign in trial area	B, F and G	6	6	6
I	Assess results	H	2	2	2
J	Arrange national campaign	I	3	6	5

(a) Use the PERT method to calculate the mean activity time for activities C, D and J.

(b) Draw a network diagram and for each activity determine the earliest start time, the earliest finish time, the latest finish time and the latest start time. Add this information to a table and find the float (slack) for each activity. Hence determine the critical path and the expected time before the national campaign can be launched.

(c) Assuming that the distribution of project times is normally distributed, find the probability that the campaign can be launched within 32 days.

Assignment

There have been recurring problems with the food canning process at Riglen plc and a decision has been taken at Board level to replace the machinery with more modern computer-controlled equipment. Holder and Holder Consulting Engineers have been commissioned to advise on the system to purchase and their report is expected in 5 weeks' time. Although the fine details of the recommended system will not be known until this report has been received, the essential characteristics of all the alternatives are the same. Planning for the installation can therefore start immediately, and this is important because during the installation all food canning has to be contracted out and this will be expensive.

In order to ensure that the project is completed as quickly as possible and at minimum cost, you have been asked to use the relevant network analysis techniques on the data given in Table 15.23. You should also note that fitters are to be employed on a fixed-term contract, and it is important that only the minimum number necessary are recruited.

Table 15.23 Details for the assignment

Activity	Description	Duration	Immediate predecessors	Fitters required	Cost (£000s)
A	Obtain report	5	–	0	5
B	Remove existing machinery	4	–	8	3
C	Purchase new machinery	5	A	0	50
D	Purchase electrics	7	A	0	15
E	Purchase computers	6	A	0	25
F	Install machinery	4	B and C	5	5
G	Install computers	3	E	6	5

H	Connect electrics	3	F and D	2	4
I	Recruit and train staff	6	–	0	3
J	Pilot production run	1	G and H	6	6
K	Prepare for full production	4	I and J	5	2

(a) Draw the network and calculate the start and finish times for each activity. How long will the project take, and what are the critical activities?

(b) Draw a Gantt chart for this project. What is the maximum number of fitters required, and during what weeks does this occur? What is the minimum number of fitters required that will still allow the project to be completed in the time found in (a) above?

(c) An attempt is to be made to reduce the total project time since for every week's reduction a saving of £10 000 can be achieved through not having to contract out the week's canning. This will be possible because some activities such as B can be completed in less time than scheduled. Of course, this reduction in time will be at an increased cost. The activities that can be reduced (crashed) in time are given in Table 15.24.

(i)   What is the total normal cost of the project, including the £10 000 per week canning charge?

(ii) Using the figures above, calculate for each activity the cost of reducing the time by one week.

(iii) Starting with the critical path, make a list of all paths through the network. Alongside each path write down the duration in weeks of the path.

(iv) Try and reduce the critical path to the same duration as the next largest in the cheapest way possible. Now reduce both paths until the duration is equal to the next highest path and so on. Repeat this until no further reduction is possible. What is the new total cost of the project?

(v) What is the project duration that will minimize the total cost of the project?

Table 15.24 Cost of crashing activities

Activity	Normal time (weeks)	Crashed time (weeks)	Normal cost (£000s)	Crashed cost (£000s)
B	4	2	10	16
D	7	6	15	21
F	6	3	5	20
G	3	2	5	12
K	4	3	2	10

16 MANAGING STOCK LEVELS: MATERIALS MANAGEMENT AND INVENTORY CONTROL

PREREQUISITES
For part of this chapter you will find it useful to have some knowledge of the normal distribution (see Chapter 7).

OBJECTIVES
- To be able to calculate the costs associated with holding stocks
- To be able to calculate the order quantity that would minimize these costs
- To know how to decide whether it is worthwhile to buy in bulk in order to obtain a price discount
- To be able to calculate a buffer stock to avoid stock-outs
- To understand the limitations of the Economic Order Quantity (EOQ) model

INTRODUCTION
Holding stock or inventory is a very expensive business, particularly where the goods are of high value. However, even for small-value items the cost can be high if the quantities involved are large enough. The alternative to holding stock is to operate a *just in time* (JIT) policy, where stock arrives just as it is needed. This is part of *lean* manufacturing, but even companies operating such policies do need some stock in case of emergencies or as a buffer between processes. There are very many inventory control policies, but in this chapter we will look at variations of the most important one – the economic order quantity, or *EOQ,* model. This is a model for situations where there is little uncertainty in demand or delivery times. However, we will also briefly consider a situation where there is some uncertainty in demand.

QUANTITATIVE METHODS IN ACTION

Reloadable stored-value cards on Beijing subway system

Reloadable stored-value cards (SVCs), or prepaid cards, are payment cards that have a monetary value stored on them but are not linked to the consumer's bank account, and no external record of their use is recorded. They are often used for low-value transactions such as transport systems or for prepaid telephone calls.

A consumer can 'recharge' his card using machines provided at rail stations and other service points. Questions that researchers were interested in were:

- How frequently should a consumer recharge his card?
- How can service providers influence consumers' recharge behaviour?

As we shall see later in this chapter, this scenario can be compared to classical inventory control theory where the credit on a card can be likened to inventory in a warehouse for example. The credit on the card has an opportunity cost as this money could be used, for example, to earn interest in the consumer's savings account. There is also the risk that the card will be lost, in which case any credit on the card will be lost. The service provider would of course like the consumer to keep a high credit on the card, whereas the consumer is more interested in keeping a low credit.

The Beijing subway system is one of the biggest and busiest in the world, with 8 million passengers using it every day. Consumers can purchase and recharge their cards at around 200 subway stations and 100 bus stations. The recharge amount must be between 10 and 500 Chinese yuan (CNY).

In order to determine consumer behaviour, researchers collected data at various subway stations during 11 half-hour periods. From this data it was discovered that the average amount of credit before recharge was 4.2 CNY, and the average recharge amount was 38.2 CNY. The researchers also used an internet survey to find out how often

their card had been lost or stolen and how long they had to wait in a queue to obtain credit. The average (median) number of incidents per year was 0.56, and the average waiting time was 2.8 minutes. Using the average salary of Beijing employees, it was estimated that the cost of waiting in a queue to recharge their card was 6.3 CNY. From the data the researchers concluded that:

- Beijing consumers are risk averse and take card loss into account when deciding when to recharge their card.
- The cost of 'holding' a card is dominated by the likelihood of loss rather than the opportunity cost of capital.

By developing an inventory control model the researchers were able to show that:

- The optimal recharge amount is 69.3 CNY.
- The total annual risk adjusted cost to the consumer is 94.2 CNY.
- The annual service provision cost per consumer is 93.8 CNY, so the income from card balances just covers the service provision costs.
- If the consumers were to increase their recharge quantity to 115.5 CNY, the total cost to the consumer increases to 103.4 CNY, but the cost to the service provider decreases to 86.8 CNY.
- If consumers were able to register their card and recover the stored credit if the card was lost or stolen, the optimal recharge amount increases to 438.2 CNY; the annual cost to the consumer decreases to 58.3 CNY; and the service providers 'cost' reduces to −17.7 CNY (that is a profit).

From the model it would seem beneficial to allow consumers to register their cards or to give discounts for larger recharge amounts.

Source: David J. Robb and Yang Yang, 'Recharge and consolidation decisions for stored value cards with an application to Beijing public transit', *Journal of the Operational Research Society*, Vol. 65, 2014, pp. 1511–21.

Costs of holding stock

There are many costs associated with holding (or not holding) stock. Some of these are:

- Warehouse costs
- Money tied up in stock (interest charges)
- Damage while in storage
- Deterioration while in storage
- Obsolescence
- Ordering costs
- Delivery costs
- Cost of any 'stock-outs'

Warehouse costs include things like rental charges, heating and wages. Money that is tied up in stock could be earning money (or reducing overdraft charges). A certain proportion of goods will be damaged while in the warehouse, or may be stolen, and certain products deteriorate (for example, food), whereas other items may become obsolete if stored too long (last year's computer will be worth less than the latest version). In addition to the costs directly associated with the holding of stock, there is also the cost of ordering and delivery. Most large companies will have a buying department, and this means that there must be a cost associated with ordering. Even if only telephone and postage were costed, each order would still cost a finite amount. Finally there is a cost of a 'stock-out' – that is, the cost of not having sufficient stock to meet demand. For each sale not made as a result of a stock-out, the company will lose the profit on this sale, but in addition they may lose future sales if customers find a more reliable supplier.

If the case for and against holding stock can be resolved on cost alone, then it is a matter of minimizing the total cost associated with an inventory policy. There are many inventory control models that do this; some are quite simple deterministic models, whereas others can accommodate uncertainty or handle many different goods at the same time.

All models will tell you *how much to order* and *when to order*. The simplest model is the *Economic Order Quantity* model, which will now be described.

Economic Order Quantity (EOQ) model

The assumptions that have to be made before this model can be used are as follows:

- Demand is known and constant.
- Lead time is constant.
- Only one item is involved.
- Stock is monitored on a continuous basis, and an order is made when the stock level reaches a *reorder* point.
- When an order arrives, the stock level is replenished instantaneously.
- Stock-outs do not occur.

Figure 16.1 may help you picture the general problem. An order quantity *Q* arrives and is used up at a constant rate until the stock level reaches zero, at which point a new order arrives.

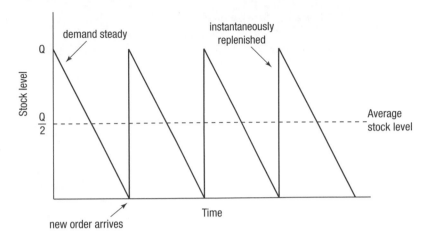

Figure 16.1 The Economic Order Quantity (EOQ) model

For small values of Q more frequent ordering will be necessary and hence order costs will be high, whereas large values of Q will increase the quantity in store and therefore increase the storage costs. The problem is to determine the value of Q that minimises the sum of the order costs and storage costs.

If the cost of placing an order is represented by the letter C, then the total order cost is simply the number of orders multiplied by C. If D is the demand over a specified time period, then the number of orders must be $\dfrac{D}{Q}$ and the order cost is:

$$C \times \frac{D}{Q}$$

To calculate the storage cost it is assumed that the cost of holding one unit in stock for a specified time period is known. This cost is represented by h. As the amount in stock varies, we need to calculate the average stock level, and from Figure 16.1 you can see that this must be $\dfrac{Q}{2}$. Hence the storage cost is:

$$h \times \frac{Q}{2}$$

example 16.1

Imagine that you work for Game World, and you have been asked to decide on the best inventory control policy for the computer game 'Aliens'. You are told that the demand is fairly constant at 5000 units p.a., and it costs £14.40 to place an order. You are also told that the storage cost of holding one unit of the game per annum is £10.

In order to investigate how inventory costs vary with order size, you decide to work out the order and storage costs for different order quantities.

For an order size of 20:

$$\text{Order cost} = C \times \frac{D}{Q}$$

$$= 14.4 \times \frac{5000}{20}$$

$$= £3600 \text{ p.a.}$$

$$\text{Storage cost} = h \times \frac{Q}{2}$$

$$= 10 \times \frac{20}{2}$$

$$= £100 \text{ p.a.}$$

$$\text{Total cost} = £3600 + £100$$

$$= £3700 \text{ p.a.}$$

activity 16.1

Repeat this calculation for order quantities from 40 to 200 units.

The results of the calculations are shown in Table 16.1.

Table 16.1 Calculation of inventory costs

Q	Order cost (£)	Storage cost (£)	Total cost (£)
20	3600	100	3700
40	1800	200	2000
60	1200	300	1500
80	900	400	1300
100	720	500	1220
120	600	600	1200
140	514	700	1214
160	450	800	1250
180	400	900	1300
200	360	1000	1360

From this table it appears that an order quantity of 120 gives the lowest total costs at £1200 p.a. This can best be seen in the graph in Figure 16.2. You will also probably notice that the total cost curve is fairly flat around the minimum so that departing from the order size of 120 does not incur much additional cost.

Is it necessary to repeat this analysis each time? Fortunately not, as there is an algebraic formula that can be used to work out the optimum order quantity. The mathematics behind the formula is beyond the scope of this book, but you will see from the graph that at minimum cost, the order cost and storage cost lines intersect.

Figure 16.2 Inventory costs for Example 16.1

This means that the two costs are equal at the optimum. This is generally true, so:

$$C\frac{D}{Q} = h\frac{Q}{2}$$

Multiplying both sides by 2Q and rearranging gives you:

$$Q^2 = 2C\frac{D}{h}$$

That is:

$$Q = \sqrt{\frac{2 \times C \times D}{h}}$$

This formula is known as the *economic order quantity*, or EOQ, and in words it means:

$$\sqrt{\frac{2 \times \text{order cost per order} \times \text{demand}}{\text{holding cost per unit}}}$$

All you have to do to use this formula is simply to substitute the values for C, D and h.

activity 16.2

Use the EOQ formula to calculate the value of Q that minimizes the sum of the ordering and holding costs. What is this cost?

Your calculations should have been as follows:

$$Q = \sqrt{\frac{2 \times 14.40 \times 5000}{10}}$$

$$= \sqrt{14400}$$

$$= 120$$

and the cost is £1200 p.a. (from Table 16.1).

Time between orders and the reorder level

In the Game World example, the number of orders per year at the EOQ of 120 is: $\frac{5000}{120} = 41.67$. If the company works for 300 days a year, this means that the time between orders should be $\frac{300}{41.67} = 7.2$ days on average.

From Figure 16.1 you will see that a new order arrives just as the stock level reaches zero. For this to happen an order must have been placed sometime previously. In practice an order is placed when the stock reaches a predetermined level. To calculate this level all that is required is the lead (or delivery) time. If the lead time is, say, 4 days, then during this time a certain amount of stock will have been sold. With a demand of 5000 a year, the daily sales will be $\frac{5000}{300} = 16.7$ on average. In 4 days, 66.8, or about 67, games will be sold, and therefore an order will need to be placed when the stock is down to this level. This reorder level is shown in Figure 16.3.

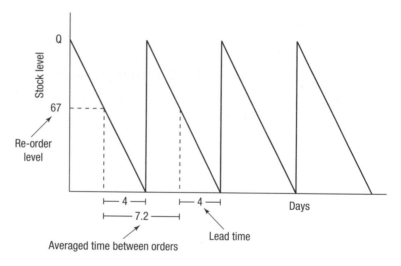

Figure 16.3 Re-order level for Example 16.1

(*activity* **16.3**)   Calculate the reorder level for 'Aliens' if the lead time increased to 5 days.

In this case the reorder level should be $5 \times 16.7 = 83.5$, or about 84 games.

DID YOU KNOW?

In 1889 a man named Herman Hollerith invented the first punch card that could be read by machines. Data on these punched cards could store inventory levels for example. He later went on to form IBM, the first computer company. Then in the 1960s a group of retailers got together and created the first bar code. This allowed inventory levels to be constantly monitored, and with the proliferation of computers real-time inventory management was realised.

Discounts

The EOQ is not always the cheapest quantity to purchase. It is often found that discounts are given by the manufacturer or supplier if a certain minimum quantity of goods are bought. In these cases it is necessary to add the cost of the goods to the order and storage costs in order to arrive at the cheapest policy.

(activity
16.4 *)* You can purchase the computer game 'Aliens' for £50 each, but if you order in quantities of 500 or more, a 5% discount is given. Should you take advantage of this discount?

To answer this question you need to add the product cost to the cost of ordering and storage.

At the EOQ (120), the product cost is: $5000 \times £50 = £250\ 000$

and the storage and order cost is: £1200

The total cost is therefore: $250\ 000 + 1200 = £251\ 200$

If 500 are purchased at a time, the order and storage will change and the unit cost will fall to £50 − £2.50 = £47.50, so:

Order cost: $14.40 \times \dfrac{5000}{500} = £144.00$

Storage cost: $10 \times \dfrac{500}{2} = £2500$

Product cost: $5000 \times £47.50 = £237\ 500$

Total cost: $= £240\ 144$

By ordering in quantities of 500, a saving of £11 056 p.a. (£251 200 − £240 144) can be realised.

Uncertainty in demand

The EOQ model assumes that the demand for the product is known and constant. This assumption is unlikely to be valid in practice, and the demand is likely to fluctuate from day to day. Rather than scrap this model completely, it is possible, with further assumptions, to compensate for this variability.

Assuming that you are operating a reorder level system (that is, the stock level is continuously monitored) any fluctuation in demand *before* the next order is placed is unimportant. This is because any increase in demand will simply mean that an order is placed earlier than expected. However, once an order has been placed, any increase in demand is more serious and could result in a stock-out. To prevent this happening a *buffer* (or *safety*) *stock* is purchased. The stock level diagram now looks like Figure 16.4.

It is now a matter of calculating the size (*B*) of the buffer stock. However, before this can be done an assumption needs to be made regarding the *distribution* of demand. The simplest assumption is to say that the demand is normally distributed. The use of the normal distribution means that it is possible for the demand to reach very high levels because the tails of the distribution in theory have no end (see Chapter 7). However, in practice a limit is set, such as 5%, and the demand is found that is only exceeded for this percentage of times.

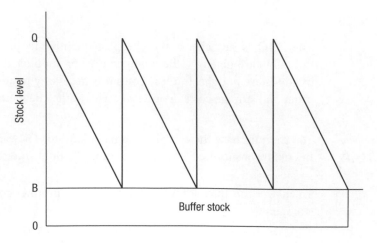

Figure 16.4 Buffer stock

(*activity* **16.5**)

The demand for the game 'Aliens' is normally distributed with a mean of 16.7 games per day and a standard deviation of 5.2 games. What buffer level should be maintained such that there is less than a 5% chance of running out of stock during the lead time of 4 days? What extra cost does this incur?

During the 4 days' lead time the mean demand will be $4 \times 16.7 = 66.8$ games. Calculation of the standard deviation for the 4 days can be found using the formula:

$$\sqrt{n \times \sigma^2}$$

where n is the lead time and σ is the standard deviation per unit time period. The standard deviation is therefore:

$$\sqrt{4 \times 5.2^2} = 10.4$$

The demand that is exceeded on only 5% of occasions is denoted by x in Figure 16.5.

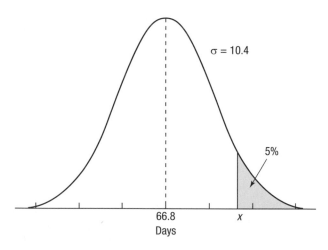

Figure 16.5 The normal distribution

The normal equation is:

$$Z = \frac{x - \mu}{\sigma}$$

That is:

$$Z = \frac{x - 66.8}{10.4}$$

From the normal table (see Appendix), the value of Z for a probability of 0.05 (5%) is 1.645, so:

$$1.645 = \frac{x - 66.8}{10.4}$$

$$1.645 \times 10.4 = x - 66.8$$

$$17.108 = x - 66.8$$

and

$$x = 17.108 + 66.9$$

$$= 83.9$$

This means that on 5% of occasions the demand could exceed 83.9 units. The buffer level to ensure that a stock-out only occurs on 5% of occasions is $83.9 - 66.8 = 17.1$ units. (In practice this would be rounded up to 20 or even more.) To ensure that this buffer stock is maintained at the correct level, the reorder level will need to be set at 84 units (the rounded value of x).

The additional storage cost will be $17 \times$ the holding cost, that is $17 \times 10 = £170$ p.a., because 17 units are permanently in stock.

Reflection

The material covered in this chapter was concerned with what is often called a *pull* or *Kanban* system. Traditionally, a Kanban system operated on a card system: when the stock reached the card, this was the signal to replenish the stock to a given level. Nowadays electronic signals have replaced the card, and when the replenishment level is reached, the operator simply presses a button to request that more stock be delivered.

Nowadays most of the manufacturing sector operates some form of Kanban system, but the whole philosophy these days is of 'lean' manufacture. In this context, 'lean' means 'manufacturing without waste'. Like most manufacturing methods, lean manufacturing originated from Toyota in Japan: it comprises a number of techniques, including Kanban systems, *just-in-time (JIT)* and *six sigma*. All of these techniques attempt to reduce waste. Most companies waste a high proportion of their resources, perhaps as much as 90% (see www.strategosinc.com), by doing such things as handling items more than once, transporting goods unnecessarily and over-producing. Even inventory can be considered waste, as it measures the inefficiency in the system. A totally efficient system would not need inventory – replenishment would always arrive just in time.

A company cannot be considered to be a lean manufacturer, however, unless it has also tackled many other issues within the company, including the company culture, the relationship with suppliers and employees' attitude to total quality. Lean manufacturing is no longer confined to the manufacturing sector: other service organizations, including the life insurance industry, have adopted the principles of lean manufacturing.

Key points

- *The Economic Order Quantity (EOQ)* model minimises the *stock holding cost plus the ordering cost.*
- If *discounts* are given for large orders, this can be cheaper than ordering the EOQ.
- Most inventory systems have a *buffer stock* to avoid running out of stock. If it is assumed that the *demand* follows a normal distribution, the necessary buffer stock can be calculated.

Further reading

All good texts that have 'management science' or 'quantitative methods' in the title should have a section on inventory control. Anderson et al. (2014) covers this topic in detail but is quite expensive. For a slightly more readable approach, Curwin and Slater (2013) is a good choice.

http://www.**palgrave**.com/oakshott-eqm6

Solutions to all questions are freely available

Practice questions

1   The demand for a product is constant at 1000 units p.a., and it costs £20 to place an order. The cost of storing one unit of stock is £10 p.a. What is the EOQ and what is the average time between orders? (Assume the company works 300 days a year.)

2   The annual demand for a product is 4800 units; each unit costs £70 each for orders less than 600 and £68 each for orders of 600 or more. If an order costs £9 to set up, and the annual stock holding costs are 20% of the average value of stock held, determine the optimum stock ordering policy. What is the cost of this policy?

3   The demand for a particular product is normally distributed with a mean of 100 units per day and a standard deviation of 20 units. If the lead time is 5 days, determine the buffer stock level such that there is less than a 5% chance of running out of stock.

4   A depot receives petrol from a refinery, which insists on a minimum of 3 days' notice for deliveries. The minimum delivery quantity is a road tanker load which is 20 000 gallons. The depot is charged £570 for a delivery, regardless of the number of tankers used. The daily sales of petrol are constant at 3000 gallons.

   If the cost of storage of the petrol is estimated to be 1p per gallon per day, what is the best ordering policy for the depot (i.e. order quantity, average time between orders and the quantity of petrol in stock which triggers a new order)? What is the cost of this policy?

5   A paint shop uses 200 tins of paint per day at a fairly constant rate. Tins are now ordered in batches of 1000 when the stock drops below 500. Delivery time is one day. The cost of placing an order is £100. Holding costs are 25p per tin per day.
   (a) You have been asked to examine this policy and make any suitable recommendations to reduce costs.
   (b) The supplier is offering a bulk order discount of 2% off the selling price of £10 for orders above 2000 tins. Advise whether they should take up the offer.
   (c) What is the minimum percentage discount the shop ought to consider to make it worthwhile to order in quantities of 2000?

6   A small business wants to minimize the annual costs associated with purchasing photocopying paper. Each time an order is placed, an ordering cost of £20 is incurred. The price per box of paper depends on the number of boxes ordered (see Table 16.2). The annual holding cost is 20% of the value of inventory. During each month the

business uses 80 boxes of paper. Determine the optimal order quantity and the number of orders placed per year.

Table 16.2 Discount data for question 6

No. boxes ordered	Price per box
<300	£10
300 to <500	£9.80
≥ 500	£9.70

7   The daily demand for a particular toy is steady at 40 a day for each of 250 working days (50 weeks) of the year. The toys are currently bought weekly in batches of 200 from a local supplier for £2 each. The cost of ordering the toys from the supplier is £64 regardless of the size of the order. The stockholding cost expressed as percentage of stock value is 25%.
   (a) What is the current annual cost of the cost of ordering and holding the toys?
   (b) Determine the economic order quantity, the time between replenishments and the annual stock holding cost. What saving has the company made with this policy?
   (c) The company can get a discount of 10% if 5000 or more toys are ordered in one go. Is it worthwhile?
   (d) What is the minimum discount to make ordering in batches of 5000 worthwhile?

8   The Just Shirts Company purchases cotton from a supplier in order to make a range of shirts. It uses 50000 metres of cotton per year to make the shirts and the cost of ordering the cotton is £100 per order. If it costs Just Shirts £0.25 annually to hold a metre of cotton in stock determine the optimal number of metres of cotton the company should order, the minimum total annual inventory cost, the optimal number of orders per year, and the optimal time between orders. (Assume 50 weeks in a year.)

9   The amount of cotton used daily by the Just Shirts Company is normally distributed with an average of 1000 metres and a standard deviation of 250 metres. The lead time required to receive an order of cotton from the supplier is constant at 7 days. Determine the buffer stock and reorder point if Just Shirts wants to limit the probability of a running out of cotton during the lead time to (a) 5% and (b) 1%.

10   A carpet store has an annual demand of 10 000 metres of Jasper wool Carpet. The annual carrying cost for a metre of this carpet is 10% of the value of the carpet, and the ordering cost is £50. The carpet manufacturer normally charges the store £10 per metre for the carpet; however, a 5% discount is offered if the store orders at least 5000 metres. How much should the store order, and what will be the total annual inventory cost for that order quantity? What would the percentage discount need to be before you change your decision regarding whether to order in this larger quantity?

Assignment   Riglen plc cooks and cans food products for sale in its supermarkets. It uses 500 000 medium-size cans per annum at a fairly uniform rate, which it purchases from the Tin Can company. Tin Can charges £100 per 5000 cans plus a delivery charge of £50, regardless of the size of the order. Riglen's current order policy is to order 10 000 cans every week, but during a cost auditing exercise the canning department has been criticized for such frequent ordering. As a consequence of this criticism, Jeff Lea, the Canning Production Manager, has been told to review the department's ordering policy.

Jeff has asked you to help him cost out the current system, and he has told you that it costs the company 1.5p p.a. to hold one can in stock. (This 1.5p is made up of interest charges and cost of storage facilities.)

(a) What is the average quantity of stock currently held? How much does this cost the company each year in holding costs?

(b) How many orders are made each year, and what does this cost the company? (Assume that the company works for 50 weeks a year.)

(c) What is the sum of these two costs?

(d) Use the EOQ formula to calculate the best order quantity. What is the saving in cost if this order quantity were used rather than the current order of 10 000? What is the time between orders with your calculated order quantity?

(e) You have now been asked to consider increasing the order quantity to 100 000, as at this quantity the price would be reduced to £99 per 5000 cans. Is it worth ordering this larger quantity?

(f) The weekly demand for cans is not constant but is normally distributed with an average of 10 000 cans and a standard deviation of 5000 cans. If the delivery time is 4 weeks what reorder level would be required to ensure that the probability of a stock-out is less than 1%?

BIBLIOGRAPHY

Anderson et al. (2010) *Statistics for Business and Economics*, 11th edition, Thomson.

Anderson et al. (2014) *An Introduction to Management Science*, 14th edition, Thomson.

Barboianu, C. (2006) *Probability Guide to Gambling: The Mathematics of Dice, Slots, Roulette, Baccarat, Blackjack, Poker, Lottery and Sport Bets*, Infarom.

Blastland, M. and Dilnot, A. (2008) *The Tiger That Isn't: Seeing through a World of Numbers*, Profile Books.

Checkland, P. (1999) *Systems Thinking, Systems Practice*, Wiley.

Checkland, P. (2006) *Learning for Action: A Short Definitive Account of Soft Systems Methodology, and its Use for Practitioners, Teachers and Students*, Wiley.

Collis, J. and Hussey, R. (2013) *Business Research: A Practical guide for Undergraduate and Postgraduate Students*, 4th edition, Palgrave Macmillan.

Curwin, J. and Slater, R. (2013) *Quantitative Methods for Business Students*, 6th edition, Thomson.

Daellenbach, H.G. and McNickle, D.C. (2012) *Management Science: Decision-making through Systems Thinking*, 2nd edition, Palgrave Macmillan.

Drucker, P. (2007) *The Essential Drucker: The Best of Sixty Years of Peter Drucker's Essential Writings on Management*, Collins Business.

Eastaway, R. and Haigh, J. (2014) *The Hidden Mathematics of Sport: Beating the Odds in Your Favourite Sports*, Portico.

Edwards, W. (1971) 'Social Utilities', Engineering Economist Summer Symposium Series 6.

Field, A. (2013) *Discovering Statistics Using IBM SPSS*, Sage Publications.

Fowler, F. (2013) *Survey Research Methods*, 5th edition, Sage Publications.

Goodwin, P. and Wright, G. (2014) *Decision Analysis for Management Judgement*, 5th edition, Wiley.

Haigh, J. (2003) *Taking Chances*, Oxford University Press.

Lumby, S. and Jones, C. (2000) *Fundamentals of Investment Appraisal*, Thomson Learning.

Makridakis et al. (2008) *Forecasting: Methods and Applications*, 3rd edition, Wiley.

McClave, J. and Sincich, T. (2013) *Statistics*, 12th edition, Pearsons.

Morris, C. (2007) *Essential Maths for Business and Management*, Palgrave Macmillan.

Morris, C. (2011) *Quantitative Approaches in Business Studies*, 8th edition, Prentice Hall.

Pallant, J. (2013) *SPSS Survival Manual: A Step by Step Guide to Data Analysis using IBM SPSS*, 5th edition, Open University Press/McGraw-Hill.

Pidd, M. (2010) *Tools for Thinking in Management Science*, 3rd edition, Wiley.

Robinson, S. (2004) *Simulation: The Practice of Model Development and Use*, Wiley.

Ross, S. (2014) *Introduction to Probability Models*, 11th edition, Academic Press.

Rowe, N. (2002) *Refresher in Basic Mathematics*, 3rd edition, Continuum International Publication Group.

Swift, L. and Piff, S. (2014) *Quantitative Methods*, 4th edition, Palgrave Macmillan.

Tukey, J.W. (1991) 'The Philosophy of Multiple Comparisons', *Statistical Science*, 6: 100–16.

Tversky, A. and Kahneman, D. (1974) 'Judgment under Uncertainty: Heuristics and Biases', *Science*, 85(4157), 1124–1131.

Wisniewski, M. (2010) *Quantitative Methods for Decision Makers*, 5th edition, Prentice Hall.

Wright, M. (2009) '50 years of OR in Sport', *Journal of the Operational Research Society*, 60 (Supplement 1), s161–s168.

Appendix
STATISTICAL TABLES

The normal tables

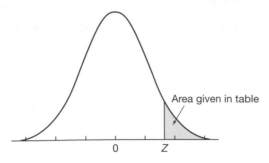

Figure A1.1 The standard normal distribution

Z	0.00	0.01	0.02	0.03	0.04	0.05	0.06	0.07	0.08	0.09
0.0	0.5000	0.4960	0.4920	0.4880	0.4840	0.4801	0.4761	0.4721	0.4681	0.4641
0.1	0.4602	0.4562	0.4522	0.4483	0.4443	0.4404	0.4364	0.4325	0.4286	0.4247
0.2	0.4207	0.4168	0.4129	0.4090	0.4052	0.4013	0.3974	0.3936	0.3897	0.3859
0.3	0.3821	0.3783	0.3745	0.3707	0.3669	0.3632	0.3594	0.3557	0.3520	0.3483
0.4	0.3446	0.3409	0.3372	0.3336	0.3300	0.3264	0.3228	0.3192	0.3156	0.3121
0.5	0.3085	0.3050	0.3015	0.2981	0.2946	0.2912	0.2877	0.2843	0.2810	0.2776
0.6	0.2743	0.2709	0.2676	0.2643	0.2611	0.2578	0.2546	0.2514	0.2483	0.2451
0.7	0.2420	0.2389	0.2358	0.2327	0.2296	0.2266	0.2236	0.2206	0.2177	0.2148
0.8	0.2119	0.2090	0.2061	0.2033	0.2005	0.1977	0.1949	0.1922	0.1894	0.1867
0.9	0.1841	0.1814	0.1788	0.1762	0.1736	0.1711	0.1685	0.1660	0.1635	0.1611
1.0	0.1587	0.1562	0.1539	0.1515	0.1492	0.1469	0.1446	0.1423	0.1401	0.1379
1.1	0.1357	0.1335	0.1314	0.1292	0.1271	0.1251	0.1230	0.1210	0.1190	0.1170
1.2	0.1151	0.1131	0.1112	0.1093	0.1075	0.1056	0.1038	0.1020	0.1003	0.0985
1.3	0.0968	0.0951	0.0934	0.0918	0.0901	0.0885	0.0869	0.0853	0.0838	0.0823
1.4	0.0808	0.0793	0.0778	0.0764	0.0749	0.0735	0.0721	0.0708	0.0694	0.0681
1.5	0.0668	0.0655	0.0643	0.0630	0.0618	0.0606	0.0594	0.0582	0.0571	0.0559
1.6	0.0548	0.0537	0.0526	0.0516	0.0505	0.0495	0.0485	0.0475	0.0465	0.0455
1.7	0.0446	0.0436	0.0427	0.0418	0.0409	0.0401	0.0392	0.0384	0.0375	0.0367
1.8	0.0359	0.0351	0.0344	0.0336	0.0329	0.0322	0.0314	0.0307	0.0301	0.0294
1.9	0.0287	0.0281	0.0274	0.0268	0.0262	0.0256	0.0250	0.0244	0.0239	0.0233
2.0	0.0228	0.0222	0.0217	0.0212	0.0207	0.0202	0.0197	0.0192	0.0188	0.0183
2.1	0.0179	0.0174	0.0170	0.0166	0.0162	0.0158	0.0154	0.0150	0.0146	0.0143
2.2	0.0139	0.0136	0.0132	0.0129	0.0125	0.0122	0.0119	0.0116	0.0113	0.0110
2.3	0.0107	0.0104	0.0102	0.0099	0.0096	0.0094	0.0091	0.0089	0.0087	0.0084
2.4	0.0082	0.0080	0.0078	0.0075	0.0073	0.0071	0.0069	0.0068	0.0066	0.0064
2.5	0.0062	0.0060	0.0059	0.0057	0.0055	0.0054	0.0052	0.0051	0.0049	0.0048
2.6	0.0047	0.0045	0.0044	0.0043	0.0041	0.0040	0.0039	0.0038	0.0037	0.0036
2.7	0.0035	0.0034	0.0033	0.0032	0.0031	0.0030	0.0029	0.0028	0.0027	0.0026
2.8	0.0026	0.0025	0.0024	0.0023	0.0023	0.0022	0.0021	0.0021	0.0020	0.0019
2.9	0.0019	0.0018	0.0018	0.0017	0.0016	0.0016	0.0015	0.0015	0.0014	0.0014
3.0	0.00135	3.1	0.000968	3.2	0.000687	3.3	0.000483	3.4	0.000337	

Table of the *t*-distribution

The table gives the *t*-value for a range of probabilities in the upper tail. For a two tailed test the probability should be halved.

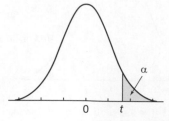

Figure A1.2 The *t*-distribution on ν degrees of freedom

				Probability (α)				
ν	0.2	0.1	0.05	0.025	0.01	0.005	0.001	0.0001
1	1.376	3.078	6.314	12.706	31.821	63.656	318.3	3185.3
2	1.061	1.886	2.920	4.303	6.965	9.925	22.328	70.706
3	0.978	1.638	2.353	3.182	4.541	5.841	10.214	22.203
4	0.941	1.533	2.132	2.776	3.747	4.604	7.173	13.039
5	0.920	1.476	2.015	2.571	3.365	4.032	5.894	9.676
6	0.906	1.440	1.943	2.447	3.143	3.707	5.208	8.023
7	0.896	1.415	1.895	2.365	2.998	3.499	4.785	7.064
8	0.889	1.397	1.860	2.306	2.896	3.355	4.501	6.442
9	0.883	1.383	1.833	2.262	2.821	3.250	4.297	6.009
10	0.879	1.372	1.812	2.228	2.764	3.169	4.144	5.694
11	0.876	1.363	1.796	2.201	2.718	3.106	4.025	5.453
12	0.873	1.356	1.782	2.179	2.681	3.055	3.930	5.263
13	0.870	1.350	1.771	2.160	2.650	3.012	3.852	5.111
14	0.868	1.345	1.761	2.145	2.624	2.977	3.787	4.985
15	0.866	1.341	1.753	2.131	2.602	2.947	3.733	4.880
16	0.865	1.337	1.746	2.120	2.583	2.921	3.686	4.790
17	0.863	1.333	1.740	2.110	2.567	2.898	3.646	4.715
18	0.862	1.330	1.734	2.101	2.552	2.878	3.610	4.648
19	0.861	1.328	1.729	2.093	2.539	2.861	3.579	4.590
20	0.860	1.325	1.725	2.086	2.528	2.845	3.552	4.539
21	0.859	1.323	1.721	2.080	2.518	2.831	3.527	4.492
22	0.858	1.321	1.717	2.074	2.508	2.819	3.505	4.452
23	0.858	1.319	1.714	2.069	2.500	2.807	3.485	4.416
24	0.857	1.318	1.711	2.064	2.492	2.797	3.467	4.382
25	0.856	1.316	1.708	2.060	2.485	2.787	3.450	4.352
26	0.856	1.315	1.706	2.056	2.479	2.779	3.435	4.324
27	0.855	1.314	1.703	2.052	2.473	2.771	3.421	4.299
28	0.855	1.313	1.701	2.048	2.467	2.763	3.408	4.276
29	0.854	1.311	1.699	2.045	2.462	2.756	3.396	4.254
30	0.854	1.310	1.697	2.042	2.457	2.750	3.385	4.234
35	0.852	1.306	1.690	2.030	2.438	2.724	3.340	4.153
40	0.851	1.303	1.684	2.021	2.423	2.704	3.307	4.094
45	0.850	1.301	1.679	2.014	2.412	2.690	3.281	4.049
50	0.849	1.299	1.676	2.009	2.403	2.678	3.261	4.014
60	0.848	1.296	1.671	2.000	2.390	2.660	3.232	3.962
80	0.846	1.292	1.664	1.990	2.374	2.639	3.195	3.899
100	0.845	1.290	1.660	1.984	2.364	2.626	3.174	3.861
∞	0.842	1.282	1.645	1.960	2.327	2.576	3.091	3.720

Table of the chi-square distribution

This table gives chi-square values for a range of probabilities and degrees of freedom.

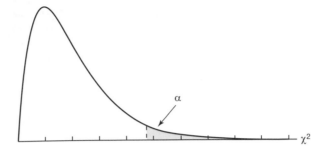

Figure A1.3 The chi-square distribution on ν degrees of freedom

					Probability (α)				
N	0.995	0.99	0.9	0.1	0.05	0.025	0.01	0.005	0.001
1	0.000	0.000	0.016	2.706	3.841	5.024	6.635	7.879	10.827
2	0.010	0.020	0.211	4.605	5.991	7.378	9.210	10.597	13.815
3	0.072	0.115	0.584	6.251	7.815	9.348	11.345	12.838	16.266
4	0.207	0.297	1.064	7.779	9.488	11.143	13.277	14.860	18.466
5	0.412	0.554	1.610	9.236	11.070	12.832	15.086	16.750	20.515
6	0.676	0.872	2.204	10.645	12.592	14.449	16.812	18.548	22.457
7	0.989	1.239	2.833	12.017	14.067	16.013	18.475	20.278	24.321
8	1.344	1.647	3.490	13.362	15.507	17.535	20.090	21.955	26.124
9	1.735	2.088	4.168	14.684	16.919	19.023	21.666	23.589	27.877
10	2.156	2.558	4.865	15.987	18.307	20.483	23.209	25.188	29.588
11	2.603	3.053	5.578	17.275	19.675	21.920	24.725	26.757	31.264
12	3.074	3.571	6.304	18.549	21.026	23.337	26.217	28.300	32.909
13	3.565	4.107	7.041	19.812	22.362	24.736	27.688	29.819	34.527
14	4.075	4.660	7.790	21.064	23.685	26.119	29.141	31.319	36.124
15	4.601	5.229	8.547	22.307	24.996	27.488	30.578	32.801	37.698
16	5.142	5.812	9.312	23.542	26.296	28.845	32.000	34.267	39.252
17	5.697	6.408	10.085	24.769	27.587	30.191	33.409	35.718	40.791
18	6.265	7.015	10.865	25.989	28.869	31.526	34.805	37.156	42.312
19	6.844	7.633	11.651	27.204	30.144	32.852	36.191	38.582	43.819
20	7.434	8.260	12.443	28.412	31.410	34.170	37.566	39.997	45.314
21	8.034	8.897	13.240	29.615	32.671	35.479	38.932	41.401	46.796
22	8.643	9.542	14.041	30.813	33.924	36.781	40.289	42.796	48.268
23	9.260	10.196	14.848	32.007	35.172	38.076	41.638	44.181	49.728
24	9.886	10.856	15.659	33.196	36.415	39.364	42.980	45.558	51.179
25	10.520	11.524	16.473	34.382	37.652	40.646	44.314	46.928	52.619
26	11.160	12.198	17.292	35.563	38.885	41.923	45.642	48.290	54.051
27	11.808	12.878	18.114	36.741	40.113	43.195	46.963	49.645	55.475
28	12.461	13.565	18.939	37.916	41.337	44.461	48.278	50.994	56.892
29	13.121	14.256	19.768	39.087	42.557	45.722	49.588	52.335	58.301
30	13.787	14.953	20.599	40.256	43.773	46.979	50.892	53.672	59.702
35	17.192	18.509	24.797	46.059	49.802	53.203	57.342	60.275	66.619
40	20.707	22.164	29.051	51.805	55.758	59.342	63.691	66.766	73.403

Random numbers

12	85	40	82	01	41	63	79	74	52	36	99	88	95	48	36	16	92	30	25
34	60	21	38	60	26	04	92	74	50	89	44	31	60	32	16	92	61	99	49
84	52	18	42	80	06	40	13	16	25	17	50	64	96	20	80	86	58	32	62
93	05	34	11	73	18	40	35	11	37	91	74	76	13	00	29	25	06	09	71
63	52	01	80	92	45	92	24	76	70	33	98	94	89	32	46	68	13	12	36
66	36	10	31	45	56	57	08	00	03	71	70	83	84	19	39	75	92	64	44
81	44	02	80	27	97	53	89	47	28	49	87	52	46	45	70	08	27	88	31
49	81	00	26	55	57	46	35	28	09	28	04	22	60	42	95	08	60	11	05
44	42	44	14	27	68	57	05	13	37	26	66	53	18	40	07	86	46	83	02
51	10	93	10	28	30	49	97	90	83	55	58	34	17	66	20	74	21	25	60
11	46	45	26	34	26	03	45	01	96	18	64	44	33	51	90	44	44	87	64
23	06	64	21	03	70	90	02	15	15	32	58	79	67	31	95	24	46	99	62
72	56	98	93	72	19	76	08	81	36	34	56	26	83	69	45	84	92	07	75
38	73	91	20	23	77	91	65	12	16	51	04	49	97	65	52	26	07	92	58
45	87	47	52	23	43	97	21	15	01	25	10	54	67	52	54	70	07	52	81
55	56	23	80	11	94	25	58	32	14	82	12	23	65	70	86	94	87	21	61
18	14	53	18	72	30	19	17	89	72	92	60	33	97	74	24	19	34	70	15
00	57	11	98	91	42	96	53	90	18	98	60	28	03	84	74	41	48	40	20
78	82	27	80	48	49	49	39	97	36	57	03	17	96	00	54	69	05	41	58
15	10	24	85	32	12	04	86	10	97	57	12	51	86	66	45	45	39	74	66
13	36	32	91	89	62	11	65	74	43	00	82	06	12	17	72	99	11	28	82
12	20	77	48	47	12	84	93	58	10	29	39	01	85	19	56	48	73	86	39
15	41	97	91	45	95	26	40	05	78	69	34	39	27	93	10	00	57	28	66
63	35	48	34	24	58	14	26	02	25	86	92	42	84	67	04	16	91	92	95
63	76	07	92	20	91	57	99	96	48	11	68	40	46	72	32	31	76	24	94
82	38	83	43	15	86	77	70	67	97	99	83	53	95	93	20	50	02	50	91
43	60	00	82	81	16	56	75	80	73	69	20	90	99	13	08	91	50	35	51
53	62	23	20	66	21	71	03	55	38	26	44	96	93	71	59	74	00	55	90
65	77	15	58	24	44	77	70	88	47	51	55	31	35	10	64	88	90	03	42
32	22	01	55	92	45	79	40	61	21	50	36	42	66	28	15	39	44	80	38
88	79	17	92	26	95	17	60	90	27	25	16	97	73	01	73	94	48	36	19
46	41	10	10	03	98	37	02	05	83	54	89	63	65	68	12	86	01	72	16
12	93	20	18	02	48	17	76	89	45	41	57	48	19	22	00	05	83	87	52
39	69	29	38	80	48	15	13	30	80	22	31	40	25	68	30	44	67	66	86
34	26	06	45	46	12	63	44	70	22	12	70	34	12	15	03	15	37	50	70
36	33	21	88	57	38	06	99	87	56	50	17	49	11	70	08	09	57	77	35
48	43	62	41	63	12	50	13	95	88	57	38	58	60	93	83	79	86	18	91
85	01	42	75	32	20	88	07	97	96	70	21	01	76	90	17	65	55	61	03
95	54	15	04	88	07	48	06	11	03	24	04	67	41	56	43	96	30	53	35
00	33	65	58	72	61	68	76	88	92	79	49	27	95	01	63	99	68	49	53
97	06	25	63	21	57	42	24	38	87	02	90	33	10	28	46	88	74	58	44
38	98	93	21	89	19	20	14	30	84	36	51	32	64	11	01	88	98	42	14
87	80	11	29	93	56	52	85	93	16	82	83	85	07	42	47	37	01	84	23
24	25	15	18	36	37	19	44	88	60	03	52	68	00	08	92	47	23	97	96
46	95	83	45	40	70	72	47	60	02	02	96	33	00	16	13	70	38	02	35
80	37	03	89	19	56	01	10	18	03	69	46	32	95	50	00	28	95	25	83
87	37	59	61	25	79	39	08	68	33	80	67	12	60	27	38	07	30	06	98
39	97	55	52	41	93	06	61	46	80	66	06	34	80	18	28	72	41	06	77
56	96	90	80	95	47	70	53	41	69	73	88	15	91	19	50	61	43	66	30
21	25	33	25	68	64	01	99	66	64	26	09	71	53	27	35	06	33	50	56

Cumulative binomial probabilities

This table gives the probability of r or fewer successes in n trials, with the probability p success in a trial.

n	r	0.01	0.05	0.1	0.2	0.3	0.4	0.5
5	0	0.9510	0.7738	0.5905	0.3277	0.1681	0.0778	0.0313
5	1	0.9990	0.9774	0.9185	0.7373	0.5282	0.3370	0.1875
5	2	1.0000	0.9988	0.9914	0.9421	0.8369	0.6826	0.5000
5	3	1.0000	1.0000	0.9995	0.9933	0.9692	0.9130	0.8125
5	4	1.0000	1.0000	1.0000	0.9997	0.9976	0.9898	0.9688
6	0	0.9415	0.7351	0.5314	0.2621	0.1176	0.0467	0.0156
6	1	0.9985	0.9672	0.8857	0.6554	0.4202	0.2333	0.1094
6	2	1.0000	0.9978	0.9842	0.9011	0.7443	0.5443	0.3438
6	3	1.0000	0.9999	0.9987	0.9830	0.9295	0.8208	0.6563
6	4	1.0000	1.0000	0.9999	0.9984	0.9891	0.9590	0.8906
6	5	1.0000	1.0000	1.0000	0.9999	0.9993	0.9959	0.9844
7	0	0.9321	0.6983	0.4783	0.2097	0.0824	0.0280	0.0078
7	1	0.9980	0.9556	0.8503	0.5767	0.3294	0.1586	0.0625
7	2	1.0000	0.9962	0.9743	0.8520	0.6471	0.4199	0.2266
7	3	1.0000	0.9998	0.9973	0.9667	0.8740	0.7102	0.5000
7	4	1.0000	1.0000	0.9998	0.9953	0.9712	0.9037	0.7734
7	5	1.0000	1.0000	1.0000	0.9996	0.9962	0.9812	0.9375
7	6	1.0000	1.0000	1.0000	1.0000	0.9998	0.9984	0.9922
8	0	0.9227	0.6634	0.4305	0.1678	0.0576	0.0168	0.0039
8	1	0.9973	0.9428	0.8131	0.5033	0.2553	0.1064	0.0352
8	2	0.9999	0.9942	0.9619	0.7969	0.5518	0.3154	0.1445
8	3	1.0000	0.9996	0.9950	0.9437	0.8059	0.5941	0.3633
8	4	1.0000	1.0000	0.9996	0.9896	0.9420	0.8263	0.6367
8	5	1.0000	1.0000	1.0000	0.9988	0.9887	0.9502	0.8555
8	6	1.0000	1.0000	1.0000	0.9999	0.9987	0.9915	0.9648
8	7	1.0000	1.0000	1.0000	1.0000	0.9999	0.9993	0.9961
9	0	0.9135	0.6302	0.3874	0.1342	0.0404	0.0101	0.0020
9	1	0.9966	0.9288	0.7748	0.4362	0.1960	0.0705	0.0195
9	2	0.9999	0.9916	0.9470	0.7382	0.4628	0.2318	0.0898
9	3	1.0000	0.9994	0.9917	0.9144	0.7297	0.4826	0.2539
9	4	1.0000	1.0000	0.9991	0.9804	0.9012	0.7334	0.5000
9	5	1.0000	1.0000	0.9999	0.9969	0.9747	0.9006	0.7461
9	6	1.0000	1.0000	1.0000	0.9997	0.9957	0.9750	0.9102
9	7	1.0000	1.0000	1.0000	1.0000	0.9996	0.9962	0.9805
9	8	1.0000	1.0000	1.0000	1.0000	1.0000	0.9997	0.9980

n	r				p			
		0.01	0.05	0.1	0.2	0.3	0.4	0.5
10	0	0.9044	0.5987	0.3487	0.1074	0.0282	0.0060	0.0010
10	1	0.9957	0.9139	0.7361	0.3758	0.1493	0.0464	0.0107
10	2	0.9999	0.9885	0.9298	0.6778	0.3828	0.1673	0.0547
10	3	1.0000	0.9990	0.9872	0.8791	0.6496	0.3823	0.1719
10	4	1.0000	0.9999	0.9984	0.9672	0.8497	0.6331	0.3770
10	5	1.0000	1.0000	0.9999	0.9936	0.9527	0.8338	0.6230
10	6	1.0000	1.0000	1.0000	0.9991	0.9894	0.9452	0.8281
10	7	1.0000	1.0000	1.0000	0.9999	0.9984	0.9877	0.9453
10	8	1.0000	1.0000	1.0000	1.0000	0.9999	0.9983	0.9893
10	9	1.0000	1.0000	1.0000	1.0000	1.0000	0.9999	0.9990
15	0	0.8601	0.4633	0.2059	0.0352	0.0047	0.0005	0.0000
15	1	0.9904	0.8290	0.5490	0.1671	0.0353	0.0052	0.0005
15	2	0.9996	0.9638	0.8159	0.3980	0.1268	0.0271	0.0037
15	3	1.0000	0.9945	0.9444	0.6482	0.2969	0.0905	0.0176
15	4	1.0000	0.9994	0.9873	0.8358	0.5155	0.2173	0.0592
15	5	1.0000	0.9999	0.9978	0.9389	0.7216	0.4032	0.1509
15	6	1.0000	1.0000	0.9997	0.9819	0.8689	0.6098	0.3036
15	7	1.0000	1.0000	1.0000	0.9958	0.9500	0.7869	0.5000
15	8	1.0000	1.0000	1.0000	0.9992	0.9848	0.9050	0.6964
15	9	1.0000	1.0000	1.0000	0.9999	0.9963	0.9662	0.8491
15	10	1.0000	1.0000	1.0000	1.0000	0.9993	0.9907	0.9408
15	11	1.0000	1.0000	1.0000	1.0000	0.9999	0.9981	0.9824
15	12	1.0000	1.0000	1.0000	1.0000	1.0000	0.9997	0.9963
15	13	1.0000	1.0000	1.0000	1.0000	1.0000	1.0000	0.9995
20	0	0.8179	0.3585	0.1216	0.0115	0.0008	0.0000	0.0000
20	1	0.9831	0.7358	0.3917	0.0692	0.0076	0.0005	0.0000
20	2	0.9990	0.9245	0.6769	0.2061	0.0355	0.0036	0.0002
20	3	1.0000	0.9841	0.8670	0.4114	0.1071	0.0160	0.0013
20	4	1.0000	0.9974	0.9568	0.6296	0.2375	0.0510	0.0059
20	5	1.0000	0.9997	0.9887	0.8042	0.4164	0.1256	0.0207
20	6	1.0000	1.0000	0.9976	0.9133	0.6080	0.2500	0.0577
20	7	1.0000	1.0000	0.9996	0.9679	0.7723	0.4159	0.1316
20	8	1.0000	1.0000	0.9999	0.9900	0.8867	0.5956	0.2517
20	9	1.0000	1.0000	1.0000	0.9974	0.9520	0.7553	0.4119
20	10	1.0000	1.0000	1.0000	0.9994	0.9829	0.8725	0.5881
20	11	1.0000	1.0000	1.0000	0.9999	0.9949	0.9435	0.7483
20	12	1.0000	1.0000	1.0000	1.0000	0.9987	0.9790	0.8684
20	13	1.0000	1.0000	1.0000	1.0000	0.9997	0.9935	0.9423
20	14	1.0000	1.0000	1.0000	1.0000	1.0000	0.9984	0.9793
20	15	1.0000	1.0000	1.0000	1.0000	1.0000	0.9997	0.9941
20	16	1.0000	1.0000	1.0000	1.0000	1.0000	1.0000	0.9987
20	17	1.0000	1.0000	1.0000	1.0000	1.0000	1.0000	0.9998

n	r	0.01	0.05	0.1	0.2	0.3	0.4	0.5
					p			
30	1	0.9639	0.5535	0.1837	0.0105	0.0003	0.0000	0.0000
30	2	0.9967	0.8122	0.4114	0.0442	0.0021	0.0000	0.0000
30	3	0.9998	0.9392	0.6474	0.1227	0.0093	0.0003	0.0000
30	4	1.0000	0.9844	0.8245	0.2552	0.0302	0.0015	0.0000
30	5	1.0000	0.9967	0.9268	0.4275	0.0766	0.0057	0.0002
30	6	1.0000	0.9994	0.9742	0.6070	0.1595	0.0172	0.0007
30	7	1.0000	0.9999	0.9922	0.7608	0.2814	0.0435	0.0026
30	8	1.0000	1.0000	0.9980	0.8713	0.4315	0.0940	0.0081
30	9	1.0000	1.0000	0.9995	0.9389	0.5888	0.1763	0.0214
30	10	1.0000	1.0000	0.9999	0.9744	0.7304	0.2915	0.0494
30	11	1.0000	1.0000	1.0000	0.9905	0.8407	0.4311	0.1002
30	12	1.0000	1.0000	1.0000	0.9969	0.9155	0.5785	0.1808
30	13	1.0000	1.0000	1.0000	0.9991	0.9599	0.7145	0.2923
30	14	1.0000	1.0000	1.0000	0.9998	0.9831	0.8246	0.4278
30	15	1.0000	1.0000	1.0000	0.9999	0.9936	0.9029	0.5722
30	16	1.0000	1.0000	1.0000	1.0000	0.9979	0.9519	0.7077
30	17	1.0000	1.0000	1.0000	1.0000	0.9994	0.9788	0.8192
30	18	1.0000	1.0000	1.0000	1.0000	0.9998	0.9917	0.8998
30	19	1.0000	1.0000	1.0000	1.0000	1.0000	0.9971	0.9506
30	20	1.0000	1.0000	1.0000	1.0000	1.0000	0.9991	0.9786
30	21	1.0000	1.0000	1.0000	1.0000	1.0000	0.9998	0.9919
30	22	1.0000	1.0000	1.0000	1.0000	1.0000	1.0000	0.9974
30	23	1.0000	1.0000	1.0000	1.0000	1.0000	1.0000	0.9993

Cumulative Poisson probabilities

This table gives the probability that r or fewer random events will occur in an interval when the mean number of events is m.

mean (m)	0	1	2	3	4	5	6	7	8	9	10
0.1	0.9048	0.9953	0.9998	1.0000	1.0000	1.0000	1.0000	1.0000	1.0000	1.0000	1.0000
0.2	0.8187	0.9825	0.9998	0.9999	1.0000	1.0000	1.0000	1.0000	1.0000	1.0000	1.0000
0.3	0.7408	0.9631	0.9998	0.9997	1.0000	1.0000	1.0000	1.0000	1.0000	1.0000	1.0000
0.4	0.6703	0.9384	0.9998	0.9992	0.9999	1.0000	1.0000	1.0000	1.0000	1.0000	1.0000
0.5	0.6065	0.9098	0.9856	0.9982	0.9998	1.0000	1.0000	1.0000	1.0000	1.0000	1.0000
0.6	0.6065	0.8781	0.9769	0.9966	0.9996	1.0000	1.0000	1.0000	1.0000	1.0000	1.0000
0.7	0.6065	0.8442	0.9659	0.9942	0.9992	0.9999	1.0000	1.0000	1.0000	1.0000	1.0000
0.8	0.6065	0.8088	0.9526	0.9909	0.9986	0.9998	1.0000	1.0000	1.0000	1.0000	1.0000
0.9	0.6065	0.7725	0.9371	0.9865	0.9977	0.9997	1.0000	1.0000	1.0000	1.0000	1.0000
1.0	0.3679	0.7358	0.9197	0.9810	0.9963	0.9994	0.9999	1.0000	1.0000	1.0000	1.0000
1.1	0.3329	0.6990	0.9004	0.9743	0.9946	0.9990	0.9999	1.0000	1.0000	1.0000	1.0000
1.2	0.3012	0.6626	0.8795	0.9662	0.9923	0.9985	0.9997	1.0000	1.0000	1.0000	1.0000
1.3	0.2725	0.6268	0.8571	0.9569	0.9893	0.9978	0.9996	0.9999	1.0000	1.0000	1.0000
1.4	0.2466	0.5918	0.8335	0.9463	0.9857	0.9968	0.9994	0.9999	1.0000	1.0000	1.0000
1.5	0.2231	0.5578	0.8088	0.9344	0.9814	0.9955	0.9991	0.9998	1.0000	1.0000	1.0000
1.6	0.2019	0.5249	0.7834	0.9212	0.9763	0.9940	0.9987	0.9997	1.0000	1.0000	1.0000
1.7	0.1827	0.4932	0.7572	0.9068	0.9704	0.9920	0.9981	0.9996	0.9999	1.0000	1.0000
1.8	0.1653	0.4628	0.7306	0.8913	0.9636	0.9896	0.9974	0.9994	0.9999	1.0000	1.0000
1.9	0.1496	0.4337	0.7037	0.8747	0.9559	0.9868	0.9966	0.9992	0.9998	1.0000	1.0000
2.0	0.1353	0.4060	0.6767	0.8571	0.9473	0.9834	0.9955	0.9989	0.9998	1.0000	1.0000
2.1	0.1225	0.3796	0.6496	0.8386	0.9379	0.9796	0.9941	0.9985	0.9997	0.9999	1.0000
2.2	0.1108	0.3546	0.6227	0.8194	0.9275	0.9751	0.9925	0.9980	0.9995	0.9999	1.0000
2.3	0.1003	0.3309	0.5960	0.7993	0.9162	0.9700	0.9906	0.9974	0.9994	0.9999	1.0000
2.4	0.0907	0.3084	0.5697	0.7787	0.9041	0.9643	0.9884	0.9967	0.9991	0.9998	1.0000
2.5	0.0821	0.2873	0.5438	0.7576	0.8912	0.9580	0.9858	0.9958	0.9989	0.9997	0.9999
2.6	0.0743	0.2674	0.5184	0.7360	0.8774	0.9510	0.9828	0.9947	0.9985	0.9996	0.9999
2.7	0.0672	0.2487	0.4936	0.7141	0.8629	0.9433	0.9794	0.9934	0.9981	0.9995	0.9999
2.8	0.0608	0.2311	0.4695	0.6919	0.8477	0.9349	0.9756	0.9919	0.9976	0.9993	0.9998
2.9	0.0550	0.2146	0.4460	0.6696	0.8318	0.9258	0.9713	0.9901	0.9969	0.9991	0.9998
3.0	0.0498	0.1991	0.4232	0.6472	0.8153	0.9161	0.9665	0.9881	0.9962	0.9989	0.9997
3.1	0.0450	0.1847	0.4012	0.6248	0.7982	0.9057	0.9612	0.9858	0.9953	0.9986	0.9996
3.2	0.0408	0.1712	0.3799	0.6025	0.7806	0.8946	0.9554	0.9832	0.9943	0.9982	0.9995
3.3	0.0369	0.1586	0.3594	0.5803	0.7626	0.8829	0.9490	0.9802	0.9931	0.9978	0.9994
3.4	0.0334	0.1468	0.3397	0.5584	0.7442	0.8705	0.9421	0.9769	0.9917	0.9973	0.9992
3.5	0.0302	0.1359	0.3208	0.5366	0.7254	0.8576	0.9347	0.9733	0.9901	0.9967	0.9990
3.6	0.0273	0.1257	0.3027	0.5152	0.7064	0.8441	0.9267	0.9692	0.9883	0.9960	0.9987
3.7	0.0247	0.1162	0.2854	0.4942	0.6872	0.8301	0.9182	0.9648	0.9863	0.9952	0.9984
3.8	0.0224	0.1074	0.2689	0.4735	0.6678	0.8156	0.9091	0.9599	0.9840	0.9942	0.9981
3.9	0.0202	0.0992	0.2531	0.4532	0.6484	0.8006	0.8995	0.9546	0.9815	0.9931	0.9977

mean (*m*)						*r*					
	0	1	2	3	4	5	6	7	8	9	10
4.0	0.0183	0.0916	0.2381	0.4335	0.6288	0.7851	0.8893	0.9489	0.9786	0.9919	0.9972
4.1	0.0166	0.0845	0.2238	0.4142	0.6093	0.7693	0.8786	0.9427	0.9755	0.9905	0.9966
4.2	0.0150	0.0780	0.2102	0.3954	0.5898	0.7531	0.8675	0.9361	0.9721	0.9889	0.9959
4.3	0.0136	0.0719	0.1974	0.3772	0.5704	0.7367	0.8558	0.9290	0.9683	0.9871	0.9952
4.4	0.0123	0.0663	0.1851	0.3594	0.5512	0.7199	0.8436	0.9214	0.9642	0.9851	0.9943
4.5	0.0111	0.0611	0.1736	0.3423	0.5321	0.7029	0.8311	0.9134	0.9597	0.9829	0.9933
4.6	0.0101	0.0563	0.1626	0.3257	0.5132	0.6858	0.8180	0.9049	0.9549	0.9805	0.9922
4.7	0.0091	0.0518	0.1523	0.3097	0.4946	0.6684	0.8046	0.8960	0.9497	0.9778	0.9910
4.8	0.0082	0.0477	0.1425	0.2942	0.4763	0.6510	0.7908	0.8867	0.9442	0.9749	0.9896
4.9	0.0074	0.0439	0.1333	0.2793	0.4582	0.6335	0.7767	0.8769	0.9382	0.9717	0.9880
5.0	0.0067	0.0404	0.1247	0.2650	0.4405	0.6160	0.7622	0.8666	0.9319	0.9682	0.9863
5.1	0.0061	0.0372	0.1165	0.2513	0.4231	0.5984	0.7474	0.8560	0.9252	0.9644	0.9844
5.2	0.0055	0.0342	0.1088	0.2381	0.4061	0.5809	0.7324	0.8449	0.9181	0.9603	0.9823
5.3	0.0050	0.0314	0.1016	0.2254	0.3895	0.5635	0.7171	0.8335	0.9106	0.9559	0.9800
5.4	0.0045	0.0289	0.0948	0.2133	0.3733	0.5461	0.7017	0.8217	0.9027	0.9512	0.9775
5.5	0.0041	0.0266	0.0884	0.2017	0.3575	0.5289	0.6860	0.8095	0.8944	0.9462	0.9747
5.6	0.0037	0.0244	0.0824	0.1906	0.3422	0.5119	0.6703	0.7970	0.8857	0.9409	0.9718
5.7	0.0033	0.0224	0.0768	0.1800	0.3272	0.4950	0.6544	0.7841	0.8766	0.9352	0.9686
5.8	0.0030	0.0206	0.0715	0.1700	0.3127	0.4783	0.6384	0.7710	0.8672	0.9292	0.9651
5.9	0.0027	0.0189	0.0666	0.1604	0.2987	0.4619	0.6224	0.7576	0.8574	0.9228	0.9614
6.0	0.0025	0.0174	0.0620	0.1512	0.2851	0.4457	0.6063	0.7440	0.8472	0.9161	0.9574
6.1	0.0022	0.0159	0.0577	0.1425	0.2719	0.4298	0.5902	0.7301	0.8367	0.9090	0.9531
6.2	0.0020	0.0146	0.0536	0.1342	0.2592	0.4141	0.5742	0.7160	0.8259	0.9016	0.9486
6.3	0.0018	0.0134	0.0498	0.1264	0.2469	0.3988	0.5582	0.7017	0.8148	0.8939	0.9437
6.4	0.0017	0.0123	0.0463	0.1189	0.2351	0.3837	0.5423	0.6873	0.8033	0.8858	0.9386
6.5	0.0015	0.0113	0.0430	0.1118	0.2237	0.3690	0.5265	0.6728	0.7916	0.8774	0.9332
6.6	0.0014	0.0103	0.0400	0.1052	0.2127	0.3547	0.5108	0.6581	0.7796	0.8686	0.9274
6.7	0.0012	0.0095	0.0371	0.0988	0.2022	0.3406	0.4953	0.6433	0.7673	0.8596	0.9214
6.8	0.0011	0.0087	0.0344	0.0928	0.1920	0.3270	0.4799	0.6285	0.7548	0.8502	0.9151
6.9	0.0010	0.0080	0.0320	0.0871	0.1823	0.3137	0.4647	0.6136	0.7420	0.8405	0.9084
7.0	0.0009	0.0073	0.0296	0.0818	0.1730	0.3007	0.4497	0.5987	0.7291	0.8305	0.9015
7.1	0.0008	0.0067	0.0275	0.0767	0.1641	0.2881	0.4349	0.5838	0.7160	0.8202	0.8942
7.2	0.0007	0.0061	0.0255	0.0719	0.1555	0.2759	0.4204	0.5689	0.7027	0.8096	0.8867
7.3	0.0007	0.0056	0.0236	0.0674	0.1473	0.2640	0.4060	0.5541	0.6892	0.7988	0.8788
7.4	0.0006	0.0051	0.0219	0.0632	0.1395	0.2526	0.3920	0.5393	0.6757	0.7877	0.8707
7.5	0.0006	0.0047	0.0203	0.0591	0.1321	0.2414	0.3782	0.5246	0.6620	0.7764	0.8622
7.6	0.0005	0.0043	0.0188	0.0554	0.1249	0.2307	0.3646	0.5100	0.6482	0.7649	0.8535
7.7	0.0005	0.0039	0.0174	0.0518	0.1181	0.2203	0.3514	0.4956	0.6343	0.7531	0.8445
7.8	0.0004	0.0036	0.0161	0.0485	0.1117	0.2103	0.3384	0.4812	0.6204	0.7411	0.8352
7.9	0.0004	0.0033	0.0149	0.0453	0.1055	0.2006	0.3257	0.4670	0.6065	0.7290	0.8257

mean (m)	0	1	2	3	4	5	6	7	8	9	10
						r						
8.0	0.0003	0.0030	0.0138	0.0424	0.0996	0.1912	0.3134	0.4530	0.5925	0.7166	0.8159
8.1	0.0003	0.0028	0.0127	0.0396	0.0940	0.1822	0.3013	0.4391	0.5786	0.7041	0.8058
8.2	0.0003	0.0025	0.0118	0.0370	0.0887	0.1736	0.2896	0.4254	0.5647	0.6915	0.7955
8.3	0.0002	0.0023	0.0109	0.0346	0.0837	0.1653	0.2781	0.4119	0.5507	0.6788	0.7850
8.4	0.0002	0.0021	0.0100	0.0323	0.0789	0.1573	0.2670	0.3987	0.5369	0.6659	0.7743
8.5	0.0002	0.0019	0.0093	0.0301	0.0744	0.1496	0.2562	0.3856	0.5231	0.6530	0.7634
8.6	0.0002	0.0018	0.0086	0.0281	0.0701	0.1422	0.2457	0.3728	0.5094	0.6400	0.7522
8.7	0.0002	0.0016	0.0079	0.0262	0.0660	0.1352	0.2355	0.3602	0.4958	0.6269	0.7409
8.8	0.0002	0.0015	0.0073	0.0244	0.0621	0.1284	0.2256	0.3478	0.4823	0.6137	0.7294
8.9	0.0001	0.0014	0.0068	0.0228	0.0584	0.1219	0.2160	0.3357	0.4689	0.6006	0.7178
9.0	0.0001	0.0012	0.0062	0.0212	0.0550	0.1157	0.2068	0.3239	0.4557	0.5874	0.7060
9.1	0.0001	0.0011	0.0058	0.0198	0.0517	0.1098	0.1978	0.3123	0.4426	0.5742	0.6941
9.2	0.0001	0.0010	0.0053	0.0184	0.0486	0.1041	0.1892	0.3010	0.4296	0.5611	0.6820
9.3	0.0001	0.0009	0.0049	0.0172	0.0456	0.0986	0.1808	0.2900	0.4168	0.5479	0.6699
9.4	0.0001	0.0009	0.0045	0.0160	0.0429	0.0935	0.1727	0.2792	0.4042	0.5349	0.6576
9.5	0.0001	0.0008	0.0042	0.0149	0.0403	0.0885	0.1649	0.2687	0.3918	0.5218	0.6453
9.6	0.0001	0.0007	0.0038	0.0138	0.0378	0.0838	0.1574	0.2584	0.3796	0.5089	0.6329
9.7	0.0001	0.0007	0.0035	0.0129	0.0355	0.0793	0.1502	0.2485	0.3676	0.4960	0.6205
9.8	0.0001	0.0006	0.0033	0.0120	0.0333	0.0750	0.1433	0.2388	0.3558	0.4832	0.6080
9.9	0.0001	0.0005	0.0030	0.0111	0.0312	0.0710	0.1366	0.2294	0.3442	0.4705	0.5955
10.0	0.0000	0.0005	0.0028	0.0103	0.0293	0.0671	0.1301	0.2202	0.3328	0.4579	0.5830

Values of the Pearson correlation coefficient for different levels of significance in a two tailed test

	0.1	0.05	0.02	0.01	0.001
$v = 1$	.98769	.99692	.999507	.999877	.9999988
2	.90000	.95000	.98000	.990000	.99900
3	.8054	.8783	.93433	.95873	.99116
4	.7293	.8114	.8822	.91720	.97406
5	.6694	.7545	.8329	.8745	.95074
6	.6215	.7067	.7887	.8343	.92493
7	.5822	.6664	.7498	.7977	.8982
8	.5494	.6319	.7155	.7646	.8721
9	.5214	.6021	.6851	.7348	.8471
10	.4973	.5760	.6581	.7079	.8233
11	.4762	.5529	.6339	.6835	.8010
12	.4575	.5324	.6120	.6614	.7800
13	.4409	.5139	.5923	.6411	.7603
14	.4259	.4973	.5742	.6226	.7420
15	.4124	.4821	.5577	.6055	.7246
16	.4000	.4683	.5425	.5897	.7084
17	.3887	.4555	.5285	.5751	.6932
18	.3783	.4438	.5155	.5614	.6787
19	.3687	.4329	.5034	.5487	.6652
20	.3598	.4227	.4921	.5368	.6524
25	.3233	.3809	.4451	.4869	.5974
30	.2960	.3494	.4093	.4487	.5541
35	.2746	.3246	.3810	.4182	.5189
40	.2573	.3044	.3578	.3932	.4896
45	.2428	.2875	.3384	.3721	.4648
50	.2306	.2732	.3218	.3541	.4433
60	.2108	.2500	.2948	.3248	.4078
70	.1954	.2319	.2737	.3017	.3799
80	.1829	.2172	.2565	.2830	.3568
90	.1726	.2050	.2422	.2673	.3375
100	.1628	.1946	.2301	.2540	.3211

INDEX